METROPOLITAN COLLEGE OF NY
LIBRARY, 12TH FLOOR
431 CANAL STREET
NEW YORK, NY 10013

Norman Podhoretz and *Commentary* Magazine

Norman Podhoretz and Commentary Magazine

The Rise and Fall of the Neocons

Nathan Abrams

Norman Podhoretz and *Commentary* Magazine

The Rise and Fall of the Neocons

Nathan Abrams

continuum

NEW YORK • LONDON

The Continuum International Publishing Group Inc
80 Maiden Lane, New York, NY 10038

The Continuum International Publishing Group Ltd
The Tower Building, 11 York Road, London SE1 7NX

www.continuumbooks.com

Copyright © 2010 by Nathan Abrams

All rights reserved. No part of this book may be reproduced, stored in a retrieval system, or transmitted, in any form or by any means, electronic, mechanical, photocopying, recording, or otherwise, without the written permission of the publishers.

Library of Congress Cataloging-in-Publication Data
A catalog record for this book is available from the Library of Congress.

ISBN: 978-1-4411-0968-2

Typeset by Newgen Imaging Systems Pvt Ltd, Chennai, India
Printed in the United States of America

Contents

Acknowledgments viii

Introduction 1

1. Taking Over 9
   Podhoretz: The Early Years   9
   Arriving   13
   Coming Apart   17
   Editor-in-Chief   21
   An Oedipal Struggle   23
   Taking Risks   28
   Softening the Hardness   30
   De-Judaizement   32
   "Kosher Baloney"   34
   Editorial Freedom   41
   Norman the Conqueror   43

2. The Revised Standard Version 49
   "Doing . . . Violence to the Truth"   52
   Not So Radical   53
   America the Beautiful   57
   Anti-Liberal Racism   60
   Hardening the Softness   67
   Incipient Conservatism   69
   Zionization and the 614th Commandment   71
   Liberal Anti-Communism Revisited   75
   Blacks and Jews   77
   Making It   81
   Climax   84
   Kulturkampf   86

3. War 93
- Podhoretz Returns — 93
- A Declaration of War — 94
- On the Offensive — 96
- Standing His Ground — 102
- "La grande peur juive" — 106
- "Literary Onanism" — 109
- "Orchestrated 'Lynchings'" — 113
- Nixonism vs. McGovernism — 116
- Political Onanism — 119
- Neoconservatism — 121
- Present Tense — 124
- Casualties — 126

4. Resurrection 133
- Resurrecting the Cold War — 133
- Reviving McCarthy — 140
- Inside the UN — 145
- Frozen Out — 146
- Double Standards — 149
- Ardent Zionism — 151
- A "Two-Bit Little Homophobic Bigot" — 155
- Insanity or Maturity? — 159

5. Empire 165
- Get Carter — 165
- Bliss — 169
- The Norman Invasion — 170
- "Podhoretz as Dr. Strangelove!" — 173
- Abusing Human Rights — 176
- A Shtetl Mentality — 178
- Tireless Fanaticism — 186
- Neo-Puritan Traditionalism — 187
- "A Farewell to Civil Rights" — 189
- Traditional Intellectuals — 193

6. Decline 199
- Betrayal — 199
- Despair — 202
- "Neanderthal[s] in Drag" — 204
- Ideologue of Zionism — 207

A False Prophet of Particularism	210
"All the Rest is Commentary"	215
Twisted Thinking	218
Confusion	222
The Conservative Crack-Up	228
Gloominess	231

7. Fall 240

Intellectual Sacrifice	240
The Gospel of American Conservatism	243
The Wrong Side of History	246
Identity Crisis	254
The Culture Wars	257
Social Darwinist Laissez-Faire Racism	261
Biblical Morality	262
Entering the Fever Swamps	264
Who's Afraid of the Religious Right?	268
"Saddam-is-Hitler"	269
"Jimmy Clinton"	275
A Hero at a Safe Distance	276
A "Counterrevolution" of the Right?	280

8. After the Fall 289

The Death of Neoconservatism	289
Sickness	291
Podhoretz's Protégé	298
Reviving Reagan	300
Life After Death?	301
Podhoretz Returns	304
Mere Posturing	306
Myth-Making	308

Conclusion 317

Bibliography 324
Index 353

Acknowledgments

This book has been so long in the making that inevitably I will forget and leave out many people who have assisted me along the way, but several names stand out deserving of praise: Richard King, Hugh Wilford, Nina Fishman, Murray Friedman, and Michael Abrams (my long-suffering father who's pretty much read every draft I ever wrote), as well as the anonymous readers whose comments have helped to improve this book immeasurably. Between them, they have given me helpful advice and suggestions but needless to say the errors are my own. Wendy Maples furnished a welcome place to edit over a summer. The University of Aberdeen and Bangor University provided congenial places to work and write, particularly the latter. And students at both universities have helped to contribute ideas which have ended up in here. I am grateful to all those who consented to be interviewed or responded to my queries by telephone, letter, and email. I would also like to thank the staff of the various libraries I used over the years: the Harry Ransom Humanities Research Center at the University of Texas, Austin; the American Jewish Archives in Cincinnati, Ohio; the Manuscript Reading Room of the Library of Congress; and the British Library. I have received financial support from various sources including The Open University, The Jacob Rader Marcus Center of the American Jewish Archives, The Harry Ransom Humanities Research Center at the University of Texas at Austin, The Myer and Rosaline Feinstein Center at Temple University and The Memorial Foundation for Jewish Culture.

I would like to thank my agent Leslie Gardner for having faith in and pushing this project when publishers were asking for books on Richard Perle and didn't even know who Norman Podhoretz was. I am also grateful to Marie-Claire Antoine and the team at Continuum.

Finally, recognition must go also to all of my parents, friends and family, as well as those others who I have met over the years. They have been pillars of support, advice, and friendship.

Introduction

During the presidency of George W. Bush an idea known as "neoconservatism" was highly influential. Certainly, many of the ideas implemented by the Bush administration had been articulated over the past two-and-a half decades by neoconservatives. The neoconservatives influenced the Bush administration's decisions on supply-side economics, tax cuts, the erosion of the wall separating church and state, bioethics, and stem cell research. Neoconservatives also held many prominent positions in the Bush administration: figures and advisors such as Deputy Secretary of Defense Paul D. Wolfowitz; the vice president's chief of staff I. Lewis Libby; National Security Council staffer Elliott Abrams; Undersecretary of Defense for Policy Douglas J. Feith; Peter Rodman, Assistant Secretary of Defense; and others like Richard Perle, John DiIulio, David Frum, David Horowitz, Murray Friedman, Leslie Lenkowsky, Leon Kass, James Q. Wilson, Daniel Pipes, Charles Horner, Samuel Huntington, Stephen Schwartz, Bernard Lewis, Michael Ledeen, and Robert Kagan.

The most significant area of neoconservative influence was foreign policy. While the administration's initial adoption of a sort of unilateralism that led it to spurn the International Criminal Court, the Kyoto accords, and the ABM treaty, among other things, mirrored the neoconservative position, the neoconservative line undoubtedly shaped the Bush administration's policy in the wake of the terrorist attacks on September 11, 2001. Suzanne Klingenstein observed the "glaringly obvious" and "astounding degree to which the neoconservatives had managed to establish their views, especially on foreign policy, at the expense of those of traditional conservatives in the Republican Party." Neoconservative ideas found expression in the Bush Administration's rhetoric and helped to revive the spirit of a Wilsonian interventionist, democratic internationalist and unilaterally globalist foreign policy implacably opposed to totalitarianism. The Bush Doctrine—the right of the United States to wage preemptive war—represented the ultimate crystallization of neoconservative thinking.[1]

The neoconservative voice was loudest in Bush's policy in the Gulf and the Middle East, as it railed against the terrorist threat of Islam.

The neoconservatives tied their Wilsonianism to what John Ehrman described as an aggressively adventurous democratic hegemonism, as they led the charge to democratize the Middle East. The neoconservatives not only wanted to spread democracy wherever they found the opportunity, but also they began recklessly (some would say) arguing that regimes like Syria and Iran should be overthrown. This line of thought was most prominently translated into policy as the Bush Administration pushed the United States into war with Iraq in 2003. Bush's repetitive 2004 election mantra of making the Middle East safe by installing democratic governments there also reflected such thinking. Suzanne Klingenstein concluded that Bush's support for the international war on terrorism and the Republican expression of support for Israel would not have been "as strong and enduring as they were without the years of preparatory work by the neoconservative intellectuals."[2]

But what does the term "neoconservative" mean? Who are we talking about and where did they come from? For almost eight years, the media and others bandied about the term "neoconservative" with little understanding of what it actually meant. It was much and widely abused. Often, the term was used to refer to any American conservative; it was also used as a synonym for "Jew" or "Zionist." Less often, but only slightly more accurately, the term was used to refer to a group of high-profile politicians and policy makers in Washington who (it is alleged) converted the Bush administration into pursuing an interventionist foreign policy aimed at Americanizing and democratizing the world. Rarely, was it correctly used to refer to two distinctive generations of high-profile American intellectuals, thinkers, writers, journalists, and politicians who have exercised a vast influence on American life and politics, most notably since the 1980s.

This book is a corrective to these misconceptions. Through a case study of the neoconservative movement's leading thinker and magazine—Norman Podhoretz and *Commentary*—it will argue that much of what has been said about neoconservatism over recent years is the product of willful distortion and exaggeration both by the neoconservatives themselves as well as their many enemies and detractors.

My account examines the origins, rise, and fall of neoconservatism through Podhoretz because he was not just its foremost intellectual but with ten books and in his 35 years as editor of *Commentary* magazine, he powerfully shaped neoconservatism. He has been described as "the conductor of the neocon orchestra." In fact, neoconservatism was Podhoretz's personal ideology, in which he pushed his own ideas for the future direction of America. In understanding Podhoretz, a figure often ignored by those who look at the contemporary neoconservative movement, we can begin to understand the origins, ideas, and intellectual pedigree of neoconservatism.

Podhoretz's vehicle (or "soapbox" as the *New York Times* called it) for the conception, gestation, birth, and transformation of neoconservatism from a small movement to a philosophy at the very center of government was *Commentary* Magazine. *Commentary* was launched in 1945 by the American Jewish Committee (AJC), the oldest and most conservative Jewish defense organization in the United States. In sponsoring *Commentary*, the AJC aimed "to meet the need for a journal of significant thought and opinion on Jewish affairs and contemporary issues."[3]

Commentary's first editor, Elliot E. Cohen, was a Southern-born Jew who had gone to Yale and had previously edited the celebrated *Menorah Journal*. Under Cohen, *Commentary* was a general and authoritative journal of the highest quality that was lively and relevant to the basic and most pressing issues on the national and the world scene and which reached a wide, if numerically small, audience. It covered matters of both universal interest and of specifically Jewish concern, in a non-Zionist intellectual, broad-based Reform Jewish contemporary tone. Cohen guided *Commentary* from a little, unknown periodical in 1945 into an important journal of intellectual thought and influence that Podhoretz inherited in 1960. Cohen established the magazine's main concerns and set the precedent of an intellectual and Jewish magazine that spoke to power for the first time. But Cohen only hinted at the possibilities of an influential policy magazine; it was Podhoretz who took the hint and turned it into a full-blown reality.

Uniquely for an institutionally funded Jewish journal in the 1940s, Cohen was granted editorial freedom. Although the philosophy of the AJC was to be implicit in the magazine's contents (its Statement of Aims printed in every issue read: "The sponsorship of *Commentary* by the Committee is in line with its general program to enlighten and clarify public opinion on problems of Jewish concern, to fight bigotry and protect human rights, and to promote Jewish cultural interest and creative achievement in America"), it was not intended to be a house organ ("The opinions and views expressed by *Commentary*'s contributors and editors are their own, and do not necessarily express the Committee's viewpoint or position"). It was designed to be nonpartisan with regard to the Jewish community politics and neither factional nor parochial in its approach, but broad and far-ranging. "With a perspicacity rare in voluntary organizations, Jewish or otherwise," wrote Podhoretz, "the AJC understood that unless the editor of the new magazine were given a free hand and protected from any pressures to conform to the Committee's own line, the result would be a pretentious house organ and nothing more." And which no one would read. The AJC had no reason in "doing anything that would parochialize the journal," or limit its appeal. It never explicitly desired the magazine to function as a public relations journal, or as a forum for its philosophies ("Its pages will be hospitable to diverse points of view and belief").[4]

According to Podhoretz, this editorial independence "consisted simply in this: no person except the editor or anyone he might voluntarily wish to consult could read articles in advance of publication or could dictate what should or should not appear in the magazine." It meant that the AJC concerned itself only with *Commentary*'s budget but did not interfere with the contents of the magazine. The journal has been seen as an exceptional enterprise in this respect: no other organization had so generously sponsored a publication and then left it to operate independently.[5]

Taking full advantage of this editorial independence, Podhoretz turned *Commentary* into an extension of his own personality. In doing so, it became an indispensable journal, the womb in which neoconservatism was conceived and gestated. It was there that neoconservative arguments were often formed and then honed. Podhoretz also learned his craft as a writer and intellectual from his years working as a junior editor at *Commentary*; he absorbed many of the elements that would form the basis of his neoconservatism: staunch anti-Stalinism and liberal anti-Communism, pro-Americanism, pro-New Dealism, pluralism and secularism, iconoclasm, anti-Jewish Establishmentism, and, perhaps above all, confidence, because *Commentary* exemplified confidence and gave the young Podhoretz assurance. These provided the props for the neoconservative model.

Eventually, however, *Commentary* took on the Podhoretz's outlook. Its history was tightly bound up with the personality of its editor, who left the imprint of his character on it. By studying the magazine we can not only understand Podhoretz better but also the wider movement of neoconservatism of which he and his magazine were a significant part.

Yet, strangely, in many of the current stories on neoconservatism, *Commentary* has been overlooked. But the magazine has played a vital part in both neoconservatism and the molding of Bush's agenda. It was in *Commentary* that what would become the props of Bush's neocon foreign policy were refined. Following the end of the Cold War, once it had become clear that Saddam Hussein and Iraq would not be permanent enemies after the first Gulf War in 1991, the magazine filled the vacated space by eagerly evoking a new category of threats: radical Arab nationalism and Islamic fundamentalism and terrorism and its sponsors like Iran, Iraq, North Korea, and Syria. It focused on the need to confront the new transnational enemy from the East, what Charles Krauthammer called the "global *intifada*."

As far back as 1989, *Commentary* argued that the terrorist danger posed by a radical, vengeful interpretation of Islam was the most urgent and ominous security menace and called for an immediate, intensified, and global confrontation of it. It warned of the hostility of Islamic militant fundamentalists to Western values, as signaled by the Salman Rushdie affair. It pointed out that Mohammed Aidid's successful defiance of the United States in Somalia in 1993 might be only one small taste of things to come. And following the bombing of the World Trade Center in February of 1993, it characterized Islamic fundamentalism as the clearest present danger and ominously predicted that, as the "fundamentalist struggle continues," the "kind of vitriol [they preach] against America" and the "systemic preaching of hatred eventually will produce violence." Even more darkly prophetic was its observation: "Manhattan's own nightmare could recur . . ." for the "World Trade Center bombing suggests, the conduct even of those fundamentalists who were once American allies and clients cannot be predicted, even in the short term."[6]

The Wilsonian ideal of making the world safe for democracy found much support and space in *Commentary*, which revived a Wilsonian streak fairly early on, dating back to the mid-1970s. In the wake of the Cold War, *Commentary* sought to ensure that the United States continued to play the part of a world power and remain involved overseas. It was part of a group of academics, intellectuals, and commentators who styled themselves as "democratic internationalists," who emphasized the necessity of American leadership in a newly unipolar world to create the conditions for peace and security through the defense and advance of democracy, and who were skeptical of international organizations and institutions. They saw the post–Cold War task of the United States was to defend democratic allies and resist aggression by fanatical states, promoting democratic transitions where possible, and supporting democratic consolidation elsewhere. After the first Gulf War, in particular, *Commentary* pushed the United States to encourage liberalization and democratization in the Middle East in order to prevent the rise of another Saddam Hussein. It called for a refashioned American crusade for world democracy in which America would be globally active.

I outline here the story of how neoconservatism grew from an unknown idea into a major influence in American politics and society by tracing the biography of Podhoretz and the history of *Commentary*. This book is structured in a roughly chronological fashion inasmuch as it covers the years from Podhoretz's birth in 1930, through his assumption of the editorship of *Commentary* in 1960, to the role he and *Commentary* have played since, continuing right up to the present. In doing so, I chart the story of

Podhoretz, the magazine, and hence neoconservatism's rise, zenith, decline, and fall. However, each chapter does not follow a strict chronological pattern, rather they operate thematically. Chapter 1 examines Podhoretz's early life and career from 1930 until the 1960s, focusing, in particular, on how Podhoretz sought to change the journal he had taken over. Chapter 2 then looks at how much of what has been said about Podhoretz and *Commentary* in the 1960s was inaccurate and that Podhoretz had not changed key fundamentals about the journal except in one key respect: he turned it into a source of antiliberal and antiblack conservatism which was consolidated as the decade progressed. It was the events of the 1960s that provided the backdrop for neoconservatism to emerge. Chapter 3 charts the shift toward neoconservatism during the 1970s as Podhoretz fought against the New Left and the counterculture, which he collectively dubbed "The Movement." Chapter 4 then looks at how, as a result of that fight, Podhoretz recycled ideas from the past and returned *Commentary* to an almost identical position (only differing in several respects) to that which it had been in when he took over.

Chapter 5 focuses on Podhoretz and *Commentary*'s zenith, when the magazine hosted the major ideologues of the so-called Reagan Revolution, and shows the importance the journal had on influencing the Reaganite agenda. Chapter 6 then traces the crumbling of Podhoretz's influence while Chapter 7 looks at his and *Commentary*'s fall, both in terms of influence and readership, a process capped by the election of President Clinton in 1992. At the same time, I examine the transmutation of neoconservatism into just a mild variant of the more orthodox and familiar conservative mainstream, what has been called "paleoconservatism," and which differs markedly from the neoconservatism of the 1970s and 1980s.

Chapter 8 reflects on the man, movement, and magazine since Podhoretz's retirement in 1995 until 2008, when he acted as the foreign policy advisor to the ill-fated and short-lived vice-presidential candidacy of Rudolph Giuliani. It examines exactly what influence the neocons had on the policies of George W. Bush and what its prospects are in the future. The final chapter, a conclusion and epilogue, summarizes Podhoretz's career and what consequences this has for our understanding of neoconservatism.

As my guiding purpose is to study Podhoretz and the genesis of neoconservatism so my coverage of *Commentary* is slanted toward those issues that led certain intellectuals to break with liberalism and become neoconservatives. These were Judaism, with special attention to Israel, including American policy toward Israel; US foreign policy and American anti-Communism, including McCarthyism; and various issues relating to the civil rights movement and race relations, including Jewish-black relations and debates over affirmative action. In the years after 1970, I give sustained attention to the cultural issues that became flashpoints during the "culture wars" in American politics such as affirmative action, homosexuality, religion and politics, feminism, and abortion. In other words, I focus on those issues that came to distinguish political conservatives from liberals in the post–Second World War era.

Finally, I pay attention to the moral and ethical responsibilities of the intellectual's vocation, for the story of Podhoretz serves as an illustration of what can happen when intellectuals get involved in politics. The independence of the intellectual and the vital need to formulate a critical stance were all-consuming issues in these years.

One note of caution: if *Commentary* does in fact possess an archive, I was not given access to it. I have thus had to rely on other sources both primary and secondary such as memoirs and personal papers. In 1995, on the occasion of Norman Podhoretz's retirement as Editor-in-Chief of *Commentary*, Irving Kristol remarked: "What Norman has done is so extraordinary that future historians will have to deal with it, and I will not try to compete with them here." While Kristol was right on one count—Podhoretz had done something "extraordinary"—he was wrong on the other: historians, thus far, have not fully dealt with it. It is my intention to complete that very project here.[7]

Notes

1. Susanne Klingenstein, "It's Splendid When the Town Whore Gets Religion and Joins the Church: The Rise of the Jewish Neoconservatives as Observed by the Paleoconservatives in the 1980s," *Shofar*, 21:3 (Spring 2003), 85.

2. Klingenstein, "It's Splendid," 85.

3. This quote is taken from a "Statement of Aims," which the AJC placed in every issue of *Commentary*. For more detail on *Commentary*, please see Nathan Abrams, Commentary Magazine 1945–1959: "A Journal of Significant Thought and Opinion" (London and Portland, OR: Vallentine Mitchell, 2006).

4. "Statement of Aims," *Commentary*; Norman Podhoretz, *Making It* (New York: Random House, 1967), 128, 133.

5. Podhoretz, *Making It*, p. 299 and quoted in Philip Ben, "*Commentary*: An American Monthly with Jewish Roots," draft article for *Maariv* (January 27, 1978), American Jewish Committee Records, Record Group 347, GEN-12 and GEN 10, YIVO Institute for Jewish Research, New York (hereafter "AJC, YIVO"). While it was never explicitly intended that *Commentary* would function either as a forum for the Committee's philosophies or as an exercise in public relations, the term "editorial freedom" belies the exact nature of the relationship between the magazine and the AJC. However, where *Commentary* has been

the subject of academic attention, these studies have not really challenged this notion of "editorial freedom." I challenge the claims to full editorial independence: the actual relationship between magazine and sponsor was perhaps more complex than suggested by the term "editorial freedom." Without going into too much detail, I will say here that *complete* editorial autonomy was never achieved. For more detail see my Commentary *Magazine, 1945-1959*.

6. Daniel Pipes, "The Ayatollah, the Novelist, and the West," *Commentary* 6:6 (June 1989), 9–17; A. J. Bacevich, "Learning from Aidid," 96:6 (December 1993), 30–33; Martin Kramer, "Islam & the West (including Manhattan)," *Commentary* 96:4 (October 1993), 33–37 and "Islam vs. Democracy," *Commentary* 95:1 (January 1993), 25–42.

7. Irving Kristol, remarks made to the friends and supporters of the magazine gathered to celebrate its Editor-in-Chief Norman Podhoretz upon the occasion of his retirement, May 2, 1995.

1

Taking Over

Podhoretz: The Early Years

Norman Podhoretz was born in 1930. He was an uncultured, scruffy, and crude Jewish kid who grew up in the very tough, poor, integrated, but, as he remembers it, racially troubled, Brownsville section of working-class Brooklyn. He was a "ghetto boy," then known as "Nifty," who would only eat overcooked meat and chicken. Hannah Arendt described him as "not civilized," as "straight out of the jungle." Podhoretz's parents had arrived in the United States in the 1920s, after the great wave of immigration had been cut off. He was raised in a lapsed Orthodox Jewish home. His father, a $60-a-week milkman, was neither learned nor pious, and did not subscribe to socialism or Zionism like so many other Jewish immigrants; he was a Jewish survivalist, enraged by assimilationist Jews.[1]

Podhoretz knew he wanted to be a writer from the age of six or seven after learning to type on an old Smith-Corona typewriter. He began by copying out stories from the newspapers, and when he got bored of that he graduated to writing his own stories and poems. Intoxicated with style, he gnawed his way like a termite through the local public library, as there were very few books in his parents' house.

Podhoretz was schooled at P.S. 28, Junior High School 178 (where he was class valedictorian in 1943 and described as having "extraordinary abilities"), and Boys High School of Brooklyn. At his father's insistence, Podhoretz also received a Jewish education, attending Talmud Torah School and Marshalia Hebrew High School. Podhoretz recorded the influence of two women on his early years: his mother, from whom he inherited his ambition and desire to "make it," and Mrs. Harriet Haft (immortalized as "Mrs. K." in his biography *Making It*), his high school English teacher, from whom he learned the world of English letters while resisting her demands for gentility. He got good grades under the wing of Mrs. Haft, and she had set her sights on Harvard where he gained admission and a scholarship. But since it did not cover room and board he entered Columbia instead, as a Pulitzer Scholar, at not quite seventeen years of age.[2]

Podhoretz spent two hours a day traveling on the subway between Brownsville and Morningside Heights. There, he lived a double life. During the day, he was a student at Columbia, studying the great works of Anglo-Saxon literature and instructed by the star professors of the day, luminaries such as Lionel Trilling, Mark Van Doren, F. W. Dupee, and Moses Hadas. At night (twice a week and the whole of every Sunday afternoon), he studied, in Hebrew, Judaism and Jewish civilization at the College of Jewish Studies, then one of the divisions of the Conservative Jewish Theological Seminary. As at Columbia, some very eminent scholars were his teachers, including H. L. Ginsberg, Abraham Joshua Heschel, and Moshe Greenberg. Meanwhile, Podhoretz soon fell under the tutelage of Trilling, one of the first Jews to gain tenure in the English department at Columbia, and a member of the New York Intellectuals who became one of the preeminent literary critics of the twentieth century. Although they were very different—Trilling was an anglicized "man of subtle grace" while Podhoretz was a Brooklyn brawling "man of anger and often uncontrollable passions"—Trilling envisaged Podhoretz as his intellectual successor and Podhoretz soon developed into his protégé. Trilling then guided and mentored Podhoretz through Columbia.[3]

Podhoretz graduated with both a BA from Columbia and a Bachelor of Hebrew Letters in 1950. He was a member of Phi Beta Kappa. Trilling then helped him to win a Fulbright Scholarship to study literature at Cambridge University in England, where he was a Kellett Teaching Fellow at Clare College. At Cambridge, Podhoretz was introduced to the highly influential academic F. R. Leavis who was possibly the most famous British literary critic of the early twentieth century. Podhoretz promptly decided to become one of his followers, who dubbed themselves as "Leavisites," and, as a result, he learned a great deal about literature from him, in particular Leavis' rigorous intellectual standards. Indeed, Podhoretz's debt to Leavis from whom he acquired his self-confessed "puritanical ferocity" was immeasurable. As he recalled:

> Though I never *sounded* like [Leavis] when I wrote—if I sounded like anyone, it was Trilling—I did to a remarkable extent learn how to respond in terms of his temperament, to think in terms of his categories, to judge in terms of his values.[4]

Podhoretz had a great engaging wit, which he very much enjoyed using. On one occasion, at tea at Newnham College, Podhoretz decided that another student of English there, a timid Englishman, was not worthy to be a follower of Leavis, and proceeded to destroy him. Podhoretz chased him into a rhetorical corner, where he admitted that he read literature because it gave him pleasure. So Podhoretz asked bluntly, if reading dirty comic books gave him more pleasure, would he switch to that? Leavis rewarded Podhoretz for his puritanical and literary ferocity with an invitation to contribute a review of Trilling's 1947 *The Liberal Imagination: Essays on Literature and Society* to his journal *Scrutiny*. Since Podhoretz was one of the few visiting Americans in Cambridge that Leavis allowed into *Scrutiny*, it was "a sort of literary knighting."[5]

Podhoretz's *Scrutiny* article prompted the then editor of *Commentary*, Elliot E. Cohen, to invite him to his office in the summer of 1952. To get such an invitation, Podhoretz must have been considered something special for, at that time, the Commentariat had a deeply equivocal and uneasy view of the academy. Most of the editors had dropped out of graduate school and were convinced that academics were boring nitpickers unable to write well because of their unhealthy fixation with footnotes. A single *Commentary* piece, on the other hand, they felt contained more thinking than a library full of doctoral theses. *Commentary* scorned academia because it preferred "high-level" journalism, the kind of writing that did not necessitate depth of knowledge or solid scholarship, but rather a tone of authority. As one contributor recalled, "anyone with a Ph.D. or close to getting a Ph.D. was under a cloud of suspicion as far as *Commentary* was concerned." Trilling had also recommended this "remarkable undergraduate" to Cohen, describing him as "a first class Hebraist (ancient and modern), a good writer, and a brilliant scholar," as well as "perhaps the very best student I have ever had." This was not faint praise as Trilling himself was brilliant, one of the most talented literary critics of his generation and one of the first Jews to gain tenure in English at Columbia.[6]

The visit offered a glimpse of the world of the nonacademic New York Intellectual. Despite the dingy, claustrophobic, cramped conditions, Podhoretz was impressed. "I would at that moment have given my life to be accepted as one of them, and . . . I felt as a girl with a secret infatuation must feel." Cohen and *Commentary* were both so alluring that Podhoretz rejected an academic career, discontinued his doctoral studies, and took up literary journalism instead. He soon befriended Robert Warshow, who became his mentor when he began writing for *Commentary*. Warshow was then the magazine's chief writer on popular culture, film and comics, and very popular within *Commentary*'s offices for his literary skill, patience, and willingness to bring out the best in young writers. Podhoretz felt that Warshow was "distinguished for an extraordinary understanding of the peculiar talents of others . . . helping a writer to realize his own intentions more perfectly."[7]

Podhoretz began contributing reviews to *Commentary* from 1953 onwards. He specialized in contemporary American fiction, even though at Columbia he had not bothered to take the single small survey course offered in American literature. Nor had he studied American philosophy, sociology, or even American history. "You seem to know something about baseball and something about novels," Cohen told Podhoretz, "So here's a novel about baseball to review," handing him a copy of Bernard Malamud's first novel, *The Natural* (1952). Podhoretz agreed "in a sustained paroxysm of enthusiasm." As he put it,

> among our most talented literary intellectuals (including just about everyone I know) reviewing is regarded as a job for young men on the make; you serve an apprenticeship as a reviewer and then you move on to bigger and more ambitious things.[8]

Meanwhile, Podhoretz graduated from Cambridge with a further BA and MA in English. His experiences as a student there meant much to him, and he said he considered it to be the single most important phase of his education.

> Some of my basic attitudes towards politics (the other of my main preoccupations as a writer and also as an editor) were shaped by the reading I did in political theory at Cambridge and much of what I saw while living in England and traveling on the continent during those crucial early days of the cold war. Finally, the opportunity to inhabit a foreign culture, and to get to know it from the inside, was not only in itself a great pleasure, but left me with a permanently altered perspective on the nature of things.

At the time, he wrote to Trilling: "It's given me a taste of the good life, of what it means to be a social being, of working in comfort and in a relaxed atmosphere; it's making me learn—in your phrase—how much more important it is to be private than public, and it's teaching me what 'private' implies." He continued to be immeasurably grateful for the opportunity for the rest of his life. Looking back, he recalled: "The years I spent at Cambridge University have had so deep and lasting an effect on me that my entire subsequent life and career would be unthinkable without reference to that experience."[9]

Arriving

Podhoretz was an *arriviste*. He was highly ambitious. As Neil Jumonville put it, "he was a young man on the make, one who wanted to assure the world of the height he was achieving." *Partisan Review* editor William Phillips, for whom Podhoretz often wrote, remembered that in those days Podhoretz "was bubbling over with enthusiasm, with energy; he wanted to know everything; he was so—I think *avid* is the word." Anxious to be liked, he could be very engaging, charming, cheerful, and upbeat with an appealing kidlike quality. Young, talented, and ferociously ambitious, he was intent on making it as one of New York's literary champions. He openly craved to be noticed, to see his name published, to be admired: "what I wanted was to see my name in print, to be praised, and above all to attract attention." And he sought to gain it with a series of uncompromising reviews which appeared in five successive issues of *Commentary* in 1953. His debut was a rather critical review of *The Natural*, which he described as possessing "artistic flaws and misconceptions" and being "a loose mixture of clichés." The review made Malamud very unhappy and it took years for Podhoretz to mend the damage. As he did many times in the future, Podhoretz offended members of the New York intellectual community, but nonetheless he was glad to be talked about. In subsequent reviews, he tore apart William Faulkner's *A Fable*, which he savaged as "so dull, tortured, above all so pretentious." As if this wasn't enough, Podhoretz moved on to destroy Faulkner's entire *oeuvre*, relegating him to the position of a minor talent.[10]

Podhoretz was very smart; he was a calculating political animal who happened, at that point, to be interested in literature, or at least that was the opening presented to him. His reviews mixed literary and political conclusions to understand what a given book "revealed about the attitudes of the author and what those in turn revealed about the general temper of the times." He never regarded literature only as an end in itself; rarely was it enough for him simply to judge its aesthetic qualities. He viewed it always as "a mode of public discourse that either illuminates or fails to illuminate the common ground on which we live." He mainly wrote on literary subjects and rarely dealt with politics, but almost everything he wrote "reflected the influence of the new revisionist liberalism of the fifties in one way or another." Podhoretz believed "in the doctrine that a work of art lived or died by the laws of its own being—aesthetic laws" and that "it must not be judged by any other standards, whether moral or political." It was "the responsibility of a serious critic to make his judgments on the basis of literary values alone." Furthermore, he felt that the

> only kind of criticism really worth writing was the kind that began rather than ended with the making of aesthetic judgments. Trilling once spoke of standing at "the bloody crossroads" where literature and politics meet, and that was exactly where I wanted to take my stand as a critic too.

Podhoretz "tried mightily to fit the image of a latter-day Trilling. His criticism was self-consciously marked by efforts at irony and complexity." At the same time, influenced by Leavis, he was "imbued with a puritanical determination to make no charitable concessions at all."[11]

Almost immediately, Podhoretz became the great hope for the future of *Commentary*, the first or only person of his generation that the veteran editors thought had the quality to become editor-in-chief of the magazine. According to Neil Jumonville,

> Much of Podhoretz's literary criticism was intelligent, brave, and provocative. He was particularly good at judging and commenting on generational trends, although the explicitly literary element of his work did not rank with that of the best of the New York group.

Norman Mailer claimed that Podhoretz was "as good as any critic in America at this kind of writing." Henry Carlisle, an editor at Alfred A. Knopf, wrote to Cohen: "I found Norman Podhoretz's piece on O'Hara and Mary McCarthy unusually interesting. Congratulations for having him on your staff. I shall be looking for more criticism by him."[12]

Not everyone was pleased with Podhoretz's reviews. One critic noted that he could hear in his essays "the tones of a young man who expects others to be just a little happy with his early eminence."[13] Irving Howe was worried about the traces of conservatism that he detected in them. One reader wrote in to accuse Podhoretz of "neglect[ing] the prime responsibility of literary criticism—to evaluate literature as an art." He went on to say: "To make the middle-class mores and culture the basic touchstone of literary evaluation is not far removed from the irrelevant evaluations of the critics of more rigid ideological persuasions, usually religious or political." And another, Maurice Samuel, complained of "the Olympian moral imperturbability of this young critic in the face of a monstrosity [which] is something like a *tour de force*."[14] Philip Rahv recalled: "He's gonna get somewhere, but he has no values and he isn't going to get any because where could he get any?" Critic Robert Brustein said, "one can detect an effort to capture for the journalist some of the novelist's prestige." And further:

> There is something poignant about this writer's effort to elevate whatever profession he happens to be pursuing at the moment, but there is something solipsistic about it too. I am certain that if Mr. Podhoretz ever went into the plumbing business, we would soon have an essay on how the toilet bowl is replacing the book.[15]

Podhoretz's breakthrough review came in October 1953, when he published a blistering critique of Bellow's *The Adventures of Augie March*. Podhoretz must have known that *Commentary*'s editors regarded Bellow with admiration, as a most promising author who, despite being Jewish, wrote American novels with an American accent. Bellow was a fellow contributor to *Commentary*, and he shared the magazine's goal of constructing postwar American Judaism along secular lines. Its editors had praised Bellow's work and hoped that he would be the first Jew to break into the American mainstream. They admired *Augie*, in particular, which had received critical acclaim and even praise from the begrudging Trilling no less. They also sympathized with the project of the book, which was "to express a new, post-thirties sense of American life very much in tune with the general intentions of *Commentary* itself." Podhoretz acknowledged that Bellow

> spoke for and embodied the impulse which had been growing among all the members of the second generation (and was the animating principle of Elliot Cohen's Grand Design) to lay a serious claim to their identity as Americans and to their right to play a more than marginal role in the literary culture of the country.

Podhoretz also knew that *Commentary* genuinely desired to see one of their own—Bellow—succeed as an important American novelist.[16]

Nonetheless, and despite Bellow's position as the preeminent New York Intellectual novelist, Podhoretz laid into Bellow in his characteristic brazen and "take-no-prisoners style." On the grounds he was impartial, not already being a friend of Bellow's, Podhoretz "trace[d] Bellow's development through his first two novels to *Augie March*" and "measure[d] *Augie* itself by how well its various intentions had been carried out." He wrote that despite "our sympathy with Mr. Bellow's ambition and our admiration for his pioneering spirit," this "should not lead us to confuse the high intention with the realization." Furthermore,

> The strain is apparent not only in many lapses, where Mr. Bellow tugs at syntax frantically, as if squeezing and twisting the language were enough to get all the juices out of it . . . the feeling conveyed by Mr. Bellow's exuberance is an overwhelming impulse to get in as many adjectives and details as possible, regardless of considerations of rhythm, modulation, or for that matter, meaning . . . His language lacks the suction to draw us into its stream.

He then added, "Mr. Bellow hasn't yet worked his way out of the non-dramatic solipsism of his earliest books: the most successfully drawn character in *Augie March* is not a human being but an ego."[17]

Podhoretz trashed *Augie* because he was eager to make a mark for himself in a world he wished to move up in. There was nothing inherently wrong with the novel, but Podhoretz calculated to junk it because it would make the most impact because, "Any praise I got and any attention I could attract would be all to the good, but it was the attention of the family [Podhoretz's term for the New York Intellectuals] I most dreamed of arousing."[18]

Podhoretz's ploy worked. The New York intellectual world sat up and took notice of him. In Podhoretz's words, "then the storm broke—so wild a storm that it took even the weatherbeaten *Commentary* staff by surprise." Bellow was furious, pleading with *Commentary* to withdraw the unsympathetic review from publication: "I beseech you in the bowels of Christ, think it possible you may be mistaken." He sent copies of his two-paged single-spaced typed petition to more than a dozen other New York Intellectuals in which he could not even bring himself to write Podhoretz's loathsome name, referring to him only as "Your young Mr. P."[19]

For Podhoretz Bellow's response and the subsequent literary outburst it had stirred up signaled success; he had attracted the attention he so conspicuously craved. For a while he became the favorite subject of gossip among the New York Intellectuals, who may have differed in their opinions, but paid attention to his pushy manner. Some three years later, according to Podhoretz, a famous American poet accosted him at a party and drunkenly threatened: "We'll get you for that review if it takes ten years." In his autobiography Podhoretz claims that:

> It had not occurred to me in my incredible naïveté that Bellow himself would take any notice of what an unknown young critic thought

of his book when everyone who was anyone had been celebrating his emergence as a major American novelist.

But was Podhoretz being disingenuous and could he have really been so naïve? While he was indeed a "young critic," the magazine he wrote for was certainly known. Rather, it would appear that Podhoretz planned that by attacking the literary doyen of the New York Intellectuals he would attract the notice he so openly coveted. After all he admitted: "Attention I had wanted? Attention I was getting." Later in life, he confessed that he had been somewhat opportunistically severe: "I haven't re-read *Augie March* in a long time, but I have mellowed considerably in the last few years, so I doubt that I would be quite as harsh today as I was when I reviewed it." Nonetheless, Podhoretz had arrived in almost exactly the fashion he had wished for.[20]

Podhoretz's sensational and bracing reviews of leading lights such as Saul Bellow in the 1950s were the means by which he achieved a reputation but, in substantive terms, they didn't represent a divergent strand of thought in postwar America. Nor was he a distinctive voice of his generation as, if anything, he was self-consciously striving to emulate the styles of Trilling, Leavis, and the New York Intellectuals. It seems that he wasn't even original; Neil Jumonville believes that this piece on Faulkner seemed derivative, largely restating Alfred Kazin's insights in *On Native Grounds*. Yet, what stood out in his reviews and which perhaps marked Podhoretz out was his precocity, particularly as the yet-to-be-published 23-year-old critic presumed to instruct older and more prolific novelists on their technique. As Gary Dorrien has put it, "Podhoretz's early writings were driven not so much by his desire to say anything in particular as by his desire to have written."[21]

As a reward for his confident outspokenness, in December 1955, Podhoretz was appointed as an assistant editor of *Commentary* at the age of 25. From the spring of 1953 until December 1955, Podhoretz had enlisted in the Army and Cohen held Irving Kristol's recently vacated position open for him during his service during which he continued to publish in *Commentary*. Despite being Trilling's heir apparent, he had forsaken his mentor by becoming a literary journalist rather than an academic.

Coming Apart

When Podhoretz returned to *Commentary*, they were not happy times. Cohen had been hospitalized for depression in 1956 and left a huge hole at the magazine that could not be filled. Cohen was perceived as an autocrat, ruling the journal dictatorially. He set the overall policy and made the final decisions. Beneath him, with the exception of the editorial assistant Sherry Abel, the editorial arrangements were egalitarian. All members of the editorial staff held the same rank of associate editor; they had an equal voice and did the same work of commissioning and editing articles, dealing with writers, voting on manuscripts, proofreading, dummying, and composing author's notes. No one was more powerful than anyone else. As Cohen had not named a successor, his absence left a vacuum.[22]

Without Cohen an awful power struggle for the succession at *Commentary* took place among those who were left at the magazine. The battle was truly ghastly recalled Cohen's niece. In Cohen's place, the AJC had temporarily appointed the brothers, Clement and Martin Greenberg, to run the magazine. The Greenbergs were in a tough situation: despite his absence, Cohen loomed large—it was even rumored that he was secretly editing the magazine from hospital—and they were further undermined by the temporary nature of their appointment. Martin in particular depended upon his job at *Commentary* and was scared to disappoint or alienate any of the AJC. For his part, Clement "was known to use his fists, not just his mouth, when he felt he had been wronged." The brothers' fears were translated into intimidating their subordinates. They did not greet Podhoretz's return warmly as they perceived him to be a particular threat; he was "genuinely gifted," according to Clement, "a better editor than any of us," unlike Cohen who "had to struggle." They made no attempt to hide their feelings that Podhoretz was a self-seeker. Clement described Podhoretz as "a technical intellectual who was on the make. He didn't give a shit about Jews. [He] has no content, has never believed in anything." His brother concurred, belittling Podhoretz as "the voice of Borough Park," a "publicity intellectual" who had no convictions. Before long they disagreed violently with him.[23]

Podhoretz was stung by the Greenberg's contempt. Richard Schickel recalled, "Norman is like a Hollywood musician, anxious to be liked, very cheerful, very upbeat. He has an appealing kidlike quality." Perhaps he realized that they had worked him out. Podhoretz felt frozen out by the brothers Greenberg, whom he thought obnoxious and mediocre, so much so in fact, that in his memoir of this period he could not bring himself to write their names, referring to them only as a composite:

> These two men happened to be so closely related that they were able to act as one man after Cohen's departure, when they assumed de facto control of the magazine. Since they also behaved as one man toward me, and because of the form this behavior took, I will be doing

no violence to the truth if I refer to them from now on in the singular, as "The Boss."

Podhoretz felt that they acted towards him in a cold, small-minded, spiteful, and remorseless fashion. He recalled that they ignored his comments on manuscripts, that in violation of traditional *Commentary* practice they suddenly presented him with galleys of articles he had never been allowed to vote on, that they did not invite him to editorial conferences, and when they did read his comments, they said nothing or told him it needed more work. Podhoretz further felt that they had reneged on the title and salary, which Cohen had promised to him, lowering his salary from $7000 to $5500 per annum and changing his title from Associate- to Assistant Editor on a six-month trial basis. Not only did Podhoretz feel that they were personally injuring him, but also that the Greenbergs were destroying *Commentary* by running it not to please themselves but to please the AJC. He considered resigning but did not want to go back to graduate school. In the end, he compromised on the title and was mollified by an annual salary of $5750.[24]

Yet, the situation was still highly volatile. There was lots of screaming back and forth between Podhoretz and the Greenbergs. It could not have been easy for Podhoretz to live through that period; he was surely miserable. Although the Greenbergs' criticisms and hostility should have inspired self-doubt, his self-belief was strong and he stuck it out, hoping Cohen would return soon. However, his resentment grew too much, and citing difficulties with the Greenbergs he offered them his resignation in 1958 "in a voluptuous emission of obscene expletives shouted at The Boss in the highest register [his] cigarette-roughened vocal chords could attain." William Phillips recalled (and he had no reason to say this) that Podhoretz behaved honorably during that awful period. Nonetheless, Podhoretz had ambitions of his own, coveting the editorship for himself. Coming to the conclusion that his position was untenable, and in an extremely effective tactical maneuver, he took his complaints to the AJC's personnel office, claiming that the Greenbergs were undoing Cohen's good work and ruining the magazine. He hid his personal ambitions by claiming he was motivated by a sense of regard for Cohen and concern for the future of *Commentary*, and in a final coup, by saying that he had no wish to return to the magazine itself, desiring only to write.[25]

The AJC accepted Podhoretz's version of events and refused to accept his resignation, launching an investigation instead. After six weeks a hearing was held, including testimony from the entire staff and any former editor they could find. During this interim, Podhoretz conducted his battle as skillfully as he could, lining up support and sympathy from everyone who would back him and attempting to behave with a combination of diffidence and fervor. He tried to hide his real motives by refusing to admit that he was actually engaged in a struggle for power, but as everyone else knew, himself included, he was charged by ruthless, naked, ambition. As he acknowledged, "I had waged a dirty fight and won, but I had also paid a price in opprobrium (the hideous reputation of ruthlessness would, I felt sure, cling to me forever)."[26]

Eventually, the Committee persuaded Podhoretz to stay by firing Clement Greenberg in 1957. Podhoretz, Martin Greenberg, and Theodore Frankel were appointed as an interim triumvirate of associate, but equal editors until Cohen returned. Frankel acted as a buffer between Podhoretz and Greenberg, but he left the magazine shortly thereafter and was replaced by George Lichtheim. Lichtheim's appointment seemed promising but the state of affairs at *Commentary* was chaotic. Podhoretz and Greenberg weren't on speaking terms and had to communicate through Lichtheim who admitted euphemistically that this was "not an ideal way of running a magazine" (blaming the AJC for this state of affairs).[27] The magazine lacked that excitement and urgency which only an overall boss or editor with strong ideas and the willingness to put them into practice could generate.

Nor did Cohen's return from hospital solve the problems of the previous two years. If anything the infighting that had occurred during Cohen's hospitalization increased, as competition to replace him was fierce. Cohen should not have returned to work; he should have stayed away. Something was lacking and he was not "the active catalyst of his earlier years," recalled Podhoretz. Cohen was a sensitive man and the infighting took its toll. *Commentary*'s offices were also a depressing place to work, very small, hemmed in, and shabby. Cohen began to show up less and less, and when he did he just sat there, doing nothing. His speech was impaired. According to Podhoretz, Cohen was a "shrunken, shaken man in his late fifties who was pitifully unsure of himself and obviously not in any shape to take the strain of running a magazine." He was paralyzed by indecision, he couldn't move. The decline in Cohen's brilliance was distressing. During a lunch with Cohen, the British historian Cecil Roth recalled "the slowness and hesitancy which used to lead up to a brilliant flash ending in nothing." Michael Wyschogrod "was more than a little frightened" by the profound depth of Cohen's depression: "Before me was one of the unhappiest human beings I had ever met."[28]

Podhoretz soon believed that, out of feelings of guilt towards Clement Greenberg, Cohen was regularly taking sides with his brother Martin. Clement recalled: "After his dose of therapy, such as it was, Elliot recognized that Martin didn't want control, didn't want to replace him; all he wanted was more comfort in his job." Podhoretz took as proof of his suspicions Cohen's rejection of an article by Robert Graves, which Podhoretz had commissioned, on the grounds that it was too controversial for *Commentary*. This episode, together with the rejection of Hannah Arendt's highly controversial article on Little Rock in 1957, convinced Podhoretz that he "simply did not belong on the staff of such a magazine." He had become more and more unhappy with the way things were going at the magazine and decided to resign. His predicament was very unpredictable. The office politics and the rowing combined with the heavy drinking at the frequent parties during that time took its toll on the young Podhoretz. He was still very young, the "runt of the litter" and seven to eight years younger than everyone else (only Susan Sontag was younger), and it was all extremely heady and too much for him. It was not an easy time to live through. Rather than repeat his earlier histrionics, and giving up his ambition of taking over as editor, he resigned and quietly left to work at Doubleday with his college friend Jason Epstein. Perhaps other factors motivated him, too. On October 21, 1956, Podhoretz had married Elliot Cohen's former secretary Midge Decter, and in doing so acquired a young family that needed supporting.[29]

Editor-in-Chief

Elliot Cohen died in May 1959 and the search for his successor began. Over the summer the AJC appointed a small sub-committee charged with finding a suitable replacement. Several other prominent intellectuals were considered as possible successors: Irving Kristol, Daniel Bell, Alfred Kazin, Clement Greenberg, Leslie Fiedler, but all turned the position down. Two final candidates were under consideration: the old adversaries, Podhoretz and Martin Greenberg. Eventually, Podhoretz was offered the job because he displayed independent vision and knew much more about Judaism than Greenberg.[30] Podhoretz wanted to be presented with the position and then rebuff it. In doing so, he wanted to rub his rejection in the face of his enemy Greenberg who wanted the job for himself. Podhoretz wrote, "I wanted the job to be offered to me, and I wanted him to know that it had been offered after I had turned it down."[31]

Against the advice of everyone he knew, Podhoretz returned to *Commentary*. He took the position of editor even though his friends thought it a dreadful mistake. Jason Epstein warned him that *Commentary* was "finished, played out, through and wondered how [Podhoretz] could even consider getting involved with a boring Jewish magazine." Others who counseled against him taking the job included Diana Trilling and Phillips, who warned him that

> it was naïve to think that the editor of *Commentary* was free to do as he pleased with the magazine: if I took the job, I would be beholden to the American Jewish Committee and forced to turn out the kind of magazine they wanted to have.

Kristol recalled telling him: "No, Norman, you don't want to be editor of *Commentary*. The magazine is okay, it's a good magazine, but it's not going anywhere, and you're on your way to being a very distinguished cultural and literary critic."[32]

Nonetheless, Podhoretz followed his own counsel. As he couldn't think of a "single reason for which I'd have respect a year from now to help me withstand the temptation of having a magazine to run," he accepted the job. He demanded "stern conditions" in return for accepting the job: complete editorial freedom, an agreement to allow him to make *Commentary* more general and less Jewish in emphasis, and a salary of $20,000. The AJC agreed to the first two terms, but knocked several thousand off his salary request. In December 1959, Podhoretz was announced as Editor-in-Chief at the age of 30. Podhoretz was "exhilarated" by the possibilities that opened up before him: "it would have been great fun to see whether I could really pull *Commentary* out of the doldrums and make it great again." Most importantly, he wrote to C. P. Snow, he was excited "by the power (which is something you can understand as my high-minded friends can't), and by the money (my income will be more than doubled)."[33]

It was entirely appropriate that Podhoretz had agreed to work for the AJC, as in many ways, it embodied all that the young Podhoretz yearned for. It was the most conservative Jewish defense agency in the United States. It was an elite organization of the Jewish "establishment": wealthy and prominent middle- and upper-class uptown Jewish leaders. It had gained access to the corridors of power, working with government authorities at the very highest levels. Editors were hired because their views (including, of course, their political views) were compatible with the AJC's. The AJC obviously saw in Podhoretz someone of similar ilk. Podhoretz, as would become clear later on, shared many of its views, even if this didn't always seem the case at times. Why else then would he accept a job with what he described as "the most establishmentarian of all Jewish organizations?" It might have seemed that the AJC took a chance on Podhoretz but eventually it turned out to be a prescient and perspicacious appointment, congenial to the sponsoring organization. This meant a Cold War anti-Communist liberal, pro-American, pro-New Deal, pluralist, secular outlook. It is no coincidence that such an outlook formed the bedrock of neoconservatism.[34]

An Oedipal Struggle

Podhoretz had inherited a moderately successful, but extremely well-edited, journal of Jewish opinion. Yet, he wanted more than that. He wanted the magazine talked about as widely as possible. He wanted to transform it into an empire. The desire to escape his slum origins, to be successful in the Gentile world of Manhattan (and eventually Washington DC) never left him ("One of the longest journeys in the world is the journey from Brooklyn to Manhattan," he wrote); it was overpowering. Podhoretz's dirty little secret was the means by which he would achieve these goals.[35]

In order to succeed, Podhoretz devised a strategy designed to breathe new life into the magazine. But to do that, Podhoretz had to make his readers believe that the Cohen years were over. He had to "make it instantly clear that *Commentary* was, to all intents and purposes, a brand-new magazine." He had to strip away the Cohen layers and rebuild the journal in his own image, on the surface at least. This meant removing any overt trace of Cohen's hand and influence. He also had to publicly reject his mentors; as Arnold Beichman put it rather astutely, Podhoretz "had to kill" Trilling, Sidney Hook, and Daniel Bell. It was an Oedipal struggle.[36]

The initial changes were cosmetic, as Podhoretz set out to modernize almost every facet of *Commentary*'s appearance. He redesigned the cover. He inserted a comma between the words "Committee" and "$1.00" on the cover because it sounded like the AJC cost a dollar. In a reversal of Cohen's policy, the author's name (in upper case) now appeared above the title of the article (in lower case). Some of the changes Podhoretz made were financial. He ran the magazine more cheaply. Where Cohen had employed four full-time editors, Podhoretz had only one. He also felt that the Business Manager, Frances Green, was incompetent, so he changed the format especially to increase advertising revenues. According to Bell, Podhoretz was a brilliant editor who understood that *Commentary*'s features and layout had become stale, and that its articles had grown dull and predictable.[37]

He then overhauled the magazine's format, and threw out its entire backlog of manuscripts. He discarded most of the 15-year-old regular departments, most notably, "From the American Scene" and "Cedars of Lebanon." He ignored the old rule that there had to be a piece of fiction in every issue and only included it if it was good enough, reducing the stories in the magazine to a mere trickle. He instituted five new departments:

"Observations," "A Commentary Report," "In the Community," "Public Affairs," and "Controversy."

Podhoretz made *Commentary* into an outlet for the expression of his views, whether he wrote them personally, or others did. John Ehrman observed, "From his appointment in 1960 until his retirement in 1995, Podhoretz ran *Commentary* as an extension of himself." He instituted his own short occasional self-penned column, "The Issue," in order to comment each month on the major articles in each issue, deliver his evaluation, and express whatever disagreements he might have had with them or elaborating on points the author had not chosen to discuss. Podhoretz intended the column to define more clearly the character of the new magazine, and indeed it did because, as the column appeared at the front and ended inside the back cover, Podhoretz had the first and last word in the magazine.[38]

Podhoretz said that he did it also to circumvent what he perceived to be Cohen's temptation to make others write for him. In reality, though, he also eventually, if not immediately, succumbed to this temptation. For Podhoretz, often a blocked writer, *Commentary* was a form of literary ventriloquism; writers became his literary surrogates, producing the type of material he desired to write. Consequently, it was perceived that many articles in *Commentary* were virtually ghostwritten. In order that the magazine said what Podhoretz wanted it to say, it continued to be a very heavily edited magazine. Podhoretz often took on a meticulous nanny role: taking a writer by the hand, furnishing him/her with clippings and ideas, being there all the way until delivery. Contributors confronted incessant and detailed suggestions for revisions, as many as they could be talked into. Manuscripts were made into "*Commentary* pieces." Such rewriting, known as "putting it through the typewriter," gave it the uniform "*Commentary* look" and distinctive writing style. It was something Podhoretz had learned from Cohen and carried with him through his years at *Commentary*. Cohen, a permanently blocked writer manqué, wrote vicariously through the writers he employed. According to Podhoretz, Cohen had used *Commentary* "as a means of coercing others, in effect, to do his writing for him." Yet, although Cohen could be overbearing and loved to rewrite, authors almost always retained their individual styles, identities, and voices. *Commentary*, it was remarked, "never came out that the magazine looked, as it later would, as though it were all written by the same hand." The great charge against *Commentary*, under Podhoretz, was that it was overedited, too rewritten, and offered an insufficient variety of style.[39]

Podhoretz brought in new staff. He hired two young graduates from the University of Chicago, Harris Dienstfrey and Ted Solotaroff, as associate editors. Solotaroff was appointed on the basis of an article he wrote on the role of the Jew in American letters, which appeared in the *Times*

Literary Supplement in 1959, and a book review for *Commentary* in June 1960. Podhoretz told him, "You didn't know what you were talking about, but you guessed right 90 percent of the time, so I figured you'd probably make a good editor." They symbolized the new breed of editor that Podhoretz attracted to *Commentary*: ambitious young men on the make like himself.[40]

The February 1960 issue, which came out under Podhoretz's imprimatur, very much had Podhoretz's stamp on it. It had a fresh, redesigned cover, with the *Commentary* masthead in a different font signaling the new editorship. Its face-lift made it resemble more closely the *Atlantic Monthly*, which was somewhat ironic as this was the AJC's initial template when it envisaged *Commentary* back in 1945. Inside, were some new names like Kingsley Davis, Judith Blake, Philip Levine, Lawrence Bloomgarden, Steven Marcus, Murray Kempton, and Mati Meged. Further changes to the format and layout were made in later issues: fewer pages per issue, increase in page size, wider margins, greater variety of typographical design, the expansion and moving of the "Letters to the Editor" section from the back to the front of the magazine and its use of three columns of text instead of two. There were also far more ads and color ads began to appear in the magazine for the first time, too. It now attracted general advertisers who had previously stayed away. Advertising pages increased from 61 in 1963 to 161 in 1964. The ads, many of which were for cigarettes, whiskeys and other luxury drinks, *treyf*, sophisticated, gourmet, and worldly delights such as lobster, as well as high-end automobiles, reflected Podhoretz's desire for worldly success and attested to the increasing affluence and embourgeoisiment of *Commentary*'s readership.

Podhoretz's major change was to try to reposition *Commentary* in the intellectual-journal market. It was his most significant attempt to wrest the magazine away from Cohen's imprint. Since he felt that the postwar liberal consensus had burned out, Podhoretz turned *Commentary*'s ideological stance into a new non-Marxist radicalism. He became friends with the literary hipster, Norman Mailer, even though three years earlier he had greeted Mailer's 1957 *Dissent* essay, "The White Negro," celebrating "hipsterism," as "one of the most morally gruesome ideas I have ever come across." He joined in Mailer's parties on Fire Island because Mailer taught him the "possibility of a new kind of radicalism—a radicalism that did not depend on Marx and that had no illusions about the Soviet Union." Podhoretz's ideological strategy, he claimed, was to abandon Cohen's hardline anti-Communism and pro-Americanism and transform *Commentary* "into a center for the revival of the long-dormant tradition of American social criticism." The new editorial program involved "criticizing existing institutions of every kind, to expose their shortcomings, their weaknesses, and their inadequacies," "a moral criticism of all existing social institutions" and a "more aggressively anti-establishment tone." It meant, wrote John Ehrman, responding "eagerly to leftist criticisms of American institutions and policies, seeing a chance to lead a new radicalism that would, in turn, reinvigorate liberalism." Podhoretz believed that radicalism provided just the sort of shot in the arm *Commentary* needed.[41]

But this radicalism was not ideologically driven. It was prompted by the same drives that led Podhoretz to savage Bellow and Malamud back in the early 1950s. As Ehrman put it, "Turning *Commentary* in a new, provocative direction also fit with Podhoretz's ambition to restore the magazine's prominence and, not coincidentally, to win additional notice for himself." Podhoretz himself admitted that it was designed "to heighten [*Commentary's*] involvement in contemporary trends and debates." Podhoretz was not a committed radical (as I will outline in more detail below), but sensing it was the hot topic in the making of the 1960s, he latched onto its bandwagon as the most efficacious way of getting himself heard.[42]

Podhoretz might have said that he had become "bored" with his own "sensibly moderate liberal ideas," borne out of a general intellectual ennui with the Eisenhower years during the late 1950s, and he might have also stated that he shared the feeling that the 1960s represented a new era, that the ideology of the 1950s was outdated and played out (even proposing a toast to the "revolutionary sixties" at a New Year's Eve Party in 1959), yet, initially, Podhoretz vacillated politically. The forthcoming election between Nixon and Kennedy was looking too close to call and Podhoretz expected little from Washington whoever was in charge. He saw very little difference between the candidates and felt Nixon and Kennedy were virtually indistinguishable in their domestic and foreign policies. The question was not who to vote for, but whether to bother to vote at all. Podhoretz published articles to this effect, with Dwight Macdonald announcing that he was abstaining.[43]

The election of Kennedy in November 1960, however, suddenly changed Podhoretz's mind. Where he was previously skeptical of the election of a new breed of young, promising, competent, agreeable, liberal politicians from both parties, even if they indicated a rejection of the sleepiness of the Eisenhower years and yearning for the energy of the Roosevelt-Truman years, Podhoretz now accepted them. Where he felt once that this new generation lacked a sense of purpose and mission, were unwilling to address the problems of modern American life, wanting not to overhaul the social system, but rather tinker with it, having replaced passion with prudence, earnestness, and blandness, symbolizing the triumph of the suburbanite as the zeal of the New Deal was superseded by the amiability of the "Smooth

Deal," he now believed JFK promised the offer of youth, hope, activity, dynamism, of social utopianism and neo-liberalism which was replacing the dull, middle-of-the-road conservatism of 1950s liberalism. He now agreed with *Commentary*'s assessment of the Eisenhower era in the late 1950s, as a decade of prosperity but also of conformity and somnolence, a "black heritage of time lost and opportunities wasted."[44]

His turnaround was prompted by the new opportunities presented by the Kennedy Administration. Where intellectuals had been rejected in the 1950s, Kennedy welcomed them to the White House, appointed them to cabinet posts, and cultivated their input into the political decision-making process. For intellectuals, Kennedy's presidency heralded a new dawn. Power and influence seemed close at hand and Podhoretz was ready and willing to be co-opted. So, Podhoretz "rode the New Frontier bandwagon," observed *Ramparts* editor Sol Stern. He chose to become, in the words of Kristol, "caught up in the zeitgeist." Tellingly, Podhoretz wrote,

> Celebrating American society may have gone hand in hand with jobs in the fifties, but criticizing it was evidently not going to mean losing these worldly goods in the nascent sixties. On the contrary, it was clearly going to bring rewards . . .[45]

There was also an element of knee jerking, whereby Podhoretz loved to resist. Podhoretz was a "counter-intellectual," someone who opposes "the adversary stance toward the general culture that intellectuals typically adopt." He was, observed Theodore Solotaroff,

> always someone, even as a young literary critic writing about Camus or Faulkner, who felt most sure of himself when he was hacking away at the prevailing opinion, the conventional wisdom. To be in an adversary position gave him energy and purpose which, at least as a writer he didn't seem otherwise to have.

His roommate at Cambridge in the early 1950s recalled, "My impression was that he was conservative then really as a reaction against the banality of the 'liberals' as he saw them. After all, he was a protégé of Lionel Trilling, who I believe was a liberal, however reflective." During this early Cold-War period, when the consensus was still overwhelmingly liberal and the heritage of Roosevelt still dominated thinking about society, being a conservative was simply a way of being an individual. Podhoretz intentionally chose to be in a "small and somewhat disreputable minority within the intellectual community." And in the 1960s, this meant choosing radicalism which was also a means by which he could hack away at the prevailing liberal anti-Communist opinion among the New York Intellectual community.[46]

Taking Risks

Podhoretz was audacious, original, and eager to innovate. He took risks. Solotaroff recalled:

> The early sixties were good years at *Commentary*. The magazine's point-of-view was a strong but flexible one. It assumed that the old *Commentary* had pretty much exhausted the "hard anti-Communist" position, that we were in a new decade with an opportunity to articulate new issues and new perspectives, mainly from the liberal left.

It was very exciting at that time, and its staff enjoyed working there. Where historians of consensus and affirmation had written for Cohen's *Commentary*—Oscar Handlin, Daniel Boorstin, and Richard Hofstadter—more dissenting voices began to contribute during the 1960s "and other names which had come to symbolize dullness or mediocrity or predictability in the minds of many stopped appearing altogether." *Commentary* under Podhoretz "was perhaps the first magazine of any size to pay serious and sympathetic attention" to the New Left. It gave space to anarchist, revisionist, progressive, and democratic socialist strains of thought as represented by the likes of Mailer, Norman O. Brown, Herbert Marcuse, Michael Harrington, H. Stuart Hughes, Edgar Friedenberg, Paul Goodman, and Staughton Lynd. These people were not in the Cohen-Trilling tradition; Cohen would have discarded their work immediately. It was these pieces that enabled the "new" *Commentary* to define itself so rapidly. As Podhoretz told a *Newsweek* reporter in 1960, "the major change since I took over is that we're more critical—critical of American society, of certain assumptions about the cold war."[47]

Podhoretz wasted no time establishing this tone and his very first issue in February 1960 serialized Paul Goodman's *Growing Up Absurd*. Goodman was an anarchist social writer who shifted the argument and political discussion in intellectual circles from foreign policy and chiefly whether anti-Communism had run its course to domestic policy after the long intellectual somnolence of the Eisenhower years, to produce a vehement assault on contemporary American society, in particular its failure to provide purposeful directions and opportunities for the youth. By connecting the contemporary sense of crisis and the institutional structure of modern society, Podhoretz felt that Goodman's analysis was "the single best description" he had read of what had happened to American youth in the postwar period and of the social situation in the 1960s. It was richer and more concrete than the standard psychoanalytic and sociological approaches, but Goodman had a hard time getting it published. Podhoretz believed Goodman's essays represented a "reawakening" of a new kind of social criticism "animated by a 'utopian' vision of human possibility" and "a good way for *Commentary* to begin a new period in its own history." Indeed, *Growing Up Absurd* was everything Podhoretz wanted for the new *Commentary*—and more: "it was the very incarnation of the new spirit I had been hoping would be at work in the world, as it had been at work in me."[48]

It was a good way for Podhoretz to begin his editorship. The sensation that Goodman caused was so great that it put *Commentary* "on the map from the very first minute." Furthermore, it was a departure from the standards of Cohen; according to Martin Mayer, Goodman had "managed to deny all the virtues represented in the past by Elliot Cohen and his magazine." Many readers loved it.

> I can't think of a more invigorating event at the beginning of this decade than the appearance of what we shall probably be calling soon "the new *Commentary*." And I can thank of no better way to signal the best intentions than to open with Paul Goodman's "Youth in the Organized Society,"

gushed one, while another added that Goodman's article was alone "worth the price of the year's subscription."[49]

Podhoretz gave space to many first-time contributors. He introduced many new writers and most of his magazine was given over to those who hadn't previously contributed to it. He cultivated cultural rather than literary criticism, and befitting the 1960s, the magazine became more political and sociological. *Commentary* thus began to appear much more sophisticated and complex. There was a much greater emphasis on economics and social affairs and a wider range of social issues than the middle period of Cohen's editorship, although it has to be said that towards the end of the 1950s more articles on these subjects began to appear. There was a much greater emphasis on reform: social, economic, and urban. There were more articles on science including psychology, psychiatry, and biology. Podhoretz published articles on a range of topics unseen in *Commentary* before: pornography, birth control, capital punishment, drug addiction, economics, and fiscal and monetary policy. He also gave space to regular monthly review sections of TV, fiction, and movies.

Because, one contributor recalled, everyone was "deep into porn" back then, Podhoretz even published articles that ran counter to his self-proclaimed Leavisite Puritanism because such Puritanism didn't fit into the new era. In "Pornography, Art, and Censorship", Goodman wrote of the "beautiful cultural consequences" that would follow from legalizing pornography. He complained about "the forbidden topic, the mockery of sacred public figures." He argued that if the legal restrictions were lifted from pornography, it would "ennoble all our art" and "humanize sexuality."[50]

Softening the Hardness

Podhoretz reined in the *hard-line* anti-Communism, correctly perceiving it to be out of kilter with the temper of the times. This shift leftwards was also the result of Podhoretz's need to wrest the magazine away from the politics and ideology of the Cohen-Trilling generation, which, by the mid-1950s, was merely repeating the message of the hard-line anti-Communist organization, the American Committee for Cultural Freedom. Podhoretz had to kill symbolically his father figures and there was no better way of achieving this than reneging on their hard-line anti-Communist politics. Rather than continuing their tradition, he softened it when he took over the magazine. The turn against Cold War anti-Communist liberalism very sharply conflicted with everything he had learned from Trilling and Cohen as a young intellectual.

Commentary's changed stand on the Cold War was most clearly articulated by the young historian, Staughton Lynd, one of the primary architects of New Left foreign policy analysis. In "How the Cold War Began," Lynd overturned previously sacrosanct US and *Commentary* orthodoxies by blaming the onset of the Cold War on America, as much as the Soviet Union, and the adoption of containment as the entire basis of its foreign policy. He presciently warned that it required the United States to ally with anti-Communist governments, regardless of their other policies. Lynd further argued that Wilsonian utopianism blocked any hope for peace with the Soviet Union. Overall, it was an extremely revisionist piece which would never have appeared in the old *Commentary* of the 1950s. Solotaroff described it as "a fire alarm" and others accused Lynd of penning "an elegantly written apology" for the Soviet Union.[51]

The revisionist theme was continued when Podhoretz initiated a series of articles, written by authors of differing points of view, on US foreign policy in the new circumstances of the 1960s. These reappraisals of US foreign policy, often taking the form of stern critiques, called for a rethinking and refashioning of relations with US allies, relations with the uncommitted nations, the relation between domestic policies and foreign policy, relations with the Communist bloc, and the supranational control of atomic power. This last area tapped into a new strain of thinking during the 1960s. Disarmament had become a key issue. Ideas like pacifism and nuclear disarmament were now considered intellectually, and articles supporting both began to appear. Many writers advocated unilateral nuclear disarmament on the part of the United States. Podhoretz began to associate with the peace movement and *Commentary* expressed a new belief in the possibility of doing something to reduce the danger of nuclear war in particular and of ending the Cold War in general. Perhaps the most important was David Riesman and Michael Maccoby's astute and critical deconstruction of Cold War policies. They argued that containment had been "distorted into a need to feel tough," creating a "climate of middle complacency and fringe hysteria." They called for disarmament as the first step to curing the "ulcer" of the Cold War.[52]

The most striking element of *Commentary*'s treatment of foreign policy was its stance on Vietnam. Under Podhoretz *Commentary* was the first magazine to seriously consider the issue and its potential ramifications. Certainly, *Commentary* had one of the longest and most consistent records of opposition to American policy in Vietnam, of all magazines. Podhoretz was one of the earliest opponents of US military intervention in Vietnam from the outset, supporting immediate unilateral withdrawal.

Podhoretz published articles severely critical of American policy in Vietnam from 1961 onwards. In that year Hans Morgenthau compared the "Laotian debacle" to France's Algeria, criticizing US policy in Southeast Asia, in particular American military involvement, as an illicit and stupid expansion of containment policy. He warned repeatedly and presciently that the application of containment to Asia would end in disaster, "bring[ing] forth more serious symptoms and will in the end bring us to the verge of national catastrophe of one sort or another." The risks outweighed the interests at stake, he argued, and commitments exceeded capabilities. France had learned this lesson in the course of a disastrous war and at the price of its democratic institutions. "Are we going to learn our lesson through reflection, or must we suffer disaster abroad and at home in order to learn it?" he wondered. In a prophetic statement, he cautioned that America's military approach, if persisted, would lead to another Korea but with conditions much more unfavorable. Such a war, he warned, "cannot be won quickly, if it can be won at all, and may well last . . . five or ten years, perhaps only to end again in a stalemate." Aside from the military risks, such a war "would certainly have a profound impact upon the political health of the nation ... The American people are bound to be at least as deeply affected by the frustrations of a Vietnamese war."[53]

Commentary consistently emphasized the use of nonmilitary means, advocating nonviolent resistance as the only viable strategic option. As force alone would not eliminate the guerrillas, it recommended the imposition of political sanctions on North Vietnam, as well as assisting the Vietnamese people to escape the oppression of the Vietcong through nonmilitary intervention like financial aid, technical assistance, and counterinsurgency advice. It was deemed imperative that the Vietnamese did the actual fighting. It wanted preventive rather than offensive action. It correctly predicted that escalation would raise the level of risk, ultimately discredit the United States, and bolster Communist accusations of imperialist interference.

This stance clearly demarcated his magazine from the intellectual competition at that time. Podhoretz's concern began very early on when other journals, newspapers, and magazines were not so bothered about the situation there; Vietnam was a highly unfashionable topic among the intelligentsia during the early 1960s. Typical of the intellectual indifference at that time were Robert Lowell and Dwight Macdonald, who cornered Podhoretz one evening, and demanded to know, "Why is your magazine so boring? Why do you keep publishing those boring pieces on Southeast Asia? Who gives a damn? Who is Hans Morgenthau?" Furthermore, opposition to US policy in those days also stood *Commentary* against the Kennedy administration and the major institutions in American life like the *New York Times*, the *Washington Post*, and the Council on Foreign Relations. Thus, within the intellectual currents of this time, Podhoretz had begun to make *Commentary* distinctive.[54]

De-Judaizement

In order to increase the magazine's appeal and circulation, Podhoretz wanted to break away from what he perceived to be Cohen's Jewish parochialism, which he says he had always disliked. One of his conditions for accepting the editorship had been an agreement to allow him to make the magazine more general and less Jewish in emphasis. He agreed to the position

> on the understanding that I had a mandate to change it from a Jewish magazine that carried a certain amount of general material to a general magazine that carried a certain amount of Jewish material. *Commentary* would continue to have a special interest in Jewish

affairs, but it would mainly be an intellectual American magazine addressing itself to the entire range of contemporary issues.

Podhoretz's reasoning betrays his real motivation: "there was no longer enough first-rate work of the kind appropriate to *Commentary* being done within the Jewish world to nourish the great magazine it ought to become." Furthermore, by becoming more general than Jewish in overall emphasis, Podhoretz distanced *Commentary* from the Cohen years and in doing so hoped to make the journal more widely appealing.[55]

Nevertheless, because Podhoretz acknowledged that a large part of *Commentary*'s success in the 1950s was attributable to its Jewishness, he didn't discard it altogether.

> By making itself into the leading Jewish magazine in America, it had also been able to win a place as a recognized institution of the national culture . . . If *Commentary* had not been a Jewish magazine, it is doubtful that it could have established itself at all.

Its "acculturated" tone of Jewishness, he concluded, had helped it to gain widespread acceptance as a magazine of general interest for it was then the only major Jewish magazine competing on the open market for circulation, expressing the Jewish outlook to the world, rather than to a Jewish audience (most other Jewish publications at that time were house organs or membership magazines). Nor could Podhoretz afford to ignore a key part of *Commentary*'s target audience—roughly 80 per cent of the subscribers were Jewish—particularly at such an early stage of his editorship. So Podhoretz simply denied publicly that *Commentary* was changing—he claimed because he thought it was "impolitic" to do so—and insisted that his magazine represented a truer picture of the condition of the American Jewish community.[56]

Podhoretz decided to push "the logic of Cohen's strategy further." He immediately removed "the single most positively Jewish feature of the old *Commentary*"—the column "Cedars of Lebanon" which reprinted classic Jewish texts—since its appeal was specifically Jewish yet strangely replaced it with "In the Community," a new column that addressed concerns of the larger Jewish community, construed in a very broad sense, covering aspects of American and Israeli Jewry. Its authors, Milton Himmelfarb and Robert Alter, wrote about subjects such as Jewish voting patterns and culture and literature, particularly current trends in Israeli literature, respectively. But Podhoretz placed a greater emphasis on articles with a general viewpoint rather than of special Jewish interest and had thus decided only to publish

Jewish material where it met his standards and not merely for the sake of it. If this meant an issue with no such material then so be it. When it was included, he insisted that his contributors address Jewish topics in a universal way, demanding that they do not assume any particular familiarity with their co-religionists when doing so.[57]

As a result, *Commentary* became broader in tone and the Jewish material which did feature, had a wider appeal. The number of specifically Jewish articles declined. For the first four years of Podhoretz's editorship, coverage of the Jewish community was infrequent at best (with the exception of "In the Community"). Podhoretz seemed to be not particularly interested in Jewish matters and fewer articles of Jewish interest appeared in it during this period than at any other time hitherto. *Commentary* therefore refused to speak for those Jews whose principal concern was simply other Jews, nor was it in the first instance a "Jewish" mouthpiece. It was not an American Jewish magazine in the usual sense, rather it was a magazine run by intellectuals who happened to be Jewish, for other intellectuals and the "common reader," Jewish and non-Jewish alike. Defending the magazine, Ruth Wisse, argued: "This was not meant to devalue internal Jewish concerns—as certain Jewish critics charged—but to encourage Jews to speak directly to the public about whatever was uppermost in their minds." In saying so, she seemed to take the words right out of Podhoretz's mouth.[58]

Compared to the last decade, *Commentary*'s coverage of Israel also declined, as Podhoretz calculated that the topic was of little interest to his readers in the early 1960s. It was as if the establishment of the State of Israel had yet to make a significant impact on the magazine. One reader wrote in to ask, "what did the Israelis do to you that *Commentary* can't forgive them after twelve years . . . ?" And when it did cover Israel, it was less concerned with the state's relationship to its neighbors but rather its strategic place in the Cold War. And there was a shift in what it published, from external and/or political affairs under Cohen, to the domestic, the internal, and the nonpolitical, such as the kibbutzim and Israeli art and culture under Podhoretz.[59]

"Kosher Baloney"

Podhoretz also continued Cohen's capacity for publishing controversial material on Jewish affairs as he realized it made an impact. Often, it seems, he deliberately took positions exactly opposite those of the wider Jewish community. In April 1961, Podhoretz devoted more than half of that month's issue to a rerun of the *Contemporary Jewish Record*'s 1944 "Under

Forty" symposium. Entitled "Jewishness & the Younger Intellectuals," its tone of ambivalence combined with rejection of the organized Jewish community was one of the most provocative and controversial issues to hit the American Jewish community in the early 1960s, provoking considerable and widespread comment and discussion. And, in "A Fund-Raiser Comes to Northrup" in March 1962, the fifth in a series of anonymous articles stretching back to the 1950s, the anonymous author decried the shocking tactics of modern Jewish fund-raising, effectively exposing the Jewish community, and questioning the very idea that the affluent American Jewish community should have "needs."[60]

Commentary continued to rail against the nostalgic sentimentalization of Jewish culture and ubiquitous popularization of American Judaism. In a review of *Mila 18*, Midge Decter called Leon Uris "a gifted writer of hardcore trash." Likewise, Irving Howe, found the Broadway version of *Fiddler on the Roof* "a tasteless jumble," "sterile," "[i]rresistible bait for the nostalgia-smitten audience," "sentimental and exploitative," which did not just reflect the "spiritual anemia" of Broadway, in his opinion, but also of the middle-class American Jews who watched it. The assault continued under Robert Alter, who railed against the vulgarization of American Jewish culture for commercial gain: "The typical involvement in Jewish culture consists of an acquaintance with gefilte fish and crass bar-mitzvahs, a degree of familiarity with overstuffed Jewish matriarchs, and a mastery of several pungent Yiddish synonyms for the male organ." And Solotaroff trashed Harry Golden, the popular editor of the *Carolina Israelite* and a widely respected commentator on Jewish life in the South, who had been discovered by Cohen and first published in *Commentary*, describing him as "the court jester of the Eisenhower Age," who dished out "soft, sloppy, equivocal thinking," "affable flatulence," "bland, homey" writing that veered away from "complexity and controversy to safe banality and nice sentiment" to soothe "anxieties, provide a confident if vague sense of direction, and preside over the evasion of issues."[61]

Commentary found it tragic that American Jewry, which it felt ought to know better, had accepted the simplicity and superficiality of crass, commercialized, vulgarized Jewishness. Philip Roth criticized many of the Jewish writers *Commentary* had championed over the previous decade, such as Malamud and Bellow. Roth also sarcastically demolished his critics who considered him a self-hater for his raw portrayal of Jews in his *Goodbye, Columbus*.[62]

These self-assured and often severe essays attracted considerable attention and provoked hostility among the wider Jewish community, particularly those who belonged to the organized framework of American Judaism like the rabbinate. Jewish readers were irritated at the manifest, and for them regrettable, tone of "shallowness and cool and detached posture," as well as "callousness and obtuseness." They complained that *Commentary* had chosen to print Jews who were "safely ensconced in their various academic jobs" and palpably ignorant of Judaism rather than any one of the "brilliant and unusually young Jewish intellectuals," who were actually competent to write about Judaism, Jewishness, and Israel. Such secular intellectuals, they protested, were much more likely to be conversant with *Fowler's Modern English Usage* and with developments in the social sciences than with Jewish religious tradition, and did not reflect the American Jewish community, and were no barometer of their feelings. One reader called it pages of wasted space, more "'baloney'—kosher, of course," while yet another found its "stench sickening." One-time contributor Jessie S. Bloom summed up the impact, "Well, keep on printing articles like the symposium. They will keep my blood stirred and I'm sure I'll find it good for the digestion."[63]

Commentary's critiques aroused anger because what Podhoretz saw as a "long overdue assessment of Jewish bourgeois gentility in American life" violated a powerful though unwritten commandment of Jewish life: "Thou shalt not reveal in-group secrets to the goyim." It had offended the public-relations concept of storytelling in which Jewish writers should portray Jews as virtuous and stay silent about the rest, lest non-Jews seize on it as ammunition for anti-Semitism. The final straw was that *Commentary* conspicuously lacked an alternative vision of Jewish cultural life to replace that being condemned. Where Cohen had suggested alternatives and future directions, Podhoretz often did not, making the attacks much starker. One reader wrote in, "I am dissatisfied with [your] attitude toward creative Jewish values." "This then was the new *Commentary*," wrote a former contributor, "the magazine that had come into being to report the dropping of the curtain on the last act of the play that was Jewish existence."[64]

While the more congratulatory elements of the Jewish community might have deplored these articles, younger Jewish intellectuals adored them. Indeed, many writers and readers were precisely attracted to the magazine because the new editorial regime had de-Judaized its contents. With these articles, wrote William Novak, the editor of *Response* magazine, "*Commentary* reached admirable new heights in understanding and analyzing what was passing for Jewish culture." Another young Jewish writer, Bernard Avishai, wrote how:

> We keenly awaited *Commentary* every month as if it were a public realm in which Jews were permitted to live on the questions . . . *Commentary* established itself as our mail-order polity; one could,

it seemed, be actively Jewish just by reading about the Jews' history, debating the place in culture of Jewish ritual law, or discerning the American "emancipation" in the elegance of the magazine's prose. And one could hope to be a good Jew by writing with virtuosity about issues that were on our minds.

Another added: "I've learned more about Jewish culture from the pages of *Commentary* than from my own experience." A further reader congratulated the real service done "in presenting Jews as fallible human beings in contrast to the semi-official policy of Jewish organizations to present an image of the Jews as someone slightly better than normal." Controversy obviously sold.[65]

This was most evident when Adolph Eichmann was kidnapped in Argentina by Israeli secret agents. Although the majority of American Jewry backed his capture and clearly supported Israel's right to try him, including Podhoretz, he gave space to discussion of the ethics of Israel's actions by high-profile Jewish luminaries who expressed their doubts. Podhoretz allowed discussion because he was equivocal on the issue, neither condoning nor condemning the execution of Nazi war criminals. As an opponent of capital punishment, Podhoretz did not advocate execution, but as a Jew he did not oppose it either. He wondered why it was that Israel was always asked to act more nobly than other nations. In stressing the unique, unprecedented, and incomprehensible nature of the Nazi crimes, he felt no conceivable punishment could possibly begin to approach adequacy. And further that any Jew who condemned the executions was in effect forgetting what the Nazis did. "All a Jew can do is hope that he is humane enough to suffer from watching men dangle at the end of a rope while at the same time being human enough to force himself to approve of the hangings because he is a Jew," he wrote. Podhoretz's equivocation was reflected in the magazine and conflicting views were presented.[66]

Podhoretz continued to court controversy over the issue. During the period between Eichmann's abduction and his trial, he ran a review of Raul Hilberg's 1961 book *The Destruction of the European Jews*, which anticipated much of what the trial later revealed. In contrast to the generally hostile reception the book received, *Commentary* found it contained "profound social content," but warned ominously that its "most surprising revelation" would be "the least welcome": the extent to which the Nazis relied upon the Jews in the machinery of extermination.[67]

But, when Hannah Arendt's articles on the Eichmann trial were published in *The New Yorker*, Podhoretz found himself in a difficult situation. As with her "Little Rock" article, she took an entirely unconventional approach to the trial, but unlike that situation Podhoretz decided to take an unsupportive position against his friend. Her twin thesis that genocide did not require monsters or pathological anti-Semites but rather that the Nazis were banal, and that the Jews acquiesced, even cooperated, in the genocide provoked a storm, causing a tremendous uproar. Podhoretz was annoyed that he had lost one of the most controversial pieces of the 1960s—Arendt had already proposed to cover the trial for *Commentary* and Podhoretz had to turn her down because he could not afford to cover her expenses. Although deeply perturbed by Arendt's articles, he was nevertheless unwilling to join those attacking her because then he would be openly in harmony with the organized American Jewish community. Furthermore, he perceived their attacks as wildly excessive, inaccurate, and emotive. Podhoretz had also learned that Arendt was becoming paranoid about what she felt was an orchestrated and directed campaign against her and he feared that if he criticized her in *Commentary* she would think he had probably been ordered to do so by the AJC and regard it as an act of betrayal. Yet, Podhoretz felt he had no choice but to respond even if it meant risking her friendship.

The piece that emerged was "Hannah Arendt on Eichmann." As his subtitle indicated ("A Study in the Perversity of Brilliance"), Podhoretz felt that Arendt's portrait of Eichmann was genuinely brilliant but he also upheld many of the criticisms of Arendt's accusers. He wrote that her arguments concerning the banality of evil were simultaneously perverse. He agreed with her accusers that there was something indecent and obscene about Arendt's line of thought which asked some difficult questions of the behavior of the Jewish leadership during the Second World War (since this implicitly included the AJC, was he also defending that agency, too?). Arendt was "all cleverness and no eloquence," "complex, unsentimental, riddled with paradox and ambiguity." He felt her "cavalier" manipulation of the evidence was "visibly tendentious," leading to "distortions of perspective." She "heavily underlines every trace of moral ambiguity she can wring out of it." She accepted Eichmann's account of himself and of his role in the Final Solution as largely true even though Harold Rosenberg had pointed out that one of the trial's extreme distortions was its presentation to the world of only the courtroom identity of Eichmann, as a defendant, which he'd refined over the years for just that sort of situation. "The brilliance of Miss Arendt's treatment of Eichmann could hardly be disputed by any disinterested reader," Podhoretz concluded. But at the same time, it demonstrated "the intellectual perversity that can result from the pursuit of brilliance by a mind infatuated with its own agility and bent on generating dazzle."[68]

Arendt felt that the AJC had put Podhoretz up to it (in order to uphold its erstwhile "hush hush" policy and to defend its wartime record).

When Podhoretz denied this, she replied, "You're lying, of course, but it was foolish of me to expect that you would be man enough to tell me the truth." Their friendship cooled considerably and Arendt never again wrote for *Commentary*, preferring *The New York Review of Books* instead. Podhoretz had irritated a brilliant contributor to the magazine to its eternal detriment, beginning a pattern that lasted well into the future. Sometime later, she asked him, "why did you do it?"[69]

Risking Old Friendships

Podhoretz did it because he calculated that the best way to win notice for himself was to court controversy. The most efficient method for achieving this was to disengage himself from his predecessor's intellectual generation. In the attempt to break away from Cohen, Podhoretz, deliberately it seemed, antagonized the older generation of the New York Intellectual community in order to create a political/ideological rift, even though many of them were his friends. His strategy operated on two levels: in the magazine and in his personal life. Anti-Communist intellectuals like the Trillings, Irving Kristol, Sidney Hook, and Daniel Bell were not happy with Podhoretz's changes, particularly his stubborn insistence on radicalism (even though, as we shall see, it was more illusory than real). They and others accused Podhoretz of having become too soft on Communism and too hard on America. They perceived his publication of the Cold War revisionists like Lynd in particular as an outrageous betrayal. Incensed, Diana Trilling wrote to Podhoretz about Riesman and Maccoby's article, describing it as "appalling." She was shocked that he had printed it and felt that he had done so merely out of cynical motives:

> I can't believe you would have ... [printed it] ... if it weren't that this is the approach to politics that you consider modern, flexible, the necessary coercive to the sterile anti-Communism of your predecessor generation. OK then, so you print it and no doubt the Zeitgeist applauds you.[70]

Even though these people were his friends, Podhoretz was nonetheless willing, even eager, to risk old friendships over his new stance. Indeed, he provoked bitter rows, calling his intellectual peers Cold War warriors and revisionists of liberalism. In turn, they accused him of forcing them out of *Commentary* and harming further the already delicate liberal anti-Communist consensus. Podhoretz's habit of courting confrontation with his former friends and mentors exploded into ugly quarrels. The first fight had broken out over Michael Harrington's 1959 *Commentary* article

"Our Fifty Million Poor," which Podhoretz liked, but Kristol hated. Bell exploded in a rage over Podhoretz's sponsorship of Norman O. Brown, whom he considered dangerous and irresponsible. Bell also perceived Henry Aiken's 1964 "The Revolt Against Ideology" to be in great measure an attack on him, as well as confused and even pointless, and he was particularly hurt that Podhoretz considered it to be one of the best articles he had read in some time. Podhoretz's own piece "The Young Generation" led to a heated squabble with Diana Trilling. Podhoretz's new regard for Mailer produced ill-tempered discussions with Philip Rahv. And philosopher Sidney Morgenbesser became so nasty and insulting that Podhoretz walked out on him in the middle of lunch.[71]

At three successive dinners Podhoretz ferociously and hysterically lashed out at his mentor Lionel Trilling, screaming that he was not a socialist at all, but a phony, and a sellout. Podhoretz attacked Trilling (as he would do repeatedly over the years) as "somehow inauthentic, suppressing his true self, feigning the false air of an English gentleman," that he "lacked the courage of his convictions, that he was faithless to his own teaching." On another night Kristol, Bell, Epstein, Trilling, Podhoretz, Hook, Marcus, Phillips, and other eminent intellectuals gathered at the Columbia faculty club. Where at previous dinners Podhoretz had vented his wrath at Trilling, this time he turned on Hook, screeching, "You're a fraud! You're not a social democrat!" Trilling went white and hurriedly got out of his seat. "Gentlemen," he said, calmly, "good evening." And he left. "He wouldn't take it any longer," said Bell. It was "the last time everyone was together." As the 1960s wore on, Trilling and his cohort had less and less to do with Podhoretz both professionally and personally as they became increasingly dismissive of each other's ideas. As Bell rather dryly remarked,

> Anyway, there it is. One more minor notch in the gunslinging of the intelligentsia. It sounds comical now and is, though doubtless somebody, someday, will write it up as a footnote to literary history as is becoming the fashion these days.[72]

Rather than being a minor notch, an emotional and ideological schism had opened up between Podhoretz and his old friends and mentor. Trilling, above all, was hurt and took it very badly. According to Mark Gerson, he perceived his former student and "protégé's flirtation with radicalism to be a direct repudiation of his tutelage," for Podhoretz had ended up promoting the very views that Trilling had spent most of his life fighting. This was compounded by the knowledge that Podhoretz was his disciple, and successor to Trilling's own mentor, Cohen. In betraying Trilling, Podhoretz's strategy of creating a gulf had worked.[73]

Podhoretz did not seem to care about his friendships. It was as if he used people for particular things at particular times and then dropped them when they no longer served a purpose. Just as he latched onto Norman Mailer (after publicly reviling his work) and Norman O. Brown, he either abandoned or publicly attacked friends like the Trillings, Bell, Arendt, and so on with alarming alacrity. These were the very people who had given him a foothold in New York intellectual life in the 1950s. The case of Trilling is instructive. Trilling lay behind Podhoretz's success at Columbia, Cambridge, and *Commentary*; his debt to Trilling was immense. But this conflicted with Podhoretz's attempt to distance himself from the Cohen generation, so rather than show gratitude, he aimed vicious ideological assaults against him, often in the form of verbal abuse. He was young, brash, and ambitious. His new stance was gaining him attention and influence. And as long as he had his wife and family behind him, it was as if he did not need anyone else. Indeed, he appeared to feel that he owed his friends and mentors nothing; he denied their patronage and insisted that he had made it on his own.

Editorial Freedom

Another key part of Podhoretz's strategy was his calculation that to appear as a radical *Commentary* must not be identified readily with such an establishment and conservative organization as the AJC. So he often took positions and printed articles deliberately at odds with their stated policies. Using the precedent set by Cohen, Podhoretz had decided to deliberately push against the boundaries established by the AJC. He had assessed that, as boss, "unless he took the risk of exercising the power implicit in that position, it would not be real."[74] Podhoretz tested the limits of his editorial independence to the full, almost to the extent of risking the AJC's patronage, as well as his job. He used such items as a gesture of defiance and autonomy, to establish *Commentary*'s ideological distance from the AJC, knowing precisely that no Jewish agency would allow this sort of thing to be printed in a conservative "house" magazine.

He refused to keep Cohen's proportion of Jewish to general articles, simply because the AJC feared a decline in Jewish subject matter. He rejected a piece by the AJC's expert on "quarantine" policy on George Linclon Rockwell, commander of the American Nazi Party, because it would be interpreted as an AJC piece. Three years later, in March 1963, he then contributed an article to *Esquire* magazine on the very same subject, expressing sentiments at odds with AJC policy. He took a position on the Eichmann kidnapping that clashed with the AJC's. Alan Stroock, a charter member of the *Commentary* Publication Committee (and one of Cohen's keenest supporters), who had until now adhered strictly to the tradition that he should be reluctant, at least in public, to comment on the contents of the magazine, was angered enough to openly express his disagreement in the magazine.[75]

In November 1964, Podhoretz decided to publish Leslie H. Farber's overtly explicit critique of the sexologist William Master's attempts to analyze the orgasm. The article contained such gems as, "At the end of the day, when his wife asked, 'How were things at the lab today?' he would reply, 'Oh, nothing, just the same old grind'" and

> Clearly, the perfect orgasm is the orgasm achieved on one's own. No other consummation offers such certainty and moreover avoids the messiness that attends most human affairs. The onanist may choose the partner of his dreams who very probably will be the Lady of the Laboratory, or he may have his orgasm without any imagined partner.

To make things worse, Podhoretz published a discussion on the letters pages on the nature of orgasm and masturbation. One reader of 16 years standing was "shocked and dismayed." AJC members were also appalled, one prominent member of *Commentary*'s board resigned in protest, and a campaign was launched to dismiss Podhoretz.[76]

Podhoretz again survived, despite his best efforts it seemed, when his attacks on the Kennedy administration's domestic and foreign policies in the face of the AJC's broad support for JFK and his New Frontier program, drew a complaint from one of Kennedy's assistants to an AJC delegation visiting the White House. Podhoretz was summoned to a meeting and told that he was jeopardizing the AJC's relations with the White House and asked to consider the harm this could do, as well as to agree to go a little easier. Podhoretz refused and offered his resignation. But the AJC declined either to fire him or to let him resign. "They therefore confined themselves to baleful shrugs of helplessness in the face of the uncontrollable young firebrand they had been imprudent enough to hire," recalled Podhoretz.[77]

Although *Commentary* was now housed in the same building as the AJC at 165 East 56th Street, it was in a world of its own on the seventh floor, and the AJC had a hard time reining in Podhoretz. Cohen had not only been much more amenable to its policies (even if he took a tougher line on Communism and liberalism than the AJC), he had also participated in its initiatives; at times it seemed that *Commentary* was a forum for airing official AJC opinions. This ended under Podhoretz. Despite the physical proximity, Podhoretz was intellectually and politically more distant from the Committee than Cohen, and Podhoretz's *Commentary* was more financially on its own than Cohen's had been, producing clear ideological gaps and strains at times.

Norman the Conqueror

Podhoretz's strategy was working. Circulation figures had risen steadily over his first few years in charge. In 1960, they were 20,000 and had risen to 25,000 the following year; by 1962 they had reached 29,000, 40,000 by 1963; and 60,000 by 1965, an all-time high, more than three times the figure when Podhoretz took over. Podhoretz bragged that readership would rise to 100,000 by the end of the decade. By virtue of what he had done at *Commentary*, and what it had done for him, Podhoretz's stock had risen. *Commentary* was a national institution and, as its editor, he was invited to banquets, parties, to join the boards of directors of committees, to appear on TV, to lecture, to consult. He was often interviewed by reporters and quoted in the press. In general, he was treated with a great degree of deference.[78]

Commentary was widely seen in Washington. White House staff regularly read the magazine. Its attacks on the Kennedy Administration were getting through loud and clear. (Despite the criticism, the President still found *Commentary* "to be one of the most stimulating and well-edited periodicals that come to my attention.") Podhoretz also had access to power. He met politicians like Bobby Kennedy, Marion Javits, and Dick Goodwin. He had so impressed or irritated the elites that the Office of Cultural Exchange at the Department of State wished to add him to their file of possible American Specialists for use in its Educational and Cultural Exchange Program. He was elected to the National Council of the Turn Toward Peace. Politicians and officials of the Johnson administration, including the president himself, often sought Podhoretz's advice.

Commentary had made it. It was now housed in handsome and impressive offices at the AJC's headquarters. The blue-paneled contemporary building with a walnut and leather lobby, a smart elevator, and five or six individual offices each with its own walnut door for the editors was a world apart from the leaking loft that had accommodated *Commentary* under Cohen. Even the receptionist was a young blonde with the cheekbones of a model and a young Al Pacino worked as an office boy for the magazine. The appointment of a new business manager, Martin Edelston, helped to arrest the magazine's deficit and for a while it was optimistically hoped that a profit might actually be made. Podhoretz took lunch at a nice French restaurant around the corner. As Solotaroff recalled on first entering, "I could see that the new *Commentary* was not just the rambunctious kid brother of *Partisan Review*, it was also the favored grandson of a very well-to-do and well-established Jewish family." Indeed, with the color ads for luxury products, the magazine itself looked more bourgeois and aspirational.[79]

Now that Podhoretz's strategy had worked, it was time to pull back and return to his instincts. As a consequence, Podhoretz devised, as we shall see, an even more controversial yet honest strategy: the open adoption of a conservatism that had been hiding beneath the surface since he took over the magazine.

Notes

1. Sidney Blumenthal, *The Rise of the Counter-Establishment: From Conservative Ideology to Political Power* (New York: Times Books, 1986), 135.

2. Ida Cohen Selavan to Nathan Glazer, April 29, 1977, Norman Podhoretz Papers, Manuscript Division, Library of Congress, Washington, DC ("NPLC"); Michael Wyschogrod, "My *Commentary* Problem—And Ours," *Judaism* 17:2 (Spring 1968), 161.

3. Norman Podhoretz, *The Prophets: Who They Were, What They Are* (New York: The Free Press, 2002), 313–14; Norman Podhoretz, *Making It* (New York: Random House, 1967), 3; Blumenthal, *The Rise of the Counter-Establishment*, 135.

4. Podhoretz, *Making It*, 80.

5. Jerry Ravetz, email to author, June 21, 2003; Podhoretz, Statement for 40th Anniversary of the Fulbright program, n.d. (c. August 1986), NPLC; Thomas L. Jeffers, "Norman Podhoretz's Discourses on America," *The Hudson Review* 54:2 (Summer 2001), 204, 207; Podhoretz, *Making It*, 80; Thomas Grubisich, "Norman Podhoretz, "New Left's Enemy From Within," *The Washington Post*, Style Section (April 11, 1971), G9.

6. Michael Wyschogrod, "My *Commentary* Problem," 150; Trilling to Cohen, December 3, 1951, NPLC; Trilling, *Proceedings of the 64th Annual Meeting of the American Jewish Committee*, May 14–17, 1970, NPLC; Nathan Glazer, email to author, July 29, 2002; Michael Wyschogrod, "My *Commentary* Problem," 149.

7. Glazer, email to author, July 29, 2002; Midge Decter, "Remembering Robert Warshow," *Commentary* 113:4 (April 2002); David Denby, "Robert Warshow: Life and Works," in Robert Warshow, *The Immediate Experience: Movies, Comics, Theatre and Other Aspects of Popular Culture* (enlarged edn. Cambridge, MA: Harvard University Press, 2001), xii; Norman Podhoretz, "The Issue," *Commentary* 29:2 (February 1960), a, 182–4; Mary Lea Schieman, interview by Bill Novak, April 29, 1974.

8. Podhoretz, *Making It*, 102; Norman Podhoretz, *Doings and Undoings: The Fifties and After in American Writing* (London: Rupert Hart-Davis, 1965), 259; Clinton Williamson, Jr., "Norman Podhoretz: The Universal Man," *The World & I* (September 1988), 669–79.

9. Norman Podhoretz, "Statement"; Podhoretz to Trilling, June 6, 1951, Norman Podhoretz to Ralph H. Vogel, August 3, 1971, NPLC.

10. Neil Jumonville, *Critical Crossings: The New York Intellectuals in Postwar America* (Berkeley: University of California Press, 1991), 195; Philips, quoted in Merle Miller, "Why Norman and Jason Aren't Talking," *The New York Times Magazine* (March 26, 1972), 105;

Podhoretz, *Making It*, p.146; Norman Podhoretz, "Achilles in Left Field," *Commentary* 15:3 (March 1953), 321–26 and "William Faulkner and the Problem of War," *Commentary* 18:3 (September 1954), 227–32.

11. Podhoretz, *Doings and Undoings*, 2–8, 11; Podhoretz, *Breaking Ranks: A Political Memoir* (New York: Harper & Row, 1979), 23.

12. Jumonville, *Critical Crossings*, 195; Norman Mailer, quoted in Stewart Hakola, "Podhoretz, Norman," in Ann Evory (ed.) *Contemporary Authors, New Revision Series*, ed. (Detroit, MI: Gale Research Co., 1982), 393; Henry C. Carlisle to Cohen, March 8, 1956, Alfred A. Knopf Archive, Harry Ransom Humanities Research Center ("HRHRC"), University of Texas at Austin, Austin, Texas.

13. Quoted in Podhoretz, *Making It*, 56.

14. Howe, quoted in Podhoretz, *Making It*, 152; Henry Wasser, Letters, *Commentary* 18:6 (December 1954), 569–70; Maurice Samuel, Letters, *Commentary* 17:2 (February 1954), 192.

15. Rahv, quoted in David Twersky, "Left, Right, Left Right: After Half a Century, Commentary Remains Defiantly Out of Step," *Moment* 20:3 (June 1995), 44; Robert Brustein, "Who's Killing the Novel?" *The New Republic* 153:17 (October 23, 1965), 22–24.

16. Podhoretz, *Making It*, 156, 161.

17. Podhoretz, *Making It*, 156 and Norman Podhoretz, "The Language of Life," *Commentary* 16:4 (October 1953), 378–82.

18. Podhoretz, *Making It*, 146

19. Podhoretz, *Making It*, 159.

20. Podhoretz, *Making It*, 160; Norman Podhoretz to Geoffrey Rans, January 23, 1964, NPLC.

21. Podhoretz, "Achilles in Left Field," 321–26 and "William Faulkner and the Problem of War," 227–32; Jumonville, *Critical Crossings*, 195; Gary Dorrien, *The Neoconservative Mind: Politics, Culture and the War of Ideology* (Philadelphia: Temple University Press, 1993), 137.

22. Walter Laqueur, interview by author, June 6, 2002; Podhoretz, *Making It*, 199–200; Wyschogrod, "My *Commentary* Problem," 154, 155.

23. Seymour Krim, "Remembering Harold Rosenberg," *Commentary* 66:5 (November 1978), 66; Clement Greenberg, interview by William Novak, May 12, 1974; Martin Greenberg, interview by William Novak, May 1, 1974.

24. Richard Schickel, quoted in Miller, "Why Norman and Jason Aren't Talking," 105; Podhoretz, *Making It*, 198.

25. Podhoretz, *Making It*, 226.

26. Podhoretz, *Making It*, 233.

27. George Lichtheim to Hannah Arendt, February 5, 1958, Hannah Arendt Papers, Manuscript Division, Library of Congress, Washington, DC.

28. Podhoretz, *Making It*, 232, 233; Cecil Roth to Sylvia Cohen, n.d; Wyschogrod, "My *Commentary* Problem," 154.

29. Clement Greenberg, quoted in Alexander Bloom, *Prodigal Sons: The New York Intellectuals and Their World* (New York and Oxford: Oxford University Press, 1986), 320; Norman Podhoretz, *Ex-Friends: Falling Out with Allen Ginsberg, Lionel and Diana Trilling, Lillian Hellman, Hannah Arendt, and Norman Mailer* (New York: Free Press, 1999), 139, 149–51.

30. Arthur Hertzberg, interview by William Novak, June 6, 1974.

31. For more detail on this episode see Nathan Abrams, *Commentary Magazine 1945-1959*: "A Journal of Significant Thought and Opinion." London and Portland, OR: Vallentine Mitchell, 2006., esp. the "Epilogue: After the Cohen Era."

32. Podhoretz, *Making It*, 274, 275; Kristol, Remarks, May 2, 1995.

33. Podhoretz, *Making It*, 283: Norman Podhoretz to C. P. Snow, December 7, 1959, C. P. Snow Papers, HRHRC.

34. Irving Kristol, *Reflections of a Neoconservative: Looking Back, Looking Ahead* (New York: Basic Books, 1983), 17; Podhoretz, *Ex-Friends*, 203.

35. Podhoretz, *Making It*, 3.

36. Podhoretz, *Making It*, 286; Beichman, quoted in Bloom, *Prodigal Sons*, 323.

37. Bell, cited in John Ehrman, "*Commentary*, the *Public Interest*, and the Problem of Jewish Conservatism," *American Jewish History* 87: 2 and 3 (June and September 1999), 163.

38. John Ehrman, "*Commentary*," in *The Conservative Press in Twentieth Century America*, (ed.) Ronald Lora and William Henry Longton (Westport, CT and London: Greenwood Press, 1999), 620.

39. Podhoretz, *Making It*, 325; Theodore Solotaroff, "The New York Publishing World," in *Creators and Disturbers: Reminiscences by Jewish Intellectuals of New York*, (ed.) Bernard Rosenberg and Ernest Goldstein (New York: Columbia University Press, 1982), 412.

40. Solotaroff, "The New York Publishing World," 410-11.

41. Norman Podhoretz, "The Beat Generation," *Partisan Review* 25 (Summer 1957), 472-79; Podhoretz, *Breaking Ranks*, 47, 322, 79; Ehrman, "*Commentary*, the *Public Interest*, and the Problem of Jewish Conservatism," 164.

42. Ehrman, "*Commentary*, the *Public Interest*, and the Problem of Jewish Conservatism," 164; Norman Podhoretz, cited in *Encyclopedia Judaica* (Jerusalem: Keter Publishing, 1971), 792.

43. Podhoretz, *Breaking Ranks*, 47; "The Issue," *Commentary* 29:4 (April 1960); Dwight Macdonald, "The Candidates and I," *Commentary* 29:4 (April 1960), 287-94.

44. For "*Commentary's* assessment" see: William V. Shannon, "Eisenhower as President," *Commentary* 26:6 (December 1958), 462-7; Karl Meyer, "Triumph of the Smooth Deal," *Commentary* 26:6 (December 1958), 461-8; William Newman, "Time Inc. Offers and Ideology," *Commentary* 28:6 (December 1959), 471-8.

45. Sol Stern, "My Jewish Problem—and Ours: Israel, the Left, and the Jewish Establishment," *Ramparts* (August 1971), 38-40; Kristol, quoted in Ehrman, "*Commentary*, the *Public Interest*, and the Problem of Jewish Conservatism," 164; Podhoretz, *Breaking Ranks*, 86.

46. Peter Steinfels, Letters, 78:6 (December 1984), 12; Solotaroff, "The New York Publishing World," 413-14; Ravetz, email to author, June 21, 2003; Podhoretz, *Breaking Ranks*, 54-55.

47. Solotaroff, "The New York Publishing World," 411; Podhoretz, *Making It*, 298; Milton S Katz, "*Commentary* and the American Jewish Intellectual Experience," *Journal of American Culture* 3:1 (Spring 1980), 159; Podhoretz, quoted in William Novak, "*Commentary* and the Jewish Community: the Record Since 1960," *Response* 7:3 (Fall 1973), 52.

48. Norman Podhoretz, "Laws, Kings, and Cures," *Commentary* 50:4 (October 1970), 30 and "The Issue," *Commentary* 29:2 (February 1960) a, 182-4.

49. Irving Kristol to Martin Mayer, March 8, 1960; Martin Mayer to Jason Epstein, March 8, 1960, NPLC; Letters, *Commentary* 29:4 (April 1960), 345–6.

50. Anonymous, interview by author, September 2, 2002; Paul Goodman, "Pornography, Art, and Censorship," 31:3 *Commentary* (March 1961), 203–12.

51. Staughton Lynd, "How the Cold War Began," *Commentary* 30:5 (November 1960), 379–89; Ted Solotaroff, interview by Novak, March 5, 1974.

52. David Riesman and Malcolm Maccoby, "The American Crisis: Political idealism and the Cold War," *Commentary* 29:6 (June 1960), 461–72.

53. Hans Morgenthau, "Asia: The American Algeria," *Commentary* 32:1 (1961), 43–47 and "Vietnam: Another Korea?" *Commentary* 33:5 (May 1962), 369–74.

54. Lowell and Macdonald, quoted in Bloom, Prodigal Sons, 337–38; Podhoretz, *Breaking Ranks*, 182–83.

55. Podhoretz, *Ex-Friends*, 157; Podhoretz, *Making It*, 278.

56. Podhoretz, *Making It*, 308.

57. Podhoretz, *Making It*, 308–309; Wyschogrod, "My *Commentary* Problem," 156.

58. Ruth R. Wisse, "The Making of *Commentary* and of the Jewish Intellectual," *Jewish Social Studies* 3:2 (Winter 1997), 33–34.

59. Alfred Ivry, Letters, *Commentary* 31:5 (May 1961), 443.

60. "Jewishness & the Younger Intellectuals," *Commentary* 31:4 (April 1961), 305–59; Evelyn N. Rossman, "A Fund-Raiser Comes to Northrup" *Commentary* 33:3 (March 1962), 218–25.

61. Midge Decter, "Popular Jews," *Commentary* 32:4 (October 1961), 358–60; Irving Howe, "Tevye on Broadway," *Commentary* 38:5 (November 1964), 73–75; Robert Alter, "Sentimentalizing the Jews," *Commentary* 40:3 (September 1965), 71–75; Theodore Solotaroff, "Harry Golden and the American Audience," *Commentary* 31:1 (January 1961), 1–13.

62. Philip Roth, "Writing American Fiction," *Commentary* 31:3 (March 1961), 223–33 and "Writing about Jews," *Commentary* 36:6 (December 1963), 446–52.

63. Letters, *Commentary* 31:6 (June 1961), 528–39; Jessie S. Bloom, Letters, *Commentary* 32:1 (July 1961), 69–72.

64. Novak, "*Commentary* and the Jewish Community," 53–57; David W. Silverman, quoted in Warren Coffy, "Faith and the Issues," *Commentary* 37:3 (March 1964), 82–5; Letters, *Commentary* 40:6 (December 1965), 30; Wyschogrod, "My *Commentary* Problem," 156.

65. Novak, "*Commentary* and the Jewish Community," 5; Bernard Avishai, "Breaking Faith: *Commentary* and the American Jews," *Dissent* 28:2 (Spring 1981), 237; Sonya Rudikoff in "Jewishness & the Younger Intellectuals," 353; Letters, *Commentary* 37:4 (April 1964), 6–10.

66. Norman Podhoretz, "The Issue," *Commentary* 30:2 (August 1960) and "The Issue," *Commentary* 29:5 (May 1960).

67. Raul Hilberg, "Nazi Bureaucrats and Jewish Leaders," *Commentary* 33:4 (April 1962), 351–56.

68. Podhoretz, *Ex-Friends*, 162–63 and "Hannah Arendt on Eichmann: A Study in the Perversity of Brilliance," *Commentary* 36:3 (September 1963), 201–8.

69. Stern, "My Jewish Problem"; Podhoretz, *Ex-Friends*, 170; and *Breaking Ranks*, 162.

70. Podhoretz, *Breaking Ranks*, 172; Trilling to Podhoretz, June 27, 1960, NPLC.

71. Podhoretz, *Breaking Ranks*, 54–55; Podhoretz, "Following Irving," page proofs, n.d., NPLC.

72. Blumenthal, *The Rise of the Counter-Establishment*, 135, 137–38; Daniel Bell, to Michael Josselson, April 24, 1964, Michael Josselson Papers, HRHRC.

73. Mark Gerson, *The Neoconservative Vision: From the Cold War to the Culture Wars* (Lanham, MD: Madison Books, 1997), 81.

74. Podhoretz, *Making It*, 227.

75. Norman Podhoretz, *My Love Affair with America: The Cautionary Tale of a Cheerful Conservative* (New York: Free Press, 2000), 146 and *Ex-Friends*, 152; Letters, *Commentary* 30:3 (September 1960), 252.

76. Leslie H. Farber, "'I'm Sorry, Dear,'" *Commentary* 38:5 (November 1964), 47–54; Letters, *Commentary* 39:4 (April 1965), 16–27; Podhoretz, *Ex-Friends*, 203–204.

77. Podhoretz, *Doings and Undoings*, 169.

78. Podhoretz, *Making It*, 303.

79. Theodore Solotaroff, *First Loves: A Memoir* (New York: Seven Stories Press, 2003), 257.

2

The Revised Standard Version

Podhoretz's Oedipal struggle—the symbolic killing of his father figures—entailed a rewriting of history through a strongly subjective filter in which the supposed successes of the past under Cohen were systematically downplayed, whitewashed, or simply ignored, and Podhoretz's own successes inflated. The crystallization of this revisionism was articulated in Podhoretz's 1967 memoir *Making It*, much of which covered the early 1960s period at *Commentary* and which has set the tone for later historians of neoconservatism, many of whom have been content to uncritically accept "The Revised Standard Version" that Podhoretz laid out before them. Podhoretz was in effect, to use his own words, "doing . . . violence to the truth."[1]

In *Making It* and subsequent memoirs (now totaling four separate, if repetitive installments), Podhoretz argued that *Commentary*'s standing had been lost over the late 1950s because the New York intellectuals had either drifted, or been pushed away, during Cohen's declining years. He wrote that the magazine was too academic, "predictable," and "listless." His suggestion that where *Partisan Review* was a magazine for "producers" of ideas, *Commentary* was intended for "consumers" was unfair in that both journals shared many of the same readers. And Podhoretz criticized Cohen for his markedly affirmative attitude toward America, placing "everything American in a favorable light" and "could always be trusted to tell its readers what was right with American society more frequently than what was wrong." Under Cohen, wrote Podhoretz,

> one got the impression that the United States of America, for all its imperfections (the persistence of discrimination against Jews and Negroes being the main one), was the best society a human nature beset and limited by its own built-in imperfections (Original Sin, in

other words—though a Jewish magazine could hardly permit itself to say so) was likely to be able to build.

But he conveniently ignored the fact that he was an editor of the magazine at that time.[2]

Podhoretz exaggerated the extent to which *Commentary* had fallen behind by 1960. In the late 1950s, after Podhoretz had left, *Commentary* had started to publish a greater number of articles dealing with specific social and economic issues like the recession, unions, urban decay, juvenile delinquency, and civil rights. A most dramatic illustration of this new tendency was the appearance in July 1959 of an essay by Harrington on poverty, "Our Fifty Million Poor," as a social and political issue in the United States. Although liberal journals rarely mentioned poverty in the 1950s, as they barely recognized that it still existed in America, assistant editor Anatole Shub had intuited that it was a fresh new issue and commissioned the article. Together with another piece in the August 1960 issue, it formed the basis of Harrington's 1962 book, *The Other America*, which was credited with launching the "war on poverty."[3]

A great deal of what Podhoretz claimed credit for had already been begun by Cohen. Cohen had established *Commentary*'s profile among the intelligentsia by harnessing its major talents. He deliberately hired and commissioned prominent intellectuals for the magazine. Managing Editor Clement Greenberg was recognized as one of the country's major art critics, and was well on his way to becoming one of the most prominent and influential internationally, too. His reputation as a prominent, acerbic, and radical critic of new American art was growing. He had been instrumental in establishing New York as a center of modern art equal in achievement and influence with Paris. He was later credited with discovering Jackson Pollock. Robert Warshow was known for his literary skill, patience, and willingness to bring out the best in writers like James Baldwin, Malamud, and Isaac Rosenfeld. The list of names that Cohen introduced to the American intellectual and literary scene is endless. He succeeded in attracting Jewish intellectuals, who had earlier completely dissociated themselves from the organized Jewish community, and who had never previously thought of discussing Jewish subject matter in an impartial, forthright, and serious fashion. Cohen exploited the reawakening of intellectual interest in Jewish culture, heritage, and history, and he provided a forum in which they could express their Jewishness. As a result, Jewishness became intellectually and culturally respectable within the intellectual community. As Podhoretz put it, many learned to "shake hands in public with their own Jewishness for the first time in their lives." Nathan Glazer acknowledged his debt to Cohen for giving him the "unrivaled opportunity to study informally but continuously the life of American Jews." In fact, so much of the journal's character had been set by Cohen that rather than deny this fact it was easier for Podhoretz to pass it off as his own achievements.[4]

Much of what Podhoretz did as an editor he learned from Cohen. In fact, there were remarkable continuities between the editors both in style and content, despite what Podhoretz has claimed to the contrary. Cohen was his editorial model and a great deal of what was said about Cohen's editorial style could also be attributed to Podhoretz, much as he would probably deny this. Podhoretz inherited Cohen's editorial setup (using a small team of talented editors to run the magazine) and continued with Cohen's form. He carried over the standards and values from the Cohen era into the way and spirit in which the magazine was edited under him and this was, in no small part, a reason for its continued success. The magazine had been edited to the very highest standards. Cohen had a mania for clarity and simplicity. He believed that in order to produce an excellent journal, articles had to be clear and simple. The more complex a subject, the simpler the execution had to be. He targeted the "common reader" and took his/her common sense very seriously. The guiding principle was that intellectuals should speak to this common reader. It was a sin therefore to use big words to impress. His advice was: "Use the simplest words to get your meaning across, but the simplest good words, not slang or provincialisms." Nothing was taken for granted. Cohen took "fanatical care" to ensure that essays unfolded logically. Points had to be made clearly and intelligibly to anyone who might pick up the magazine. Writers had to persuade, inform, but never condescend or show off. Cohen's approach to editing derived from his belief that it was his aim "not to tell people what to think, but to give them the material to think with."[5]

Consequently, Cohen exercised a high degree of editorial intervention. All articles had to pass through his close editorial scrutiny. Podhoretz recalled that "virtually no article ever appeared in *Commentary* without some trace of his hand." Manuscript editing was considered important because of Cohen's concern for clarity and insistence on literary polish and not least because many of its contributors were specialists who lacked the skills of literary exposition or whose native language was not English. For Cohen, the whole took precedence over the individual parts. Accordingly, no writer was considered so important that his/her piece was ever featured. The title of each article was always stressed above the name of its author, even when that author was as famous as Jean-Paul Sartre or George Orwell. No writer was indispensable.[6]

Like Cohen, Podhoretz strongly objected to reportage. He was never interested in mere factual recitation; he wanted insight and experience. He demanded articles that were infused with immediate urgency and the passion of the moment, heat, and emotion, but with a simultaneous coolness of mind and a perspective that the historian might bring. This editorial style also involved an effort to publish pieces that were simultaneously interesting to the specialist and the lay reader, as Podhoretz also appealed to that mythic "common reader" who was intelligent, patient, receptive to careful argument, and exposition. So, Podhoretz strove for clarity, distinctiveness, and economy both as a writer and an editor. He wanted his and the magazine's prose to always drive toward a point, regardless of the graces of expression or the richness of texture. He wanted to make a case as decisively as possible. This was learned from Cohen; as Theodore Solotaroff put it, "Now this standard did not begin with Norman."[7]

While Podhoretz undoubtedly changed *Commentary*, some of these alterations were not as sudden or dramatic as he has made out. Many were incremental. The first issue under Podhoretz's editorship in January 1960 still listed Cohen as editor and was very much modeled in his image, as a testament to him, and included many common Cohen contributors. It was not until the February issue that the redesigned cover signaled the new editorship. And, only in the September 1963 issue did the major changes to the format and layout of *Commentary* occur.

Nor were the links to the Cohen days completely severed. Understandably piqued by Podhoretz's appointment, Martin Greenberg had already resigned but Podhoretz not only kept on Milton Himmelfarb (an AJC staffer and regular contributor under Cohen), but promoted him to Contributing Editor, and Frances Green, Anatole Shub, and Sherry Abel (whom he promoted from Editorial Assistant to Managing Editor) were all retained. Abel was a particularly important connection to the Cohen years, as she guided Podhoretz in his first few years as editor, helping him through the transition from "old" to "new" *Commentary*. Only one new face appeared in the supposedly "new" editorial lineup and that was Harris Dienstfrey. *Commentary* continued to include familiar New York Intellectual faces and Cohen regulars like Trilling, F. W. Dupee, Richard Chase, Alfred Kazin, Arthur Koestler, Irving Kristol, I. B. Singer, and George Lichtheim, alongside the new contributors Podhoretz introduced, resulting in a strange blend of old and new.

"Doing ... Violence to the Truth"

Some of What Podhoretz has said is erroneous. He recalled that there were not "more than a handful of articles" in *Commentary* on the death camps while Cohen was editor but a perusal of the magazine shows that scores of articles and reviews were published. Podhoretz even republished eight of them in *The Commentary Reader* in 1966! He stated that he chucked out poetry altogether, yet poetry continued to appear in the magazine. He said he had been trying to publish Goodman in the magazine since 1955, but Goodman had appeared ten times during Cohen's editorship. He also wrote that his friends were whispering that Staughton Lynd was soft on Communism, so in order to gauge Lynd's real outlook, he invited him to his apartment one evening and they talked until nearly dawn. Podhoretz then concluded that Lynd was more sympathetic to China than to the Soviet Union but was far more benevolent towards Communism and more hostile toward America than he had suspected. Lynd, however, says that the two never met and that there was no political break. Simply, he moved to Atlanta in the fall of 1961 to begin teaching at Spelman College. He was teaching four or five courses while trying to complete his doctoral dissertation and did not have the time to write. Finally he dated Irving Howe's now famous article "The New York Intellectuals" to the early 1970s when it was actually published in 1968. In these seemingly trivial instances, does Podhoretz's memory fail him (he even admits, "Memories are short") when such facts can be easily checked or are they the product of willful distortion?[8]

Not So Radical

Most significantly, however, Podhoretz and his former friends among the New York Intellectual community exaggerated the extent and nature of his radicalism. Podhoretz says that he took the magazine to the Left in 1960, but the reality is *Commentary* and Podhoretz did not have such a clear-cut editorial line at that time. It was neither Left nor Right. And it wasn't centrist either. Rather, it was an amalgam of all three as Podhoretz experimented during the early 1960s. While Podhoretz encouraged and published Goodman, Lynd, Brown, Marcuse, he had drawn the line at Mailer, only giving in to him after two years of resistance, and when he did allow him into the magazine, he did so only an informal, bimonthly basis. Furthermore, Mailer was restricted to politically safe Jewish topics. Even then, after six installments, Mailer was dropped. Podhoretz was happy to have Mailer as a friend, attend his parties, but he was not prepared to let him publish regularly in his magazine. Podhoretz claims that he had one eye on the AJC, for Mailer was "too wild" for a magazine sponsored by the most conservative of all Jewish organizations, and that he was "being careful not to jeopardize the institution for which I was responsible or my position in it by moving too far too fast in a culturally radical direction." But, given his track record of publishing articles contrary to AJC positions, and given some of those others he published, it is much more likely that Podhoretz was not the convert to the New Left as he has made out in his various memoirs. Only in his latest one has he come close to admitting the truth of the matter: "I was never even entirely at one with the friends and colleagues and collaborators I acquired when I became the editor-in-chief of *Commentary* in 1960," although to which ones he is referring is not entirely clear. Podhoretz had merely created the illusion of an intellectual gulf between him and the older generation. There were differences, of course, but they were not as great as have been made out.[9]

Although Podhoretz really did publish some rather radical and New Left-progenitor type of writing, he himself was hesitant to join them. He was highly critical of some of the New Left's attitudes and ideas. He refused to publish the Students for a Democratic Society's (SDS) "Port Huron Statement" of 1962 because he disapproved of its naïve simplicity, rejecting it as too "vulgar, infantile, and altogether intellectually unworthy for publication in *Commentary*." (Ironically, he later regretted his decision not to publish it as "the worst judgment of my entire editorial career.")[10]

He was a severe critic of the Beat poets and writers. He attacked what he perceived to be the morally disturbing aspects of Mailer's work, when the other New York Intellectuals had adopted him as a genius. He dismissed Jack Kerouac and the Beats at the height of their vogue in a 1958 essay, which amounted to an outpouring of hatred. He regarded them as exceptionally naive, callow, and immature. He condemned them as nihilistic "Know-Nothing Bohemians," calling them a mindless "non-generation," who "know nothing, stand for nothing, believe in nothing." They were "hostile to civilization" and worshipped "primitivism, instinct, energy, 'blood,'" as well as "mystical doctrines" and "irrationalist philosophies." He charged that their disdain for traditional, middle-class morality translated into a dangerous nihilism: "the revolution of the spiritually underprivileged and the crippled of soul—young men who can't think straight and so hate anyone who can." For Podhoretz, the message of their animosity toward private property and the middle class was clear: "Kill the intellectuals who can talk coherently, kill the people who can sit still for five minutes at a time, kill those incomprehensible characters who are capable of getting seriously involved with a woman, a job, a cause." Podhoretz put down the entire group of younger writers, insisting, among other things, that they were lazy and spoiled. Recalling an argument with Podhoretz, William Phillips was surprised at the strength of his intransigence, alarm, and outburst. "It struck me at the time as a very vivid and disturbing example of the conservative impulse to preserve the older order against the new barbarians, to preserve moral values, aesthetic standards, and social order."[11]

Podhoretz's attack on the Beats, apart from being motivated by a conservative impulse, also had personal roots. He knew and disliked many of them individually. He later wrote of the class antagonisms he felt from them, recalling "the homosexuals with their supercilious disdain of my lower-class style of dress and my brash and impudent manner." One of those, Allen Ginsberg, had been a fellow undergrad in the English department at Columbia, and while working as an assistant editor on *Columbia Review*, had altered a poem Podhoretz had submitted to the magazine without asking Podhoretz's permission, publishing the revised version. Podhoretz reacted furiously: he severed his links with Ginsberg. They split and went their separate ways. Had it not been for Ginsberg's collegiate crime, reckoned Neil Jumonville, Podhoretz "might have grown much closer to the Beat outlook he later hated so much" and might well have run with the Ginsberg-Kerouac crowd. Instead, when Ginsberg went on to become a very influential figure in the making of the counterculture, Podhoretz became a very prominent enemy. It appears that he never forgave Ginsberg for this student sin. The injury was compounded when Podhoretz returned from England. The Beats, led by Ginsberg, were the new avant-garde and their work replaced ironic detachment with howling. The styles of Leavis and Trilling, which Podhoretz tried so hard to blend and emulate, had suddenly become outdated, and Podhoretz had been left behind.[12]

Podhoretz had never changed his mind completely. He had only been a theoretical Socialist at Columbia, but given his hectic schedule he probably had little time to act upon it. The anti-Communist liberalism of Trilling, Dupee, and Richard Chase had influenced him deeply, and by the time he graduated he had been converted into a passionate partisan of the new Cold-War liberalism, at once pro-American and anti-Communist. His experiences in Europe and of writing for the anti-Stalinist *Partisan Review* confirmed his politics. He had not changed certain assumptions about the Cold War either. He still considered himself an anti-Communist. After all, at Diana Trilling's prompting, he had joined the hard-line anti-Communist outfit the American Committee for Cultural Freedom (ACCF), and he did not doubt that "Soviet Communism represented the greatest threat on the face of the earth to intellectual and cultural freedom." He still thought that the Soviet Union's ultimate goal was global domination and that the only obstacle in its path was America. He also found the notion of the existence of a peace party in the Soviet Union highly dubious. Khrushchev's actions may have led to a perceptible thaw in the Cold War, but he had brutally suppressed the Hungarian Revolution.

> It wasn't that I thought the hard anti-Communist position had been proven wrong; on the contrary, never for a single moment did I doubt the soundness of ideas about the character of Stalin's regime inside

the Soviet Union or about his aggressive designs on the rest of the world, or about the need for a determined American resistance to those designs.[13]

While Podhoretz did not fully agree with the hard-line anti-Communist stance, he had not fully rejected it either. Simply put he supported the liberal objective of containing Communism, but embraced a selective rather than an unlimited approach. For all his cultural wandering, Podhoretz remained a committed anti-Communist at heart, distinguishing him from many New York Intellectuals who went through a youthful flirtation with Communism, often of the Trotskyite variety. He attributed his immunity to the good fortune of being born too late (1930) to have entertained illusions about the USSR, and to the profound example of Trilling, who defended liberalism against totalitarianism. The rejection of totalitarianism was another constant in Podhoretz's career, even when he turned toward radicalism at the end of the 1950s. His conversion against hard-line anti-Communism, therefore, was not and could never have been wholehearted.

Even his position on Vietnam accepted the basic premises of anti-Communism. He never questioned the need to contain Ho Chi Minh or the continuing resistance of the Communist advance. Podhoretz saw nothing wrong with trying to prevent a Communist takeover. He still supported the policy of containment because "that policy had saved Western Europe from the barbarism and misery which had become the lot of every country in the world with the misfortune to fall under Communist rule." Rather, Podhoretz opposed intervention on tactical rather than political or moral grounds. He thought that there was very little chance of succeeding in this particular case. He did not oppose the principle of containment underlying intervention in Vietnam, but denied its practical applicability. Under the tutelage of Hans J. Morgenthau, then the leading exponent of the *Realpolitik* point of view in America, Podhoretz had adopted an essentially anti-utopian position on Vietnam. He maintained simply that it was a conflict from which the United States could not emerge victorious. Deeper US military involvement in the region was too complex to be effective; such action would only produce another Korea but with more casualties. In the words of General Maxwell Taylor, it was "the wrong war in the wrong place at the wrong time."[14]

Podhoretz wavered on other key issues. When his own mind wasn't made up he decided to air all sides of the debate. Compared to later years, his willingness to publish a range of opinions and the appearance of the differing voices from the New Left to the moderate and hard-line anti-Communists in *Commentary* reflected his prevarication and uncertainty on the issues during his first years as editor. It meant that the magazine's pages were often host to acute divergences, but this experimentation was also refreshing. This occurred particularly over issues affecting foreign affairs, for example, the issue of nuclear deterrence that led to a rather sharp exchange when Sidney Hook (along with others) rejected H. Stuart Hughes' call for unilateral disarmament.[15]

Podhoretz also tempered some of the more radical critiques with some old-fashioned 1950s orthodoxy for he had never entirely discarded the "old" contributors. Despite the disgust of his old friends, and possibly as a result of it, Podhoretz continued to publish their views, too. He ran essays from familiar Cohen contributors like Alfred Kazin, Dwight Macdonald, Harold Rosenberg, David Bazelon, William Barrett, Leslie Fiedler, Irving Howe, Daniel Bell and Nathan Glazer; hard-line anti-Communists and others from the ACCF like Sidney Hook; and even right-wingers, such as Robert Nisbet, who was described as "one of the most thoroughly conservative scholars in America." In the same issue that Riesman and Maccoby referred to the "ulcer of the cold war" and criticized the United States' role in it, hard-line anti-Communist Richard Lowenthal argued that Khrushchev was indeed Stalin's logical successor and that the Soviet Union was still a totalitarian state. Leon Lipson and Nehemiah Jordan dismissed Riesman and Maccoby's claims stating that, "'Peaceful coexistence' is a Soviet synonym for the cold war." Cold Warrior Moshe Decter disagreed with Lynd's analysis of how the Cold War started, presenting the Orthodox point of view. This position was extrapolated several times by Theodore Draper, who argued that still, in 1961 and, indeed more than ever, the Soviet Union entertained "unlimited aims." For all the complaining of the liberal and hard-line anti-Communists, then, the radical material was toned down by the inclusion of more moderate, liberal, and hard-line voices.[16]

Overall, suggests historian of neoconservatism Mark Gerson,

> the experimentation with utopian foreign policy ideas in *Commentary* was limited. Theoretical pacifism may have found a home in the pages of several issues, but realism was the governing philosophy of most actual discussions of serious policy. The real radicalism in the early years of *Commentary* [under Podhoretz] was not found in the realm of foreign affairs . . . [17]

America the Beautiful

In addition to anti-Communism, certain other fundamental ideas remained in place. Podhoretz had never given up on America as it seemed that some of those in the New Left had. He had never stopped favoring liberal democracy in particular the American version of it. He continued to see it as the greatest structure in which to extend and realize social transformation. As Nathan Glazer put it, "we valued the country, the role it had played in international affairs, its ability to handle complex domestic problems, its stability in the maintenance of democratic procedures, its capacity for change and correction." Furthermore, Podhoretz had consistently stressed that while he may be radical, his radicalism did not challenge certain basic values: pro-Americanism, anti-Communism, and cultural excellence. He stated:

> Even when I was at my most radical, I still loved America, and my utopian aspirations were directed at perfecting, not destroying, it. It went without saying that there were problems and flaws, above all the plight of the blacks and the poor, but I was confident that they could be effectively addressed through programs of radical reform within the going political system.

The aggressive anti-Americanism he witnessed at Cambridge pushed him into the role of patriotic defender of his country. More than anything else, either pro-Communism or neutralism, Podhoretz detested anti-Americanism. For him, it was always the more dangerous enemy.[18]

Besides, the radicalism then showcased by Podhoretz in *Commentary* shared much with conservatism. *Commentary* began to attack government centralization and concentration of power. Many of those who published in the magazine believed in minimal government and the redressing of social problems through local rather than state initiative. In, possibly, the first ever piece of his to appear in America, British economist and anti-industrialist E. F. Schumacher assailed the desirability of economic growth. Ten to fifteen years later, he was to become perhaps the most influential critic of the growth in the English-speaking world and the most famous exponent of the view that "small is beautiful." "This was a radicalism that had a good deal in common with conservatism," explained Glazer:

> the bias against government intervention in various areas, the willingness to let people decide for themselves how to spend their money, the belief that the theoretical and political structures reared by liberals to control policy in the foreign and domestic realms would no longer work, the allergy to Communist repression, the attraction toward the small.

Even Goodman's *Growing Up Absurd* had emphasized the anti-bureaucratic and the small. *Commentary*, then, according to Gerson, remained fairly conservative on issues concerning politics and social institutions, and did not question the fundamental tenets of American politics and did not advocate any type of socialist economics. Capitalism was criticized, but only when it fit directly into the rubric of cultural criticism. And no alternative was offered in its stead.

Podhoretz had decided to "place limits on the types of radicalism that *Commentary* showcased ... even when he was presented with good opportunities to stretch those boundaries."[19]

Likewise, *Commentary* repeatedly scrutinized and criticized current domestic policy, as Podhoretz began to assume an increasingly oppositional stance toward the White House. Nothing was left unexplored: the economy, unemployment, taxation, public expenditure, monetary policy, welfare programs, and civil rights. He began to see the Kennedy administration as an enemy. Indeed, he saw the entire liberal establishment, of which the administration was merely the political arm, in this light. And when Johnson became President, *Commentary* articulated an increasingly counterstance. Many of the Jewish New York intellectuals who made up the Commentariat, including Podhoretz, were wary of the Texan and did not trust him. Consequently they scrutinized him much more than they did Kennedy. Since politics had come to the fore in the 1960s, another bimonthly department, "A Washington Commentary," written by economist Oscar Gass and devoted to the analysis of important domestic issues, was instituted, as *Commentary* became a more explicitly political magazine. Much of this analysis was devoted to attacking LBJ. Podhoretz himself had turned away from literary criticism by this point, becoming a political animal, and almost completely rejecting his earlier life.

Podhoretz's conversion to radicalism should not therefore be overstated. It is no coincidence that in the latest anthology of Podhoretz's writings (*The Norman Podhoretz Reader*), only scattered examples of this alleged radicalism are provided. Other than some hindsight glimpses (from *Breaking Ranks*, Podhoretz's 1979 "political memoir"), the only radicalism on display in the book are a few discouraging words about America: in his famous 1963 article "My Negro Problem—and Ours" (which will be discussed in more depth below) and in essays on Saul Bellow's novels and Huckleberry Finn. That is because Podhoretz's radicalism was cultural/literary-intellectual rather than political, involving not much more than taking many radical writers seriously. Gerson hit the nail right on the head when he wrote, "The real radicalism in the early years of *Commentary* was ... of cultural criticism." Podhoretz's own words when he wrote of taking *Commentary* in "a *culturally* radical direction" reinforce this point. *Commentary*'s politics were uncertain during the early 1960s because

Podhoretz's *political* radicalism was never complete, if it even really existed. Indeed, even Podhoretz called it "a false position" that "inhibited [his] sentiments and ideas."[20]

Podhoretz's own silence is further confirmation of his ambivalence toward radicalism. If it didn't come from the gut, Podhoretz admitted, he couldn't fake it. He could not write what he didn't really believe. So, rather than counterfeit a radical stance in the early 1960s, and reveal his *real* feelings, he chose to stay silent instead and let others do the writing for him. Only eight months after it began, his self-penned column, "The Issue," ceased and Podhoretz became impotent literally—unable to write a word—for two years. An anecdote from 1960 also reveals how Podhoretz and *Commentary* really felt about the radicals: one evening in Union Square, he went to address a left-wing meeting about Vietnam with his Assistant Editor Marion Magid. She surveyed the audience ("that bedraggled-looking assemblage") and whispered to Podhoretz: "Do you realize that every young person in this room is a tragedy to some family or other?" It was most telling that during Podhoretz's "radical" phase, the National Executive Director of the Jewish War Veterans wrote in 1963, "I can't draw the line between Podhoretz, *Commentary*, and the American Jewish Committee as you do . . . *Commentary* is identified in the public mind as one of the spokesmen of the American Jewish Committee point of view."[21]

Podhoretz's leftism, if it indeed ever really existed, then, was surely a means to distance himself from Cohen and his intellectual generation, to attract new readers, and adopt a counterintellectual posture, while winning extra attention for himself. As his son, John, said much later, "The classic rule of thumb is that if you are an intellectual ideological magazine, you do better in opposition than you do if your views are reflected by people in power." Yet, so as not to completely alienate some older readers, Podhoretz included essays that reflected the anti-Communism of an earlier decade to temper the more revisionist pieces. The inclusion of both was also a way of moving *Commentary* away from the reputation of intellectual homogeneity it had begun to acquire at the end of the 1950s under Cohen and then the Greenbergs (and Podhoretz himself since he was also an editor then).[22]

Anti-Liberal Racism

In reality, Podhoretz's editorship actually gave rise to an anti-liberalism which led to the publication in *Commentary* of a substantial number of pieces attacking so-called liberal dogmas. Podhoretz never subscribed to one of the basic premises of liberalism and radicalism in the early 1960s—integration—because he did not believe that integration would ever be achieved in the United States. His own experiences growing up had convinced him that whites and blacks living together only exacerbated the hatred that existed, rather than ameliorating it, and that such hatred existed for good historical, social, political, psychological, and reasons, rather than just on ignorance and bigotry, on both sides of the racial divide. He felt that white resistance combined with black impatience meant that blood would spill before integration would succeed. He despaired of the drive toward it. And felt that the "old civil-rights movement had run its course" and that "a 180-degree change in direction was needed."[23]

Yet, despite his personal beliefs, Podhoretz still printed a range of opinions on the issue of Civil Rights. Given the prominence of Jews in the Civil Rights movement, and *Commentary*'s charter to assist in the fight against bigotry and to protect human rights, Podhoretz could not afford to ignore the topic and continued the trend established by Cohen. He recognized that this was a key topic for the next decade and tied in nicely with his desire to increase *Commentary*'s profile. "Certainly," observed Harvey Teres, the "magazine owed a good part of its wide influence during the 1960s to its willingness to address the controversial subject of race relations, especially relations between African Americans and Jews." Moreover, Podhoretz could not yet reveal his true beliefs and turn *Commentary* fully into an anti-integrationist magazine.[24]

So Podhoretz was, on the surface, broadly supportive of the aims and the tactics of the Civil Rights movement. He still supported the basic goal of the Civil Rights movement: the securing of previously denied fundamental civil and constitutional rights for blacks. *Commentary* articles still tended to be positive in content and encouraging of the movement, supporting its aims and cooperation between blacks and whites. It welcomed the Civil Rights Act of 1964 for example. Although not all of *Commentary*'s writers were upbeat and optimistic, in none of these articles nor in any of the others published in this period, was there any suggestion that the effort toward equal rights for blacks ought not to be undertaken. *Commentary* may have occasionally criticized particular aspects of the movement or expressed pessimism about its chances for success, but always on the understanding that the cause they were discussing was noble and correct.

This superficial support belied a deeper anti-left and antiblack agenda. Podhoretz's general encouragement for integration and civil rights masked an underlying prejudice. Under Cohen, there had been articles examining culture, literature, and the arts by critics like Bertram Wolfe, Irving Howe,

Steven Marcus, James Baldwin, Jervis Anderson, and John Thompson, reflecting Cohen's greater concern with the African American experience and culture. In contrast, only a handful of such articles appeared since Podhoretz took over in 1960 (although to be fair he had asked Baldwin to contribute and Baldwin gave his article to the *New Yorker* instead) and comparatively little fiction or literary criticism touched upon race or the African American experience. Indeed, very little space was given over to African American writers and African American literature. *Commentary* thus failed to cover adequately the complex of attitudes and values found in the black community; it neglected precisely those African American writers who might have opened up their world to a wider audience; it did not take note of the important role that literature has played in the politics of race in the United States; and by not giving equal voice to African Americans in the debate on race, it was not the product of both whites and blacks. Instead, with the occasional exception, Podhoretz published white academic political scientists, social psychologists, sociologists, and historians whose main interest was in producing studies centered on public policy designed to assist Administration policymakers. Such contributors tended to engage in the academic and policy debates, rather than those emanating from the African American community, particularly the nonacademic community. Typical of this approach was a three-hour discussion on Civil Rights, held in March 1964, compressed into the article, "Liberalism and the Negro: A Round-Table Discussion," involving three white academics (Nathan Glazer, Sidney Hook, and Gunnar Myrdal) to the one token black (Baldwin). Even Podhoretz admitted he didn't know what Hook was doing there, as he was no expert on race relations.[25]

Podhoretz also began to question the contemporary and faddish fashion for antiracist protest and Civil Rights activism. In his own words, he threw his weight behind "the very first stirrings of a turn in the black community away from the leaders whose strategic goal was integration and whose tactics consisted of pushing for legislation and appealing to the courts." In June 1960, Podhoretz published the testimonial of a disillusioned University of Chicago undergraduate who had enthusiastically picketed in front of a local Woolworth's store. Not only was this the first time *Commentary* had paid any serious attention to the sit-in movement, but in doing so it lent little support to it. In April of the following year, he ran an article assaulting the traditional, largely middle-class leadership of the Black community, as represented by the NAACP and the nonviolent movement. The piece enraged the NAACP (and surely the AJC, which was very close to the NAACP), which deemed the article so inflammatory that it censured Podhoretz for publishing it.[26]

Podhoretz criticized progressive Jewish liberalism in a series of what Michael Staub called "concerted attacks already launched by *Commentary* in 1960–61 against a Jewish engagement with racial justice concerns." Lucy Dawidowicz argued that there wasn't any concern for social justice in Judaism or any link between Jewish faith and Jewish activism. Emil Fackenheim condemned progressive Jewish pleas for social justice as false. Milton Himmelfarb charged that Jewish liberals lacked a healthful self-respect when they defended the constitutional rights of Rockwell. He even went as far as to suggest that this liberal impulse might threaten Jewish communal survival. And Solotaroff ridiculed Harry Golden, the longtime champion of southern Jewish antiracist activism, in a "devastating attack." Together, asserted Staub, these essays amounted to "a remarkable variety of antiprogressive arguments" and an "antiprogressive liberal strategy," and at the very point that Podhoretz was supposed to be a leftist.[27]

The most explicit and blunt statement of this anti-left and antiblack ideology came in 1963 with Podhoretz's extremely controversial essay, "My Negro Problem—and Ours." It was the first essay Podhoretz had written entirely in his own voice. Podhoretz's article had three aims: to critique integrationism, to accuse white liberals of hypocrisy on Civil Rights, and to suggest that miscegenation was the most desirable outcome. "With daring bravado," wrote Staub, Podhoretz "sought to denigrate liberal Jewish antiracist activism while it also shamelessly—via its shamefulness—presented camouflaged sentiments—however thinly—just one shade shy of white racism" through a "particular case study of uninhibited self-expression."[28]

Podhoretz reminisced about his own experience of racism, as a child growing up poor in a racially integrated neighborhood of Brooklyn during the 1930s. In his account, he dwelt not on ideas of solidarity or friendship between blacks and Jews but on the rift dividing them. He recalled being "repeatedly beaten up, robbed, and in general hated, terrorized, and humiliated" by blacks. His black best friend Carl hit him on way home from school one day and announced that he wouldn't play with him anymore because he killed Jesus. In presenting Jews (himself) as the victims, Podhoretz turned the thinking that had characterized the black-Jewish relationship for over a decade at least entirely on its head. Podhoretz further confessed that he still feared, hated and envied blacks, albeit not with the same intensity he did as a child. He described his feelings of envy for what seemed like their superior masculinity, physical grace and beauty, and their undisciplined upbringing, which seemed to embody the free, reckless, masculine, and erotic values of the street. He admitted that he was "afraid of Negroes" and that he "hated them with all my heart." He was still apprehensive of them but knowing that the police were on his side he felt shame, guilt, fear, resentment and self-contempt. He knew, too, that his hatred had not entirely disappeared because of

> the insane rage that can stir in me at the thought of Negro anti-Semitism; I know it from the disgusting prurience that can stir in me at the sight of a mixed couple; and I know it from the violence that can stir in me whenever I encounter that special brand of paranoid touchiness to which many Negroes are prone.[29]

His essay then turned into a diatribe against white 1960s liberalism. Podhoretz was convinced that white Americans were "twisted and sick" in their feelings toward blacks. He accused whites of hypocrisy and "self-deception," whose "abstract commitment" to the cause of civil rights "will not stand the test of a direct confrontation." Such people fled the inner cities for the suburbs, sending their children to private rather than integrated public schools. He wondered why blacks would want to survive as a distinct group when their history and color had been nothing but a stigma. He concluded that integration would only occur for blacks if color were erased, if it does "*in fact* disappear": "and that means not integration, it means assimilation, it means—let the brutal word come out—miscegenation . . . I believe that the wholesale merging of the two races is the most desirable alternative for everyone concerned." In a final twist of the knife, he wrote,

> In thinking about the Jews I have often wondered whether their survival as a distinct group was worth one hair on the head of a single infant. Did the Jews have to survive so that six million innocent people should one day be burned in the ovens of Auschwitz? It is a terrible question and no one, not God himself, could ever answer it to my satisfaction.[30]

The article was offensive to liberals, Jews, and blacks. Although Podhoretz printed letters from readers expressing both support and contempt, he refused to run rebuttals, even denying the AJC's attempt to redress the balance with a more sympathetic article on quotas. Nonetheless, despite the uproar, Podhoretz considered it to be the best piece of writing he had ever done. He reprinted it a few years later in *The Commentary Reader*, an anthology published on the occasion of the magazine's 20th anniversary in 1966, and described it as the most radical act of the radical phase of "new" *Commentary*. If "My Negro Problem," then symbolized Podhoretz's radicalism of the early 1960s, it was a radicalism of antiliberalism and prejudice.

Not only did the article reveal the limits of Podhoretz's supposed leftism, but also it demonstrated his complex personality. Podhoretz had commissioned James Baldwin to write an article about the growing Black Muslim movement and paid him in advance for it. After several discussions Podhoretz learned that Baldwin had instead submitted the article ("Letter from a Region in My Mind") to *The New Yorker* for a larger audience and a greater fee ($12 000 compared to the $600 fee *Commentary* typically offered). Podhoretz felt betrayed and furious with Baldwin. He met with Baldwin who encouraged him to give vent to his real feelings. Podhoretz also aimed at a sensation. He knew it would get him "into a certain amount of trouble" and eagerly anticipated the "angry protests." He was not disappointed. *Commentary* received over three hundred letters compared with the ten or twenty that a controversial article usually generated, indicating a range of reactions from those who branded him a racist to those who hailed him a moral hero. Dozens of articles and editorials commenting on the piece were printed in other magazines and newspapers.[31]

Podhoretz had poured scorn on liberal Jewish antiracist activism. His act of unrestrained articulation disguised a stark anti-left and antiblack ideology. In his invoking of the analogy of the Nazi Holocaust of European Jewry so soon after the Eichmann trial, Podhoretz implicitly sought to discourage Jewish support for African American struggles for social justice. Indeed, Podhoretz mocked wavering white and Jewish liberalism, and this theme gradually snowballed over the coming years, as he and *Commentary* began to fit the description of the very white liberals he derided. His essay marked a new phase of open disagreement between black and Jewish intellectuals, as it ominously hinted at future developments and anticipated the debates of the second half of the 1960s.

Commentary now argued that Jewish liberal advocacy for Civil Rights posed dangers for Jewish group survival. It critiqued the idea that Jewishness and liberal activism might have something in common. Leading the charge was Nathan Glazer, whose prominence and emergence as one of the key writers on Civil Rights did much to shape the magazine's discussion. Glazer predicted an ominous future based on a sharp increase in hostility between blacks and Jews: the old frictions between Jews and lower-class blacks had grown to be more widely shared by a substantial part of the new black middle-class, as well as white-collar and leadership groups. Rather than focusing on the points of resemblance between Jews and blacks, Glazer concentrated on the contrasts, often resorting to echoing stereotypes about both blacks and Jews in the course of his analysis.

In so doing, the call for Jewish self-interest began to emerge. Glazer argued that black demands for equality and integration posed a new challenge to the Jewish community because, if met, they would destroy Jews' ability to maintain the integrity of their own communities. He suggested that rather than fighting together for legislation that advanced the interests of both groups, Jews must resist black demands for preferential treatment, since such demands, in producing equality for all, dismantled all the gains Jews had made. For the first time in *Commentary*, Glazer had clearly articulated specifically *Jewish* discomfort with the new course of the Civil Rights movement, signaling the retreat of some Jewish liberals from the cause. His essay marked the last threshold of social optimism in the magazine and at least one longtime reader and contributor noted this tendency with some dismay: "The editors might well consider whether an article like Mr. Glazer's serves any useful purpose in preserving the liberal image of *Commentary* or the concern for justice and good inter-group relations in which the magazine has done such outstanding service." *Commentary* had begun to publicly resign from interracial commitments, turning solely to Jewish concerns where they clashed with black ones. It attacked the liberal Jewish stand on school desegregation because it saw an irreconcilable tension between granting full civil rights for blacks and a first-rate education for Jews. It signaled a refusal to identify with blacks.[32]

The symposium "Liberalism and the Negro" was typical of this approach. The panelists Hook, Myrdal, and Glazer ganged up on Baldwin, publicly challenging his status as a spokesperson for the African American community, leading to an awkward, heated discussion. Baldwin, it seems, had been set up: he was isolated, a black face in a sea of white academics. He stood out, and not just for his color, but also by his activist stance, having been directly involved in the Civil Rights movement, speaking publicly, raising funds, and talking to journalists, unlike the others. Baldwin wondered out loud about "what the hell he was supposed to say to them in there about all this sociology and economics jazz." Podhoretz admitted that he had done this on purpose to expose the vast divide between Jews and blacks. The symposium marginalized African American voices and demonstrated that if moderate blacks like Baldwin and Kenneth Clark (who was also in attendance) couldn't even get through to the white "professional liberals," then what on earth would they do about those whites who were less eloquent. It was one of the first salient public events at which the scarcely suppressed anger between African Americans and their white, frequently Jewish, allies emerged. It heightened the call for Jewish self-interest that was beginning to emerge as advanced by Glazer. From the letters *Commentary* received in response, it was clear that the magazine was diverging from the African American and working class communities. The African American protest magazine *Liberator* was frightened by the symposium, noting that the "liberals" had lost touch with reality and were ignorant of what the real problems were. Podhoretz said the symposium "didn't work," but it seemed to have been deliberately designed to prove the point he had made a year earlier in 1963.[33]

Over the years 1965 and 1966, Podhoretz took full advantage of the high level of public interest in civil rights activity and urban rioting to publish articles advancing his antiliberal, antiblack agenda. The number of articles on topics like integration and racial equality peaked. During this explosive period, Bayard Rustin emerged as a key writer on Civil Rights. Rustin was a strange addition to *Commentary*. Rustin was black, at a time when Podhoretz preferred white voices on this subject, and he was a moderate integrationist and strong advocate of black-white cooperation (he had organized the March on Washington in 1963 and was a close associate of Martin Luther King and socialist labor leader A. Philip Randolph). Yet, Rustin was included because he articulated congenial views. In line with Podhoretz's thinking, Rustin repeatedly jabbed at the liberal conscience and agreed that integration alone would not solve the problems of the black community. At the same time, he also opposed violent resistance as Podhoretz was likewise troubled by what he viewed as a radical takeover of the black power movement.

Podhoretz astutely picked Rustin because of his long and honorable history as a Civil Rights activist. What better way to attack the Civil Rights movement than to use one of its most recognized and leading tacticians? Together with his color, it conferred some legitimacy on Podhoretz's anti–Civil Rights strategy. Furthermore, Rustin was no longer in step with the new generation emerging from the African American community. Rustin was seemingly only speaking to white, liberal voices. *The Liberator* observed that, "Rustin has shown himself to be more and more out of step with the masses of people he purports to understand and lead. It almost seems that he is now an official civil-rights ambassador for the Johnson administration." Another pointed out the unfortunate "decline of Bayard Rustin as a philosopher who is listened to by the black people," because he could not see that "his banner of liberalism cannot compete with the concept of 'black power' in the struggle against racism. Its cerebral call . . . cannot stand against the visceral appeal of 'we blacks.'"[34]

Hardening the Softness

Alongside a growing antiliberalism was the growth of anti-Communism in the magazine during the early 1960s. Symptomatic of that trend was the less frequent appearance of Staughton Lynd in the magazine. In a particularly shrewd maneuver, Podhoretz used Lynd to criticize William Appleman

Williams' *Tragedy of American Diplomacy*. What better than to use one of the architects of New Left foreign-policy analysis to attack the leading revisionist? Podhoretz also wanted to use Lynd to criticize Goodman for the same reason as Lynd had a very strong influence on the thinking of young leftists. Podhoretz's use of him to criticize these leftists had showed insight, and indicated that, as early as 1960–1961, Podhoretz was resisting, not at that time the antiwar movement, but the beginnings of the whole upsurge that became the New Left. At the time of the Cuban Missile Crisis in October 1962 there was a noticeable shift in the magazine's politics. "By that time the magazine began to pull back," Solotaroff recalled. "I always felt it was at just that point when *Commentary* began to close up its 'opening to the left' and resume the hard line which was to grow harder from year to year." Writers like Nathan Glazer, Oscar Gass, George Lichtheim, and Daniel Patrick Moynihan commenced to be as favored and influential as the increasingly radical Lynd, Morgenthau, and Goodman had been two are three years before and the latter now began to appear more irregularly.[35]

The gradual seep of anti-Communism into *Commentary*'s analyses of foreign affairs turned into a greater flood by the mid-1960s. Lichtheim, like Glazer, was another link to the Cohen years and signaled a return to the hard-line anti-Communism of the 1950s. They took increasingly trenchant and hawkish positions which returned *Commentary* to the Cold War paradigms of the 1950s. In his regular bimonthly column, "Public Affairs," which he had taken over from Morgenthau who had conducted it for the past three years, Lichtheim contributed a series of dogmatically anti-Soviet and anti-Maoist articles in which he claimed that Peking and Hanoi were happy to allow the war in Vietnam to drag on as it suited them to do so.

Commentary argued that the United States could not pull out now for the cost of withdrawal in 1965 could very well be a large nuclear war in the future. It believed the civil war in Vietnam was under Communist direction, serving the general Maoist strategy of world revolution. Since Peking and Moscow were behind the guerrilla activity, the United States must stay to fight a limited war. Dredging up notions of "appeasement" and "Red Fascism" from earlier decades by comparing March 1965 to March 1936 when Hitler reoccupied the Rhineland, it opined that a "take-over by Ho Chi-minh's men in Saigon would probably make the Nazi occupation of Vienna and Prague look like a picnic." If the United States withdrew from Vietnam, it had also to abandon its allies in Laos, Thailand, and Malaya, which it could not do, for Communist victory in those countries would strengthen the appeal of this tactic in the world Communist movement and be used by Soviets in the Middle East, Africa, Latin America, and even Europe.[36]

Podhoretz's anti-Communism led him to continue to oppose the Vietnam War. With no hope for a reversal of American policy in Vietnam, the policy of escalation was rapidly undermining America's international reputation, as well as the Cold War anti-Communism that he had grown up with and still respected. Consequently, as America's role in Vietnam escalated, so did Podhoretz's opposition to it and *Commentary*'s interest in foreign affairs during the latter half of the 1960s was absorbed by Vietnam, which was proving to be a major diversion from the resurrection of anti-Communism. This practical rather than moral opposition to the war increased the distance between Podhoretz and the New Left.[37]

Incipient Conservatism

By 1964, as some of the ideas Podhoretz had helped to disseminate in *Commentary* spread faster and further than he had anticipated, becoming dominant in the universities, and well on their way to achieving the same position in the media, Podhoretz shifted course. As a "counterintellectual," someone who preferred to hack away at the prevailing intellectual opinion, Podhoretz did not want to be drawn into the ranks of the majority (not yet at least) where he did not feel at ease. His counterstance was boosted by the student unrest of 1964 and the spread of the increasingly influential counterculture values. The resulting revolts, demonstrations, and uprisings across American campuses horrified him. As student protest spread across the country, Podhoretz saw it as a threat to the very existence of the academy and to the values it embodied, which he cherished. The student revolt at Berkeley in 1964 stood out for him in particular. Shocked by the radical assault on the universities, Podhoretz published Glazer's denunciation of the student activities at Berkeley ("What Happened at Berkeley?") in March 1965, and, in doing so, established the beginning of *Commentary*'s systematic opposition to the radical movement.

Podhoretz increasingly believed that the New Left's critique of American society was superficial and facile. He felt that radical thinking was almost completely misguided, littered with error and confusion, based on ignorance and arrogance, no more than cheapened and vulgarized rehashings of the thought of the 1890s and 1930s. Not only was it not regenerating liberalism, but it was also actually having the opposite effect of threatening to destroy it. He became increasingly disturbed by a "certain tone or emphasis" which insisted on reanalyzing the "clichés of the fifties" while surrendering to those of the thirties. He recoiled at the anti-Americanism of the New Left, outraged by comparisons between Nazi Germany and "Amerika." When he first heard such analogies coming from the lips of a close friend with whom he was dining at an expensive restaurant, Podhoretz lost his temper and stormed out. As he left, he shouted in a very loud voice that if his friend felt that way, he should consider emigration the only honorable course. He also refused to accept the then prevalent New Left notion that American society was dispiritedly and irredeemably corrupt. And, he was saddened by the failure of liberalism to counteract these disturbing trends.[38]

Commentary echoed Podhoretz's recoil from Leftist anti-Americanism, as Podhoretz began moving *Commentary* in the opposite direction to the one he said he had taken in 1960. The magazine underwent a significant transformation in terms of tone and viewpoint, as Podhoretz gave vent to his real feelings, particularly in its articles on blacks, racial integration, and Civil Rights. As a sign of this change, Werner J. Dannhauser, a conservative graduate and student of the influential conservative philosopher Leo Strauss at the University of Chicago, joined the staff in November 1964, as the "token conservative" in the offices at that time. A hawk on foreign policy and a "proud and passionate foot soldier in the ranks of the [1960s] counterrevolutionaries," he had grave doubts over the "Negro question," in particular the direction of black radicalism. Although Dannhauser denied that Podhoretz appointed him on a political basis (he said that Podhoretz took him on Marion Magid's recommendation as a smart and able person with deep Jewish and Zionist roots and knowledgeable on intellectual and European history), there was something prognostic about his employment: not only did it point to the future direction of the magazine, but it indicated where it was already heading. From 1966 onward a series of articles by Tom Kahn, Glazer, and Rustin denounced the New Left movement. Remarks like Daniel Patrick Moynihan's observation that the "liberal left can be as rigid and destructive as any force in American life," spoke for much of the Commentariat and became commonplace in the magazine's pages.[39]

As a sign of the increasingly open antiliberalism of the magazine, relations among the magazine's staff were becoming more and more problematical. Podhoretz compensated for his earlier silence, as Cohen had done before him, by throwing himself into the work of the magazine with a greater fury than every before. He became increasingly independent of the other editors and his editorial hand ever heavier. The more progressive editors in turn became more resentful, suffocated by the magazine's new line. Eventually Harris Dienstfrey resigned because, as he put it, "there wasn't enough oxygen." He felt uncomfortable, out of place, and "cramped and a bit stifled" by Podhoretz's "strict and intense conception of what the magazine should be." After Dienstfrey left feelings of solidarity in the office had begun to decline and the bonds of the early part of the 1960s started to come apart. Solotaroff's relationship with Podhoretz became tense. A "real left-winger," Solotaroff, had developed "a strong negative feeling about the magazine's politics" and he "sharply disagreed" with Podhoretz. He also clashed with the conservative Dannhauser, particularly over the latter's hawkish pro-Vietnam War stance, leading to heated arguments. In April 1966 Solotaroff decided to leave the magazine, as he felt marginalized, a "loner" on it staff now that Dienstfrey had gone. Podhoretz's overbearing editorial nature combined with his increasingly antiliberal and antiradical editorial line produced a symbolic revolving door at the entrance to *Commentary*'s offices as staff came and went throughout the 1960s.[40]

Zionization and the 614th Commandment

A series of events then confirmed Podhoretz's new adversarial stance and drove his magazine further against New Left radicalism. The key turning point was the Six Day War of 1967. Podhoretz did not perceive himself to be "in the first instance" a "Jewish" intellectual. Rather he considered himself to be an American intellectual who openly accepted his Jewish roots and was proud of them. Podhoretz knew both Hebrew and Yiddish, and by his own admission, he was "better educated in Jewish things than most of the Jews who were in that world, even those who knew something." But his writing often reflected mixed feelings and emotions about his Jewish upbringing and education. In a 1955 review he had written: "A part of me still broods on the mystery of my own Jewishness." In the following year he suggested that the lesson of Sholom Aleichem is that Jewishness inheres simply in the Jews and not in any ideology or doctrine that seeks to "explain" or "define" them. Jewishness was not a matter of values or essential characteristics of race or nationality or both, it was nothing abstract, neither a civilization nor a peculiar kind of religion. Jewishness was simply the way Jews behaved, their manners and habits, and attitudes. By 1961, however, he wrote: "I will register my conviction that one ought to feel a sense of 'historic reverence' to Jewish tradition." Yet, in 1963, Podhoretz asked, "In thinking about the Jews I have often wondered whether their survival as a distinct group was worth one hair on the head of a single infant." His use of the terms, "the Jews" and "their," betrayed a tone of ambivalence, alienation, and distance. Podhoretz's inner battle with his Jewish identity raged and it was reflected in the pages of *Commentary*.[41]

As for where he stood in relation to Israel, Podhoretz was neither a Zionist nor an anti-Zionist. He did not agree with Jewish socialist, reform, assimilationist, or orthodox rejections of the State, but neither did he agree with the non-Zionists and the binationalists. He did believe, however, that the Holocaust had proved incontrovertibly and conclusively that Jews required a secure haven from persecution and death in which Jews were the majority and enjoyed full sovereignty. Nevertheless, he had no great love for the refuge that had actually been created. He had never "been at ease in Zion." He had felt like a foreigner when he visited Israel for the first time in 1951, even though he spoke fluent Hebrew, and knew as much about the history of the country as he did about America. It was a "foreign," "alien" place, he wrote. (And, despite four Israeli grandchildren and an Israeli son-in-law, this feeling never changed.) He wrote to Lionel Trilling that a visit to Israel left him "with a slightly bitter taste" in his mouth and that Israelis were "a very unattractive people . . . gratuitously surly and boorish . . . [and] arrogant."[42]

But when the combined military forces of the Arab armies massed on Israel's borders in May 1967 Podhoretz's mood underwent an intense, widespread, abrupt, radical, and unpredictable change. Suddenly, long dormant feelings of Jewishness were aroused. Podhoretz realized that he was a Jew no matter what. The grave danger to Israel dominated his thoughts and emotions almost to the exclusion of all else. Previously ambivalent about both his Jewishness and Zionism, he felt simultaneously proud of Israel, as well as vulnerable, lending an immediacy and direct personal concern for Israel's plight. The State of Israel may have been established in 1948, but it was not until now that Podhoretz began to feel a profound sense of solidarity with it. Israel suddenly became a very strong focus for his Jewish emotional loyalty as the Six Day War reinforced Podhoretz's identification with the state. He now felt a new sense of "literal implication in the destiny of Israel" and a

> determination to resist any who would in any way and to any degree and for any reason whatsoever attempt to do us harm, any who would diminish us or destroy us, any who would challenge our right and our duty to look after ourselves and our families, any who would deny us the right to pursue our own interests or frustrate us in our duty to do so. We would from now on stand our ground.[43]

Reflecting its editor's mood, *Commentary*'s August issue opened with no less than four articles on Israel. For the first time in its history, the magazine unequivocally began to radiate a sense of belonging to a worldwide Jewish people with Israel as its spiritual center. For *Commentary*, the events leading up to the war had shown for the second time in quarter of a century that Jews were being threatened with annihilation, while it seemed the world stood by. Christians appeared indifferent to the cause of Israel's survival in the Middle East. Confronted with the horrifying prospect that Israel might be annihilated, comparisons began to be made with the Holocaust. After 20 years of Jewish self-confidence in America, there was a sudden belief that anti-Semitism was not something of the past, but a real and present danger. A revulsion against the passivity of the Jewish victims of the Nazis was felt, and faced with the specter of a second genocide within the space of a single generation, the *Commentary* was determined that the past was not going to be repeated. If Israel was to go down, Podhoretz felt, let it go down fighting. The Jewish people had not been completely vanquished in Auschwitz, and it would not happen in modern Israel either. The Six-Day War, in particular the trauma of the dark days of the two long weeks preceding it, had jolted Podhoretz and that experience produced a deeply felt need to confront the Holocaust in religious terms.[44]

In terms of *Commentary*'s response, one article in particular stood out from the rest. In his essay, "Jewish Faith and the Holocaust," theologian Emil Fackenheim connected the Six Day War and Israel to the Shoah to produce a new, emergent quasi-religious "Holocaust consciousness." Fackenheim argued that Jews now had a duty to observe a "614th Commandment": "*Jews are forbidden to grant posthumous victories to Hitler.*" This meant that Jews "are commanded to survive as Jews, lest the Jewish people perish." With this one article, written in the wake of the Six-Day War, and with his 614th commandment, Fackenheim, more than anyone else, contributed to making the Holocaust a basic element of Jewish theological reflection. It marked, according to William Novak, the transformation of *Commentary* away from "a magazine whose policies had been, in past years, somewhat less sensitive to the particular demands of Jewish history and culture." Until 1967, Israel and the Holocaust—which served merely as an illustration of the manifestation of evil and was used to strike at optimistic theologies—possessed no special significance for *Commentary*'s thought, whether religious or secular; no meaning was contained in them and they were not related in any fashion to Jewish survival. The Six Day War in 1967 and Fackenheim's response in *Commentary* changed all that, setting *Commentary*'s new tone.[45]

Fackenheim's article deeply influenced Podhoretz's thinking in particular. For Podhoretz only Fackenheim had begun to appreciate the significance of the Holocaust. It had such a major effect on Podhoretz that he referred to it in his speeches and writings time and time again. Podhoretz sought to obey Fackenheim's 614th commandment by promoting an inward-looking Jewish particularism:

> That is to say, I think that Jews must once again begin to look at any proposal for policies from the point of view of the Jewish interest, and

must once again begin to ask what the consequences, if any, of any proposal or policy are likely to be so far as the Jewish position is concerned.

Furthermore, he resolved that,

in taking upon myself the yoke of this commandment, to obey it by relentlessly championing the Jewish state against its political and ideological enemies, who, wittingly or not, were working to destroy it . . . On a lesser level, I also took it upon myself to stand up for Jewish interests in America whenever they were disregarded or threatened.

As letters to the magazine pointed out, Podhoretz had wrapped himself up in an insular and "blanket emotional equation of all opposition to Israel with the murderous anti-Semitism of the Nazis." Thereafter, Podhoretz's—and therefore *Commentary*'s—credo became, "Is it good for the Jews?"[46]

Particularism was a new idea to *Commentary*. For the first 20 years of its existence from 1945–1965 it had stressed universalism, but now the magazine embraced particularism with a new zeal and fervor unseen since the 1930s. Milton Himmelfarb wrote: "We learned the old truth that you can depend only on yourself . . . We relearned the old, hard truth that only you can feel your own pain." It was as if Podhoretz and other Jewish intellectuals were repenting for past sins of universalism and for turning their backs on their Jewishness. "Under the aegis of this idea," wrote Podhoretz, "*Commentary* would become more aggressive than it had ever been before in defending Jewish interests both at home and abroad, even as, with regard to the overall balance of subject matter, it would remain a Jewish magazine with a special emphasis on issues of particular concern to Jews." As a result of the Holocaust and the Six Day War and the events surrounding it Podhoretz returned to the position of what he had once scorned as the Jewish parochialism that he had been so keen to reject and purge from Cohen's *Commentary* when he took it over in 1960. Now, all things were to be viewed through the prism of Jewishness.[47]

It marked a new phase in Podhoretz and *Commentary*'s thought. Following Israel's victory in the war, Podhoretz and many of his fellow editors and contributors were converted into Zionists. Prior to 1967 Israel, US foreign policy, and Jewishness had largely trodden separate paths in *Commentary*, occasionally overlapping but never for long. Now, by the autumn of 1967, those paths melded into a complex that set *Commentary*'s tone for the next three decades at least, as Israel became a central cause. *Commentary*, like much of American Jewry, became much more focused on Zionism. And there was a greater attempt to understand the internal concerns of American Jewish life, from the inside, rather than from a position of detachment. Podhoretz and *Commentary*'s aloofness toward the American Jewish community of the previous 20 years began to break down.

Podhoretz's new found Zionism further confirmed his recoil against the New Left. While Podhoretz and *Commentary* were becoming more supportive of Israel the New Left was turning against it. The Six Day War helped to diminish some New Left support for Israel because it had transformed the Israelis from being victims into victors and hence, by some New Left logic, victimizers. Israel was deemed an imperialist or a neo-imperialist instrument. It didn't help that SNCC referred to Israel as "illegal" and as "oppressors," and black militant H. Rap Brown declared, "we are not anti-Jewish . . . We just don't think Zionist leaders in Israel have a right to that land." In response to the New Left's negative response to Israel's victory in the 1967 war Podhoretz published two articles by Robert Alter and Martin Peretz on the New Left's position on Israel in *Commentary* in consecutive issues. Peretz was a wealthy 1960s radical, who had strong ties to the New Left and one of its journals *Ramparts*, but when the New Left National Conference for New Politics he helped to organize descended into anti-Semitism, he walked out. Still shaken, he wrote a vehement and scathing condemnation in *Commentary* of the New Left's "hyperbolic and egregious" "verbal and tactical excesses" which had reached "new heights of righteous arrogance and absurdity." Indeed, both articles caricatured the New Left's position on Israel as a picture of a chauvinistic, militaristic, brutal, callous, victimizing, and bellicose state. They lumped together all New Left spokesmen into one amalgam without analyzing any of their positions individually. The distinctions between the old and New Left were also deliberately blurred. It was a very unusual tactic for Podhoretz to publish two such similar articles thus indicating the strength of his feeling on this issue.[48]

Liberal Anti-Communism Revisited

The next step in Podhoretz's emerging antiliberal and anti-New Left agenda was the exposure in the spring of 1967 of the CIA's covert funding of artistic and intellectual endeavor in the 1950s—including sponsorship of the Congress for Cultural Freedom (CCF) and the ACCF—through a series of dummy and front foundations. While *Commentary*, as far as we know, was not a recipient of such monies, many of the Commentariat were for they had been members of both the CCF and the ACCF, occupying prominent positions in both organizations, and they had written for *Partisan Review* and *Encounter*, all of which were revealed to be in receipt of government monies. Both Podhoretz and Decter, for example, had been flown at the expense of the Farfield Foundation—a conduit for CIA funds—to Acapulco to participate in various anti-Communist cultural activities. As a result, many intellectuals were effectively charged with complicity in governmental propagandizing, exacerbated by the fact that *Commentary* writers in the late 1940s and early 1950s had argued for just such initiatives before they came into being.

In response to the accusations and allegations flying around, Podhoretz took the customary *Commentary* reaction: he published a symposium, "Liberal Anti-Communism Revisited." Since he wanted to save and shore up hard-line anti-Communism which seemed to have been discredited by the destructive nature of the war in Vietnam, Podhoretz stacked the symposium with those veteran liberal anti-Communists with whom he had fallen out during the early part of the decade when he had flirted with leftism to refute those charges. Podhoretz welcomed back names that hadn't been seen in *Commentary* for a while: Sidney Hook, Daniel Bell, and Lionel and Diana Trilling. He was rewarded as their contributions to the symposium justified the hard-line anti-Communist liberalism that was so prominent in the *Commentary* of the 1940s and 1950s, as they scrambled to prove their intellectual autonomy either by claiming ignorance of the CIA's sponsorship or insisting that even though CIA funds were accepted, it had in no way compromised the editorial independence of their journals or affected their opinions. They argued that CIA backing of cultural projects, if a disaster, was a necessary one, but that revelations of CIA patronage did not "prove that liberal anti-Communism has been a dupe of, or a slave to, the darker impulses of American foreign policy." They insisted on the importance of liberal anti-Communism which had not been compromised by CIA sponsorship. As Hugh Wilford pointed out, "there was an element of self-exculpation in all this."[49]

Many of *Commentary*'s readers were unconvinced of its attempts at repentance. "Every last one of the cold war liberals who entered your essay contest sold out to the CIA, the Pentagon, and/or the State Department years ago. And they remain bought off and unrepentant to this day," wrote one. Another called the symposium "pathetic and macabre," perceptively adding, "so the *danse macabre* of the liberals goes on in measured steps from left to center and maybe beyond . . ." And the readers were right; it was this symposium, which finally convinced Podhoretz to renege fully on his flirtation with radicalism and cement the change to an anti-Communist, antiliberal, anti-New Left, and antiblack ideology that had been brewing since the early 1960s.[50]

The symposium had also given Podhoretz a way to make up with those former friends, mentors, and colleagues he had once argued with, as he now needed such people on his side. Inviting them to contribute allowed him to make amends, and say sorry, albeit in a roundabout and indirect way. As a mark of his reversion, where Podhoretz had once symbolically killed his hard-line anti-Communist father figures, he now resurrected and readopted them. In doing so, *Commentary* increasingly reflected their anti-Communist Cold War politics as they articulated their Cold War stance and tried to regenerate a renewed faith in America and take on the revisionist historiography of the New Left. Further articles expressed this posture as Podhoretz published former liberals, like him, now turning to the right.

Blacks and Jews

The third stage in Podhoretz's development was his perception of the machinations of the New Left. His ill-feeling towards the New Left was increased by the student revolts at Columbia University in April 1968. These were the first of their kind to hit a major private university in America. Although student revolts were nothing new by that point, the revolt at Columbia, in particular, affected Podhoretz. It brought student protest to New York, the home of the eponymous intellectuals in general, and to Podhoretz's alma mater in particular. When the students occupied key campus buildings the hurt he felt was intensely personal because he had a special bond with the university. It was there that he met Trilling and received his undergraduate education. Worse, his friends and mentors, the Trillings, were still there. If this wasn't enough, the protest mixed radical student politics with racial overtones.

This racism further delegitimized the New Left in Podhoretz's eyes. As the New Left increasingly associated with the more radical and militant members of the Civil Rights Movement, Podhoretz became increasingly fearful of both. He became more concerned with the means being used to achieve racial equality, dreading the new hard-edged black militancy of Black Power that had emerged to mark the departure point from the Civil Rights era of Martin Luther King because it was accompanied by the emergence of a vociferous black anti-Semitism. Nonetheless, as Black Power became more prominent, the New Left moved to support it and courted the poorest urban blacks as revolutionary material. The New Left had also become gradually more focused on the racist aspects of American society, and was preoccupied with legitimating and assisting black militancy in the ghettos.

When these trends had reached a new phase in 1968, as many New Leftists openly supported the Black Panthers, Podhoretz became even less enthusiastic about the Civil Rights Movement and much more critical of it. He felt that black demands, such as affirmative action and equality of results, were excessive, and that Black Power's increasingly militant stance was obliterating any chance of equal opportunity for blacks. Accordingly, *Commentary* voiced its unease about the direction the movement was taking. As the first clear sign of his new stance, Podhoretz ran Jervis Anderson's "Race, Rage and Eldridge Cleaver" in December 1968. Other than a short piece by George Dennison in February 1965 about the black playwright Le Roi Jones, it was the first article to deal directly with the unpleasant manifestations of hate and extremism by the new black movement, as symbolized by Cleaver. Podhoretz also dropped the moderate, integrationist Bayard Rustin, who sincerely struggled to keep the black-Jewish alliance together. Rustin's conspicuous absence from *Commentary*, particularly in light of his prominence over the past few years, highlighted the degree to which the debate on race and Civil Rights in the magazine was coming to an end.

For *Commentary* relations between blacks and Jews had been in steady decline since the mid-1960s and had become even worse since the death of Martin Luther King, reaching an all-time low. As Murray Friedman pointed out in the magazine, although King had called anti-Semitism "anti-man and anti-God," placing a particular burden upon blacks to end it, his words were not heeded and black anti-Semitism was growing. It didn't help that black anti-Semitism was interlaced with the New Left's negative response to Israel's victory in the Six Day War, as expressed by SNCC and others. With the death of King, no other black leader seemed willing to combat the growing anti-Semitism within the black community. Indeed, the anti-anti-Semitism of James Baldwin and King was being replaced by the overt anti-Semitism of black leaders like Jesse Jackson, Roy Innis, LeRoi Jones, Eldridge Cleaver, Stokely Carmichael, Wilfred Ussery, and Andrew Young.[51]

This was most clearly demonstrated, Podhoretz felt, during the New York City teachers strike in the Ocean Hill-Brownsville district of Brooklyn in 1968. Black-Jewish relations were particularly exacerbated because the strikes highlighted this growing black anti-Semitism. Black militants accused white teachers and public school administrators of being racists. Many of those accused were liberal Jews who had marched in Civil Rights demonstrations. Black militants then seized control of the school district's governing board, employing fierce anti-Semitic rhetoric to rationalize the dismissal of Jewish teachers. In response, New York teachers went on strike three times to protest against the unfair treatment, including physical violence and unexplained expulsion, meted out to them. An unprecedented situation of polarization occurred between the two groups represented by the United Federation of Teachers (many of whom were Jewish) on the one hand and the "community leaders" (many of whom were black) on the other. For Podhoretz, the strike brought black anti-Semitism into widespread public view and showed that blacks were ready to advance their civil rights at the direct expense of Jews. Although black-Jewish relations had been steadily eroding, they had never sunk this low and there was much consternation expressed in the pages of *Commentary* by Earl Raab, Maurice Goldbloom, Murray Friedman, and Carl Gershman among others. Along with many other Jews of his generation, Podhoretz feared that black anti-Zionism coupled with New Left radicalism would set off a fresh wave of anti-Semitism in the United States.

The number of articles on this topic in *Commentary* illustrated Podhoretz's growing apprehension over developing discord between blacks and Jews and the manifestations of anti-Semitism in black extremist movements. The magazine pointed out that the development of an anti-Semitic ideology within the Civil Rights Movement had abruptly caused the Jewish Question, dormant since the end of the Second World War, to reappear once again. The Black Power movement had succeeded in reintroducing political anti-Semitism as a fashionable item in the American public arena, which, if allowed to grow unchecked, would have an incalculable effect on Jewish lives. Podhoretz raised the specter of an anti-Jewish alliance, a union between the privileged and the underprivileged against the Jews. *Commentary* warned that Jews should be concerned more clearly than ever before and that the Jewish imperative for independent self-survival was never more legitimate.

The Golden Age, the two decades immediately following the war when anti-Semitism was virtually nonexistent, had ended to be replaced by fear and suspicion. Jews found themselves alone, with no allies on the Left, liberal or radical, or within the Establishment. The situation was now extremely serious indeed and warranted a more concerned Jewish response than anxiety and nervousness. *Commentary* asked if American Jewry was in crisis as, "more and more people have become apprehensive about the security of Jews in America." The magazine had struck a chord that would recur henceforth, as increasingly fears about Black Power were intertwined with fears for Jewish security.[52]

Podhoretz openly called for Jewish self-interest. *Commentary* proposed that Jews vote with the right wing while abandoning their traditional liberalism and concern for the (black) underdog. It warned that the Jewish community must develop a "more self-conscious focus of group interest" and begin asking seriously, "Is it good for the Jews?" This appeal to Jewish parochialism was increasingly accompanied by negative assessments of the black community. African Americans were collectively portrayed as simultaneously passive and volatile: while they did not do enough to help themselves, they were, at the same time, unwilling to put up with the slow pace of legislative and social reform. Furthermore, unlike in previous decades, black leaders were denied the opportunity to respond or provide a sympathetic representation of African American life that could have raised awareness among *Commentary*'s readership.[53]

At the same time, *Commentary* disparaged those Jews who continued to support the Civil rights movement, as self-hating masochists who clung to a cause even though blacks had angrily rejected their help as both unnecessary and condescending long ago. This view reached its apotheosis in an essay by Nathan Glazer. In "Blacks, Jews and the Intellectuals," in April 1969, Glazer attacked young Jewish radicals and the continued Jewish commitment to black activism. He coupled criticism of black anti-Semitism with an even stronger attack on "a white, predominantly Jewish, intelligentsia," who "abetted and assisted" militant blacks. "I do not want to deprive blacks of all the credit for the mood of violence that hangs over the country and frightens almost everyone," he wrote, "but we must acknowledge that white intellectuals, and that—to repeat—means in large measure Jewish intellectuals, have taught violence, justified violence, rationalized violence." Blurring the stark differences within the Jewish radical movement, he repeatedly compared Jewish radicals to Nazi perpetrators. He reserved particular ire for Jewish radicals whom he blamed for facilitating the "expansion and inflammation of anti-Semitism among blacks." It was not surprising that many of these were regulars for New Left publications but a number of them (viz. Norman Mailer, Edward Friedenberg, Susan Sontag, Theodore Solotaroff) had earlier contributed to or worked at *Commentary*, too.[54]

By the late 1960s, the comparatively unrestrained enthusiasm of *Commentary*'s treatment of Civil Rights under Cohen in the 1940s had disappeared completely. It had been supplanted by a tough, hardheaded line of thought that evaluated black anti-Semitism as a major menace to Jews and called on Jews to act appropriately in their response to it. The specter of black anti-Semitism had a galvanizing effect on many of the more prominent members of the Commentariat like Glazer and Himmelfarb. Their response to the problem of black anti-Semitism was to attack it head-on and scold American Jews for their perceived disinclination to identify the potentially dangerous effects of anti-Semitism in the black movement. *Commentary* urged Jews to learn from their historic experience of Nazism and in combating anti-Semitism that showed Jews must act in their own self-interest and to protect their own communities. Conspicuous by its absence from these articles in 1969 was the liberal appeal for black-white cooperation and that was frequently found in the writings of Rustin and other moderates in earlier years. *Commentary* was clearly turning inward and increasingly offered rationales for withdrawing support for Civil Rights. Podhoretz and his magazine had become that very type of white liberal he had castigated in "My Negro Problem" back in 1963, whose—to use Podhoretz's words—"abstract commitment to the cause of Negro rights will not stand the test of a direct confrontation." Ralph Ellison even accused *Commentary*'s writers of being "new apologists for segregation."[55]

Making It

While New Left anti-Americanism and black anti-Semitism alienated Podhoretz from radicalism, driving him towards the right, some of the reasons behind his shift were more personal rather than strictly political. Podhoretz had a sense of loss. Being too young, he missed out on the highly charged politics and intellectual debates of the 1930s, which pitched Stalinists against anti-Stalinists, particularly in the alcoves of City College. Nor did he participate in the fight against Henry Wallace in the following decade. When he reached maturity in the 1950s, the "end of ideology" had replaced the politics of earlier years and, as we have seen, he had no sympathy with the bohemian radicals of his generation like Ginsberg and Kerouac, many of whom he knew and disliked from his student days at Columbia. Podhoretz's desire to discover a struggle he could join seemed to be finally answered in his rejection of radicalism and he compared the current conflicts to "the struggles of the *Partisan Review* circle over Stalinism in the 1930s."[56]

The most personal factor driving Podhoretz out of the radical camp, however, came when he published his infamous memoir *Making It* in 1967. *Making It* was an auto-case history, a biographical and uncritical celebration of America of the 1950s and early 1960s, precisely the type of thing which Podhoretz said he had rejected in the early 1960s. In a similar fashion to the fiction he had railed against in *Commentary* and elsewhere, Podhoretz depicted himself as the postwar Jewish hero who had achieved social and material middle-class success by the tender age of 30. He aligned himself with his bourgeois suburban Jewish readers rather than his intellectual contemporaries. And, as if to alienate the latter, he lifted the veil on what he called the intellectuals' "dirty little secret"—that "lust for success which . . . had replaced sexual lust . . . especially for the writers, artists, and intellectuals among whom I lived and worked."[57]

Those of Podhoretz's friends who saw the draft book begged him not to publish it. He showed the manuscript to Epstein who responded, "If I were God, I'd drown it in a river." Podhoretz then sought his mentor's approval and presented his manuscript to Trilling, "anxiously awaiting his judgment." Trilling's verdict was absolute and shattering. "Do not publish this book," he advised. "It is a gigantic mistake. Put it away and do not let others see it." Podhoretz next turned to Bell, Trilling's close friend and another authoritative figure among the New York intellectuals. If you must publish this Bell said, then add a final chapter showing some ironic distance, some perspective on yourself. Even Podhoretz's agent would not touch the manuscript, refusing to represent him (despite the commission). His publisher rejected it as well, as if Podhoretz had "handed him something obscene," forfeiting the large advance he had already given Podhoretz. Only one person liked it: Willie Morris, editor-in-chief of *Harper's*, and it is no coincidence that Morris was not part of the New York intellectual community, being a Southern gentile.[58]

Nonetheless, despite protests and advice from his friends not to publish the book and, in the face of overwhelming opposition, he went ahead and proceeded to publication. Why he did this is an illustration of Podhoretz's complexity. In his own words, he hoped *Making It* to be "a Big Book"— "a frank, Mailer-like bid for literary distinction, fame, and money all in one package." But did he hope to achieve this by provoking his intellectual contemporaries in the same way as he had done some fourteen years earlier when, as a young and relatively unknown writer, he deigned to attack darling of the New York Intellectuals, Saul Bellow? If so, then Podhoretz's scope this time was far wider, reflecting his new position as the Editor-in-Chief of *Commentary* rather than merely one of its junior contributors. He didn't just have one intellectual in his sights, this time he had the entire community. Or was it another attempt at the same honesty which motivated him to write "My Negro Problem?" Or was it part of his oedipal journey: the completion of the process of symbolically killing his intellectual fathers and mentors that he had begun in 1960 when taking over *Commentary*? What was going through his mind? Perhaps the answer is: all of these things.[59]

The book provoked an intellectual storm of hostility. No other nonfiction book of the previous decade had received so many venomous reviews. For a while, *Making It* replaced Vietnam as the main topic of conversation at New York dinner parties. The New York Intellectuals greeted the book with either embarrassed silence or outright snickers. At the eye of the storm was Podhoretz's confession of his "dirty little secret": his unremitting drive for success. Although he had been honest, he had tried to exculpate himself by claiming that this lust was shared by all of his intellectual contemporaries. Podhoretz was hurt by his friends' reactions to the book.

Their reviews of *Making It*, in Podhoretz's opinion, exuded hatred. He must have felt like an outcast, alone, and betrayed by his friends.

The biggest and most personal blow came when the book was reviewed by the *New York Review of Books* (NYRB). Its editor, Podhoretz's erstwhile friend Jason Epstein, gave the book to Edgar Z. Friedenberg to review—a New Left writer whom Podhoretz had regularly published in *Commentary*—possibly because Podhoretz had started to reject his manuscripts. Friedenberg's review was less than flattering, concluding damningly,

> we may surely hope that successive volumes will permit us to follow the career of this remarkable young man. And they may be more mellow; sometimes, as we age, memory softens our perception of reality. In *Podhoretz Returns* and *Son of Podhoretz*, the monster may turn out to have a heart of gold.[60]

Podhoretz felt Epstein had betrayed him. He believed that his friend should have endorsed his book. Not only had Podhoretz and Epstein been friends since their days together as undergraduates in the English department at Columbia during the late 1950s, but also Podhoretz had left *Commentary* to work for Epstein at Doubleday. When Epstein left Doubleday, Podhoretz performed what he felt to be the ultimate act of friendship by refusing Epstein's vacated job. In the early 1960s, Podhoretz even offered his friend a post at *Commentary* (but Epstein insisted on being "co-editor-in-chief" so the arrangement collapsed).

Furthermore, Podhoretz had been instrumental in establishing the NYRB. He had speculated with Epstein over the years to produce "a serious newsprint paper" like the *Times Literary Supplement* with Podhoretz as editor. Podhoretz took an active part in the early discussions and was a member of the inner circle that eventually launched the NYRB. There had been talk of him leaving *Commentary* to become editor of the new journal. His flair for iconoclastic and reputation-destroying book reviews earmarked him as a natural choice for the position. (Podhoretz says that had he wanted the post he would have got it but based on past experiences, he was skeptical of whether this new venture would be a success and didn't want to give up the editorship of *Commentary*.) But Podhoretz was never directly offered the post and nor did he ask for it. Instead, Robert Silvers, whom Podhoretz had tried to recruit for *Commentary* three years earlier, became editor on Podhoretz's recommendation. At the same time, the NYRB was increasingly becoming the mouthpiece of the New Left. In an illustration of this shift, in April 1967, Epstein's "The CIA and the Intellectuals" suggested that the anti-Communism of the Left was responsible for the war in Vietnam, or at least created a climate of opinion favorable to it. Nevertheless, Podhoretz still felt that Epstein should have repaid his earlier acts of kindness by giving his wholehearted endorsement to the book. But Epstein didn't, and Podhoretz felt let down. Podhoretz thereafter was surely driven by a determination to get even with Epstein, the NYRB, and the whole New Left for the humiliation he had suffered at their hands over *Making It*.

Climax

By 1968 Podhoretz's mind was pretty much made up. The Six-Day War, the New Left's negative response to Israel's victory in it, the student revolts at Columbia, growing black anti-Semitism, and the New York school strike had progressively converted Podhoretz to the view that the New Left was a treacherous influence, combining a deadly force of anti-Americanism, antiliberalism, and anti-Semitism. Moreover, Norman Mailer's April essay in *Commentary*, "The Battle of the Pentagon," warned Podhoretz of the risks of the violence, which words like those of Mailer, had activated. The hostile reception of *Making It*, in particular Epstein's betrayal and Friedenberg's review in the spokes-journal for the New Left—the NYRB— was the final straw. On top of that came the series of critical, shocking, and traumatic events that defined the end of the decade: the Tet Offensive of January which was the final collapse of a long, mistaken policy in Vietnam; LBJ decided not to rerun for the presidency in March; Martin Luther King was assassinated in April, followed by Robert F. Kennedy in June; and in the summer, the chaotic Democratic Convention took place.

It was at that point that Werner Dannhauser left to return to academia, as if his work in converting the journal to his conservative viewpoint was now completed. When Dannhauser had joined in 1964 he had been the token conservative on staff, but four years later he saw that *Commentary* was moving toward the conservative mainstream. Where Dannhauser had once clashed with Podhoretz and Solotaroff on Vietnam and black radicalism, now Solotaroff had gone and Podhoretz was largely in agreement with Dannhauser.

Podhoretz "realized that to really make it, to achieve genuinely meaningful success, he would have to mount a campaign against the detractors of his way of life." This meant lashing out at the New Left, even if they were his friends. The NYRB was now clearly identified as a supporter of the New Left. Since the NYRB supported radicalism, the counterculture, and leftism, so Podhoretz turned his personal feelings of hurt, anger, and betrayal towards Epstein in particular on to the movement his journal espoused in general.[61]

Podhoretz now began to devote as much attention to the wrongs of the New Left and the antiwar movements, as to the ills of the war. Indeed, the former started to swamp the latter. *Commentary* pointed to the similarities between the New Left and the far right, arguing that there was little actual difference, and warning that the enemies of the Jews were now to be found on both sides of the political divide. The Right had remained silent during the Six Day War, even if its more moderate elements had supported Israel, while the Left was only differentiated by its hostility. *Commentary* called for legally sanctioned dissent instead of more radical alternatives. It opposed radical anti-Vietnam intellectuals like Mailer, Chomsky, McCarthy, and Macdonald, and who wrote in the NYRB and other radical publications.

As *Commentary* turned its fire toward the New Left, basic differences of opinion that had previously been verbalized and settled in pages of the magazine, using the old symposium format, now became irreconcilable rifts that descended into harsh personal feuds. Issues were reduced to personal and moral arguments, frequently resorting to the tactic of *ad hominem* character assassinations. What was formerly rational and reasonable disputation degenerated into personal vendettas and mudslinging, often dredging up the past. Acrimony entered the debate, and intellectual relations became progressively worse, as *Commentary*'s backlash became more vocal in response to the New Left's antiwar rhetoric of "moral disgrace," "immediacy," and "devouring of national energy." Irving Howe and Michael Harrington led the anti-New Left attack on the left flank, while Nathan Glazer, Irving Kristol, and Daniel Bell led the incipient neoconservative flank on the right. Glazer's emotional article, "The New Left and its Limits" in July 1968, marked the shift from an attitude of superiority to one of outright antagonism. In newly developing neoconservative terms (namely, the orderly and efficient management of institutions and bureaucracies), something that featured much more frequently in the coming decade, Glazer questioned the New Left's patriotism and vigorously attacked its underlying philosophical premises. America had its flaws, he argued, but its accomplishments were in fact much greater than its shortcomings.

> Ultimately, my disagreement with the radical Left comes down to this: I see no Gordian knot to be cut at a single stroke, the cutting of which would justify the greatest efforts (as in the past it has seemed to justify great horrors).

Glazer argued that although the war in Vietnam was a huge mistake, it had nonetheless happened, and it was not worth tearing down American political or social structures because of it. He had drawn the limits, the line over which he, Kristol, Bell, Podhoretz, and other members of the Commentariat were not going to cross.[62]

In October 1968, Irving Howe launched a devastating counterattack against the New Left and the NYRB. Howe wrote from the position of insider; he had been one of the NYRB's most prolific contributors and a leading protester against the war. But he felt threatened by the emergence of a "new sensibility" and lashed out at its totalitarianism, its refusal of nuance and observation, its political primitivism, its innocence, its simplicity, its psychology of unobstructed need, its lack and refusal of complexity, its Emersonian romanticism, its impatience, its contempt for rationality, and its hedonism. These tendencies were characterized by a rising younger generation of New Left intellectuals like Mailer, Brown, Marcuse, and McLuhan. In a sign of how far *Commentary* had moved since the early 1960s, Howe trashed these "pop poppas of the new," the very people Podhoretz had championed in *Commentary* when he took over its editorship in 1960. Howe lashed out at them as "ambitious, self-assured, at ease with prosperity while conspicuously alienated, unmarred by the traumas of the totalitarian age, bored with memories of defeat, and attracted to the idea of power." Such intellectuals stood in "absolute opposition" to his peers for they mixed "sentiments of anarchism with apologies for authoritarianism; bubbling hopes for 'participatory democracy' with manipulative elitism; unqualified populist majoritarianism with the reign of the cadres." He moved on to the NYRB, which blended "campus 'leftism' and East Side stylishness." A "snappish and crude anti-Americanism" had "swept over much of its political writing," which had helped to produce "a kind of rhetorical violence, a verbal 'radicalism,' which gives moral and intellectual encouragement to precisely such fashionable (self-defeating) talk." Finally, Howe ended by announcing that the intellectual and generational split was a "Kulturkampf," the most serious challenge of the last 25 years which required a "coherent response," "a sustained confrontation," and "an austere and sharp criticism."[63]

Kulturkampf

Commentary articles at the end of the decade tended to spell out wreckage and doom. They signaled a new, more aggressive and crisis-oriented tone. The restrained, rational, and qualified language of an earlier era was replaced by a new vocabulary of catastrophe and belligerence. This only got worse in the coming decade, as Podhoretz declared an-all out war on the New Left and the counterculture.

Notes

1. Norman Podhoretz, *Making It* (New York: Random House, 1967), 198.

2. Norman Podhoretz, *Making It*, 286-7, 283, 130, 294-5 and *Breaking Ranks: A Political Memoir* (New York: Harper & Row, 1979), 79.

3. Michael Harrington, "Our Fifty Million Poor," *Commentary* 28:1 (July 1959), 19-27; and "Slums, Old and New," *Commentary* 30:2 (August 1960). After Dwight Macdonald had praised the book for 40 pages in *The New Yorker*, Harrington was deluged with requests for articles, speeches and media interviews. The book became required reading among social scientists, government officials, student activists, and intellectuals. Economic adviser Walter Heller gave a copy to President Kennedy, who may have read it before ordering a federal war on poverty three days before his death.

4. Podhoretz, *Making It*, 99-100; Nathan Glazer, "Introduction," in *American Judaism* (Chicago: The University of Chicago Press, 1957), ii.

5. Elliot Cohen to Mandel Cohen, January 30, 1934, letter in author's possession; "Magazine of Quality," *Time* (January 29, 1951)[internet edition]; Fern Marja, "*Commentary*'s Number One," *New York Post Home News Magazine* (February 17, 1949), 1.

6. Norman Podhoretz, "Preface," in *The Commentary Reader: Two Decades of Articles and Stories*, ed. Norman Podhoretz (New York: Athenaeum, 1966), ix, viii.

7. Theodore Solotaroff, "The New York Publishing World," in *Creators and Disturbers: Reminiscences by Jewish Intellectuals of New York* (ed). Bernard Rosenberg and Ernest Goldstein (New York: Columbia University Press, 1982) 412-13.

8. Norman Podhoretz, *My Love Affair with America: The Cautionary Tale of a Cheerful Conservative* (New York: Free Press, 2000), 147; Staughton Lynd, emails to author, May 28 and 29, 2002; Norman Podhoretz, *Ex-Friends: Falling Out with Allen Ginsberg, Lionel and Diana Trilling, Lillian Hellman, Hannah Arendt, and Norman Mailer* (New York: Free Press, 1999), 141, 33, 12, 174.

9. Podhoretz, *Ex-Friends*, 203; *My Love Affair*, 141; and "Laws, Kings, and Cures," *Commentary* 50:4 (October 1970), 30.

10. Mark Gerson, *The Neoconservative Vision: From the Cold War to the Culture Wars* (Lanham, MD: Madison Books, 1997), 81; Podhoretz, *Breaking Ranks*, 174, 197; Michael Wyschogrod, "My *Commentary* Problem—And Ours," *Judaism* 17:2 (Spring 1968) 161; Norman Podhoretz to James Gatsby, March 13, 1962, Norman Podhoretz Papers, Manuscript Division, Library of Congress, Washington, DC .

11. Norman Podhoretz, "The Beat Generation," *Partisan Review* 25 (Summer 1957) 472-9 and "The Know Nothing Bohemians," *Partisan Review* (Spring 1958), 305-18; William Phillips, *A Partisan View: Five Decades of the Literary Life* (New York: Stein & Day, 1983), 244-5.

12. Jacob Heilbrunn, "Norman's conquest: why Rudy Giuliani loves Norman Podhoretz," *Washington Monthly* (December 1, 2007) [internet version]; Neil Jumonville, *Critical Crossings: The New York Intellectuals in Postwar America* (Berkeley: University of California

Press, 1991), 194; Paul Berman, "Allen Ginsberg's Secret: What he did with Norman Podhoretz at Columbia," Slate.com (June 5, 1997).

13. Podhoretz, *Breaking Ranks*, 91, 38–41, 204.

14. Podhoretz, *Breaking Ranks*, 338, 174.

15. Sidney Hook, H. Stuart Hughes, Hans J. Morgenthau, and C. P. Snow, "Western Values and Total War: An Exchange," *Commentary* 32:4 (October 1961), 277–297.

16. Richard Lowenthal, "Totalitarianism Reconsidered," *Commentary* 29:6 (June 1960), 504–12; Leon Lipson and Nehemiah Jordan, "The Cold War," *Commentary* 30:4 (October 1960), 340–4; Moshe Decter, "The Origins of the Cold War: An Exchange," *Commentary* 31:2 (February 1961), 142–59; Theodore Draper, "Beyond Berlin," *Commentary* 32:5 (November 1961), 302–10 and "Five Years of Castro's Cuba," *Commentary* 37:1 (January 1964), 25–37.

17. Gerson, *The Neoconservative Vision*, 80.

18. Nathan Glazer, "On Being Deradicalized," *Commentary* 50:4 (October 1970), 76; Podhoretz, *Ex-Friends*, 47.

19. E. F. Schumacher, "A Humanistic Guide to Foreign Aid," *Commentary* 32:5 (November 1961), 414–21 and "Economism," *Commentary* 36:1 (July 1963), 81–4; Nathan Glazer, "On Being Deradicalized," *Commentary* 50:4 (October, 1970) 74–80; Gerson, *The Neoconservative Vision*, 80–1.

20. Gerson, *The Neoconservative Vision*, 80; Podhoretz, *Breaking Ranks*, 320, 321.

21. Norman Podhoretz, *World War IV: The Long Struggle against Islamofascism* (New York: Doubleday, 2007), 81; Joseph F. Barr to Fineberg, March 1, 1963, Solomon Andhil Fineberg Papers, American Jewish Archives, HUC-JIR, Cincinnati, Ohio ("AJA").

22. Deborah Solomon, "The Legacy," *New York Times* (December 9, 2007) [internet version].

23. Podhoretz, *My Love Affair*, 171, 175.

24. Harvey Teres, *Renewing the Left: Politics, Imagination, and the New York Intellectuals* (New York and Oxford: Oxford University Press, 1986), 22.

25. Teres, *Renewing the Left*, 223.

26. Podhoretz, *My Love Affair*, 175; Ted Dienstfrey, "A Conference on the Sit-ins," *Commentary* 29:6 (June 1960), 524–528; Julian Mayfield, "Challenge to Negro Leadership," *Commentary* 31:4 (April 1961), 297–305; Letters, *Commentary* 32:1 (July 1961), 72–5.

27. Michael E. Staub, *Torn at the Roots: The Crisis of Jewish Liberalism in Postwar America* (New York: Columbia University Press, 2002), 65, 59, 66–9; Lucy S. Dawidowicz, "Middle-Class Judaism: A Case Study," *Commentary* 29:6 (June 1960), 492–503; Emil L. Fackenheim, "The Dilemma of Liberal Judaism," *Commentary* 30:4 (October 1960), 301–10 and "Apologia for a Confirmation Text," *Commentary* 31:5 (May 1961), 401–10; Theodore Solotaroff, "Harry Golden and the American Audience," *Commentary* 31:1 (January 1961), 1–13.

28. Staub, *Torn at the Roots*, 73.

29. Norman Podhoretz, "My Negro Problem—and Ours," *Commentary* 35:2 (February 1963), 93–101.

30. "My Negro Problem—and Ours," 93–101. He further antagonized liberals by writing,

"I suspect whites of self-deception who tell me they have no special feeling toward Negroes. Special feelings about color are a contagion to which white Americans seem susceptible even when there is nothing in their background to account for the susceptibility. Thus everywhere we look today in the North, we find the curious phenomenon of white middle-class liberals with no previous personal experience of Negroes—people to whom Negroes have always been faceless in vice—discovering that their abstract commitment to the cause of Negro rights will not stand the test of a direct confrontation . . . There are the writers and intellectuals and artists who romanticize Negroes and pander to them, assuming a guilt that is not properly theirs. And there are all the white liberals who permit Negroes to blackmail them into adopting a double standard of moral judgment, and who lend themselves—again assuming the responsibility for crimes they never committed—to cunning and contemptuousness exploitation by Negroes they employ or try to befriend."

31. Norman Podhoretz to C. P. Snow, January 7, 1963, C. P. Snow Papers, Harry Ransom Humanities Research Center; Norman Podhoretz to Kenneth B. Clark, January 4, 1963, Kenneth B. Clark Papers, Manuscript Division, Library of Congress, Washington, DC.

32. Nathan Glazer, "Negroes and Jews: The New Challenge to Pluralism," *Commentary* 38:6 (December 1964), 29–34 and Glazer's contributions to "Liberalism and the Negro: A Round-Table Discussion," *Commentary* 37:3 (March 1964), 25–42; Letters, *Commentary* 39:6 (June 1965), 8.

33. Nathan Glazer, "Liberalism and the Negro," *Commentary* 25–42; Marvin Elkoff, "Everybody Knows His Name," *Esquire* 62:2 (August 1964), 120, 121; Letters, *Commentary* 38:2 (August 1964), 8–12.

34. Norman Podhoretz, Letters, *Commentary* 40:4 (October 1965), 12.

35. Lynd, emails to author, May 28 and 29, 2002; Solotaroff, "The New York Publishing World," 413–14.

36. Solotaroff, "The New York Publishing World," 413–14; George Lichtheim, "Vietnam and China," *Commentary* 39:5 (May 1965), 56–9; Donald S. Zagoria, "China's Strategy," *Commentary* 40:5 (November 1965), 61–66; Oscar Gass, "The World Politics of Responsibility," *Commentary* 40:6 (December 1965), 85–90.

37. Strangely, though, Podhoretz had chosen to remain silent on the Tonkin Gulf Resolution of August 7, 1964. He made no public editorial statement, unlike other intellectual journals such as the liberal Catholic *Commonweal*, which praised the resolution, and *The New Republic*, *The Nation*, and *The Progressive*, which all denounced it. In fact, nothing on Vietnam was said until January 1965. When Podhoretz did publish an article on Vietnam, it was to point out the bureaucratic and policy-making confusion rather than to denounce the war in David Halberstam's "Getting the Story Straight in Vietnam," *Commentary* 39:1 (January 1965), 30–4. The launch of the sustained bombing of North Vietnam in Operation Rolling Thunder in February 1965 produced another dilemma for Podhoretz. Although he opposed further Communist expansion in Southeast Asia, he had doubts about the direction American policy was taking. He was against the United States taking over command from South Vietnam, sending in more and more troops, and eventually B-52 bombers to bomb the North. Confusion led to silence on this point and a series of feature articles on Southeast Asia appeared in the magazine without immediately addressing the bombing of the North. But concern over US policy grew in the magazine, and confidence in the LBJ's government began to erode, bringing *Commentary* into greater conflict with the administration. See Donald S. Zagoria, "Communism in Asia," *Commentary* 39:2 (February 1965), 53–8; J. K. Galbraith, "An Agenda for American Liberals," *Commentary*

41:6 (June 1966), 29–34; Robert R. Tomes, *Apocalypse Then: American Intellectuals and the Vietnam War, 1954–1975* (New York: New York University Press, 1998), 58. Taking stock of Johnson's Presidency in June 1965, *Commentary* found his foreign policy unsatisfactory because Vietnam had reduced the United States' international prestige to the lowest point in recent memory. The bombing of North Vietnam and the use of napalm had antagonized world opinion. It charted the catalog of errors committed by LBJ in Vietnam and condemned him for not negotiating a settlement similar to that in 1962 in Laos. See Maurice J. Goldbloom, "Foreign Policy," *Commentary* 39:6 (June 1965), 47–55.

38. Podhoretz, *Making It*, 317; Podhoretz, *My Love Affair*, 174, 175, 177.

39. Werner J. Dannhauser, "Review of *Cornell '69: Liberalism and the Crisis of the American University*, by Donald Alexander Downs," *Academic Questions* 12:4 (Fall 1999), 87–89; Werner J. Dannhauser, interview by author, August 22, 2003; Daniel Patrick Moynihan, "The President and the Negro," *Commentary* 43:2 (February 1967), 43.

40. Harris Dienstfrey, email to author, May 18, 2002: Ted Solotaroff, "The New York Publishing World," 413–15; Solotaroff, interview by William Novak, May 5, 1974; Werner J. Dannhauser, interview by author, August 22, 2003. In April 1960 Lichtheim had rejoined as a contributing editor. In May 1960 Shub left and Howard Fertig became an Assistant Editor. In April 1962 Rhoma Mostel replaced Brenda Brown as an Editorial Assistant and then in June of that year, Dienstfrey left. By September, Richard Lincoln had replaced him, but had left by February 1963. In April, Marion Magid, a young theatre critic living in New York City, joined as Assistant Editor, Edelston became the Business Manager, and Dannhauser had joined as an Assistant Editor in November 1964. In December 1964, Sylvia Roseman became Circulation Manager. In July 1965, Rhoma Paul became Editorial Assistant while David L. Ackerman became the Advertising Manager. In September, Ackerman had left and was not replaced. In November Florence Victor replaced Rhoma Paul and Sylivia Roseman had left to be replaced by Promotion Manager Rita Lintz. In March 1966 Dannhauser and Magid became Assistant Editors. In April Florence Victor had left. In December 1966 Neal Kozodoy had joined as an Assistant Editor, while Lawrence M. Craner became Advertising Director and Ronald Greene the Circulation Manager. By January 1967 Craner had left. In October 1967, Kozodoy was promoted from Assistant to Associate Editor. In March 1968 a new position of "Typography" was created and filled by Ira Teichberg. New positions of Assistant to the Editor and Editorial Assistant were established and given to Martha Goldstein and Kathie Gordon respectively. In July 1968 the new post of Production Manager was occupied by Bruce Lodi and in November there were two new Associate Editors, Brenda Brown and Peter Shaw and Dannhauser had left to teach at Cornell. During that year, Kozodoy was promoted to the new title of Executive Editor. By October 1969, Peter Shaw had left and Mary Ann Brussat became Editorial Assistant. And in December 1969 Susan Zimmerman became Editorial Secretary.

41. Podhoretz, quoted in David Twersky, "Left, Right, Left Right: After Half a Century, *Commentary* Remains Defiantly out of Step," *Moment* 20:3 (June 1995, 57; Norman Podhoretz, "Jewish Culture and the Intellectuals," *Commentary* 19:5 (May 955), 451–7; "Sholom Aleichem: Jewishness is Jews: The Unregenerate Tribe," *Commentary* 16:3 (September 1953), 261–3; "Jewishness & the Younger Intellectuals," *Commentary* 31:4 (April 1961), 310; "My Negro Problem," 93–101.

42. Twersky, "Left Right, Left Right," 42; Podhoretz, *Ex-Friends*, 155–6; Norman Podhoretz, "In Israel, With Scuds and Patriots," *Commentary* 91:4 (April 1991), 19–26.

43. Norman Podhoretz, "A Certain Anxiety," *Commentary* 52:2 (August 1971), 4–10; Theodore Draper, "Israel and World Politics," *Commentary* 44:2 (August 1967), 19–48; Walter Laqueur, "Israel, the Arabs, and World Opinion," *Commentary* 44:2 (August 1967), 49–59; Amos Elon, "Letter from the Sinai Front," *Commentary* 44:2 (August 1967), 60–8; Arthur Hertzberg, "Israel and American Jewry," *Commentary* 44:2 (August 1967), 69–73.

44. Milton Himmelfarb, "The 1967 War," 44:4 (October 1967); See Laqueur, "Israel, the Arabs, and World Opinion," 55; Hertzberg, "Israel and American Jewry," 69–73.

45. Emil L. Fackenheim, "Jewish Faith and the Holocaust," *Commentary* 46:2 (August 1968), 30–6; William Novak, "*Commentary* and the Jewish Community: the Record Since 1960," *Response* 7:3 (Fall 1973), 58. In August 1966, for example, *Commentary* had dedicated an issue to the state of Jewish belief but in its hundred or so pages questions concerning Israel and the Holocaust were conspicuously absent; not only did the editors fail to ask them, but also many of the symposiasts failed to raise them. Israel was hardly mentioned at all; indeed, one respondent observed that the fourth-generation Jews of the 1960s were even embarrassed by what they perceived as "Zionist demands," preferring to give to nonsectarian, American charities, rather than Israeli ones. The Holocaust was mentioned more often but still the references to "Auschwitz" and "the crematoria" were scattered and vague. The closest the symposium came to asking about the Holocaust was the question: "Does the so called 'God is dead' question . . . have any relevance to Judaism? What aspects of modern thought do you think pose the most serious challenge to Jewish belief?" Professor Jacob Neusner even equated Auschwitz to Hiroshima, Stalingrad, Coventry, Berlin, and Dresden, denying its uniqueness and specificity. In his own lengthy contribution to the symposium, even Fackenheim did not take more than a passing note of the Holocaust. As late as 1966, therefore, the full impact of the Holocaust had not made a deep impression in American Jewish life. See Michael A. Meyer, "Judaism after Auschwitz: The Religious Thought of Emil L. Fackenheim," *Commentary* 53:6 (June 1972), 55–62; "The State of Jewish Belief," *Commentary* 42:2 (August 1966), 71–160 and *The Condition of Jewish Belief: A Symposium Compiled by the Editors of* Commentary *Magazine* (Northvale, NJ and London: Jason Aaronson, 1995).

46. Norman Podhoretz, "The State of World Jewry," *Commentary* 76:6 (December 1983), 38.

47. Norman Podhoretz, "Is it Good for the Jews?" *Commentary* 53:2 (February 1972), 7–11; Milton Himmelfarb, "In the Light of Israel's Victory," 44:4 (October 1967), 57; Podhoretz, *Ex-Friends*, 167–8.

48. John Ehrman, *The Rise of Neoconservatism: Intellectuals and Foreign Affairs, 1945–1994* (New Haven and London: Yale University Press, 1996), 38; Robert Alter, "Israel & The Intellectuals," *Commentary* 44:4 (October 1967), 46–52; Martin Peretz, "The American Left and Israel," *Commentary* 44:5 (November 1967), 27–34.

49. "Liberal Anti-Communism Revisited: A Symposium," *Commentary* 44:3 (September 1967), 31–79; Hugh Wilford, *The New York Intellectuals: From Vanguard to Institution* (Manchester and New York: Manchester University Press, 1995), 202–3.

50. Thomas D. Bryant, J. Menkes, Letters, *Commentary* 44:6 (December 1967), 6.

51. Murray Friedman, "Black Anti-Semitism on the Rise," *Commentary* 68:4 (October 1979), 55.

52. Milton Himmelfarb, "Is American Jewry in Crisis?" *Commentary* 47:3 (March 1969), 33–42.

53. Himmelfarb, "Is American Jewry in Crisis?" 33–42.

54. Nathan Glazer, "Blacks, Jews and the Intellectuals," *Commentary* 47:4 (April 1969), 33–9.

55. Leslie Fiedler, "'A Very Stern Discipline': An Interview with Ralph Ellison," *Harper's* 234 (March 1967): 76–95.

56. Podhoretz, *Breaking Ranks*, 210.

57. Podhoretz, *Making It*, 55 and *Breaking Ranks*, 223, 227.

58. Epstein, quoted in Philip Nobile, *Intellectual Skywriting: Literary Politics and the New York Review of Books* (New York: Charterhouse, 1974), 12; Sidney Blumenthal, *The Rise of the Counter Establishment: From Conservative Ideology to Political Power* (New York: Times Books, 1986), 137–8.

59. Podhoretz, *Making It*, 356, 55.

60. Edward Z. Friedenberg, "Du côté de chez Podhoretz," *New York Review of Books* 10:2 (February 1, 1968), 11–13.

61. Jumonville, *Critical Crossings*, 198–9.

62. Nathan Glazer, "The New Left and Its Limits," *Commentary* 46:1 (July 1968), 31–9.

63. Irving Howe, "The New York Intellectuals: A Chronicle and a Critique," *Commentary* 46:4 (October 1968), 29–51.

3
War

Podhoretz Returns

For the first time in the ten years since he took over as editor, Podhoretz requested a vacation. After having worked twelve hours a day for six days a week, he felt he deserved it. In the summer of 1970 he took three months paid leave from *Commentary*, holed up by himself in the country, and wrote a book about the volatile politics of the 1960s. During this break he did a great deal of thinking. "A lot of things came together," he recalled. "I came out with a much clearer idea, if you will forgive my pomposity, of what my duty was—to tell the truth, as I saw it." When Podhoretz returned, one of the *Commentary* staff recalled, "he was loaded for bear and, not at all incidentally, for Jason Epstein and *New York Review*. He reminded some of us of Moses coming down from Mount Sinai, but his commandments were not limited to 10 . . ." Podhoretz had made the decision to fight New Left and counterculture radicalism in all its manifestations. In his own words, his "growing doubts about radicalism had coalesced and come to a head in a conviction so blazing that it ignited an all-out offensive" in *Commentary*. He had decided that the time had come to declare full-scale war against what he called "The Movement."[1]

Where Podhoretz had once flirted with Leftist cultural-literary radicalism, he now turned his back on it completely. He was not so much "born again" as reborn, returning to the politics he had held as a student during the 1950s: anti-Communism, pro-Americanism, and Leavisite Puritanism. "In short, in turning against the liberal consensus on domestic issues," he wrote, "I was finding my way towards a political position that was in some essential respects more consistent with everything I had been educated to believe as a student of literature."[2]

Podhoretz severed any remaining links with radicalism however tenuous they were in reality. Of course, he had never been entirely in agreement with those radical friends, colleagues, and collaborators he acquired and courted when he became editor in 1960, and by the end of the decade he found himself almost completely out of sympathy with them. He despised their "barbaric hostility to freedom of thought." He hated their "nihilism" as expressed in the "terrorism" of the Weather Underground, the "ideology of 'revolutionary suicide' preached by the Black Panthers, and in the spread of drug addiction among the affluent young." "Essentially," he continued,

> my disillusionment with the New Left took place over its anti-Americanism. I had been very critical of the American involvement in Vietnam, and *Commentary* was among the first to criticize that involvement. But I was never anti-American. My falling out with the New Left in the 60's was like the break with the Communist party for radicals in the 30's.

As a young man, Podhoretz believed in "trying to change the world." He had criticized the words of Edmund Wilson, who had admonished his fellow writers and intellectuals to give up "trying to improve the world or make a public impression," to forget about "transforming human society," or "realizing the Kingdom of God on earth." Now, ten years later, in 1970, he had changed his mind. He was convinced that intellectuals had

> a far greater stake in the maintenance of a liberal democratic order than they had ever realized, and that they themselves were mortally threatened by the radical effort to undermine and ultimately destroy that order as it existed in the United States.[3]

A Declaration of War

At the celebration of *Commentary*'s 25th anniversary in May 1970, Podhoretz issued his battle cry. The cementing of his ideological shift necessitated the language of combat.

> [W]e are at war, not in Indo-China . . . we are actually at war in the United States . . . we in this culture, in this country, are at war and in fact we have even now begun to experience actual physical casualties of that war, that is dead bodies . . .

Invoking the AJC's statement of aims—appearing at the front of every issue of *Commentary*—he declared, "now more than ever" it was *Commentary*'s mission to enlighten and clarify public opinion in the war in which he was engaged. His tactics were simple: "calling things by their proper names and thereby helping to redeem the corruption into which so much political, cultural, ideological, intellectual discourse has fallen." He went on to say that it must be clear exactly "who the contending armies are and what exactly they are fighting about." Podhoretz identified those "ignorant armies" that were "charging by night." He expressed his determination to assume a militant and aggressive posture, to "lift the sword" and so "smite those who are in an unholy alliance to destroy American democracy." With a final clarion call, he concluded,

> we hope to be responsible, bold, militant and continue to be in the service of that which is conducive to the health and vitality and beauty of this culture rather than to its disease, its sickness, its decay or its death.

Podhoretz radiated his sense of excitement at the forthcoming battle: "I always felt I was holding the line; now I'm on the offensive." With what had become his favored posture of characteristic self-assurance he proclaimed, "If you want to know the truth, the truth is I know I'm going to win."[4]

Podhoretz steered a course for war. He declared his rebirth and without delay converted his magazine to his new cause. Using his editorial freedom as Cohen had done before him, Podhoretz imposed a heightened regimentation on the magazine. He mercilessly extirpated opposing views and overhauled the magazine to fit his new hard-line vision of militarized us-against-them mentality. Experimentation and debate within the ranks was halted as topics that the magazine had discussed liberally over the years were expunged. *Commentary* from now on was to stop covering both sides, and a clear chain of command and editorial line were established.

Podhoretz also drastically altered his lifestyle to fit his new militant stance. From being a heavy drinker, who attended as many parties as he could in the late 1950s and early 1960s, he gave up alcohol altogether in 1970. Daniel Patrick Moynihan compared this to Babe Ruth benching himself during his home-run-hitting season; Moynihan admired Podhoretz as the only Jew who could drink an Irishman under the table. As a mark of his reversion Podhoretz went back to his old mentor, Lionel Trilling, for help. His Oedipal journey had ended and now Podhoretz had decided that it was time not to kill his symbolic fathers but his radical peers instead.[5]

Podhoretz sensed and seized the opportunity. He compensated for missing out on the intellectual struggles of the 1930s and the 1940s. In comparing the New Left of the 1960s to the Stalinism of the 1930s he was able to live out a heroic fantasy in which he could lead the remnants of the New York

Intellectuals, in his own words, as a "general," in the counteroffensive against the Movement. His language became increasingly conflict-orientated, as he directed the campaign from the front. Where he had written little during the previous decade, he revived his dormant self-penned column ("The Issue") and renamed it "Issues." From this "promontory," he issued clear "commands" to his "troops." His monthly diatribes set the polemical tone for *Commentary*'s ruthless, confrontational, and highly personal attacks on radicals, many of whom had been friends.

On the Offensive

In June 1970, Podhoretz officially launched the counteroffensive. He embarked on a scorched-earth campaign, a systematic assault against the Movement. He relentlessly strafed Movement positions. He did not just attempt to rebuff the Left but to eradicate it altogether. His conception of the enemy was deliberately hazy; his targets were broad. It was all-inclusive, covering almost the entire spectrum of American liberalism to the hardest radicals. While ideologically motivated, his recoil was at times reactive and instinctive and not always neat and consistent. Podhoretz loathed the New Left and its view of America. His hatred of it cannot be overestimated. Podhoretz considered the Movement to be destructive and ultimately dangerous. New Left radicalism was corrupting America's institutions and society. It was a repudiation of liberalism that was irrevocably carpet-bombing the infrastructure of American society, destroying its youth, and wreaking damage on its institutions. For Podhoretz, the "idealism" of the counterculture was self-interested, unctuous, hypocritical, ludicrous, snobbish, insensitive, lacking in imagination and curiosity, and smug. He saw in its sensibility only "a nihilistic assault" that "terrorized" all standards and values. As a sign of his obsession, in the December 1970 issue he published three consecutive articles on the topic. Podhoretz wanted to break the link between the New Left and the young because it suggested that the future then belonged to radicalism. He wanted to consign the Movement to oblivion because it endangered the entire nation.[6]

Commentary furiously attacked on every front, pursuing a roll call of targets. It struck out sharply, in a defiantly provocative style, criticizing every strand of sixties radicalism: its political, cultural, educational, social, artistic, and foreign policy ideas and attitudes, its institutional structures, and its literary and intellectual heroes—the New Leftists, Black Panthers, Women's Liberation, educational theorists, "literary revolutionism"—and other "new age" notions like ecology and population control, student unrest, proposed housing, education, and welfare legislation, anti-Americanism, antidemocratic elitism, anti-bourgeois values, anti-Semitism, counterculture "apologists," proponents of "apocalyptic thinking." It perceived them all as threats to reason and intellectual discourse.

According to George Nash, "virtually every issue of *Commentary* crackled with at least one-right wing liberal analysis of social issues." Articles had significant titles like "The Limits of Social Policy," "Is Busing Necessary?" "Liberty and the Liberals," "Growth and Its Enemies," "Liberalism vs. Liberal Education," and "Quackery in the Classroom." They compared the New Leftists to the various Communist thinkers in the 1920s and 1930s who had helped to pave the way for Hitler and implied that those who claimed the US government was fascistic were laying the groundwork for another Nazi dictator. Repression in America was a myth and, in any case, a desired response to radicalism. And even this was not enough, as *Commentary* writers began to invent distorted and imaginary portraits of New Left characters: "The Radicalized Professor," "The Activist Cleric," "The Liberated Woman," "The Advocate," and "The Communard." These were no more than caricatures and stereotypes to be fired down in a volley of vitriol.[7]

Commentary then raked over the battlefield, dispatching the wounded. Book reviews finished the job that articles started, as even the reviewers were given their orders, and every book was paired with a reviewer who was dictated to praise or attack it, depending on what the situation demanded. Almost every inch of available space in the magazine was utilized to destroying the intellectual foundations of the Movement.

Podhoretz closed ranks and relied on an increasingly small cadre. He purged any perceived traitors, collaborators, and weak links. Like his editorial predecessor at *Commentary*, Elliot Cohen, had done from the late 1940s onwards, many of those who had written for *Commentary* for more than a decade were swiftly expelled from its pages. Compared with the last decade, his core staff remained remarkably stable and constant. Neal Kozodoy filled the rank of Executive Editor; Marion Magid was Managing Editor; and Brenda Brown, Milton Himmelfarb, and Robert Alter remained associate editors.

Commentary drew its firepower from recruiting those who had once been part of the Left. Intellectuals who had been deradicalized by New Left radicalism and black anti-Semitism eagerly joined the fight, as did those who were naturally antipathetic to radicalism. These included Nathan Glazer, Midge Decter, Dennis Wrong, Michael Novak, Jack Richardson, Walter Goodman, Bayard Rustin, Dorothy Rabinowitz, Samuel McCracken, Edward Grossman, David Horowitz, Peter Collier, Diane Ravitch, Daniel Patrick Moynihan, Alexander M. Bickel, Irving Kristol, Hilton Kramer,

Seymour Martin Lipset, James Q. Wilson, Robert Nisbet, Leslie H. Farber, William Barrett, Joseph Adelson, Joseph W. Bishop, Jr., Paul Seabury, Charles Frankel, Jeane Kirkpatrick, Roger Starr, Daniel Bell, Paul Weaver, Suzanne Weaver, Edward Jay Epstein, Theodore H. Draper, Robert W. Tucker, Edward Luttwak, and Walter Laqueur. Many of these intellectuals were zealous fighters, hurt by a movement of which they had once been a part. They took up combat positions on the front line, as Podhoretz deployed tireless squadrons of infantry, backed up by artillery which never ran out of ammo. They kept the Movement pinned down to its positions.

A new generation of young, potentially conservative intellectuals was recruited. Chester Finn, Joshua Muravchik, Carl Gershman, Penn Kemble, Elliot Abrams, Scott McConnell, John Earl Haynes, Arch Puddington, Joseph Epstein, and Linda Chavez, among others, had been scarred and damaged in skirmishes with the Left on the college campuses. The Young People's Socialist League proved a particularly fertile recruiting ground for Podhoretz; when its young members became disillusioned with socialism, they found a home in *Commentary*.

This group of writers was far from ideologically or politically homogenous. It ranged from neoconservatives like Daniel Bell and Irving Kristol to democratic socialists like Irving Howe, but they were all united in their hatred of the New Left. Podhoretz deliberately published these writers because many of them were former radicals who had been identified or associated with the Left, both old and new, and thus spoke with the authority of the insider. Their knowledge of the Left would stand them all in good stead for the fight. The vehemence of their backlash against the New Left was motivated by the perception that they had been its sacrificial victims, its martyrs. Richard Herrnstein had been accused of racism by the SDS after a 1971 article on the genetic basis for IQ; James Q. Wilson fell victim to a similar campaign which may have cost him his chance to become Harvard's Dean of Arts and Sciences; and Edward Banfield was hounded from a chair he had accepted at the University of Pennsylvania. Jeane Kirkpatrick suffered the same fate (twice, no less), when she was driven off the stage during the course of her Jefferson lecture at Berkeley and another lecture scheduled for Smith College was cancelled altogether.

Such treatment at the hands of the Left motivated their embittered and enraged attacks. Their attacks were heavy-handed. They were guilty of overkill, as the magazine became preoccupied with unmasking conspiracy and the sinister forces behind it. They displayed all the characteristics of the recently converted zealot. Their tone, verging on the conspiratorial, encouraged a sense of disproportion and outrage. It was pontificating, defensive, elitist, distressed, defiant, obstreperous, aggressive, truculent, and hysterical. They felt isolated and desperate, as if they were the last defenders of America against a hostile incursion of radical New Left and countercultural Visigoths. They took their lead from Podhoretz who, with typical modesty, saw himself as to blame for nurturing the rise of the Movement. He never let it be forgotten that under his stewardship, *Commentary* had introduced Goodman, Marcuse, Mailer, Brown, and others to the American public. He had created them and now he could destroy them, or so he thought.

The campaign continued with extraordinary intensity over the first three years of the 1970s. Calm and consideration were replaced by fire and brimstone. *Commentary*'s politics became much more personalized, as Podhoretz and his cohorts used its pages to carry on intellectual spats and to deepen feuds and rivalries. A tone of viciousness and malice replaced the dynamism of the early sixties and the groundbreaking articles disappeared as everything was reduced to an attack on the Movement. The consequence was that both in public and private, intellectual discourse often descended to a personal, *ad hominem* level.

Podhoretz was driven by personal demons. Once very close both socially and ideologically to Epstein and his NYRB, Podhoretz had since fallen out with both. The betrayal of NYRB's review of *Making It* together with their ideological divergences over CIA-sponsorship during the Cultural Cold War (Podhoretz supported it, Epstein did not) and Tom Wolfe's 1970 book *Radical Chic* (Epstein hated it, Podhoretz praised it) prompted Podhoretz to locate the command center of the Movement at the NYRB. Podhoretz's anger was possibly further antagonized by jealousy, as the NYRB had stolen the limelight from *Commentary*. The NYRB, a journal he said he had helped to create, was now more successful than all of the other New York Intellectual journals combined. Its circulation of almost 100,000 was one-and-a-half times greater than *Commentary* and ten times more than other key intellectual publications like *Partisan Review* and *Dissent*. Not only had the NYRB surpassed *Commentary* in circulation, it had also done so in prestige as the forum for America's intellectuals: a 1972 study ranked *Commentary* behind the NYRB, as the highest influential intellectual publication in America. *Commentary* was forced to admit, "No other intellectual magazine has ever achieved so widespread an acceptance in America or the prestige that goes with such acceptance." As the author and hero of *Making It*, which admitted his "dirty little secret" of self-interest, Podhoretz surely resented the fact that his old friend Jason Epstein had gained greater attention and material success than he had done—and through the espousal of radical causes at that.[8]

Podhoretz ordered Dennis Wrong to produce a surgical strike, resulting in "The Case of the *New York Review*" in November 1970. Podhoretz chose Wrong because he was ostensibly more disinterested. Podhoretz also offered him a higher fee than normal. The piece was so important to Podhoretz that he spent more time on the article than he did by his own sedulous, line-by-line editing standards. Even though it went out under Wrong's name, it was perceived that Podhoretz most likely wrote a good deal of it. Some felt they could point to whole paragraphs written in Podhoretz's unmistakable style. Even Wrong wished he had developed his own ideas more fully, but Podhoretz had browbeaten him into being more aggressive, as the article was being used as an instrument of his personal revenge in Podhoretz's increasingly personal vendetta with Epstein.

Wrong listed the journal's war crimes. He took the NYRB's 1967 issue, featuring a diagram of a Molotov Cocktail on its cover just after a series of bloody riots in the Black ghettos of the North had broken out, as his starting point. In a lengthy analysis of its contents and politics, Wrong claimed the NYRB had become, "a vehicle of what might be called haut New Leftism." He described it as a tone of "extravagant, querulous, self-righteous anti-Americanism," which provided the basis for "an extreme and bitter repudiation, marked by an unmistakable touch of Schadenfreude, of a great deal more in American life." In a charge that would later be leveled at *Commentary*, Wrong accused the NYRB of becoming "thoroughly predictable," relying on a decreasing number of writers, and providing them with a "cloak of intellectual respectability." He concluded, apocalyptically, that the NYRB had precipitated a "confrontation on all fronts between the Movement at its arrogant, mindless worst and the demagogic, patrioteering Right." And that "the menace of politicized will," created by the NYRB, "feeding on its own self-righteousness, thrusting blindly forward in a frenzied activism until it finds or creates the resistance it seeks," will find "a consummation which, now as then, can have disastrous consequences for all of us." Podhoretz felt that it was, "'Almost exactly the sort of article I had in mind." He offered reprints at 50 cents each (with a 20 percent discount on orders larger than 25) because he wished to have it as widely circulated as possible. As Alexander Bloom has pointed out, "No other editorial comment was necessary."[9]

Underlying Wrong's entire article was the proposition that the NYRB's editors were calculating, scheming, deceitful, devious, opportunistic self-seekers, with "one eye on the Dow-Jones of radical fashion and the other on the market profile of their journal's audience." As Ruth Wisse put it, the NYRB's "responsiveness to fashion makes it the Women's Wear Daily of the American intelligentsia." But it is possible that these comments were a form of subconscious transference and projection. When Wisse and Wrong (and Podhoretz) damned the NYRB they could also have been referring to *Commentary* and its editor. One could also argue that Podhoretz's ideological shifts had "one eye on the . . . market profile of their journal's audience." When Podhoretz took over *Commentary* in 1960, he shifted away from the liberal anti-Communism of the 1950s and toward the new radical fashion. It allowed him to be a counterintellectual to his symbolic fathers of an earlier generation. Similarly in the 1970s, his shift away from the New Left and toward the right was a maneuver designed to throw *Commentary* into an oppositional stance. It demarcated the magazine from its intellectuals competitors like *Partisan Review*, *The Nation*, *The New Republic*, and *Dissent* which were all shifting leftwards, as the NYRB had done. Podhoretz wanted to differentiate his product in the magazine market and relocate *Commentary* in a completely alternative part of the ideological scene. While it could be argued that Podhoretz was alienating his magazine form its prime target audience—the predominantly leftwing intelligentsia—at the same time, he was tapping into the preexisting market of conservatism as well as the newly emerging one of deradicalized Leftists. As Peter Steinfels put it, it was in effect "a struggle for turf and attention." If anyone was responsive to intellectual fashions, surely it was Podhoretz.[10]

Podhoretz launched a further attack on Epstein. When Epstein published a book on the Chicago conspiracy trial, which resulted from disruptions at the 1968 Democratic convention, Podhoretz saw this as an opportunity to get even for Friedenberg's review of *Making It*. When a frequent reviewer for *Commentary* requested to review it, Neal Kozodoy responded, "Oh, no. We have something special in mind for that book." Instead, Podhoretz assigned Yale law professor Alexander Bickel to the task. Essentially a review elevated to a status of leading article, Bickel dissected the book, describing it as a pretentious argument by insinuation, sleight of pen, and lacking in candor. Podhoretz had got his revenge. What little, if anything, of their friendship that had survived by this point, was extirpated.[11]

It was not the only friendship that was to end. If *Commentary* was no longer popular among leftist intellectuals, Podhoretz also found himself avoiding and being avoided in his social circles. Most of his former friends and acquaintances ostracized him. Angry with him, they called him names, from "traitor" to "crazy." Some of them thought he had literally gone mad and one even went to his wife and suggested to her that he should be institutionalized or, otherwise, he'd end up committing suicide. Podhoretz has written that he felt very lonely and isolated and missed his old pals of whom he said he had been terribly fond. Yet, nevertheless, he said he saw no alternative. Either he moved to the right or shut up. But Podhoretz did not seem to care at the time, as he exhibited a quasi-religious fervor: "far from feeling persecuted in those days, I experienced the special happiness that comes from breaking out of a false position and giving free rein to previously inhibited sentiments and ideas," he wrote in his memoir of that period. He denied, however, that "this new clarity" had turned him into a "political zealot," but that is exactly what he had become and the price he paid was vilification and even social shunning. He was now cut off from some of the most fashionable and in some ways most influential circles in New York.[12]

Yet, his desire to win attention for himself was working. The mainstream media, which usually ignored the squabbles, spats, antics, and eccentricities of the intelligentsia, began to sit up and take notice. There was an enormous amount of talk about *Commentary* in the press—both sympathetic and hostile—that had built up over the past 12 months, and far more than at any other period in the magazine's history. The major East Coast newspapers focused on *Commentary*'s break with the New Left. In November 1970, the *Wall Street Journal* devoted a long article on its editorial page to discussing *Commentary*'s new tone. It was pleased to announce that "a pro-American type of intellectual is starting to speak up." And a couple of days later the *New York Times* joined in. The ultra-conservative *National Review* acclaimed the February 1971 "Revolutionism and the Jews" issue and sent out the message, "C'mon In, the Water's Fine." *National Review* approved of *Commentary*'s new stance and extolled *Commentary* as a maturing conservative magazine and a key friend in the anti-New Left campaign. It noted that such a posture "would have been unthinkable in the pages of *Commentary* even a few years ago. But the journal has affected its *volte face* from support to disparagement of the radicals with remarkable skill." A new era in *Commentary*'s intellectual life had been signaled, and as the magazine contributed to the increasing intellectual polarization, so the larger society beyond it changed as well.[13]

Standing His Ground

Podhoretz took up the values of anti-Communism, Zionism, the middle class, and democratic capitalism and established the ground that he would defend at all cost. He argued that a large part of the solution to the problems of the 1906s lay in the restoration of tradition, authority, and restraint. He celebrated the dull and unexciting culture of ordinary bourgeois America. He stood up with self-confidence against those whom he identified as cultural barbarians: those opponents of middle-class values whose influence was spreading far beyond the college campuses where the critics of such values flourished. He complained that the "new sensibility" had erased distinctions between high, mass and low culture, creating a treacherous cultural relativism. "There is no longer a consensus as to what is good, what is bad, what is important, what is minor, what is significant, what is trivial, and how one tells the difference." Such an atmosphere of "confusion" was "surely damaging and dangerous." He opposed the atmosphere on the campuses and warned of the "threat" of "Balkanization along ethnic lines of our sense of the culture," which was already happening in the universities in the form of various programs of ethnic and women's studies. He felt it was "an epidemic of cowardice, together with an enormous panic to get on the right side of what looked like a triumphant revolution," an intellectual "failure of nerve," that had abdicated in the face of the New Left challenge. Intellectuals had abdicated their responsibilities and Podhoretz saw it as his task to contribute a new clarity and to reiterate values of high culture and critical sensibility, and even of old-fashioned literary scholarship.[14]

Podhoretz had returned the magazine to its 1940s and 1950s position, which, according to Mark Gerson "embodied a chastened liberalism." Despite a brief diversion during the 1960s, Commentary had returned to its former Cohen-era path of uncritically celebrating America despite its imperfections. Obsessed with anyone and anything to the left of him, Podhoretz overlooked important issues like Vietnam, racism, institutionalized corruption of business, politics, and the military, and ecological disaster. Podhoretz's new anti-New Left backlash had blinded him and Commentary to the very real evils which the New Left was trying to address. Its readers noticed a continuing neglect of some of the most crucial social issues of the day and a "major blind spot" in its editorial policies.[15]

Podhoretz, though, had moved far beyond a "chastened liberalism," to a "mild conservatism" to use Nathan Glazer's words. As if to explain himself, Podhoretz published Glazer's account of his disaffection from liberalism and his transformation from "mild radical to mild conservative." Like conservatism, Commentary had become largely unconstructive. It stopped proposing solutions; it became pessimistic and destructive and suggested nothing in its place. Podhoretz had been too busy fighting a war against the New Left and the counterculture to provide a coherent, alternative, ideological vision. Instead, his positions were reactive, instinctive, determined as a mirror opposite to what his perceived enemies believed. The letters poured in, complaining of Commentary's "bitter whining." The editors of Partisan Review detected a growing conservatism, a querulous tone, and a marked suspicion of any deviation from Podhoretz's regimented line. The writings of Midge Decter and Dorothy Rabinowitz stood out in this respect. Despite Commentary's praise for his work, even Tom Wolfe remarked, "They're congenitally negative."[16]

Reflecting Podhoretz's more ascetic, alcohol-free lifestyle, Commentary showed a much more puritanical influence. Sex and pornography had long been an interest of Podhoretz's, cropping up frequently in the magazine during the 1960s (much to the chagrin of the AJC). As a student Podhoretz had been very sexually aggressive, and proud of it; on the boat over to England, he said he needed to find a woman before he landed, and he did. But as the permissiveness of the 1960s skyrocketed (in his opinion), he replaced his sexual aggression with a new chasteness. Podhoretz felt that it the time was right to resurrect the moral and sexual Puritanism he had learned from Leavis at Cambridge—who was a Puritan par excellence—that he had publicly suppressed hitherto. The Devil, Podhoretz wrote, "seduces us into sterility not with denunciations of the generative act but with promise of sexual riches and sexual delights free of all troublesome consequentiality: onanism and sodomy, copulation without end and without issue." Even though Podhoretz tended toward an absolutist position on freedom of speech, he found it increasingly hard to defend in the face of the spread of hardcore pornography. And no doubt with the Beats in mind, many of whom he had met while a student at Columbia, Podhoretz pursued an antidrugs policy, calling marijuana "very harmful indeed," and echoed the words of Samuel McCracken that it was "the lethal enemy of any intellectual community" and "more apocalyptically as the lethal enemy of life itself."[17]

In his attack on the New Left, Podhoretz also pursued an antifeminist agenda. Apart from viewing feminism as a road to socialism, he had a detectable and rather shocking bias against women, and consequently it was as if he wished that feminism would just go away. When writing about Lillian Hellman in particular, and to a lesser extent Hannah Arendt and Diana Trilling, he exhibited what seemed to be a compulsive need to mention their sex lives, affairs, and lovers. When describing Mary McCarthy, for example, he couldn't resist mentioning that Philip Rahv was her lover or that she was "our leading bitch intellectual." Indeed, running throughout his articles on such women was a rather bitchy (and it might be added, salacious) tone.[18]

Commentary thus dismissed feminism as "a coercive movement toward androgyny," tarred by its connection to "all sorts of left-wing causes." It referred to the "irrationality" of contemporary feminism and its "dogma." It rejected educational equality and objected to any change in the curriculum and through the courts, as "feminist ideology." Indeed, its articles on feminism and women were often cynical and angry antifeminist diatribes, nothing more than assaults upon all the advances women had made in the past few decades in asserting their rights as full members of society, and making scant use of scientific data in support of their arguments. They were flimsy apologies for sexism which indicated a tendency to see any tampering with social institutions as tantamount to inviting a disastrous collision with nature. *Commentary* was culpable of particularly specious reasoning which attempted to prove that the biological, genetic, and hormonal differences of women made them less equal than men. It assumed and defended inherent male superiority and dominance, proclaiming systematic discrimination against women to be a myth.

Commentary repeatedly portrayed feminists as egomaniacal anarchists set on savaging the American family. It criticized feminism for its efforts to blur differences between the sexes, its denigration of motherhood, its indiscriminate nastiness toward men, and its contempt for femininity. It argued that mothers should stay out of the workforce and tend to their children, implying that women who did so were family-hating feminists. It assumed the traditional male role of breadwinner and that all women were genetically programmed to be good mothers. Women were all alike, an undifferentiated mass with uniform and identical needs, aptitudes, aspirations, drives, emotional patterns, and reactions to motherhood and family. Western society had put too little emphasis on full-time motherhood, it contended, and as a consequence rates of divorce and poverty were higher.

Commentary attempted to efface the dignity of the feminist movement by calling it the "woman question" and by mercilessly scolding and denouncing those women who had aspirations beyond home and family. Midge Decter's "The Liberated Woman," represented a deliberately provocative, overly generalized portrait, or better caricature, of the eponymous female. Letters poured in, complaining that it was "biased and prissy," "snide," "catty," "supercilious," "condescending," "frivolous," "vindictive," "immoral." It set up a "straw woman, making her the pampered little bitch we all know and love." Vivian Gornick of *The Village Voice* wrote:

> And even though the piece bears Midge Decter's name it smacks so entirely of *Commentary*'s contemporary view of the world that [the] unmistakable impression is that it was written in the magazine's editorial rooms... Every time *Commentary* sets out to observe any of the numerous and, God knows, legitimate social-protest movements that are tearing our lives apart, it ends up sounding like a Jewish mother, arms folded across her fat breasts, mouth compressed into her fat face, saying: "After everything I've done for you, this is what I get back!" For, in the view of fat and self-satisfied *Commentary*, what is behind all the social stirrings, all the churning and screaming and profound injustice thousands of people feel characterize their daily existences, is merely the dissatisfactions of a handful of ungrateful and maladjusted middle-class children.

Jane Larkin Crain continued the attack, this time lashing out at "feminist" fiction. Harold Bloom even managed to invoke Jewish mystic tradition to condemn feminism, wondering why the demoness Lilith (believed to strangle babies) had not become "the patroness of some of the more extreme manifestations of the women's liberation movement." The offensive was rounded off by Michael Novak's "verbal thrashing" of Susan Brownmiller's 1975 book *Against Our Will*, which denounced rape. Brownmiller replied to Novak saying: "The Nut of the Year award goes to Michael Novak for his review of *Against Our Will*. As for the rest of you at *Commentary*, tsk tsk." And another reader in response asked, "With such acrimonious female colleagues, who needs male chauvinism?" An anti-women agenda had become a staple of *Commentary*'s conservative anti-New Left thought.[19]

"La grande peur juive"

After his previous ambivalence on the subject, Podhoretz now openly declared his interest as a Jew. As Rabbi Balfour Brickner wrote most eloquently,

> *Commentary*, under the aegis of its editor, Norman Podhoretz, is the most glamorous of the latest crop of Jewish converts. After years of supercilious sneering at Judaism and Jewish life in America, after years of condescension toward matters Jewish, after years of deliberately trying to "make it" as a generally intellectual, but decidedly not Jewish affirming journal, *Commentary* has now decided to convert. Now the magazine and its editor pose as the great defenders of Jewish survival, and they do so in such extremely conservative terms that some of us who have been Jewish survivalists for a long, long time, can only cry out: "Heaven help us! Preserve us from our new allies." If Jewish survival in America depends upon the cynical intellectual posturing of those who have only recently discovered the virtues of Jewish ethnicity but who display little if any real awareness of the complex tensions and balances that Judaism contains at its deeper levels, then we are indeed in great trouble![20]

At the end of the last decade, Podhoretz had declared that the shaping force for his politics would hereafter be the question, "Is it good for the Jews?" What he once considered to be "a mentality no broader than the horizons of the tribe" and a "ridiculously parochial question," was now "a useful guide to thought." He thought that Jews must once again begin to looking proposals and policies from the point-of-view of the Jewish interest, and must once again begin to ask what the consequences, if any, of any proposal or policy are likely to be so far as the Jewish position is concerned.[21]

While Podhoretz did not advocate a retreat into "a self-regarding parochialism," he did suggest that the Jewish interest should be the first rather than the last consideration. Recalling a phrase Elliot Cohen had written almost fifty years earlier, Podhoretz argued, "In the brassier age aborning, Jews will either ask, Is it good for the Jews? and act on the answers, or else they may wake up one day to find themselves diminished, degraded, discriminated against, and alone." Podhoretz had fully converted to the philosophy that Jews must devote themselves to themselves and to Jewish things exclusively. He was suggesting nothing less than "the Jews stand alone." He had become guilty of a narrow, self-serving ethnicity as the basis for Jewish particularism, and retreated into a religious, as well as social and political conservatism. There was an inward turn in *Commentary*, an insistence on the defense of separate Jewish interests, an emphasis on what made Jews different from Americans.[22]

Commentary now operated on *"la grande peur juive."* It became increasingly obsessed with anti-Semitism in radical quarters. Reading *Commentary* in the early 1970s, one would imagine that Jews were living in a climate of fear. Previously, the history of Jews in America was seen as a success story but the "golden age" had come to an end, *Commentary* told its readers, asserting that the prevailing liberal directions were becoming increasingly inhospitable for Jews. American Jews represented as an endangered species, who were no longer treated as equal citizens, and whose physical safety could no longer be assured even. A subtle "new anti-Semitism" existed in America (rather than the "old" defamatory variety). Hostile references to Jews in the media had markedly increased. Hostility was directed toward Jews on a "corporate" level, even among those who would genuinely and angrily reject anti-Jewish stereotypes. American Jews were now lonely and exposed. Words like "deadly" and "anxious" began to creep into article titles. *Commentary* pessimistically inferred that American Jewry was imminently and massively threatened by intermarriage which had reached large-scale proportions. Its assessment was bleak, exaggerating the issue of survival, tending toward panic. Where in earlier years *Commentary* had castigated Jewish liberals and Leftists for misusing the term genocide to describe the treatment of African Americans, it now freely and loosely was using it to describe what Jews were doing to themselves, as intermarriage became a key concern.[23]

Commentary's new Jewish affirmation expressed itself in an ardent opposition to any manifestation of Jewish radicalism and even liberalism. It railed against American Jewish support for birth control, abortion rights, and many aspects of the sexual revolution. It launched a rallying cry to lift Jewish fertility rates. The crusade for American Jewish women to bear even larger numbers of Jewish children found its most aggressive and persistent standard-bearer in Milton Himmelfarb. "No one worked harder, longer or more passionately than Himmelfarb to advance the view that Jews needed urgently to up their numbers," pointed out Michael Staub. As far back as 1963, Himmelfarb had looked at the ominous costs of low Jewish fertility rates ("The Vanishing Jews") and blamed them on the attitudes of the Reform and Conservative rabbis. By the 1970s Himmelfarb had become even more zealous and vocal. He argued ever more emphatically that Jewish women were not grasping how critical it was that they have Jewish children.[24]

There was a search for themes that could promote Jewish solidarity and stem the hemorrhage of assimilation and intermarriage. Accordingly, new threats were manufactured. *Commentary* devoted ten pages to the non-issue of Christian evangelist conversionist and missionizing efforts, even though it had never been a significant factor in the defection of Jews away from Judaism. Later in the decade, *Commentary* returned to the theme, using overly polemical and charged terms, accusing those who dissented from its line of "accommodationism." Jewish communal groups were criticized for their little effort. *Commentary* scaremongered and articles expressing fear, anxiety, and impotence began to grow in number.

Podhoretz now felt obligated to persuade his co-religionists that radicalism was their enemy. He wanted to organize liberal Jewish opinion to be less tolerant of those attitudes he felt would destroy the Jews if left unchecked. He wanted to expose the threats to Jews: black anti-Semitism, youth, and radicalism, New Left anti-Zionism, the Soviet Union, Arab revolutionaries, and Euro-Communists. "Jews," he argued, "should recognize the ideology of the radical Left for what it is: an enemy of liberal values and a threat to the Jewish position." Threats to Jews came from within the community, too. He exposed Jewish "apologists" for the Movement. Any Jews who supported radical change were cast as anti-Semites and self-haters who should be proclaimed non-Jews, and other Jews should not enter into dialogue with them. Podhoretz imposed an editorial line that stated that those who embraced the universal over the particular were "self-haters" masquerading as "self-affirmers." He reprinted Gershom Scholem's "The Holiness of Sin," which had appeared in Hebrew 34 years earlier. Although many readers understood it to be an attack on Stalinism,

Podhoretz made it clear that it had more to do with the revolutionary spirit of the 1960s. The ideological fight against the radical Left, Podhoretz argued, was a fight for Jewish security in America. Feeling more nervous and anxious than ever before, *Commentary* thus was "determined to extirpate any phenomenon associated with or influenced by countercultural trends, root and branch," wrote Irving Greenberg, "as any such association *ipso facto* cancels out the good in any aspect of such phenomena," even if it was Jewish.[25]

Podhoretz even devoted a whole issue to the subject of "Revolutionism and the Jews." He adopted the right-wing tactic of lumping the entire Jewish Left together for the purposes of denigration, condemning the function of liberal Jews in the New Left movement. Glazer had earlier written that while such Jews did not directly engage in New Left violence, the money that they gave to such causes bred violence nonetheless. He now pointed out that Jews were disproportionately represented in the pernicious movements that supported drug legalization, pornography, liberalization of abortion laws, unilateral peace in Vietnam, welfare rights, busing, and other liberal and radical causes during the 1960s and early 1970s. Together with Walter Laqueur, he anticipated a recoil against the New Left once the Vietnam War ended. They warned that, since Jews were so disproportionately represented in the New Left, the result would be an anti-Semitic backlash. They pointed out that Jewish interests could no more be served by the extremism of the Left than they could be by the extremism of the Right. Those committed to Jewish interests had to oppose the enemies of those values on the Left.[26]

"Literary Onanism"

Commentary attacked other manifestations of New Left, radical, or countercultural-influenced Judaism. Reflecting this sense of urgency, it turned on any Jews it believed were guilty of masochistic self-hatred and/or anti-Semitism. The most prominent victim of this new editorial policy was Philip Roth, as he became a key target in this specifically anti-Jewish-New-Left campaign. The 1969 publication of *Portnoy's Complaint* was for Podhoretz a literature of self-loathing because, in building upon the derogatory portrayal of Jews that Roth had pioneered (in *Commentary*) in his short stories in the late 1950s, it was deemed to be "bad for the Jews." Roth was deemed also to embody a particularly harmful form of everything that was wrong with the 1960s—what was called the New Class—a distinctive social and technocratic elite that was fundamentally hostile to the moral values of the average American and the enemy of American interests.

Its members read *Portnoy's Complaint* since it was a representative and perfect outburst of the ethos of the New Class, which was newly emergent and began coming to consciousness of itself as a class around the time Roth first appeared in 1959. *Portnoy's Complaint* shared their distinctive "snobbery and self-righteousness" and by replacing high culture with the counterculture, it had become their zeitgeist text. In turn, Roth owed his centrality to his perfect embodiment of its ethos because that elite set the cultural style and political program for 1960s America. Roth was the exemplification of New Class' flashiness and liberal attitudes toward the family, drugs, Communism, busing, affirmative action, and job quotas; he was the New-Class writer *par excellence*.[27]

Podhoretz acted like a god, attempting to create and destroy authors at will. He claimed to have discovered Roth's early and as yet unknown work, giving him his literary debut in the magazine, while an assistant editor in the late 1950s. As Editor-in-Chief, he later published Roth's defenses of his work ("Writing American Fiction" and "Writing about Jews") against the author's Jewish detractors who were used to something more public-relations minded and self-congratulatory. Yet, now, Podhoretz allied with Roth's critics initiating a campaign against Roth. It was a mark of how far Podhoretz had changed from his risk-taking days of the early 1960s, when he flirted with cultural and literary radicalism. The editor, who had published Roth, Goodman, Mailer, Brown, and Farber, on topics such as sex and pornography, had now turned against his earlier self.

Roth was viciously and repeatedly attacked in a form of "virtual warfare" in the magazine, which lasted for decades, each time he produced a new book. *Commentary* dealt with Roth in a personal and reductive fashion, in a species of one-dimensional criticism, bordering on character assassination that would become *Commentary*'s increasingly favored tactic against its enemies henceforth. Podhoretz and Howe, in a rare moment of agreement, recanted their earlier praise for Roth. They both described him as a "tendentious writer" who was always bent on making the same point over and over again. They found him "tiresome," "nagging," "attitudinizing," "deeply marred by vulgarity", "impatient," "snappish," "dismissive," "raucous," and "self-aggrandizing." John W. Aldridge called Roth's *oeuvre* "literary onanism" and Marie Syrkin charged him of delighting in Nazi racial defilement "right out of the Goebbels-Streicher script." Such attacks continued will into the 1980s when Ruth Wisse wrote that Roth had "atrophied into a stereotype and become an artistic liability" and Joseph Epstein that Roth's work resembled "the rebellious outcry of a claustrophobic fourteen-year-old boy."[28]

Roth took these critical beatings over the years, but the deepest and nastiest of all came from Howe, put up to the job by Podhoretz. In "Philip

Roth Reconsidered" in December 1972, Howe opined: "The cruelest thing anyone can do with *Portnoy's Complaint* is to read it twice." He called it "an assemblage of gags," "a shriek of excess," "a vulgar book . . . full of contempt" and "afflicted with claustrophobia of voice and vision." Howe, wrote Epstein,

> quite consummately eviscerated all Roth's work . . . its effect was as though Dr. Howe, working over the corpus of Roth's work, had removed all the patient's major organs, leaving only a small portion— that one short story—of the spleen.

If Howe's 1972 essay had left Roth in the "spiritual equivalent of intensive care," wrote in a reader, "then Mr. Epstein's elective surgery is clearly intended to dispatch the patient to the morgue. No longer can he say that Howe's was the 'unkindest cut of all,'" as Epstein's "skilled vivisection lays bare all the parts . . ." In a private letter to Bernard Malamud, Roth wrote,

> I don't see *Commentary* because there's a loathsome creature named Joseph Epstein who reviews books for them, and another named Ruth Wisse, less loathsome, but more idiotic and narrow, if that is possible. There are no philistines like those Jews over there, and for me enough's enough.[29]

Podhoretz pursued other Jewish New Left figures. When Rabbi Arthur Waskow dared to submit an article to *Commentary* which pushed for a new Jewish radicalism ("The Shabbat was the first general strike, a holy general strike; let us build an Age of Shabbat!"), Podhoretz leapt into action probably not least for the chutzpah Waskow displayed in sending it to him in the first place. For Waskow represented a pernicious and specious confluence of radicalism and Judaism, whose thinking was, in the words of Robert Alter, "self-loathing and self abasement masquerading as an expression of self-affirmation," "the crude political rape of a religious tradition," and "homiletic hypocrisy." Podhoretz felt that Alter's comments were "too gentle to do justice to the truly abominable case at hand" for it "might more accurately be considered a contribution to the literature of Jewish anti-Semitism." Waskow and other radicals, he opined, "belong to the tribe of the wicked son" whose teeth should be set on edge because they emphasized the universal over the particular, and sought to use the Jewish historical experience "as a point of departure for political activism."[30]

Podhoretz was attempting to destroy the option of a radical perspective for young Jews, but all he succeeded in doing was illustrating the yawning gap between the magazine and the Jewish youth it was trying to influence.

He found it difficult to convince many Jews—both young and old—that not only was the radical domestic agenda a serious threat, but also that they had a moral duty—both to themselves and America—to oppose it. His publication of Marshall Sklare's review trashing *The Jewish Catalog* (1973), a do-it-yourself book that provided practical self-help information on how to live a Jewish life, illustrated the divide. The book was a major public event in American Jewish life: it was accorded instant recognition by the American Jewish community, granted "classic" status, and sold out five times.[31]

Hostile and angry letters disapproving of *Commentary*'s shrill, callous, vicious, smug, niggling, nitpicking, and snide tirades that substituted malice and personal abuse for reasonable thought poured in. Readers accused the magazine of "intellectual overkill," "name-calling," "facile generalizations," "vengeance," spite, and distortion. The "grumpy" tone of Sklare's article in particular won him little support, and in an exchange of letters in *Commentary*, not one respondent took his side. Indeed, such Jewish figures as Irving Greenberg, Trude Weiss-Rosmarin, William Novak, and Michael Berenbaum attacked him. Alfred Marcus of *Response* magazine felt,

> To be the subject of a *Commentary* assault is an honor that every self-respecting individual, book, or movement should covet. Certainly it is jealousy that generates such venom and hostility. Destroying reputations seems to be *Commentary*'s favorite pastime. Unable to present an image of positive Jewish values and of a satisfying Jewish life style, it is forever falling into empty negativity.

Rabbi Balfour Brickner added that *Commentary* betrayed an

> unutterable chutzpah in presuming to judge who among their fellow Jews is "kosher" and who is "treif"—who falls within the pale and has strayed beyond the *Commentary* line—who should be tolerated and who should be wiped out. Editor Podhoretz has the litmus paper, and he gives out the new Jewish seal of Good Housebroken Approval. An intellectual pseudo-Jewish McCarthyism, presided over by *Commentary*, is something new and ugly under the sun!

In attacking the possibility of a Jewish radicalism, *Commentary* had simply become, noted Sol Stern, a "bellwether for the thinking of the Jewish Establishment—the rich, assimilated Jews who run the major Jewish organizations and make the 'Jewish opinion' that the mass media picks up," reflecting only the interests of those "American Jews who have made it here and don't want anyone rocking the boat."[32]

"Orchestrated 'Lynchings'"

Podhoretz's new Jewish self-interested parochialism manifested itself an ardent opposition to quotas and affirmative action. In the first two years of the new decade, *Commentary*'s interest in the issue of Civil Rights fell considerably to the point of almost disappearing. In 1970 only two articles appeared and over the following year there were none. In 1972, the issue returned but with a new concern—affirmative action and quotas—and four articles addressed that issue. Nominally, *Commentary* was in favor of ending racism and correcting injustice against blacks, but in practice, its coverage of black issues was generally limited to attacks, not on racism, but on programs to end it. Podhoretz made *Commentary* the intellectual center of opposition to affirmative action and quotas not least because they were planks of the New Left's program. The magazine provided a forum for those wishing to attack prevailing affirmative-action programs, as well as racially-conscious employment and academic selection. Opponents of quotas embraced the magazine to produce a long and consistent opposition. Quotas and affirmative action became *the* civil rights issue in *Commentary* during the 1970s, and far more space was devoted to this subject than any other.

Podhoretz had initially supported Kennedy's original special efforts to recruit qualified blacks and to help unqualified blacks compete on an equal footing and to encourage institutions to make a concerted effort to be inclusive of all people. However, when affirmative action had become a series of programs and benefits intended to give preference to people based upon their race, such treatment violated one of Podhoretz's fundamental beliefs: that an individual should not be judged on the basis of an involuntary characteristic. He opposed the admission of unqualified persons in order to fill a predetermined quota and concluded that quotas and proportional representation by group were not in the best interest of Jews. He feared that, as a Jew, a quota system designed to overcome discrimination against blacks would almost certainly result in discrimination against Jews. Podhoretz vigorously defended the concept of a meritocracy against its critics. He wrote that quotas violated traditional American ideals and savaged the very idea of the government programs designed to help the disadvantaged.[33]

Podhoretz was uncompromisingly opposed to any affirmative action to favor blacks, with or without formal quotas. *Commentary*'s pages were repeatedly filled with piercing denunciations of affirmative action and quotas, which were attacked throughout the 1970s from every conceivable angle. Those articles dealing with race relations directly attacked the means employed by government, busing, quotas, and scatter site housing, to achieve racial equality. Nathan Glazer criticized the enforced school busing experiment to achieve racial integration by documenting its failure to achieve its intended results; not only had it not led to increased racial harmony but also it had not improved academic performance for black and white children. Blazoned across the cover of the February 1972 issue were the words, "How Washington Enforces New Discrimination in the Name of Equal Opportunity." Inside, Podhoretz saw an increase in discriminatory practices against Jews in civil-service employment and university admissions and hiring as a result of quotas. Peal Seabury opposed the efforts of the Department of Health, Education, and Welfare to compel universities to hire equal numbers of women or lose federal aid. And Elliot Abrams argued that, by following a system of preferential treatment and proportional representation of nonwhites and women, the Equal Employment Opportunities Commission had violated the law.[34]

Commentary argued that those who suffered the most from affirmative action programs were the intended beneficiaries. It predicted that they would constantly feel the need to prove their ability, while those who were not lined up to benefit from affirmative action programs would react bitterly when they lost out to a member of a preferred group on the basis of race. It pointed out how affirmative action had led to the substitution of the word "disadvantaged" for "blacks" or other minorities when "not all minorities are disadvantaged, and not all those disadvantaged are minorities." Other *Commentary* contributors demonstrated that affirmative action originated merely as a means for companies to recruit people from different racial and ethnic backgrounds by advertising job positions clearly and widely.

Podhoretz loved to shatter what he perceived to be the great liberal commitment to Civil Rights. So *Commentary* had placed its imprimatur on antibusing, antidesegregation sentiments. The source of support for quotas was attributed to white liberal racism, in particular a "don't blame the victim" philosophy. Ben J. Wattenberg and Richard M. Scammon felt that although blacks had made extraordinary socioeconomic progress, the liberal community had been silent on the issue or denied it. Instead liberals suggested that blacks were now worse off than ten years ago because their public policy was to mute any public acknowledgment or celebration of black accomplishments in order to maintain moral and political pressure on the administration and on public opinion. Furthermore, liberals continued to assert that America was a failure and that things were as bad as ever, and maybe worse. Richard Herrnstein challenged what he saw to be the prevailing academic orthodoxy of environmentalism by stating his belief in the inheritability of IQ. Such sentiments were, noted Philip Brantingham, "like a red flag to the Establishment intellectuals of America. Whenever your contributors write an article that flouts a liberal myth, outraged letters sealed with froth, come pouring in."[35]

Commentary's anti-affirmative action stance also helped to sharply divide the Jewish and African American communities. Naturally, blacks responded bitterly to *Commentary's* attacks on such programs. They felt that Jewish former liberals like Podhoretz defended the interests of those who had already made it. Having completed their integration into American society, the Podhoretzes had come to identify with its prevailing racist patterns in exchange for inclusion in the white majority. They suspected that Jews had backed off from civil rights activities because they were now "making it" and it would become a primary cause of black anger against Jews. And while couched in the rhetoric of the constitutional commitment to govern without preference to any by reason of color, or religion, or national origin, they were right in feeling that *Commentary's* arguments often came down to Podhoretz's formulation at the beginning of the decade, that they weren't good for the Jews. Many readers became convinced that *Commentary* was not just moving away from the policy of affirmative action but retreating from the goal of racial equality itself. One even described the magazine's articles on these topics as "orchestrated 'lynchings.'"[36]

In turn, Podhoretz countered that blacks did not deserved Jewish help because of the revival of black anti-Semitism. Black leaders had acquiesced and even encouraged anti-Jewish and anti-Israel sentiments and anti-Semitism had become more respectable than at any time since the Holocaust. The failure to this "black perspective" to critical examination, argued *Commentary*, was the result of a particular kind of liberal racism which exempted "black" ideas from scrutiny. *Commentary* reminded its readers that Martin Luther King had decried anti-Semitism and called upon blacks to end it, and that when black anti-Semitism had emerged in the mid-1960s the NAACP, CORE, and King all condemned it publicly. But, it lamented, King's words had not been heeded and no such condemnation had been heard since. Instead, with a few exceptions like Bayard Rustin, black leaders had endorsed, rationalized, or actually promoted the expression of anti-Semitism.

Commentary refused to accept that, while there had always been black anti-Semitism, Jewish opposition to affirmative action had compounded it.

Instead, it argued that quotas were only one form of affirmative action and were opposed by the overwhelming majority of Americans, including most blacks. It then warned its Jewish readers that they would find themselves on the opposing side to those blacks. Jews, it cautioned, must be more "considerably more hard-headed and willing to risk confrontations, coming down hard on automatic anti-Israel positions and anti-Semitic posturing that even moderate blacks have so easily slipped into." They would have no choice but to resist black anti-Semitism while not retreating from opposition to quotas. Within only ten years, then, Podhoretz had undone *Commentary*'s liberal and sympathetic relationship with the Civil Rights movement.[37]

Readers found it distressing that the magazine had joined a broad and often-hysterical alliance. It was particularly saddening, they pointed out, that the spokesman for this position was Nathan Glazer who, in the past, had written sympathetically about integration and ethnic pluralism. Irving Howe charged that *Commentary* "habitually denied or minimized" the distinction between affirmative action and quotas in a campaign to meld them. He felt that it was "An odd paradox" that "such leading journals as *Commentary* . . . appear to be somewhat, perhaps a good deal, more conservative than their sponsors." Howe was right: the magazine did equate quotas with affirmative action even though the two were not synonymous, and this failure to distinguish between them evoked an emotional response against *any* form of affirmative action (even if it didn't involve the "tragedy" of quotas, as *Commentary* liked to call them). Irving Levine, director of national affairs at the AJC during the 1970s, distanced the agency from the magazine and rejected the accusation that Jews led the charge against affirmative action. *Commentary*, then, may have become the most widely quoted organ of Jewish opinion in America, but it did not speak for all Jews on these issues least of all its sponsor.[38]

Nixonism vs. McGovernism

As the 1972 presidential election approached, although he was a registered Democrat, Podhoretz was unsure about voting for the Democratic Party. His wife recalled "a state of combined fear and disgust" about what had become of it. George McGovern's nomination as the Democratic presidential candidate in 1972 had horrified Podhoretz. There was, in part, a personal dimension to this feeling. In the mid-1960s, McGovern had invited Podhoretz to dinner at a French restaurant. McGovern got there early and, as he sat down, he noticed two striking women sitting behind him and two ugly, heavily made-up women facing him. When Podhoretz arrived, McGovern joked about the women: "Norman, you get to look at those good-looking ones while I have to look at those turkeys." Podhoretz glared and mumbled "That's my wife." McGovern apologized but Podhoretz scowled throughout the meal, obviously hurt by McGovern's comment.[39]

Podhoretz also despised McGovern for political reasons. McGovern signaled the victory of the antiwar and countercultural left. McGovern was the product of the ideological currents that arose out the New Left in the 1960s. As a college student, McGovern had backed Henry Wallace in 1948, making him, in Podhoretz's opinion, a Stalinist fellow traveler. And McGovern had voiced opposition to Vietnam. Furthermore, McGovern and his supporters were identified with a more skeptical approach toward Israel but a positive approach toward quotas. As a consequence, Podhoretz described McGovern as "patronizing, unsympathetic," and "hostile to the feelings and beliefs of the majority of the American people." A new category of "McGovernism" was invented and, under Podhoretz's direction, *Commentary* became its foremost enemy. To Podhoretz McGovern's followers were members of the despised New Class.[40]

Nonetheless, if there was still a chance of it getting elected, Podhoretz was not ready to let go of the Democratic Party just yet, even if it had been heavily compromised by McGovern. In spite of his personal and political feelings toward McGovern, Podhoretz gave each candidate in the 1972 election equal backing, running conflicting essays on the forthcoming presidential election. Nathan Glazer endorsed McGovern while Milton Himmelfarb, Irving Kristol, and Gertrude Himmelfarb supported Nixon. The latter three argued that Nixon had done more for Israel than any other American president and was a proven friend. For his part, Podhoretz tried to persuade liberals that Nixon's achievements had done more and more to deserve, if not their affection, then at least a diminution of their dislike, while his administration had been friendly to Jews in a variety of important ways. He painted the forthcoming election as a contest between the traditional culture and the counterculture. This was far more support than the Republicans had ever previously received from the magazine, usually a stronghold of the Democrat Party.[41]

Podhoretz eventually voted for Nixon, as did other "deradicalized" intellectuals like Sidney Hook and Irving Kristol. It was a significant moment for Podhoretz as it was his first Republican vote ever and demonstrated how far he had shifted his outward stance since 1960. Podhoretz surely also wanted to be near power: he calculated that Nixon's victory in 1968 was the beginning of the "bringing together [of] a new Republican majority that would, like the Roosevelt coalition which served as its obverse model, freeze the opposition out of power for the next generation or more."

Yet, only three years earlier in 1969 Podhoretz had been embarrassed when vice-president Spiro Agnew quoted from *Commentary* in defense of his own position. Podhoretz published a letter dissociating the magazine from Agnew, saying it would be most unfortunate if the Vice-President's approving reference to *Commentary* were taken as implying that the magazine is in agreement with him. In that same year, *Commentary* had produced an ambiguous assessment of the new Nixon administration. In the following year, he was equivocal about Nixon's record on foreign policy. Thus, only three years after Podhoretz had no use for Nixon he had turned around and supported him. It either showed how much Podhoretz had changed or how far he was prepared to shape his politics to fit the new political realities. It also helped that in 1968 Podhoretz's good friend, Daniel Patrick Moynihan, a veteran member of the Commentariat and lifelong Democrat, had accepted an offer from the newly elected Nixon to serve in the White House as a special advisor on domestic affairs, and then as ambassador to India. In turn, Moynihan recommended Podhoretz to the Nixon administration as a potential ally.[42]

With Nixon elected again and with the emergence of a Republican majority, Podhoretz and *Commentary* never looked back. Podhoretz realized that Nixon and the Republicans were not just a temporary blip but also represented the future, and if he was to translate his editorial success into actual power and influence, it was them he needed to court. Conservatism had begun to develop as a sizeable and respectable intellectual movement in the late 1960s—and the election of Nixon was a great boost as much as it was a blow to liberals. The political pendulum had swung in the direction of the Right, and a new, more developed right wing could now be detected among the American intelligentsia. Writing in *Commentary*, William Pfaff even raised the possibility that the left had become obsolete through its own success. "Perhaps a new agenda had emerged—issues which not only supplanted traditional liberal reform, but make it irrelevant." Podhoretz thus looked on Nixon's victory as a defining moment in his political philosophy in particular and in the orientation of American life in general.[43]

As a mark of this change, whereas Podhoretz had publicly expressed unkind thoughts about the rightward-leaning journal, *The Public Interest* (which had been founded in 1965), he had effected a rapprochement with it and its editors, Irving Kristol and Daniel Bell, began to appear in *Commentary* once again. Podhoretz published others like Frank Kermode, Nathan Glazer, Robert Heilbroner, Seymour Martin Lipset, Werner Dannhauser, and Moynihan whose writings also betrayed conservative thinking. *The Public Interest* may have led the way in the shift rightwards, pushing toward conservatism, but *Commentary* soon caught up and overtook it as a key journal in this respect. With a great deal of help from *Commentary* in general and Podhoretz in particular, conservatism in a new form, was fully restored as a viable political movement in the coming decade.

Political Onanism

If Philip Roth had been guilty of "literary onanism," then *Commentary* was guilty of the political version. In his courting of Nixon, Podhoretz went to great lengths to justify his vote for him. He whitewashed Nixon's record. Readers pointed out that there was no real evidence that Nixon was a friend of Israel or that he had done more for Israel than any other American president, as the only pro-Nixon public statement by an Israeli official (Ambassador Yitzhak Rabin) was promptly and unequivocally repudiated by the Israeli government. They further suggested that Podhoretz had overlooked the first three years of the Nixon administration whereby he refused to deliver Phantom jets as promised and authorized by LBJ unless Israel rolled back to her pre-1967 borders. Podhoretz had also ignored Nixon's record on civil liberties, Vietnam, Supreme Court appointments, Civil Rights, foreign policy, his attempt to bully and control the press, to bug the Democratic headquarters, and the squelching of all disagreement at the Republican Convention. In his attempt to court the Nixon White House, *Commentary* was guilty of rewriting the Nixon record.

Podhoretz's support for Nixon even led him to ignore the Watergate crisis and its impact on American life until the scandal had long since passed its climax. It took Podhoretz a long time to publish a piece on Nixon and Watergate and when he did its impression was slight. The piece by Lipset and Earl Raab minimized the acts committed by the White House and reduced the whole affair to an analysis of Nixon's psychological behavior. Indeed, they seemed to blame the political system itself for Watergate rather than Nixon personally when they wrote that it "was symptomatic of a deep strain in American society, of which Nixon has come to seem the almost perfect embodiment" and "the United States, and the Nixon administration, had an appointment with Watergate." In an even more revisionist piece, history professor James Nuechterlein sought to rehabilitate Nixon by stressing that there was more to his administration than Watergate. Paul Johnson described Watergate as "a mess and nothing more" and suggested that the Nixon administration's record of misuse of power "was no worse than that of Truman and Eisenhower and considerably better than Franklin D. Roosevelt's" and that there "was none of the personal corruption which had marked the rule of Lyndon Johnson, let along the gross immoralities and security risks of John F. Kennedy's White House." "In essence," he concluded, Watergate was a "media *Putsch*" "as ruthless and anti-democratic as any military coup by bemedaled generals with their sashes and sabers." *Commentary* thus had become more adept at anticipating the needs of government than those of the intellectuals; rather than speaking *to* power, *Commentary* began to speak *for* it.[44]

Sick of watching what he saw as his friend's sycophantic opportunism, novelist Joseph Heller pilloried Podhoretz in print. Podhoretz had, as Heller saw it, to grovel more and more cravenly before President Nixon, "as if rehearsing for the engulfing, mandible-straining blow job that he would later bestow on Ronald Reagan," wrote Christopher Hitchens. Heller cut off their friendship and initially rebuffed Podhoretz in a letter to *The Nation*, indicating his disgust with Podhoretz's political transformation. In his 1979 novel *Good as Gold*, Heller smashed the point home with lethal force. Heller's portrait of Podhoretz was damning and exaggerated yet insightful nonetheless. Podhoretz was caricatured as Lieberman, a sad, overweight, friendless editor of a magazine that nobody read.

> All through college Lieberman's dearest wish for the future had been to manage a small intellectual magazine. Now he had his magazine, and it wasn't enough. Envy, ambition, and dejection were still ravaging what few invisible good qualities he might have been born with.

Lieberman was disliked even by the few friends he had. "Not many people other than the President allowed Lieberman into their homes for dinner. If the White House was going to be so unparticular, Lieberman was not the person to dismiss the opportunity." Lieberman was also forever producing "still another soiled clump of hastily written pages he felt certain would make an important book." Heller satirized Podhoretz's dirty little secret—his careerism and desire for success—and the means by which he was prepared to get it: his switching of positions at will and his various ideological flip-flops. Lieberman "loved getting his name in the papers," and was willing to say whatever was needed to get it. He longed for attention and was openly fawning toward the Nixon administration in which he craved a position or even just an invitation for dinner. He was prepared to say whatever was needed to get it. "Get me a CIA grant," requested Lieberman, with absolutely no feeling that such secret money from the government would compromise his intellectual integrity. "'There is nothing wrong with accepting money for supporting positions I would advocate anyway.'/'And what are the positions you will advocate?'/'Whichever ones they want me to.'" By that point, Lieberman's politics were "all for a totalitarian plutocracy, backed by repressive police actions when necessary—as long as the men on top were good to Jews like himself and let him have a little—and called it neoconservatism."[45]

Neoconservatism

Podhoretz delighted in the utter completeness of McGovern's defeat in the 1972 election. But there was still work to do as McGovernite forces had captured the Democratic Party. Podhoretz hoped to take back the party from these insurgents and helped to establish the anti-McGovern Coalition for a Democratic Majority (CDM). It was a group of unrepentant anti-Communist and pro-Israel hawks, backing Democratic Senator Henry ("Scoop") Jackson of Washington, as he represented a staunchly aggressive anti-Soviet cold warrior and pro-Israeli champion within the party, who hoped to win the Democrats and the liberal community in general over to their way of thinking in opposition to the McGovernite liberals. They saw the defeat of McGovern by Nixon—one of the worst in the country's history—as an opportunity to remind the Democrats of their commitment to the policies of FDR, Truman, and JFK, as well as to reiterate their opposition to the New Left and all those legislative and judicial measures (in particular, affirmative action) they perceived were intended to "overturn the country's essential philosophical and political underpinnings." The CDM believed that the Democratic Party had been punished by the voters for having "come to be unduly influenced by forces and ideas both unrepresentative of and hostile to traditional Democratic principles." They called "for a return to that very Democratic tradition which, abandoned by the forces temporarily in control of the national Democratic party in 1972, was usurped in some measure by the Republicans." They sought to recapture the leadership of the Democratic Party through political mobilization of what they considered to be the party's silent majority, proceeding on the assumption that their views reflected the sentiments of a majority of Democratic voters. At the same time, they wanted to fend off the influence of "New Politics" movement within the Democratic Party as represented by those who nominated McGovern. The CDM's manifesto was drafted by Podhoretz, many of the Commentariat joined the organization, and *Commentary* became an outlet for its views.[46]

Podhoretz published members of the CDM, who sounded the alarm over the deterioration of US defenses and the buildup of Soviet military capability, warning that these trends, if not reversed, would lead to a period of Soviet military superiority. The CDM's views were certainly reflected in *Commentary*'s hawkish stance on Israel. Israel, as a political cause, became a substitute for religion for *Commentary*'s secular Jews. Podhoretz and others mobilized their support behind Jackson. Jackson's aides, Richard Perle and Elliott Abrams attempted to torpedo any effort by the Nixon (and later Carter) administration to improve relations with the Soviet Union or to launch peace efforts in the Middle East. At this time, Israel became one of the most important elements on Podhoretz's agenda, particularly when war broke out again in October 1973. Podhoretz's support for Israel increased exponentially. Like the Six Day War before it, the Yom Kippur War had much the same impact as in 1967: Podhoretz became even more "Zionized." In a series of provocative articles in successive issues from January to March 1974, *Commentary* compared the Yom Kippur War to Second World War and intimated that the West should not be fooled by the illusion of détente for *Commentary*, which had successfully duped America. While Nixon and Kissinger were basking in the warmth of their false impressions, the Soviets had heated up a war in the Middle East. Podhoretz saw it as his task to shatter this illusion and a total of eight articles on Israel were published over three consecutive issues. Overall, *Commentary* took a more hard-line stance and pessimistic outlook on the Middle East than other journals like *Time*, *Newsweek*, and the *New York Times*. Where those journals felt that Sadat and Egypt were moderate, *Commentary* was unconvinced. This skepticism helped to shape the emerging neoconservative coalition that emerged as a counterforce to McGovern.

The neologism "neoconservative" was originally invented by Michael Harrington and the editors of *Dissent* to designate right-wing socialists, namely their old friends who'd moved to the right. It was meant as an insult, along the lines of "running dog" or "fellow traveler," or perhaps to suggest "neo" as in "neo-Nazi" or "neo-liberal." It was soon applied to anyone who had once been on the Left but had since shifted rightwards. Irving Kristol famously described a neoconservative as a liberal who had been "mugged by reality." Thereafter it was used to describe those liberal anti-Communists who found themselves outnumbered and alone with the Democratic Party in America. They hoped to stop liberalism's drift to the left and anchor it within the moderate center. The neocons emerged as a significant counterforce after the 1972 victory of George McGovern. For many of them, his nomination was the final straw in a series of developments that alienated them from the Left. At that time, though, many of those designated as "neos" were not happy with this description. They were uncomfortable with any association with conservatism and almost none of them were Republicans. They were accustomed to the Democratic Party. As Seymour Martin Lipset wrote, the term "was invented as an invidious label to undermine political opponents, most of whom have been unhappy with being so described."[47]

The neocons were far from ideologically or politically homogenous. They ranged from conservatives to social Democrats and to democratic socialists, but they were all united in their hatred of the New Left and the counterculture of the 1960s. "Though the enemy is ostensibly Communism and the Soviet Union," wrote Theodore Draper,

> what really stirs the "neo" to a sort of holy wrath is anything that can be blamed on liberals. There is not much he can do about getting at the Soviet Union, but home-grown liberals are readily available as targets of his rancor. It is *de rigueur* for a "neo" who was formerly a liberal to be particularly unforgiving in his anathemas upon liberals. Against this enemy the "neo" goes into battle as if in a civil war, with more than a hint that those who differ are really serving the enemy. A disagreement over policy comes to resemble a quasi-religious war rather than a legitimate secular dispute . . . The remaking of history plays a large part in this apocalyptic drama of good and evil because the older "neo" has repented and recanted transgressions that he committed as a liberal or leftist. No one raises his blood pressure more than the liberal with whom he once shared the same views—about the Vietnam War, for example—but who has stubbornly refused to admit grievous error and recant publicly. The present frustrates "neos" because it resists their unconstrained adventurism; only in historical reinterpretations can they indulge themselves in ideological imperatives and infallible hindsights. Thus their treatment of history is peculiarly guilt ridden, with the guilt often displaced on to others.[48]

What made neos "conservative" was their committed pro-Americanism that recoiled from the anti-Americanism of the New Left. Like ordinary conservatives (often designated in America as the "Old Right" or "paleo-conservatives"), they rejected redistributive schemes imposed through government planning. They opposed what they perceived to be the more dangerous manifestations of economic and civil rights measures like quotas, affirmative action, busing, open admissions, community control, environmentalism, prisoners' rights, women's lib, abortion, gay lib, pornography, and the counterculture. They were wary of large government (except in military terms, of course). They supported the cultivation of excellence and the maintenance of meritocracy. They espoused traditional family, moral, and religious values, the work ethic, equal opportunity, and a vision of America as a free-market society in the New Deal mould. They were committed anti-Communists. The opposed détente, Strategic Arms Limitation Talks, feared the failure of nerve in US foreign policy, the Vietnam syndrome, and Third World rhetoric about Western guilt and neocolonialist oppression. They were concerned with the Left's attacks on the inequalities of liberal capitalism, the corruption of middle-class culture, and the sickness of American society itself. They wanted to actively resist the arguments of those who found America irredeemably corrupt and in need of radical moral or institutional reconstruction.

They were "neo" because of key components that distinguished them from conservatives of the Old Right, also known as "paleoconservatives." They were once on the left; in the 1930s and 1940s many were Trotskyite or subscribed to the modernist leftism of the anti-Stalinist *Partisan Review*. They supported a liberal, interventionist and activist foreign policy that aimed, in the words of Woodrow Wilson's formulation, "to make the world safe for democracy," rather than the Old Right realpolitik or isolationism. They supported a strong federal government, New Deal social market capitalism, and commitment to secular, scientific modernity and the welfare state of FDR, Truman, and LBJ, as well as the civil rights tradition of Martin Luther King. They were Zionist and staunch supporters of Israel, but they were also committed secularists. They were pro-immigration. And finally most, but not all, were Jewish New Yorkers. If paleos favored Governor Ronald Reagan, neos liked Daniel Patrick Moynihan. Where paleos read the *National Review* and followed William F. Buckley, neos read *Commentary* and *The Public Interest* and followed Podhoretz and Kristol.

As a result of the emergence of neoconservatism old friendships were broken and new battle lines were drawn among the New York Intellectuals. What to some seemed just another New York Intellectual squabble actually determined political alignments in the 1970s. Once again, America's intellectual community began to realign itself following *Commentary*'s lead. Not only did many contributors depart from the magazine, disagreeing with its new political stance, but also its shift helped define a newly emerging movement of moderate or disillusioned liberals, known as neoconservatives, such as Bell, Glazer, and Moynihan, providing them with a prominent outlet for their views. By the early 1970s, Podhoretz promoted the new political alignment of neoconservatism. Just as Cohen had provided a home for liberal anti-Communism in the 1950s, so Podhoretz gave one to neoconservatism in the 1970s. *Commentary*'s hard-line anti-Leftism meant that it became a haven for those Cold War liberals and Democrats who felt that the forces of McGovernism had misdirected their party. Podhoretz provided a means to air their objections.

Present Tense

Because of its neoconservative turn, the AJC correctly perceived that *Commentary* no longer spoke for the majority of the American Jewish community, and that its rightward shift was too unrepresentative. *Commentary* had moved too far from its original conception. The AJC realized that its child had left the fold and was rejecting parental advice. *Commentary* was the brilliant but wayward Jewish son who had married out of his liberal faith, even if he seemed to be becoming more overtly Jewish again. Podhoretz had been given too much editorial freedom and, unlike his predecessor, Elliot Cohen, had proved much tougher to rein in. Since the early 1960s Podhoretz had printed articles at odds with AJC positions. In granting the magazine editorial freedom, the AJC had not and could never have foreseen that its editor might turn so conservative. Such a suggestion in 1945 would have been treated with incredulity. The AJC had grown increasingly frustrated with Podhoretz. Its executive vice-president, John Slawson, would no longer call Podhoretz by his name, referring to him simply as "the present editor." Podhoretz recalled, "I've given them a lot of trouble on the right-wing swing, and on the scarcity of Jewish articles, also the lack of immediate response to Watergate and this whole mess in Washington." The AJC's Richard Maass wrote to Podhoretz expressing his concern over the magazine's "tendency towards a 'line,'" pleading, "if *Commentary* is to have a line then why can't it be the AJC line?" He also registered his protest about the increasing tendency of *Commentary* to reflect what he saw as conservative to reactionary views on matters of domestic US policy. Whereas in earlier years the magazine had solicited articles from authors on subjects pertaining to Civil Rights, civil liberties, and moral decay, it now seemed that these subjects have been avoided for a long time.[49]

Commentary took such a hard right-wing line that the AJC felt the need to launch a new liberal journal that would achieve some balance. *Present Tense: The Magazine of World Jewish Affairs*, edited by Murray Polner, was born in 1973 to be everything *Commentary* was not. Published by the Committee's Foreign Affairs Department, *Present Tense* was a quarterly magazine of world Jewish affairs. It was designed to further the AJC's commitments to promote Jewish life and culture, protect Jewish security, and advance human rights, as well as to provide information and analysis on matters of Jewish concern throughout the world. The magazine's "Statement of Purpose" was illuminating as it indicated what it felt the neocon *Commentary* was not:

> In sponsoring *Present Tense*, the American Jewish Committee aims to meet the need for a journal that will broaden American Jewry's understanding of the condition of world Jewry. The magazine will publish popular articles and reportage, expressing a wide diversity of opinion on the situation of Jews in countries around the world, the special problems of Israel, the relationships among Jewish

communities, and those issues and events in the United States and abroad which affect Jewish life and institutions.

Commentary was no longer hospitable to diverse points of view hence the need for a journal that encouraged a wide diversity of opinion. According to Polner, the AJC founded *Present Tense* "because *Commentary* wasn't Jewish enough." *Commentary* was under increasing criticism for not paying sufficient attention to Jewish affairs and *Present Tense* was the AJC's attempt to rectify this situation by focusing on Jews around the world, a subject which was at one time of enormous interest to *Commentary*, but which had generally been ignored for the past ten years or so. *Present Tense* wanted a more positive emphasis on Jewish life, including Judaism's sense of compassion, morality, social justice, and ethics. Unlike *Commentary*, *Present Tense* writers did not have to take any specific line in order to appear in its pages. It wanted to be more factually based than *Commentary*, which often substituted opinion for fact, and it didn't simply want to take a political focus. *Present Tense* was less cerebral, less academic, less highbrow, less dry, warmer, more middlebrow, more Jewish, more *heimish*. In contrast to *Commentary*, *Present Tense* was openly liberal on political issues, filling the space that *Commentary* had long since vacated.[50]

Casualties

By 1973, the worst of the fighting was over, as *Commentary*'s all-out assault on the New Left died down. Podhoretz felt victorious. His self-penned column then stopped, his work done, and barely a peep out of him was heard for the next three years. His campaign against the New Left transformed *Commentary* into the most efficient journal of antiradical criticism in America. In Podhoretz's own proud words, *Commentary* had become "perhaps the single most visible scourge of the Movement within the intellectual community."[51]

Yet, *Commentary* was also a casualty of this war. As one reader pointed out: "To climb up the flag-pole and sing the 'Star-Spangled Banner' isn't even good rhetoric. It's simply a sign that Podhoretz has stopped thinking." Neil Jumonville observed that Podhoretz "had become the Sidney Hook of the third generation, a Johnny-one-note who lacked Hook's intellectual power." Podhoretz's attitudes had hardened into a rigid ideological stance that seemed to deny there were any real social problems in America requiring even modest attempts at reform. He had retreated. Dennis Wrong referred to Podhoretz's "indiscriminate delegitimation of the Left" and

Commentary's ideological "monomania" which made it "as wearisomely predictable as the doctrinaire and sentimental Left against which it discharges so much energy." By that point, *Commentary* began to suffer from narrowness, becoming much more predictable and repetitive. It suffered from what Irving Howe had accused the NYRB of being back in 1968: refusing nuance and reveling in simplicity. While still well edited, it became much less interesting to read for some, since there were so few surprises and so little ambivalence or complication. Writing in *Response* magazine, Ernst Pawel observed, "what used to be a magazine of ideas has withered into the peristalsis of an *idee fixe*." All one had to do to establish *Commentary*'s position on any topic, noted Peter Steinfels, was simply to establish the New Left or counterculture position (or make one up, particularly by use of stereotype, exaggeration, caricature, and distortion) and turn 180 degrees in the opposite direction. This stretched to include fiction and book reviews for everything in the magazine was subordinated to its new ideological line, even when such a formula became absurd like William J. Bennett's defense of competitive sports against suspected countercultural disregard for them, or the dangers posed by E. L. Doctorow's *Ragtime*. In the service of his war against the New Left, Podhoretz had taken *Commentary* on a u-turn from variety, complexity, ambiguity, nuance, and thoughtfulness to a new neoconservatism built more on anti-Left backlash than on any serious social engagement, in which personal convictions were translated into unassailable truth.[52]

The imperatives of the war against the New Left led to the replacement of the best and most articulate and intelligent writers by the most reliable writers, regardless of their intellectual abilities, even if they were second- and third-rate. In his 1974 book, *The American Intellectual Elite*, Charles Kadushin tabulated lists of contributors to leading American "intellectual" publications, narrowed the names down to 200, and in a series of queries or interviews asked his subjects who the most influential intellectuals were. Some of the most highly rated (by others in this publishing circle), included Arendt, Bell, Bellow, Chomsky, Goodman, Hofstadter, Howe, Kristol, Mailer, Marcuse, Podhoretz, Riesman, Silvers, Sontag, and Trilling. Most of these had published in *Commentary* at one point or another. However, since 1970, quite a few of those names had cased to write for the magazine altogether. The retreat to parochialism and the foregrounding of supposed Jewish interests scared off many other writers. Podhoretz may have made tactical inroads in the battle against the Movement, and it may have been more financially stable than in any time in its history (being practically in the black) but qualitatively his magazine was suffering, a casualty in the war of the 1970s.[53]

Bill Novak, editor of *Response*, wrote to Trude Weiss-Rosmarin: "One hears so much about the boredom of *Commentary* and the disatisfaction [*sic*] of readers, it sometimes seems only a matter of months until it grinds to a halt. Do you think it will continue?"[54]

Notes

1. Podhoretz, quoted in Thomas Grubisich, "Norman Podhoretz: New Left's Enemy From Within," *The Washington Post*, Style Section (April 11, 1971), G1; Merle Miller, "Why Norman and Jason Aren't Talking," *The New York Times Magazine* (March 26, 1972), 109; Podhoretz, *Breaking Ranks: A Political Memoir* (New York: Harper & Row, 1979), 302, 305.

2. Norman Podhoretz, *Breaking Ranks*, 172.

3. Norman Podhoretz, *My Love Affair with America: The Cautionary Tale of a Cheerful Conservative* (New York: Free Press, 2000), 141; "Laws, Kings, and Cures," *Commentary* 50:4 (October 1970), 30; Podhoretz, *Breaking Ranks*, 321; quoted in Philip Ben, "*Commentary*: An American Monthly with Jewish Roots," American Jewish Committee Records, Record Group 347, GEN-12 and GEN 10, YIVO Institute for Jewish Research, New York (AJC, YIVO).

4. Norman Podhoretz, quoted in *Proceedings of the 64th Annual Meeting of the AJC*, May 14–17, 1970, Norman Podhoretz Papers, Manuscript Division, Library of Congress, Washington, DC (NPLC) and Robert L. Bartley, "A Most Improbable 'Conservative,'" *Wall Street Journal* (November 10, 1970), 18.

5. Norman Podhoretz, Book TV, January 7, 2001.

6. Norman Podhoretz, "The New Hypocrisies," *Commentary* 50:6 (December 1970), 5–6; "Intellectuals at War," *Commentary* 4:4 (October 1972), 8; "Like Fathers, Like Sons," *Commentary* 50:2 (August 1970), 21.

7. George H. Nash, *The Conservative Intellectual Movement in America Since 1945* (New York: Basic Books, 1976), 327.

8. Julie Hover and Charles Kadushin, "Influential Intellectual Journals: A Very Private Club," *Change Magazine* 4:2 (March 1972), 38–47; Dennis Wrong, "The Case of the *New York Review*," *Commentary* 50:5 (November 1970), 49.

9. Wrong, "The Case of the *New York Review*," 49–63; Podhoretz quoted in Philip Nobile, "A Review of the *New York Review of Books*," *Esquire* (April 1972), 114, 119; Alexander Bloom, *Prodigal Sons: The New York Intellectuals and Their World* (New York and Oxford: Oxford University Press), 36.

10. Ruth R. Wisse, "The Anxious American Jew," *Commentary* 66:3 (September 1978), 47–50; Peter Steinfels, "The Cooling of the Intellectuals," *Commonweal* (May 21, 1971), 255–61.

11. Alexander M. Bickel, "Judging the Chicago Trial," *Commentary* 51:1 (January 1971), 31–40.

12. Podhoretz, *Breaking Ranks*, 320, 321; James A. Nuechterlein, "Life at the Intellectual Barricades," *Worldview* (April 1980), 27; Howard Schaeffer, "Eastsider Norman Podhoretz: Editor of *Commentary*," *The East Side TV Shopper and Restaurant Guide*, n.d., 25.

13. Bartley, "A Most Improbable 'Conservative,'" 18; "C'mon In, the Water's Fine" *National Review* (March 9, 1971), 249-50; "Split in the Family?" *National Review* (December 15, 1970), 1335.

14. Norman Podhoretz, "Culture and the Present Moment: A Round-Table Discussion," *Commentary* 58:6 (December 1974), 31-50.

15. Mark Gerson, "Norman's Conquest: A Commentary on the Podhoretz Legacy," *Policy Review* 74 (Fall 1995), 64-8.

16. Nathan Glazer, "On Being Deradicalized," *Commentary* 50:4 (October 1970), 21-8; "Art, Culture and Conservatism: A Symposium," *Partisan Review* 39 (Summer 1972), 431-45; Wolfe, quoted in David Brock, *Blinded by the Right: The Conscience of an Ex-Conservative* (New York: Three Rivers Press, 2002), 303.

17. Jerry Ravetz, email to author, June 21, 2003; Podhoretz, "Speak of the Devil," *Commentary* 51:4 (April 1971), 6; Norman Podhoretz, "Living with Free Speech," *Commentary* 54:5 (November 1972), 6-8; Norman Podhoretz, "Seducer of the Innocent," *Commentary* 51:6 (June 1971), 4, 6; Samuel McCracken, "The Drugs of Habit & the Drugs of Belief," *Commentary* 51:6 (June 1971), 43-52.

18. Norman Podhoretz, *Ex-Friends: Falling Out with Allen Ginsberg, Lionel and Diana Trilling, Lillian Hellman, Hannah Arendt, and Norman Mailer* (New York: Free Press, 1999), 146.

19. Midge Decter, "The Liberated Woman," *Commentary* 50:4 (October 1970), 33-44; Vivian Gornick, *Letters, Commentary* 51:2 (February 1971), 12-36; Jane Larkin Crain, "Feminist Fiction," *Commentary* 58:6 (December 1974), 58-62; Letters, *Commentary* 59:5 (May 1975), 22; Harold Bloom, "Kabbalah," *Commentary* 59:3 (March 1975), 65; Michael Novak, "A Radical Feminist," *Commentary* 61:2 (February 1976), 90; Susan Brownmiller, Letters, *Commentary* 61:5 (May 1976), 4-12.

20. Rabbi Balfour Brickner, Letters, *Commentary* 51:6 (June 1971), 8.

21. Norman Podhoretz, "'Is It Good for the Jews?,'" *Commentary* 53:2 (February 1972), 7-12.

22. Ibid.

23. Philip Nobile, "A Review of the New York Review of Books," *Esquire* (April 1972), 112; Michael E. Staub, *Torn at the Roots: The Crisis of Jewish Liberalism in Postwar America*. (New York: Columbia University Press, 2002), 275.

24. Staub, *Torn at the Roots*, 261.

25. Norman Podhoretz, "A Certain Anxiety," *Commentary* 52:2 (August 1971), 4-10; Letters, *Commentary* 51:6 (June 1971), 8; Irving Greenberg, Letters, *Commentary* 59:3 (March 1975), 18.

26. Nathan Glazer, "Blacks, Jews, and the Intellectuals," *Commentary* 47:4 (April 1969), 33-9; Nathan Glazer, "The Role of the Intellectuals," *Commentary* 51:2 (February 1971), 55-61; Walter Laqueur, "New York and Jerusalem," *Commentary* 51:2 (February 1971), 38-46.

27. Norman Podhoretz, "Laureate of the New Class," *Commentary* 54:6 (December 1972), 4-7; Mark Shechner, *After the Revolution: Studies in Contemporary Jewish-American Imagination* (Bloomington and Indianapolis: Indiana University Press, 1987), 203-20.

28. Peter Shaw, "Portnoy & His Creator," *Commentary* 47:5 (May 1969), 77-99; Letters, *Commentary* 48:1 (July 1969), 14; Podhoretz, "Laureate of the New Class," 4-7; John W. Aldridge, "Literary Onanism," *Commentary* 58:3 (September 1974), 82-86; Marie Syrkin, Letters, *Commentary* 55:3 (March 1973), 8; Robert Alter, "Defaming the Jews," *Commentary* 55:1 (January 1973), 77-82; Ruth Wisse, "Philip Roth Then and Now," *Commentary* 72:3 (September 1981), 56-60; Joseph Epstein, "What Does Philip Roth Want?" *Commentary* 77:1 (January 1984), 62-67.

29. Howe, "Philip Roth Reconsidered," *Commentary* 54:6 (December 1972), 69-77; Epstein, "What Does Philip Roth Want?" 62-67; Letters, *Commentary* 77:4 (April 1984), 14. Roth to Malamud, August 13, 1984, Bernard Malamud Papers, HRHRC. Roth was deeply hurt by Howe's attack in particular, battling in "the spiritual equivalent of intensive care." He was scarred for life, with a pain that would not go away, Roth was upset because Howe had initially promoted him and had attacked the very same people that Roth did. But Howe had since switched sides and Roth hated him for it; he never forgot or forgave this attack. Roth responded in the best way he knew how. In his *My Life as a Man*, he lampooned Podhoretz's obsessions. "And what will *Commentary* make of this confession? I can't imagine it's good for the Jews." But Roth was so crushed that it wasn't enough so he composed an entire novel, *The Anatomy Lesson*, to dispatch a critic undeniably modeled after Howe. In it, Roth described Howe's review as "the unkindest review of all, embedded, indelibly." "Sooner or later there comes to every writer the two-thousand-, three-thousand, five-thousand-word lashing that doesn't just sting for the regulation seventy-two hours but rankles all his life," he wrote. Howe's attack had made "Macduff's assault upon Macbeth look almost lackadaisical" and Roth had been "lucky as to come away with decapitation. A head wasn't enough for [Howe]; he tore you limb from limb." Philip Roth, *The Anatomy Lesson* (London: Penguin, 1986), 78, 68, 69.

30. Arthur I. Waskow, "*Malkhut Zadon M'herah T'aker*," *Judaism* 20:4 (Fall 1971), 404; Robert Alter, "Appropriating the Religious Tradition," *Commentary* 51:2 (February 1971), 47-54; Norman Podhoretz, "The Tribe of the Wicked Son," *Commentary* 51:2 (February 1971), 6-10.

31. Marshall Sklare, "The Greening of Judaism," *Commentary* 58:6 (December 1974), 51-57.

32. Rabbi Balfour Brickner, Letters, *Commentary* 59:3 (March 1975), 18, 20; Letters, *Commentary* 51:6 (June 1971), 8; Sol Stern, "My Jewish Problem—And Ours: Israel, the Left, and the Jewish Establishment," *Ramparts* (August 1971), 38, 40.

33. Podhoretz, *Breaking Ranks*, 301-2; Norman Podhoretz, "The Intellectuals & the Pursuit of Happiness," *Commentary* 55:2 (February 1973), 7-8. See also Martin Mayer, "Higher Education for All? The Case of Open Admissions," *Commentary* 55:2 (February 1973), 37-47. J.J. Goldberg, *Jewish Power: Inside the American Jewish Establishment* (Reading, MA: Addison-Wesley Publishing Co., 1996), 321.

34. Glazer, "Blacks, Jews, and the Intellectuals," 33-9; Nathan Glazer, "The Limits of Social Policy," *Commentary* 52:3 (September 1971), 51-8; and "Is Busing Necessary?" *Commentary* 52:3 (March 1972), 39-52; Podhoretz, "'Is It Good for the Jews?'" 7-12; Paul Seabury, "HEW & the Universities," *Commentary* 53:2 (February 1972), 38-44; Elliot Abrams, "The Quota Commission," *Commentary* 54:4 (October 1972), 54-7.

35. Ben J. Wattenberg and Richard M. Scammon, "Black Progress and Liberal Rhetoric," *Commentary* 55:4 (April 1973), 35–45; R. J. Herrnstein, "On Challenging an Orthodoxy," *Commentary* 55:4 (April 1973), 52–62; Philip Brantingham, *Letters, Commentary* 55:4 (April 1973), 32.

36. Murray Friedman, *What Went Wrong? The Creation and Collapse of the Black-Jewish Alliance* (New York: Free Press, 1995), 267–68; Letters, 59:3 (March 1975), 8.

37. Murray Friedman, Letters, *Commentary* 69:2 (February 1980), 20.

38. Irving Howe, "Liberalism & the Jews: A Symposium," *Commentary* 69:1 (January 1980), 47–48; Irving Levine, Letters, *Commentary* 54:1 (July 1972), 20–22.

39. Midge Decter, *An Old Wife's Tale: My Seven Decades in Love and War* (New York: Regan Books, 2001), 122–23; Sidney Blumenthal, The Rise of the Counter-Establishment: From Conservative Ideology to Political Power (New York: Times Books, 1986), 127.

40. Norman Podhoretz, "What the Voters Sensed," *Commentary* 55:1 (January 1973), 4–6.

41. Norman Podhoretz, "McGovern and the Jews: A Debate," *Commentary* 54:3 (September 1972), 43–51; Podhoretz, "Between Nixon and the New Politics," *Commentary* 54:3 (September 1972), 4–8.

42. Podhoretz "The New American Majority," *Commentary* 71:1 (January 1981), 19–28. The experience of Richard Pipes seems instructive here. He wrote: "In 1971, when the Democratic Party nominated George McGovern for the presidency I found myself in a quandary because I was a registered Democrat and had always voted Democratic, yet I felt I could not in good conscience cast a ballot for a man so unsuited for the post of chief executive. Even so, I hesitated to support Richard Nixon, his Republican opponent. 'What would you do in my position, Isaiah [Berlin]?' I asked. He thought for a moment and responded, "I would vote for Nixon but tell no one." Richard Pipes, *Vixi: Memoirs of a Non-Belonger* (New Haven & London: Yale University Press, 2004), 69.

43. William Pfaff, "The Decline of Liberal Politics," *Commentary* 48:4 (October 1969), 45–51.

44. Seymour Martin Lipset and Earl Raab, "An Appointment with Watergate," *Commentary* 56:3 (September 1973), 35–43; James Nuechterlein, "Watergate: Toward a Revisionist View," *Commentary* 68:2 (August 1979), 38–45; Paul Johnson, "In Praise of Richard Nixon," *Commentary* 86:4 (October 1988), 50–53.

45. Christopher Hitchens, "Unmaking Friends: Norman Podhoretz as Crumb," *Harper's Magazine* (June 1, 1999), 73–6; Joseph Heller, *Good as Gold* (New York: Simon & Schuster, 1979), 12, 59, 47, 60, 158, 221–22, 427.

46. Podhoretz, *Breaking Ranks*, 355, 339; Twersky, "Left, right," 45; Decter, *An Old Wife's Tale*, 122–23; Podhoretz, "The New American Majority," *Commentary* 71:1 (January 1981), 28; James Nuechterlein, "Neoconservatism & Irving Kristol," *Commentary* 78:2 (August 1984), 43–52.

47. Jonah Goldberg, "The Neoconservative Invention," *National Review* (May 20, 2003) [internet version].

48. Theodore H. Draper, "Neoconservative History," NYRB (January 16, 1986) [internet version].

49. Norman Podhoretz, interview with Bill Novak, June 5, 1974; Richard Maass to Norman Podhoretz, November 24, 1975, AJC, YIVO.

50. Murray Polner, quoted in David Twersky, "Left, Right, Left Right," *Moment* 20:3 (June 1995) 59.

51. Podhoretz, *Breaking Ranks*, 305–6.

52. Norman Podhoretz, Letters, *Commentary* 51:1 (January 1971), 21–8; Neil Jumonville, *Critical Crossings: The New York Intellectuals in Postwar America* (Berkeley: University of California Press, 1991), 200; Dennis Wrong, Letters, *Commentary* 76:2 (February 1983), 4–10; Ernst Pawel, "Smugness in Eden, Is it Good for the Jews? *Commentary* on the Jewish Scene," *Response* 7:3 (Fall 1973), 39–48; Peter Steinfels, *The Neoconservatives* (New York: Simon & Schuster, 1979), 21.

53. Charles Kadushin, *The American Intellectual Elite* (Boston: Little, Brown, 1974), 30.

54. Bill Novak to Trude Weiss-Rosmarin, January 15, 1971, Trude Weiss-Rosmarin Papers, American Jewish Archives (AJA).

4

Resurrection

Of course *Commentary* did continue. However, its alleged victories against the New Left and the counterculture were pyrrhic. It may have won many battles, but it did not emerge unscathed. Its previously sturdy intellectual infrastructure lay in ruins, as Podhoretz had discarded the magazine's thoughtfulness and consideration and replaced it with a new, militant stance. Showing a lack of imagination, Podhoretz ran out of vision and returned to the past. The gaps in erudition were patched up with a reprise of warmed-over 1950s ideology. Podhoretz used the same ideas, themes, and language and merely recycled them. He had returned *Commentary* to almost exactly the same spot as it had been in when he took it over. Yet, in doing so, the magazine became extremely influential among the cohorts of neoconservatives. Indeed, through *Commentary*, Podhoretz further refined the neocon agenda, but it was not so much a forward-looking vision as a regressive look back to the past.

Resurrecting the Cold War

In his campaign against the New Left, Podhoretz wanted to resurrect hardline anti-Communism. But, in terms of foreign affairs, Vietnam was the one stumbling block to its revival. Podhoretz sensed that he could not yet rehabilitate the Cold War ideology while simultaneously criticizing the Vietnam War. It remained to be cleared up, and Podhoretz found it difficult if not impossible to address other problems until the Vietnam issue was resolved. The strategy, according to Frederick Tomes, was to first demand withdrawal from Vietnam in order to reestablish the credibility of the policy out of which intervention had grown in the first place: containment. In order to reassert control over US foreign policy, *Commentary* had then to wash its hands of the issue of the Vietnam War and insist that the first order of business was to halt the war immediately. What followed were intensified demands in the magazine for such a course of action. Podhoretz, who had been critical of American policy in Vietnam from 1965 through early 1968, calmly began to urge a negotiated pullout on American terms. In 1969, speaking in New York City, Podhoretz had publicly and firmly stated his desire for a withdrawal from Vietnam for the first time. In 1970, Podhoretz stated it was time to end the war and his calmness was replaced by frequent and bitter denunciations of the "wanton" US involvement.[1]

Yet, Podhoretz had no desire to see a North Vietnamese victory or an American defeat. He was disgusted with what he saw as his former Leftist friends' "gleeful anticipation not just of a North Vietnamese victory but of an American humiliation"; he certainly did not share their wish to see America disgraced. Podhoretz may have opposed the Vietnam War from its outset, but he hated the antiwar movement even more and refused to associate himself or his magazine with it, despite their shared goals. When, in the early 1960s, Podhoretz had opposed an indiscriminate act of American intervention in the fight against Communism, by the early 1970s, in contrast, when the war was winding down, he opposed an equally indiscriminate American withdrawal from the fight against Communism in the future. Instead, he advocated a negotiated settlement, one that would bring about an American withdrawal while allowing South Vietnam to exist in peace as a non-Communist democratic country. It was only toward the end of the war, when a Communist victory seemed certain and threats were being made by the Nixon administration to resume large-scale bombing of the North, that Podhoretz finally gave up and wrote a piece, with a "heavy heart," in which he reluctantly said that an American defeat would be preferable to a return of the B-52 bombers over North Vietnam. He opposed "Vietnamization" since it meant "the indefinite and unlimited bombardment by American pilots in American planes of every country in that already devastated region." Instead, Podhoretz called for "a complete and immediate American withdrawal . . . from the air as well as the ground."[2]

Podhoretz then struggled to establish an interpretation of the war as the product of well-meaning errors in judgment and general good intention. He had always opposed the war on political rather than moral grounds. So, although he called the war in Vietnam a "mistake" and "disastrous" and had been opposed to it from the very beginning, he explicitly avoided using terms like "criminal," "immoral," or "evil" to describe US intervention. Podhoretz felt that the war was tragically ill-conceived, the product of intellectual error and incompetence. He certainly did not agree with the view promoted by the New Left that the war was the product of a deep-rooted

American malaise. Instead, he concluded that, although the application of anti-Communism to South-East Asia had been misguided and incorrect, the overall rationale of US foreign policy was not. He wrote:

> wrong as the war the US fought in Vietnam was ... it was not wrong in the purposes for which it was fought ... That the American military intervention in Vietnam ended in failure, and worse than failure, is an argument not against those purposes but against the lack of wisdom with which they were in that instance pursued.

Vietnam, then, may have been "an illegitimate and unintelligent expansion of the policy of containment," but the strategy was still sound. Podhoretz thus exonerated all those anti-Communists who'd initially supported the war.[3]

With the Vietnam War out of the way, Podhoretz could then turn his attentions to re-fighting the early Cold War of the 1940s and 1950s. Indeed, he echoed the Truman Doctrine of 1947 when he wrote:

> In resisting the advance of Soviet power, then, we are fighting for freedom and against Communism, for democracy and against totalitarianism ... In sum: the conflict between the US and the Soviet Union is a clash between two civilizations. More accurately, it is a clash between civilization and barbarism ... since the defeat of fascism in World War II, Communism has emerged as the single greatest threat to liberty on the face of the earth ... To oppose Communism in the world of ideas and ideologies is therefore in itself a necessary condition of fighting for human rights; anyone who fails to oppose Communism forfeits the intellectual and moral right to speak in the name of human rights.

Podhoretz had clearly articulated his return to the Cold War equation of: Communist = totalitarian = bad; anti-Communism = good. Only American power, he argued, could contain the malignant spread of totalitarian Communism. He thus reimposed a hard-line anti-Communism on the magazine, echoing its obsession of the 1950s. His prime concern was to forge a new and revived Cold War foreign policy in the post-Vietnam era. *Commentary* articulated a renewed and updated version of the 1940s and 1950s anti-Communist campaign to counteract Soviet expansionism. It invoked the father of containment, George Kennan, and repeated his rhetoric from an earlier generation. It was no coincidence, therefore, that much of *Commentary*'s foreign-policy analysis elicited comparisons with the George Kennan's "X" articles in *Foreign Affairs* that originally outlined the theory of containment.[4]

Podhoretz led the way in trying to convince the United States that the Soviet Union was a deadly foe. In his first public utterance since May 1973, Podhoretz gave a speech before the Council on Foreign Relations in 1976. He later expanded these sentiments in an essay published in *Commentary* as "Making the World Safe for Communism," which ended his three-year silence in the magazine. In his speech Podhoretz described the Cold War as "a clash between two civilizations. More accurately, it is a clash between civilization and barbarism." Communism, he stated, had "enslaved every people which has had the misfortune to be forced to live under it—and there is still not a single case of any people freely choosing by majority vote to live under it." The Soviets were "the most determined and ferocious and barbarous enemies of liberty ever to have appeared on the earth." Worse still, they had "entered into a period of active imperialist expansion" and were on their way to achieving both conventional and nuclear superiority. Without effective resistance, he apocalyptically warned, "nothing will stop them conquering the earth," because the current isolationist consensus in the United States and the "greening" of US foreign policy was "exposing the rest of the world to Soviet domination." Podhoretz felt that America had to take a stand against Communist totalitarianism. Looking back "to the past for inspiration," he hailed the "vital center" of 1948–49, as the model for foreign policy in 1975–76, for it had established "a bipartisan consensus in support of anti-Communist intervention." He recommended the use of American power "to make the world safe for democracy."[5]

Podhoretz called for a vital center, activist, interventionist foreign policy along the lines of the postwar containment policy. He opined that the polarization of the Cold War years had returned as that the world was split into two opposing camps. He called for an uncompromising moral position rather than a flexible pragmatic approach to the world. Month after month, Podhoretz wrote and published articles that, in his own words,

> on the one side, made the case for a more vigorous American response to the Soviet threat and, on the other, tried to explain to a generation whose memory had gone dim what it was that was being threatened and why we had a sacred duty to do everything in our power to defend and uphold and—again—celebrate it.

Podhoretz sought and succeeded in ultimately reclaiming the intellectual legitimacy of anti-Communism in order to renew it. Indeed, the intellectual case for a revived militant, militarist Cold War posture came more from *Commentary* than from anywhere else, increasing its popularity with certain elements on the Right, as well as the disillusioned and deradicalized Cold War liberals on the Left now known as neoconservatives. For them, Podhoretz was the clairvoyant prophet crying in the wilderness. He may have increasingly begun to sound like the more strident and conservative William Buckley, but it was *Commentary* that gave legitimacy to this position rather than Buckley's anti-Communist journal *National Review*. As evidence of this, the fourteen-page article in *Foreign Affairs* singled out *Commentary*, especially writer Carl Gershman, as one of the chief culprits in bringing about a state of confrontation between the United States and the Soviet Union.[6]

Commentary once again took a hard-line anti-Communist stance, rejecting reconciliation in favor of a huge increase in conventional and nuclear weapons, and advocating the need to deploy US military power if and where necessary. It did not go so far as to suggest direct American military engagement, but had no moral qualms in recommending it if the need so required. It called for an end to the détente, the policy of compromise, reconciliation, and peaceful coexistence with the USSR that had originated under Nixon, in 1950s-style rhetoric, frequently invoking the concept of Soviet imperial expansion. In apocalyptic language typical of *Commentary* of that time, it argued that détente was an illusion, hiding Soviet aims, and which had comforted Americans at a time when US power was in retreat. The United States was beguiled by détente, which had to be discarded for a more realistic assessment that Communism was "a system based on terror and total power," and that it was in "an imperial, expansionist phase." There was little evidence, *Commentary* argued, that Soviet hostility to the West had substantially diminished. The rapid development of Soviet naval forces with an expanding interventionist capability could be used to impede the flow of oil to Europe and also be converted to political leverage. There was, therefore, no escape from a policy of containment, as there was a continued need to contain Soviet power. *Commentary* sought to rally the United States to confront and fight the Communist enemy, advocating a new containment, not that of the Truman Doctrine, but one more demanding than hitherto. It even made the case for the use of military force to protect US national interests. For example, in response to the 1972 oil embargo, Robert Tucker recommended military rather than political measures to secure and ensure America's oil supply, which was under threat from the Arab oil-producing nations, while reducing dependence on Middle Eastern oil as much and as soon as possible.[7]

At the same time, in resurrecting the early Cold War, Podhoretz had positioned *Commentary* in his favorite counterposition: arguing against the intellectual grain. A renewed isolationism borne out of the Vietnam War was deemed to be the intellectually respectable position in the mid- to late-1970s. A "Vietnam Syndrome"—the belief that the use of American military force was both morally indefensible and bound to fail—had begun to develop among America's intellectual, foreign-policy and political elites, liberal and conservative alike, albeit for opposite reasons. Nothing more illustrated this than Tucker's article recommending the use of force to protect US oil supplies which provoked worldwide discussion and press reaction. The oil issue was so delicate that the AJC wanted to be absolutely, and to the fullest possible extent, dissociated from the article. When the AJC's president was informed of its forthcoming publication, he said, "We must have nothing whatever to do with this." The NYRB described the article as "criminal nonsense" and "irresponsible." Earl Ravenal in *The New Republic* called it "proposals of international armed robbery", and Irving Howe referred to Tucker's "weird scenarios" for invading the Arab oil-rich countries. Podhoretz was "amazed" and "surprised" by the amount of press coverage it received since discussion in the newspapers of magazine articles was rare.[8]

Podhoretz further argued that isolationism threatened to block an effective containment of the Soviet Union. Although he was happy that direct US participation in the Vietnam War had ended, any pleasure or comfort that he might have gained from this knowledge was rapidly being destroyed by the growth of the Vietnam Syndrome. Podhoretz believed that a general misunderstanding of the significance of the Vietnam War had created this post-Vietnam "failure of nerve" and "loss of political will" to take on the Soviet Union. Podhoretz allowed writers to use *Commentary* as a forum for attaching such notions. *Commentary* feared the growing Cold War revisionist and neo-isolationist drift of US foreign policy. It dreaded that realism and disillusionment were replacing idealism, that American expectations were being trimmed, that American exceptionalism and its sense of mission were waning. It noted with alarm that a new "intellectual-industrial complex" had produced a "greening" of US foreign policy, the desire to de-emphasize American military and political power in favor of economic and moral strength. The overwhelming stress of articles by Tucker, Edward Luttwak, Daniel Patrick Moynihan, Podhoretz, and Walter Laqueur was to reject the proposition that the American national will had been seriously damaged as a result of recent failures to assume responsibility. They warned of a major danger of retreating into isolationism and away from internationalism, from concern with democracy abroad, at a time when foreign defeats and the Soviet Union's perceived strength had scared many Americans and led some intellectuals to call for reaching an agreement with the Soviet bloc. Those intellectuals whose faith in American exceptionalism had declined had begun talking of "the overextended society" and "the culture of narcissism." *Commentary* stood in opposition to them and warned of the dangers of "accepting the limitations of American power" and even "surrendering the exercise of power altogether." It warned that the end of involvement in Vietnam was not the end of foreign policy.[9]

A new mood permeated *Commentary*. Its articles were generally pessimistic and unanimous in pointing to the loss of American power. A whole issue of the magazine was devoted to a symposium, "America Now: A Failure of Nerve?". Podhoretz worried that recent developments had enormously significant implications for the future of the United States in particular and of Western civilization in general. The experience of Vietnam marked the tragic end of an era. Fifteen years ago, the United States promised to "pay any price, bear any burden, meet any hardship," he noted, "to assure the survival and the success of liberty." Today, however, in the wake of its traumatic experience in Vietnam, the United States was "mild," "passive," and "reluctant" in the face of other, more fundamental threats to its security and economic welfare. Such threats would almost certainly have been met with either the threat or the use of force in the past but instead today among the political, cultural, and commercial elites there was a growing tendency to question the legitimacy of American civilization, its character, its past record, and its future prospects. Podhoretz's fear that the country was suffering from a "failure of nerve" and a "loss of political will" was barely concealed.[10]

Overall, contributors emphasized America's failure to understand world affairs and the lack of a clear notion of America's purpose as a nation. They demonstrated an almost "uniform pessimism," suggesting they were tired and confused, even frightened. The respondents used the symposium to vent against their bugbears: Nixon, Kissinger, US-Soviet relations, the US role in Vietnam, the press, and intellectual chic. Repeating Cold War formulae, Midge Decter argued that the "Vietnam Syndrome" could not be allowed to govern US foreign policy for if the country "ceases to continue that struggle . . . a vast proportion of the earth's surface will to one extent or another eventually be Bolshevized." Such remarks reflected *Commentary*'s new direction, a revived variation on the old liberal anti-Communist consensus of the Cold War.[11]

Christopher Lasch felt that *Commentary* was calling for a revival of "gunboat diplomacy" and "worried obsessively about whether American 'nerve' and 'will' were equal to the requirements of world leadership and believed that it was necessary to test their own nerve and will in the face of every 'challenge.'" And Ronald Steel added, "Relax, *Commentary*.

Just because the U.S. has not bombed or invaded anyone this week does not mean that Western civilization is tottering on the brink of ruin."[12]

Reviving McCarthy

Alongside his commitment to resurrecting 1950s-style containment, Podhoretz wanted to revive Cold War domestic anti-Communism, too. Indeed, *Commentary* became the place for reconstructing the past and rewriting history through a filter in which supposed errors of history were whitewashed or exculpated. The title of one article neatly summed up Podhoretz's strategy: "Revising the 50's." The Vietnam War was recast as a noble and necessary affair and the classic anti-Communist text, *The God That Failed* (1950), was admonished for its softness. Any dissenting literature on the Cold War domestic anti-Communist campaign of the 1950s was dismissed as distorted, as *Commentary* became the place for hammering out the neoconservative interpretation of the past. By attempting to restore and defend the anti-Communism of the 1950s, *Commentary* was seeking to justify its resurrection in the present.

Accordingly *Commentary* re-contested the domestic political battles of the 1950s. It attacked what it perceived to be the academic and journalistic bias toward the Soviet Union and China. It traduced the wartime record of the Old Left. It pilloried anyone who popularized a revisionist historical outlook. It renewed its long-dormant attacks on fellow-travelers, describing them as "collaborators with barbarism" and guilty of a "shameful betrayal of values and common decency." It warned that Americans must be wary of those who were soft on Communism, and forgive the sins of those who could be relied upon to fight Communists and their sympathizers, real and alleged, inside the government and out. It attacked "'one-eyed liberals,' who could see injustice only through the left eye, who were keenly aware of the evils of the system under which they lived and even flourished but were blind to the sweeping inhumanities of the Soviet system." It railed against "the new Soviet apologists" of the Left who were "so intently working to recast the Soviet image in a more positive light." It frequently reminded readers of the extent of Stalin's crimes, never missing an opportunity to do so, even in its movie reviews. It equated Stalin and Hitler, resurrecting a favorite Cold War trope of conflating Nazism and Communism. It pointed out that the Bolsheviks were the first to set up concentration camps on a mass scale, and that the death rate in the Soviet gulag was probably as high as that in the Nazi concentration camps. At one point, the magazine even built a flimsy and circumstantial case that Stalin bore a major responsibility not only for having presented Nazi Germany with a model for mass murder, but also for actually cooperating in the Holocaust itself. When it came to articles on the Left, malice oozed from virtually every paragraph. Clearly, for *Commentary*, the Cold War was not over and still needed to be fought.[13]

The era of Senator McCarthy was revived and defended. *Commentary* exonerated many of the leading liberal anti-Communists of the 1950s who had contributed to the magazine. Hard-line Cold War Intellectuals like Sidney Hook, Irving Kristol, Diana Trilling, and Louis Berg were praised as committed "adversaries" of McCarthy, who

> did not rationalize his conduct, but instead attacked liberals and progressives for shortcomings which in the review benefited his demagogic assault on American institutions. Indeed Hook, Kristol, and others, by refusing to grant the Right a monopoly on the issue of anti-Communism, were the true enemies of McCarthyism, while those (like the editors of the *Nation*) who denied that American Stalinism was a problem merely afforded McCarthyism free rein. As for those who kept the party line or who devoted their political energies to the cause of the Soviet Union, and then attempted to pose before HUAC as defenders of American principles, they were not foes of McCarthy at all. To the contrary, they were the props on which he built his insidious career.

Conversely, *Commentary* attacked anyone who attempted to defame its own record as "soft" on Communism.[14]

Two figures in particular were targeted. The first focus of attack was Podhoretz's ex-friend Lillian Hellman. Podhoretz was again motivated by personal feelings, borne out of his former friendship with Hellman but which had dissolved into disrespect. To make matters worse, in her 1977 autobiography *Scoundrel Time*, Hellman had accused *Commentary*'s editors and writers of doing nothing to protest against McCarthy. Podhoretz was outraged and commissioned Nathan Glazer to defend *Commentary*'s somewhat shabby role during the McCarthy period in response to Hellman's claims. Glazer responded:

> The fact that what Lillian Hellman says about *Commentary* . . . is untrue—the fact that articles against McCarthyism were published . . . should not have to be mentioned in any honest discussion. To be forced to defend oneself in this way is no less demeaning than being forced to sign a loyalty oath. I could list such articles, including one by myself in *Commentary* when I was a member of the editorial

staff ["The Method of Senator McCarthy"], but that would be beside the point. For opposition to McCarthyism was so taken for granted by magazines like *Commentary* . . . that the main intellectual contribution they could make was to examine and clarify the many questions surrounding the phenomenon.

His defense, though, was unconvincing. Readers wrote in to say that Glazer exaggerated the menace Communist conspiracies posed in the 1940 and 1950s, that his claims didn't wash, and that they were mere excuses smacking of "too much" self-justification defending his record as an editor. Irving Howe attacked Glazer's "feeble" attempt to retrospectively exonerate the magazine from Hellman's accusations. He felt that Hellman was "largely right" for, "[t]wo of its leading editors, Elliot Cohen and Irving Kristol, while not giving their approval to McCarthy, went some lengths to dismiss the idea that the Wisconsin demagogue constituted a serious threat to American liberties."[15]

Podhoretz later solicited a further series of reviews and articles to discredit Hellman and her "pernicious" claims. Eric Breindel wrote that "accuracy is not her strong point" and that she was guilty of "substantive distortion." Samuel McCracken read Hellman's series of memoirs to check whether Mary McCarthy's judgment of Hellman as a bad and dishonest writer, that, "[e]very word she writes is a lie including 'and' and 'the,'" was true. He concluded that Hellman consistently misrepresented facts, reporting on various people she knew inaccurately, and had a "contaminating effect on our knowledge of our times": "she has manipulated millions of readers and moviegoers into admiring her as an ethical exemplar, and as a ruthlessly honest writer." Former leftists Peter Collier and David Horowitz had another go at her:

> Hellman had for many years cut her conscience to fit Stalin's fashions. She postured as an innocent and naïf, someone who might have been in Moscow during the worst moments of Stalin's trials of the 30's but knew nothing about them.

Podhoretz was pleased to describe the result of these attacks as "an utterly devastating indictment that made mincemeat of the reputation Lillian had acquired."[16]

The second target was Howe himself because he dared to uphold Hellman's claims. Also, because *Commentary* aimed to undermine American Socialism it harshly attacked Howe for he was the American Socialist par excellence. Furthermore, Howe was a former contributor to *Commentary* so it was a means of distancing the magazine from him. In a polemical, faultfinding review of Howe's autobiography *A Margin of Hope* (1982), using the *ad hominem* style that had become the magazine's staple style, Midge Decter smeared Howe, his book, and American Socialism since the 1930s. She aimed to destroy Howe's reputation as a writer, an intellectual of standing authority, and a public personality. She called his account of the 1950s "distorted." She hoped to convince her readers that Howe's works were overrated, that he wrote little or nothing of value, that he was evasive, furtive, and disloyal, both as an American and a Jew, a person to be viewed with contempt, while conveniently ignoring what he wrote for *Commentary*. Ironically, she even taxed Howe and his comrades for not having anything "new or arresting to say," something which *Commentary* had been guilty of for years. Similarly, she deplored Howe's lack of "intellectual manners" and ascribed his deficiency in literary decorum to the Trotskyite training and radical activism of his student days, while overlooking the fact that this was also true of many of the older generation of *Commentary* writers. But the facts were unimportant here, for behind her lofty façade, Decter's main objection was Howe's attacks in his book on *Commentary*'s record on McCarthyism and on the neocons for "selling out" and abandoning the Old Left. Readers detected "her lustily vengeful spirit" conducted in a tone of "shrillness and shrewishness." She wrote, noted one, as if "conducting a star-chamber investigation or prosecuting a defendant at the bar." Another pointed out: "The space and prominence given to her article facilitated its use as a weapon of a prearranged character assassination." The style harked back to the late 1940s, it was a "form of literary terrorism," "a page out of the book of Joe McCarthy."[17]

Podhoretz dug up more Cold War skeletons. He printed articles vilifying the Rosenbergs, even though they had been executed in June 1953. Their guilt was assumed to be unarguable, a position which the magazine had held to since Lucy Dawidowicz's 1952 article "Anti-Semitism and the Rosenberg Case." Nathan Glazer described Ronald Radosh and Joyce Milton's 1983 book, *The Rosenberg File*—in which they described how their conviction that the Rosenbergs were innocent changed on the basis of a lengthy study of the case, in particular the mass of documents released under the Freedom of Information Act—as "superlative." There was no miscarriage of justice, they argued, the FBI did its work carefully and its evidence was sound, and the case was properly presented. Thirty-four years after their trial, "there can be no doubt as to the guilt of the Rosenbergs... There can be no argument against the jury's verdict." The sentence may have been excessive, but even then it was in large part because of the political activism of the Communist Party: many people who were uneasy at the death sentence refused to become associated with the demand that the Rosenbergs be spared lest they be linked with Stalinism. Similarly, the magazine raked over the Hiss case, arguing his guilt. It reiterated that Hiss was still a Communist, while Whittaker Chambers was "courageous" and his autobiography "one of the most remarkable philosophical and literary documents of our age." *Commentary* was bent on thwarting any hint that these cases may be linked with a repressive political system.[18]

Commentary's ideological animosity widened to include a whole range of ordinary liberal Democrats. This included targets like the *New York Times*, and former contributors like Daniel Bell. Howe charged that *Commentary* and many of its readers had "veered so sharply to the Right in its politics," as betrayed by its "incessant polemics against the 'intellectuals' and 'liberals' whom they see as undermining the will to oppose Communism." For him and others, Podhoretz's fiery yearning to resurrect anti-Communism smacked of repression at home and wild recklessness abroad.[19]

In publishing such articles and reviews, Podhoretz was clearly disavowing completely his own earlier, heretical, doubts about anti-Communism. In his *Making It*, Podhoretz had expressed a sense of shame in his participation in the persecutions of the 1950s:

> There can be little question that the hard anti-Communists were more concerned with fighting what they took to be misconceptions of the nature of Soviet Communism than with fighting the persecution to which so many people were being subjected in the early fifties; and it shames to say that I shared fully in their brutal insensitivity on this issue.

But he had since changed his mind so that by 1976, he wrote very matter-of-factly about these persecutions, seeing their benefits in "transforming what might have seemed a remote abstraction into a clear and present danger, so that sending money to Europe or sending troops to Korea could be represented as necessary measures of self-defense against a danger which had already moved inside the gates and even, as it were, under every bed." Podhoretz was attempting to revive the legacy of McCarthyism in order to resurrect its good name as a guiding ideological theme for his magazine. In this way, he hoped to erase any tarnishing of anti-Communism. Yet, in doing so, in style and substance, *Commentary* merely offered "warmed-over McCarthy."[20]

Inside the UN

Meanwhile, as befitting his preferred counterintellectual posture, Podhoretz imposed an anti-Third World radicalism line on the magazine. A particularly influential writer in this regard during this period was Daniel Patrick Moynihan. Toward the end of his service as US ambassador to India, Moynihan took up Podhoretz's suggestion that he write about America's increasingly isolated position at the United Nations. The result was the essay "The United States in Opposition" in March 1975. Moynihan argued that the United States' ignorance of the prevailing ideology of open anti-Americanism in the United Nations had made it ineffective in dealing with the Soviet-bloc Third World dictatorships and the Arab nations. He deplored the acquiescence, oversensitivity, and passivity of US diplomats, particularly at the UN, who, in their eagerness to win popularity in the Third World, had been too modest about their accomplishments and too quick to submit to unflattering accounts of their faults. He argued that the time had come for the United States to stand up for itself against such (self-) abuse. To do this, the United States had to accept that it was in a minority and "go into opposition" at the UN, making a stronger, more aggressive defense of liberal democratic principles when they came under attack. It must deliberately and consistently bring its influence to bear on behalf of defending and expanding liberty. It must cease to bend over backwards toward the Third World and treat it as an equal, using candor and toughness where appropriate. "American spokesman [should come] to be feared," he argued, "for the truths he might tell."[21]

Given the political atmosphere at that time Moynihan felt that only Podhoretz could edit this essay and that only he would publish it. In an unprecedented move, Podhoretz announced its release in a press conference held on February 26, 1975. The article was provocative and was widely read. It created a sensation that attracted widespread attention. Moynihan would never write anything more directly influential. The article's spirited defense of Western principles came out at a time when the US-backed South Vietnamese and Cambodian governments were on the brink of crumbling. Various newspapers and TV and radio stations picked it up, and it received a rush of media criticism, which condemned it as Cold War rhetoric. Even the Central Committee of the Soviet Union translated it into Russian. Secretary of State Henry Kissinger read it and called to congratulate Moynihan for his "staggeringly good" article. He immediately brought it to the attention of President Gerald Ford and persuaded him to appoint Moynihan as US ambassador to the UN so that he could translate his theory into practice. By May 1975, no more than two months after the article's appearance, Moynihan was installed at the UN, putting into practice what his essay had proposed. Moynihan had become the first neocon to defend Podhoretz's ideas from the floor of the United Nations. Podhoretz's power was growing.[22]

Moynihan had taken the job at the height of the anti-Zionism, anti-Semitism and anti-Western sentiment in the UN. In his stormy eight months there, Moynihan pursued a strategy of aggressively defending American ideals and interests and, in relations with other countries, rewarding the nation's friends and punishing its enemies. This was never more evident than in November 1975 when Ugandan dictator Idi Amin took to the floor of the UN to deliver a speech that maintained that "the United States of America has been colonized by the Zionists who hold all the tools of development and power." Amin called upon the United States to "rid their society of the Zionists," and for the UN to pursue the "extinction of Israel as a state." The UN delegates responded with a standing ovation and passed Amin's accompanying resolution that "Zionism is a Form of Racism and Racial Discrimination." When Moynihan replied to the UN resolution, Podhoretz's influence was clearly felt for, in drafting his response, Moynihan had turned to him for advice. Podhoretz actually wrote most of the speech, which Moynihan addressed to the UN. The speech's staunch defense of the United States, Israel, and liberal democracy made Moynihan so popular in New York that he used the position as a platform to build a political base among Jewish voters in that city, which he then used to launch his campaign in that state for the Senate. He was elected to the Senate in the following year. Moynihan was so grateful for Podhoretz's advice and assistance that he dedicated his memoirs of his service at the UN, *A Dangerous Place*, to him. And the *National Review* concluded that Podhoretz had "played a major role in the political emergence of Mr. Moynihan." Moynihan's success demonstrated Podhoretz's increasing reach as his intellectual influence was being translated into tangible political power.[23]

Frozen Out

Despite Podhoretz's growing success, the election of Jimmy Carter in 1976 was a setback. Like Johnson before him, Carter was an outsider, a southerner, but who also stood in opposition to everything that Podhoretz advocated. Nonetheless, true to his deepest (and basest) instincts and in spite of his ideological views, Podhoretz courted Carter. Shortly after the election, the heavily neocon CDM presented Carter with a list of 60 prominent individuals seeking appointments in the administration among them many neocons like Jeane Kirkpatrick and Nathan Glazer. But in a heavy blow to the neocons, Carter appointed only one member of the group to a governmental position: Peter Rosenblatt, and as special negotiator to Micronesia. The CDM was "completely frozen out" signaling its complete defeat. Podhoretz then concluded that, having failed to secure one significant appointment, the general ideological tone of the Carter administration was New Leftist and McGovernite. Consequently, Podhoretz, with the help of the CDM, determined that Carter would have to be dislodged and consequently *Commentary* became the driving force behind a coordinated effort to weaken public support for the president. He launched another all-out offensive in the magazine against Carter, in particular his foreign policy agenda, accelerating the political transition of the neocons from the Democratic to the Republican Party.[24]

Commentary launched vehement attacks against every single strand of Carter's foreign policy. Everything Carter did was attributed to weakness and liberalism. As Carter did not share Podhoretz's view of a Soviet expansionist threat and worse still desired a more cooperative relationship with Moscow and softened America's stance, the magazine painted a picture of a leaderless country. It charged that Carter had no clear idea of America's role in world affairs. In its absence he substituted "vague trends and contradictory statements," which were "a source of bewilderment" and "a great deal of confusion." It attacked his efforts to improve US relations with the Soviet Union. Carter's appointment of Andrew Young as UN ambassador came in for particularly heavy criticism. *Commentary* objected to everything about Young: his anti-anti-Communism, his denunciations of US "militarism" and "imperialism," his opposition to the use of American military power under any circumstances, his readiness to justify Soviet despotism as a product of economic backwardness or to blame Amin's tyranny on Western colonialism, his benignly relativistic attitude toward Third World dictatorships of the Left, his absolutistic assurance about right-wing dictatorships. Young reflected the conventional wisdom of the New Politics, he embodied what *Commentary* called the "psychology of appeasement," as well as the racial climate in the country. Walter Laqueur asked: "Can anything be said to the credit of the administration's record in foreign policy?"[25]

Under Carter, argued *Commentary*, the West was in danger of becoming "Finlandization." Indeed, the term "Finlandization" became a favorite *Commentary* codeword following Carter's election. "*Commentary* and its conservative readers saw the phrase as containing such profound truth about geopolitics that it was repeated as a mantra," observed John Patrick Diggins. "Rarely has a metaphor about the fate of a country been so manipulated in a combination of word play and spectral evidence." The term referred to the "special relationship" between Finland and the Soviet Union. It meant appeasement by Finland of its powerful neighbor to the extent that the country could no longer be defined as neutral and independent in the traditional sense, because its sovereignty becomes reduced. *Commentary* felt that the nominally autonomous but actually submissive stance of Finland in relation to the USSR and its perceived veto power over Finnish foreign and domestic policy represented a dangerous and intolerable political paradigm. Furthermore, it argued that the Soviet Union's medium-term objective was the "Finlandization" of the whole of Western Europe, to control it not quite as a satellite, but which was politically subservient nonetheless in return for a degree of freedom—and this process required the neutralization of US power. Podhoretz took the position to its extreme, fearing "Finlandization from within" and even the "Findlandization of America."[26]

Many of *Commentary*'s criticisms of Carter were voiced through a long-running drive against the second strategic nuclear arms treaty with the Soviet Union, SALT II. Articles with titles like "The Illusions of SALT II" began to appear. SALT II was, asserted *Commentary*, "an expression of American acquiescence in the Soviet drive for overwhelming military superiority." Podhoretz was particularly influenced here by the Team B report in 1976. Team B was an independent commission of experts, appointed by George Bush (then Director of the CIA under President Ford) in response to the growing rightwing clamor to assess the Soviet nuclear capability and strategy to provide an alternative assessment of the Soviet strategic threat as a counterpoint to the CIA's analysts (known as Team A). Team B believed the CIA's assessment was faulty. It disapproved of arms control as a political tool. It insisted on building up first offensive nuclear forces and then anti-nuclear defenses. This was based on the premise that the Soviet Union held a different view of the utility of nuclear weapons, regarding them as guarantors not of peace but of victory, from that of the United States. It obliged the CIA to revise its estimates of Soviet intentions, and shaped its warning of the Soviets' arms and resolve superiority and opposition to the SALT II treaty. Podhoretz then published Team B experts. Team B's Chairman, Richard Pipes, a professor of History and former director of Harvard's Russian Research Center began contributing to the magazine, setting its tone on the Soviet threat.[27]

Worried by Team B's findings, Podhoretz joined the Committee on the Present Danger (CPD). The CPD was an allegedly politically independent and nonpartisan organization, which despised McGovernism, as currently represented by Carter, and was dedicated to restoring an "informed and objective discussion of national security issues." The belief in Soviet expansionism underpinned the Committee's thinking; it felt that Soviet leaders were "even more ambitious than Hitler." The CPD promoted a range of strategic weapons (like the B-1 bomber Carter had cancelled) to preempt and guard against the Soviets, in particular, the Soviet nuclear arsenal. The Soviet Union was a threat, the CPD argued, but the real enemy was within. Weapons were only as good as the will to use them, which seemed to be dissipating by the day. Like Podhoretz, the CPD harked back to an earlier era, the two decades proceeding Second World War, when America committed itself to containment of Communism. It was, noted historian Michael Sherry, a "new nostalgia." Many other neocons, including Midge Decter, Jeane Kikpatrick, Richard Pipes, and Paul Nitze, a Cold War strategist who had also sat on Team B, joined the CPD. Through his relationship with members of the CPD, Podhoretz and *Commentary* began to wield greater political influence.[28]

Space was given in the magazine to express CPD views and *Commentary* became the platform for many of the Committee's most important pronouncements, just as *Foreign Affairs* had once been for the old foreign-policy elite. Edward Luttwak argued that the unilateral arms control pursued by the US since 1964 and the bilateral efforts that culminated in the 1972 agreements diminished American security and, as a result, the United States may now be approaching a new period of acute instability. Pipes pointed to the divergent policies held by the United States and the Soviet Union: where the United States believed in Mutually Assured Destruction, the Soviets emphatically asserted that that the better-prepared country, in possession of a superior strategy, could win and even emerge viable. Pipes insisted on paying heed to Soviet doctrine, arguing that the US strategic community arrogantly, ignorantly, and dangerously shrugged off this doctrinal discrepancy. SALT thus missed the point. Five days after the *Washington Post* carried excerpts from this article, Pipes was attacked by a *Post* columnist, as a member of "the military-industrial complex" who spreads "rank hysteria in scholarly garb."[29]

Double Standards

One of the key points of attack was Carter's human rights policy, particularly his perceived failure to distinguish between totalitarian and authoritarian regimes. The Communist threat was so deadly, according to *Commentary*, that the United States must ally itself with anti-Communist regimes, no matter how right-wing, dictatorial, authoritarian, and repressive they were. It recommended, in a close replication of the attitudes and stances of the 1950s, interference in the internal affairs of other countries whenever and wherever deemed advisable in the name of anti-Communism. It called for an activist foreign policy to advance and protect the values of democracy and liberty including, if necessary, interfering in the internal affairs of other nations to save a democratic regime. It attempted to draw a distinction between authoritarian regimes (those that did not support Communism) and totalitarian regimes (Communist governments). Nathan Glazer wrote, "there is something truly special about Communist governments which separates from the run-of-the-mill authoritarian regimes and military dictatorships." He justified American allegiances with authoritarian states like Chile, Spain, Portugal, and Greece in order to defend western Europe from the Soviet Union.[30]

The most notable rationalization of such action was Jeane Kirkpatrick's "Dictatorships and Double Standards" essay of November 1979. It was an acerbic and searing indictment of Carter's foreign policy, in particular its moralism. The failure of the Carter administration's foreign policy, she wrote, was

> now clear to everyone: in the thirty-odd months since his inauguration there had occurred a dramatic Soviet military build-up, matched by the stagnation of American armed forces, and a dramatic extension of Soviet influence in the Horn of Africa, Afghanistan, Southern Africa, and the Caribbean, matched by a declining American position in all these areas . . . The U.S. has never tried so hard and failed so utterly to make and keep friends in the Third World.

In a twist on Glazer's distinction between authoritarian and totalitarian regimes, Kirkpatrick argued for supporting "traditional" (authoritarian) rather than "revolutionary" (totalitarian) autocracies, calling for realism about their nature and relation to American national interests. Traditional authoritarian governments were less repressive than revolutionary autocracies, she postulated, and, as they "are more susceptible of liberalization," they could internally change while totalitarian regimes never could. Also, authoritarian regimes were "more compatible with U.S. interests" and thus even the most repressive regimes in the world could be supported as long as they could be seen as allies in the struggle against Communism. Consequently, Kirkpatrick called for a "realistic policy" to protect American interests because "morally responsible people recognize that there are degrees of evil."[31]

Such ostensibly value-free analysis led Kirkpatrick to excuse the very real abuses of authoritarian regimes. Nicaragua under Somoza and Iran under the Shah sometimes invoked martial law to arrest, imprison, exile, and torture their opponents, as well as "relied for public order on police forces whose personnel were said to be too harsh, too arbitrary, and too powerful." But this could be excused because they were not only anti-Communist, they were positively friendly to the United States, sending their sons and others to be educated in US universities, voting with the United States in the United Nations, and regularly supporting American interests and positions even when these entailed personal and political cost. The embassies of such governments were active in Washington social life, and were frequented by powerful Americans who occupied major roles in these nations, diplomatic, military, and political life. Not only did this article crystallize neocon thinking for the next decade but also its importance and influence was to become demonstrably clear.[32]

Ardent Zionism

In Podhoretz's rerun of the 1950s in the magazine, one element was different: Zionism. Once direct US military intervention had ended and the US had withdrawn from Vietnam in 1973, that issue all but disappeared from *Commentary*'s pages and the topic dropped from its radar. In its place, Israel dominated Podhoretz's foreign policy thinking. Podhoretz's Jewish affirmation manifested itself in an ardent Zionism and *Commentary* became progressively more concerned with the position of Israel. For the first time in its history, Zionism was foremost in *Commentary*. Once again the magazine had been turned around completely. From a position of clear non- and even anti-Zionism in the 1940s and 1950s, and coolness and ambivalence in the 1960s, *Commentary* was now openly "very supportive" of Israel in the 1970s.[33]

Podhoretz felt that the old arguments about the legitimacy of the Zionist position were no longer relevant; the debate was over. Yet, Israel suffered from a conspicuous lack of support in the intellectual circles, particularly those of the Left, so Podhoretz led the campaign to launch an intellectual defense of Israel and to weaken the anti-Zionist flank of the New Left. Podhoretz felt that it was his task to persuade liberal intellectuals to recognize Israel as the only stable and democratic state friendly to the United States, as well as the only champion of human rights, in the Middle East. He mobilized a cohort of pro-Israel writers from around the world. He increasingly developed Israeli writers to write about Israel more than ever before. Hillel Halkin, Shlomo Avineri, Amos Oz, and Amos Elon regularly appeared in the magazine alongside their American and European counterparts like Walter Laqueur, Robert Alter, and Milton Himmelfarb.

Podhoretz argued that there was an inextricable link between US military strength and Israel's survival. He believed that Israel's security required a strong American commitment to internationalism and defense. Conversely, American isolationism represented a direct threat to Israel's well-being. He argued for a continued American commitment to the security of Israel and against cutting military budgets in order to ensure that this commitment could be carried out. Indeed, he suggested that Israel was the democratic frontier of the West in the Middle East. An American foreign policy dedicated to the survival and success of liberty was good for both Israel and United States. Only a militarily strong and perpetually interventionist America could guarantee the security of Israel. The upshot was that a strong Israel was a "strategic asset" as far as American interests in the Middle East were concerned, helping Washington to contain Soviet expansionism in the region, as continued American support for Israel weakened the Soviet position. This was soon reduced to a dogma: what is good for Israel is good for America, and vice versa. The magazine, at Podhoretz's prompting, developed justifications for greater US military expenditure and military aid to Israel. The United States should commit itself to Israel because, in Glazer's words, "the United States defends democracies, and it defends the independence of small, threatened nations." America should also support Israel because of its "large commitment to the defense of freedom" and because "democracies are better than authoritarian and totalitarian states."[34]

Commentary's defense of Israel was part of its larger argument that the United States could not survive alone as the sole democracy in the world once its allies and supporters had been taken over or nullified by pro-Soviet forces. Laqueur inquired "Can freedom and traditional American values survive once the lights go out on the rest of the world?" No, replied Podhoretz for the United States could not survive in a world "given over to barbarism and misery." Glazer suggested that such a world would be "dangerous and depressing". "For us," he added, "the world is a safer and more congenial place with such [democratic] societies in it," thus it was the duty of the United States "to support the shrinking island of democracies in the world." Podhoretz claimed that this wasn't an "expression of simple Zionism." "I support Israel," said Podhoretz, "because I believe that such support is good American policy." Elsewhere Podhoretz further elaborated:

> Where *Commentary* may be said to differ from American Jews on the question of Israel is that we call for the defense of Israel not because it is a Jewish state, but because it is a democracy . . . in defending Israel, the United States is defending itself.

Podhoretz argued that "a strong, confident" Israel was an "indispensable ally" to the United States and "a vital factor in any program to protect our own legitimate national interests."[35]

Podhoretz, though, feared that in the post-Vietnam climate, America might forgo its military support of Israel. "If the United States will not defend a democratic country like Israel," he inquired, "whom will we defend?" He outlined the ominous consequences of the failure to do so. "Betrayal of Israel by the United States would be only the beginning," he warned. "After that would come the betrayal of Western Europe and Japan. My conviction of this is that we must not do this. The United States must defend these countries." He therefore railed against those who proposed the cuts in the defense budget as working against the best interests of the United States and Israel. Since there was a direct relationship between Israel's security and the level of American military spending, any reduction in the US defense budget would make it increasingly difficult for the United States to supply Israel with the tools it needs for its own defense.[36]

Podhoretz's writings on Israel became increasingly pessimistic and sensationalist, deliberately invoking inflammatory analogies between Israel and Vietnam and Israel and Czechoslovakia, to heighten feelings of paranoia and insecurity. In "The Abandonment of Israel," he argued that weakening American support for the Israeli position towards a policy of one of one-sided and intolerable moral pressures on Israel would lead not to peace but disaster, even nuclear war in extremis. If nuclear war should ever erupt in the Middle East it would be the fault of the United States and others who,

> under cover of self-deceptions and euphemisms and outright lies are "negotiating over the survival of Israel" instead of making the survival of that brave and besieged and beleaguered country, the only democracy in the Middle East and one of the few left anywhere on the face of the earth, the primary aim of their policies and the primary wish of their hearts.

Commentary even proposed that Israel develop its nuclear capability, which would simultaneously diminish its reliance on the United States, while deterring Arab governments harboring hostile anti-Israel guerrilla movements.[37]

Commentary repeatedly laid into Carter's Middle East policy for effectively ending the US-Israeli special relationship and for provoking fear rather than hope. It was critical of Carter's efforts to accommodate Palestinians' national aspirations and to achieve a peace settlement between Israel and Egypt at Camp David, railing against his initiatives, as an example of "How Not to Make Peace in the Middle East." Carter alienated the neocons because he did not seem committed enough to Israel's security for

Commentary's liking. In particular, National Security Adviser Zbigniew Brzezinski was its *bête noire* in the Carter administration.

Podhoretz generally let go of his critical faculties when it came to the topic of Israel. He took a one-sided approach of defending the state as if it could do no wrong. At times, he merely repeated the standard Israeli line. Furthermore, he took the view that any criticism of Israel, even constructive criticism, resulted in policies that strengthened the hands of its enemies while isolating, weakening, and forcing the Israelis into a desperate corner. He condemned the attitude of those who applied a double standard to Israel, pressing it to accept conditions which nobody dreamed of demanding of any other people, as anti-Semitism. Anyone who questioned *Commentary*'s Zionist dogma or who opposed Israel policies was labeled an anti-Semite or self-hater who unwittingly lent their support to Israel's enemies.

Podhoretz even took the position that American Jews had no moral right to criticize Israel's security policies. Following the election of the hard-liner Menachem Begin of the hawkish Likud Party as Israeli prime minister in 1977, Podhoretz argued that since Israeli policies literally involved the life and death of the state and its people, only those whose lives were actually on the line had the standing to participate in the public debate over them. Any American Jew who wanted to acquire such standing only had to board a plane for Tel Aviv and claim citizenship under the Law of Return. Conversely, those American Jews who attacked Israel until that time merely provided cover for the ideological enemies of Israel and even outright anti-Semites who, Podhoretz claimed, were overjoyed at being able to quote Jews instead of having to rely exclusively on their own easily discounted forms of vilification.

Podhoretz urged American Jews to ask the United States to support Israel and to do whatever is in its power to see that Israel survives, even if it put American Jews in an exposed and embarrassing position. *Commentary* invoked the Holocaust to mobilize Jews behind Israel, to push them into a more positive identification with Israel. "Never again, we meant, would we let others fool us or would we fool ourselves about the intention of those who intended to destroy the Jews," wrote Milton Himmelfarb. "Never again, would we lean on that broken reed, enlightened opinion. Never again would we do less than all we could do. Never again would we expose ourselves to our own reproaches for having done less."[38]

"As Likud policies alienated more and more liberal Jews," wrote David Twersky, "Podhoretz's views hardened." Unlike the rest of the New York Intellectuals and the Jewish community, Podhoretz dismissed the notion that Begin's election would derail the peace process, if indeed the Arabs were ready for one. Instead, Podhoretz attacked Jewish and non-Jewish critics of Begin, in fact, anyone who took an alternative stance to *Commentary* including AJC staff members if necessary. The magazine even had the chutzpah to attack Knesset Members like Abba Eban and other Israelis who dared criticize Begin, as lending comfort to the enemy. However, because of its rightward-leaning, pro-Likud politics, *Commentary* found it hard to convince a skeptical and overwhelmingly liberal American Jewish community of its Jewish value. Readers complained that *Commentary* published "distressingly little material about modern Jewish culture, theology, and philosophy, history, or even internal communal issues . . ." *Commentary*, charged its critics, had "run out of creative ideas for protecting and revitalizing Israel and Jewry" for it was "more important to protect their own institutional self-interests than to encourage an intelligent discussion about how to protect and revitalize Israel and the Jewish people." Its general turn to the Right and its attacks on Jews cost the magazine many of its best writers on Jewish affairs. For example, Arthur Hertzberg, the rabbi who had presided at Podhoretz and Decter's wedding stopped contributing to the magazine thereafter. In the late 1970s, Podhoretz began to fill the vacuum with articles, both by himself and others, the screaming and angry tone of which seldom encouraged sensible dialogue.[39]

A "Two-Bit Little Homophobic Bigot"[40]

By this point Podhoretz had become obsessed with "deviant" sex, clearly linking it to what he perceived to be political deviancy. He was especially fascinated by sodomy and homosexuality. Podhoretz said he deplored the rise of homosexuality for it struck at the very survival of society through its power to undermine the institution of the family.

> My position on gay rights has to do with my fear of the rise and spread of tendencies in this society and in this culture which undermine in a very drastic way the possibility of maintaining the family as the key institution of our society, and of raising our children and our grandchildren in a context which makes it possible for them to live and take their place in the natural chain of the generations.

But, in reality, Podhoretz's homophobia derived in large part from a Leavisite Puritanism that raged and subsided in a complex fashion. Now it suited him to deploy it as an anti-Left political strategy.[41]

Few, including Podhoretz, had taken the modern gay movement, born in the Stonewall Riots at a New York bar in 1969, seriously at its inception. To them it seemed nothing more than a camp joke. Yet, when so many of the causes of the 1960s had faded or been defeated, gay liberation refused to do so and moved from beyond the fringe to the mainstream. The speed of this advance disorientated Podhoretz and the neocons as thousands of years of prejudice were being challenged in little more than a generation. The neocons knew they could not simply lie back, and *think* of retaking America, but actively get the sordid business of homosexuality out of the way. The war against it, as much as the war against the Soviet Union, was what drove them from their beds in the morning. Gay bashing became endemic among the neocons, extending from their public writings to their private salon gossip.

Podhoretz allowed his writers to trash the sexuality of the heroes of the counterculture—Paul Goodman, Norman O. Brown, and Norman Mailer—conveniently forgetting that they had found their voice in *Commentary*. He thought Mailer made far too much of sex in his writing and decried his penchant for anal intercourse; he was bothered and embarrassed by Mailer's attribution of "a veritably metaphysical significance to the act of heterosexual anal penetration." Motivated by a sense of Puritanism and old-fashioned views about sexuality, Podhoretz indulged in a kind of prurient righteousness, a hidden delight in finding "repulsive" passages in others' works, particularly John Updike, Philip Roth, and Mailer, often reducing their work to simply writing about sex. Joseph Epstein made much of Mailer's sexual proclivities:

> Everything in this novel builds up to someone penetrating someone else in one orifice or another, usually with a good deal of humiliation involved for one of the parties, a sense of triumph for the other . . . The connection between buggery and excrement is not shirked in this loathsome book in which excrement is intended to have magical, even divine, properties.[42]

Homosexuality, above all, became a discernable concern in *Commentary*. Typical article titles read, "Forster as Homosexual." The magazine reiterated the "horrors" of homosexual acts as the magazine linked them to the New Left and the counterculture. Epstein wrote, "Many of the Pied Pipers of the youth rebellion of the late 60's were homosexuals," somehow implying that Leftist politics derived from homosexual anger, and both were invalid products of "sexual and political adventurism." Leftist writing was viewed through the prism of its authors' homosexuality, as being central to their work. Gore Vidal's Leftist political views and anti-Semitism were attributed to his homosexuality. Podhoretz's animus against Allen Ginsberg and the Beats may have also been in part due to their homosexuality which

Podhoretz connected to their politics. Back in 1958 he had written that homosexuality was Ginsberg's "preserve" before quoting a line of his poetry ("who let themselves be fucked in the ass by saintly motorcyclists, and screamed with joy"). The once-favored Paul Goodman was "hauled up before [the] court of sexual orthodoxy." "The good society for Goodman started at the groin," wrote Epstein. "*Homophobia* is an overused term," opined Paul Notley, "but Joseph Epstein was guilty of it. He was literally afraid of homosexuals." Typical of the neocons at this time, Epstein had declared in 1970, "If I had the power to do so, I would wish homosexuality of the face of this earth."[43]

The nadir of *Commentary*'s homophobia was Samuel McCracken's "Are Homosexuals Gay?" in January 1979 in which McCracken set out to expose what he perceived to be the myth of the happy, well-adjusted homosexual, to deny that homosexuals were, in fact, "gay." His solution for homosexuals was that they get better by either becoming heterosexual or cease all sexual activity altogether. As more than one reader pointed out, "These facile generalizations are of course the ancient clichés of invincible prejudice that willfully ignores the diversity of the human condition, even among homosexuals." *Commentary* further expressed its fears of homosexuality with an article by Decter, "The Boys on the Beach." A purported examination of the militant Gay Lib movement, it amounted to little more than an impressionistic description of the male homosexual lifestyle, as recounted through her youthful personal experiences of "the homosexual community" on Fire Island, which she took as representative of the entire gay community in America.[44]

Overall, *Commentary*'s articles on such subjects betrayed bigotry and ignorance. They resorted to stereotyping and blaming-the-victim analyses usually directed against Jews and blacks. They characterized gays as a single, undifferentiated mass and profiled an entire group on a highly atypical sample thus failing to do justice to the complexity of the gay experience in America. They provided little or no evidence, cloaking their essays in anecdote and autobiographical reminiscence. Their generalizations were never qualified nor did they admit that they were based solely on conjecture and hearsay. And the sources used were themselves highly selective and atypical. There was no reasoned analysis, no documentation no substantiation, but brimming with stereotypes and generalizations. They trotted out all of the clichés, that homosexuals were desperate, promiscuous, pathetic freaks, doomed to suicide, alcoholism, drug abuse and sadomasochism, death wishes, adolescence. These pieces, written by those with little authority or experience of the subject, were full-scale attacks on the gay community, which unfortunately played into and lent credence to American bigotry and homophobia. Furious respondents accused the magazine of "replicating the historical patterns of modern anti-Semitism" in its attack on homosexuals, and the *Gay City News* felt that it even read like an "Elders of Zion" against gays.[45]

Commentary had sunk to a new low in the mire of conservative reaction and intolerance, as Podhoretz published notorious and homophobic rants against homosexuality in his magazine. Neocons and conservatives alike loved the articles that opposed homosexual emancipation. The pieces provided an illicit thrill of bellowing "Bugger!" and certainly, there was an element of prurience in the explicit details of homosexual activity that Podhoretz printed. But far from being an isolated topic or the result of simple prejudice, Podhoretz's (like his wife's) homophobia was central to his anti-New Left, anti-counterculture, right-wing neocon project. After all, those responsible for The Movement and all that was wrong with America, said *Commentary*, were either gay or sexually deviant, people such as the Beats, Allen Ginsberg, Paul Goodman, Gore Vidal, and Norman Mailer.[46]

Homosexuality was linked to appeasement, as *Commentary* frequently compared the world situation of the 1970s to that of the 1930s. Appeasement was used to explain the current foreign policy. Hard-line Cold Warrior Sidney Hook wrote that the attitudes of the Left toward Communism in the 1970s were far worse than those of the Western liberals who had appeased Hitler in the 1930s. Where the destructive effects of appeasement could not have been forecast in the 1930s, now there was no excuse. Warning of a return to the earlier decade, Podhoretz and other neocons invoked the term "appeasement" almost to the point of obsession. "We are threatened by a new Munich, and I will have no part of a new movement of appeasement," he wrote. Podhoretz likened the "Vietnam Syndrome" to "the culture of appeasement" present in "England in 1937." For Podhoretz, the "culture of appeasement" included the "kind of women who do not want to be women and . . . men who do not want to be men." The abandonment of "proper manhood among homosexual writers of the 1920s," in England had paved the way for appeasement. The nation had nurtured a "culture of appeasement," argued Podhoretz, a "national mood of self-doubt and self-disgust" which he compared to the one that had prevailed in the 1930s in the face of fascism.[47]

By conflating homosexuality with deviant politics and appeasement, Podhoretz had produced a right-wing device to explain America's perceived malaise over the past two decades. The device allowed his contributors to vent their anger on the New Left movement of which many of them had been a part. Ironically, though, this may have been one prejudice they shared with and carried over from their Movement days. Elements of the New Left had felt that homosexuality was a "capitalist perversion" that would be corrected on the glorious day. Its heroes like Mao's Red Guards castrated "sexual degenerates," while Fidel Castro was almost as vicious. Yet there was an element of opportunism about all of this. Podhoretz was willing to publish articles and reviews from gay contributors like Bayard Rustin (whose homosexuality was never mentioned in the magazine at this time), while other contributors espoused homophobia. As Douglas Charles, put it, "Anything to discredit the Left in their eyes, right?"[48]

Insanity or Maturity?

In a letter to the magazine, reader Benno Weiser Varon summed up the 1970s for Commentary.

> When doomsday comes, the readers of Commentary will have one advantage over other Americans: they won't be surprised... Walter Laqueur, Edward N. Luttwak, Richard Pipes, Carl Gershman, Robert W. Tucker, Theodore Draper, Daniel Patrick Moynihan, Bayard Rustin, and others have conjured up enough horsemen for two apocalypses.

And Peter Steinfels pointed out

> *Commentary's* world is not a happy one. Blazoned across the envelope received by a potential subscriber is the single world SANITY—in two-inch letters. After quoting a harebrained bureaucratic regulation from the Polish government, the promotional letter begins: "Dear Fellow Inmate, Don't Laugh. Life in this part of the world hasn't been much saner." In the midst of madness, however, *Commentary* offers "sane thinking" and "uncommon rationality." The magazine will do "our best to restore your faith in Reason and Sanity too." The return postcard repeats the message: Subscribe to *Commentary*, "In the Interest of Sanity." (Recent postcards, with the same message, have also expressed *Commentary's* feelings by reproducing nineteenth-century engravings of schoolteachers or headmasters harassed by unruly children.)

"This is a remarkable self-revelation," wrote Steinfels.

> Magazines are given to claiming that they are right when others are wrong, stimulating when others are dull, bold when others are timid, thoughtful when others are superficial. But "sane" when others are... what? Such a stance is not conducive to political dialogue.

Nothing, he added, better demonstrated the mentality of the magazine than its promotional literature. "A promotional mailing reveals both a journal's self-image and its calculated estimate of the potential audience's state of mind; it expresses, in brief, the mental world in which a journal exists."[49]

Commentary had "grown up" in this period (some might say "matured") and, as Ruth Wisse noted, "[u]nderlying and informing all of the arguments that *Commentary* has mounted since 1970 is the changed posture of the intellectual from adolescent to parent." What this meant was that by the end of the decade, *Commentary* had come back full circle to some of the ideas it displayed under Cohen in the 1950s. Its neoconservatism did not markedly differ from the hard-line anti-Communism of the immediate postwar era. But now it had a new Puritanical dimension: homophobia, anti-feminism, anti-abortion, anti-liberalism, and anti-Black.[50]

Believing that his ideological enemies in "The Movement" were either dead or defeated and *Commentary* victorious, Podhoretz now turned his attention on greater sights: empire-building. Podhoretz had transformed *Commentary* into the most influential English-language Jewish magazine in history and indeed into one of the most prominent journals in the United States. *Commentary* added influential ideas to the wider foreign policy debate, helping to shape the public understanding of the performance of the American defense establishment, as well as set the parameters of American foreign policy thinking in the mid- to late 1970s. Its contributors were now major participants in national discussions, and it received increased attention and had much success during the 1970s. But Podhoretz wanted more. He wanted to translate his success and the access of his ideas to policy makers and the public into real political power, and this is what he did in the coming decade, greatly assisted by the influence and visibility of the neoconservatives he published in the magazine's pages.

Notes

1. Robert R.Tomes, *Apocalypse Then: American Intellectuals and the Vietnam War, 1954–1975* (New York: New York University Press, 1998), 195; Norman Podhoretz, "First Things, and Last," *Commentary* 50:1 (July 1970), 27.

2. Norman Podhoretz, *My Love Affair: The Cautionary Tale of a Cheerful Conservative* (New York: Free Press, 2000), 172–4 and "A Note on Vietnamization," *Commentary* 51:5 (May 1971), 6–9.

3. Podhoretz, quoted in Merle Miller, "Why Norman and Jason Aren't Talking," *The New York Times Magazine* (March 26, 1972) 35, 104; Norman Podhoretz, "Vietnam and Collective Guilt," *Commentary* 55:3 (March 1973), 4–6.

4. Norman Podhoretz, "The Future Danger," *Commentary* 71:4 (April 1981), 29–47.

5. Norman Podhoretz, "Making the World Safe for Communism," *Commentary* 61:4 (April 1976), 31–42.

6. Podhoretz, *My Love Affair*, 183; Dimitri Simes, "The Anti-Soviet Brigade," *Foreign Policy* 37 (Winter 1979/80), 28–42.

7. Carl Gershman, "After the Dominoes Fell," *Commentary* 65:5 (May 1978), 47–54; Theodore Draper, "Appeasement & Détente," *Commentary* 61:2 (February 1976), 27–38; Robert W. Tucker, "Oil: The Issue of American Intervention," *Commentary* 59:1 (January 1975), 21–31.

8. I. F. Stone, "War for Oil?" *New York Review of Books* (February 6, 1975), 7; Earl Ravenal, "Fear of Force in the Middle East: The Oil Grab Scenario" *New Republic* (January 18, 1975) [online version]; Irving Howe, "America Now: A Failure of Nerve? A Symposium," *Commentary* 60:1 (July 1975), 45, 16–87; Podhoretz, interview by Judith Goldstein, February 19, 1975, Norman Podhoretz Papers, Manuscript Division, Library of Congress, Washington, DC (NPLC).

9. Peter L. Berger, "The Greening of American Foreign Policy," *Commentary* 61:3 (March 1976), 23–7.

10. Podhoretz, "America Now," 16

11. Midge Decter, "America Now," 30; Letters, *Commentary* 60:5 (November 1975), 4–15.

12. "America Now," 16–87.

13. Steven Kelman, "Stalinophilia," *Commentary* 56:1 (July 1974), 67; Louis Berg, "McCarthy as Buccaneer," *Commentary* 56:2 (August 1973), 82; Arch Puddington, "The New Soviet Apologists," *Commentary* 76:5 (November 1983), 25–31.

14. Eric M. Breindel, "Progressives' Progress," *Commentary* 75:3 (March 1983), 81–4.

15. Nathan Glazer, "An Answer to Lillian Hellman," *Commentary* 62:6 (June 1976), 36–9; Letters, *Commentary* 62:3 (September 1976), 4–8; Irving Howe, "Lillian Hellman and the McCarthy Years," in his *Celebrations and Attacks: Thirty Years of Literary and Cultural Commentary* (New York: Harcourt Brace Jovanovich, 1979), 209.

16. Eric M. Breindel, "The Communists & the Committees," *Commentary* 71:1 (January 1981), 46–52; Samuel McCracken, "'Julia' & Other Fictions by Lillian Hellman," *Commentary* 77:6 (June 1984), 35–43; Peter Collier and David Horowitz, "McCarthyism: The Last Refuge of the Left," *Commentary* 85:1 (January 1988), 36–41; Norman Podhoretz, *Ex-Friends: Falling Out with Allen Ginsberg, Lionel and Diana Trilling, Lillian Hellman, Hannah Arendt, and Norman Mailer* (New York: Free Press, 1999), 134.

17. Midge Decter, "Socialism and Its Irresponsibilities: The Case of Irving Howe," *Commentary* 74:6 (December 1982), 25–32; Letters, *Commentary* 76:2 (February 1983), 4–10; Letters, *Commentary* 75:4 (April 1983), 12–15.

18. Nathan Glazer, "Verdicts of History," *Commentary* 76:3 (October 1983), 66–70; Eric J. Sundquist, "'Witness' Recalled," *Commentary* 86:6 (December 1988), 57–63.

19. Howe, "America Now," 16–87.

20. Podhoretz, *Making It*, 291; Podhoretz, "Making the World Safe for Communism," 32; Letters, *Commentary* 70:3 (September 1980), 4–12.

21. Daniel Patrick Moynihan, "The United States in Opposition," *Commentary* 59:3 (March 1975), 31–44 and "Was Woodrow Wilson Right? Morality and American Foreign Policy," *Commentary* 57:5 (May 1974), 25–31.

22. Daniel Patrick Moynihan, *A Dangerous Place* (Boston: Little Brown, 1978), 37; H. Joachim Maitre, "Mit *Commentary* gegen die Kentauren" ("With *Commentary* against the Centaurs"), *Die Welt* (December 14, 1979), 27; James Nuechterlein, "The Moynihan Years," *Commentary* 110:3 (October 2000), 29–36.

23. Mark Gerson, *The Neoconservative Vision: From the Cold War to the Culture Wars* (Lanham, MD: Madison Books, 1997), 171–2; "Et Tu Moynihan," *National Review* (August 5, 1983) [online version].

24. Norman Podhoretz, *Breaking Ranks: A Political Memoir* (New York: Harper & Row, 1979), 355, 339.

25. Walter Laqueur, "The World and President Carter," *Commentary* 65:2 (February 1978), 56–63.

26. John Patrick Diggins, "*Commentary*'s Cold War on Liberalism," paper delivered at the "*Commentary*, the American Jewish Community and American Culture" conference, March 11, 2003; Walter Laqueur, "Europe: The Specter of Finlandization," *Commentary* 64:6 (December 1977), 37–46; Letters, *Commentary* 65:5 (May 1978), 6, 8; and "A Postscript on Finlandization," *Commentary* 95:1 (January 1993), 53; Norman Podhoretz, *The Present Danger* (New York: Simon and Schuster, 1980), 58.

27. Eugene V. Rostow, "The Case Against SALT II," *Commentary* 67:2 (February 1979), 23–32.

28. John Ehrman, *The Rise of Neoconservatism: Intellectuals and Foreign Affairs, 1945–1994* (New Haven and London: Yale University Press, 1996), 112; Michael S. Sherry, In the Shadow of War: the United States since the 1930s (New Haven and London: Yale University Press, 1995), 353.

29. Edward N. Luttwak, "Why Arms Control Failed," *Commentary* 65:1 (January 1978), 19–28; Richard Pipes, "Why the Soviet Union Thinks It Could Fight and Win a Nuclear War," *Commentary* 64: 1 (July 1977), 21–34; Letters, *Commentary* 64:2 (August 1977), 4–26; Sherry, *In the Shadow of War*, 352–3.

30. Nathan Glazer, "American Values and American Foreign Policy," *Commentary* 62:1 (July 1976), 32–7 and "The Exposed American Jew," *Commentary* 59:6 (June 1975), 25–30.

31. Jeane Kirkpatrick, "Dictatorships and Double Standards," *Commentary* 68:5 (November 1979), 34–45.

32. Jeane Kirkpatrick, "Dictatorships and Double Standards," 34–45. Kirkpatrick's thesis was less original than she thought/claimed. Although widely credited with formulating the distinction between "authoritarian" and "totalitarian" regimes even if she used the terms "traditional" versus "revolutionary" autocracies, and inclined to take the credit for herself, Kirkpatrick had merely popularized rather than originated the distinction. Her article was "overpraised," according to Garry Wills, not least because the distinction had become popular in certain conservative circles long before her article appeared in November of 1979. Ernest Lefever, who would go on to lead the Reagan administration's first assault of Carter's human rights policy, had formulated it for the Heritage Foundation well over a year before her article had appeared. Later, her arguments proved unfounded, too. See Garry Wills, *Reagan's America: Innocents at Home* (London: Heinemann, 1988), 348.

33. Podhoretz, *Breaking Ranks*, 349.

34. Glazer, "The Exposed American Jew," 25–30.

35. Walter Laqueur, "The West in Retreat," *Commentary* 60:2 (August 1975), 48; Podhoretz, "Making the World Safe for Communism," 38, 39; Glazer, "American Values and American Foreign Policy," 35, 36; Podhoretz, quoted in Ben, "*Commentary*."

36. Norman Podhoretz, "The Abandonment of Israel," *Commentary* 62:1 (July 1976), 27.

37. Podhoretz, quoted in Ben, "*Commentary*"; Podhoretz, "The Abandonment of Israel," 23–31.

38. Milton Himmelfarb, "Never Again!" *Commentary* 52:2 (August 1971), 73.

39. David Twersky, "Left, Right, Left Right," *Moment* 20:3 (June 1995), 58; Letters, *Commentary* 63:6 (June 1977), 4–14; Letters, *Commentary* 60:4 (October 1975), 7.

40. Franklin E. Kameny, Letters, *Commentary* 103:3 (March 1997), 3–26.

41. Podhoretz, quoted in Alan M. Dershowitz, *Chutzpah* (New York and London: Simon and Schuster, 1991), 202–3.

42. Podhoretz, *Ex-Friends*, 195, 196, 35–8; Norman Podhoretz, "The Know-Nothing Bohemians," *Partisan Review* 25 (Spring, 1958) 305–18; Epstein, "Anti-Americanism & Other Clichés," *Commentary* 75:4 (April 1983), 60–3; Epstein, "It's Only Culture," *Commentary* 76:5 (November 1983), 56–61; Epstein, "Mailer Hits Bottom," *Commentary* 76:1 (July 1983), 62–8; Joseph Epstein, "Sex and Euphemism," *Commentary* 77:4 (April 1984).

43. Joseph Epstein, "Paul Goodman in Retrospect," *Commentary* 65:2 (February 1978), 70–3; Joseph Epstein, "What Makes Vidal Run," *Commentary* 63:6 (June 1977), 72–5; Paul Notley, "*New Criterion*," in *The Conservative Press in Twentieth Century America*, ed. Ronald Lora and William Henry Longton (Westport, CT and London: Greenwood Press, 1999), 608.

44. Samuel McCracken, "Are Homosexuals Gay?" *Commentary* 67:1 (January 1979), 19–29; Midge Decter, "The Boys on the Beach," *Commentary* 70:3 (September 1980), 35–48.

45. Freiderich Koenig, Letters, *Commentary* 70:6 (December 1980), 12, 13; *Gay City News* (January 17–23, 2003) [online version].

46. Nick Cohen, "Pink power sinks the Tories," *The Observer* (November 10, 2002) [internet version].

47. Sidney Hook, "America Now" 41; Podhoretz, quoted in Philip Ben, "*Commentary*: An American Monthly with Jewish Roots," draft article for *Maariv* (January 27, 1978), American Jewish Committee Records, Record Group 347, GEN-12 and GEN 10, YIVO Institute for Jewish Research, New York (AJC, YIVO); Norman Podhoretz, "The Culture of Appeasement," *Harper's* (October 1977), 25, 31, 32.

48. Douglas Charles email to author, March 23, 2004.

49. Peter Steinfels, Letters, *Commentary* 69:6 (June 1980), 6–7; Steinfels, *The Neoconservatives* (New York: Simon & Schuster, 1979), 79–80.

50. Ruth R. Wisse, "The Making of *Commentary* and of the Jewish Intellectual," *Jewish Social Studies* 3:2 (Winter 1997), 38. Unlike the majority of American Jews, *Commentary* opposed abortion. Full-page ads for the Non-Sectarian Committee for Life regularly appeared in the magazine throughout the 1970s, getting increasingly shriller as the decade progressed. Magda Denes skillfully presented the abortion question in such a way as to provoke guilt among those readers who supported the right to choose. It was surely no accident that Dorothy Rabinowitz's "Portrait of a Survivor" of the Nazi death camps followed Denes' article. "The parallels are obvious, and ironic," noticed one reader.

"Otherwise viable human beings are legally placed in a non-human category, and then efficiently, rationally, and scientifically exterminated." See Magda Denes, "Performing Abortions," *Commentary* 62:4 (October 1976), 33–7; Letters, *Commentary* 62:6 (December 1976), 4–6; Letters, *Commentary* 63:2 (February 1977), 22–5; Letters, *Commentary* 63:1 (January 1977), 18–22.

5

Empire

In 1980, with the election of Ronald Reagan, *Commentary* entered its finest hour. It represented the zenith of Podhoretz's empire. The Reagan era was *Commentary*'s place in the sun. Neoconservatism had reached its height and Podhoretz's empire-building was complete, as many neocons became Reaganauts. The decade of fighting against the New Left, McGovernism, and liberalism had ended in victory. After the civil wars of the 1970s, reconstruction was complete; *Commentary* crossed the Potomac, and marched on Washington, right up to the steps of the Capitol, and straight into the White House. In the years that followed, Podhoretz and *Commentary*'s ideas on a range of topics were translated into concrete Administration policy.

Get Carter

Before the triumphant march on Washington, one problem remained to be gotten out of the away: Jimmy Carter. The campaign against the Left, which had occupied *Commentary* over the past decade, could not be considered over until Carter had been driven from office. Furthermore, victory was not sealed until a Republican president was returned to the White House after what Podhoretz felt was the illegitimate "coup" of Watergate that toppled the rightful Nixon from the throne.

Commentary carried on railing against Carter in the first year of 1980. It constructed a giant straw man merely in order to tear him down. In a comprehensive hatchet job—a term often used by *Commentary*'s disgruntled readers to describe its articles—it wrote of the softness and ineptitude of the Carter administration particularly its "humiliating" "capitulation" in the Iran hostage crisis of November 1979. It was particularly irritated with Carter's Middle East policies, considering them to be deliberately anti-Israel. The world according to *Commentary* was now a more dangerous place in the aftermath of Carter's massive failure of policy.[1]

More than any other intellectual publication, *Commentary* helped to convince the public that the Carter Administration had utterly failed to comprehend or to deal effectively with the Soviet political, economic, and military threat. On the issues of Afghanistan, Nicaragua, arms control, European neutralism, and the meaning of the Vietnam experience, Podhoretz and the neocons were influential, aiding and abetting the shift of important members of the American intelligentsia to neoconservatism. Moreover, traditionally liberal magazines like the *New Republic* were now beginning to echo *Commentary*'s point of view. And, its anti-Carter campaign marked it out compared with the other leading conservative magazines of the day: David Brock found magazines like the *American Spectator* too "foppish" and "Anglophilic," whereas *Commentary* was marked by "intellectual vigor and fiery polemics."[2]

Nonetheless, Podhoretz was still willing to court presidential power. His chance came when Carter tried to woo neocon support. As he was running for office again in 1980, and facing a drop in the polls, as well as a challenge from Senator Edward Kennedy in the Democratic primaries, Carter felt he could use the backing of the neocons whose support he was losing. It was a sign of their growing influence that Carter felt he so badly needed their help. Consequently, one morning in 1980 Carter invited key neocons, including Podhoretz, Decter, their son-in-law, Elliot Abrams, and Jeane Kirkpatrick to the White House to win their electoral patronage. In turn, despite their disgust with Carter, and as a measure of their complexity, they accepted the invitation. The meeting went badly ("silly," recalled Decter) as the neocons clearly expected Carter to persuade them while he anticipated the exact opposite. When the neocons refused, Carter became visibly annoyed and left the meeting red-faced without having secured their support. Given that, with only one or two exceptions, the neocons had by then lost all interest in saving the Democratic Party one can only wonder why they attended in the first place. Opportunism seems to be the only answer. It would thus be interesting to have seen what the outcome would have been if, as Peter Rosenblatt suggested Carter should have done, that is appoint a number of them.[3]

Stunned by Carter's intransigence—but then what else did they expect?—the neocon delegation departed the White House, agreeing that any hopes of working with Carter had been "dashed." Kirkpatrick firmly told Decter, "I am not going to support *that* man." She promptly faced the TV cameras and announced that she was going to back Reagan. One by one, other neocons discarded what was left of their already diluted liberalism, crossed the point of no return, and defected to the Republican camp to assist Reagan's campaign. Abrams also signed up and *Commentary* contributor Ben Wattenberg became Reagan's campaign speechwriter.[4]

Disgusted with Carter and the Democratic Party, Podhoretz stepped up his anti-Carter campaign and put his full weight behind Reagan. He enthusiastically joined the Republican campaign because of Reagan's declared willingness to counter Soviet global aggression combined with the Democrats' confusion over America's world role. Just as he had once eschewed the thought of voting Republican, Podhoretz now could not countenance the idea of backing the Democrats under Carter. As Arnold Beichman wrote, "The only way I could support the 1980 Democratic presidential candidate, is if he should be Daniel P. Moynihan."[5]

Podhoretz personally contributed to Reagan's campaign by publishing two more books in 1980. The first, *Breaking Ranks: A Political Memoir* was a sequel to *Making It* in which Podhoretz charted his ideological transformation from liberalism to neoconservatism. Podhoretz told "the whole story of how and why I went from being a liberal to being a radical and then finally to being an enemy of radicalism in all its forms and varieties." As Podhoretz had chosen the wrong side, he repudiated it completely, right down to its essential principle—social solidarity: "The politics of interest," he wrote, was "the only antidote to the plague" of sixties radicalism. *The Present Danger*, on the other hand, seemed simply to be a piece of campaign literature endorsing Reagan's bid for the presidency. Together, the books were a crystallization of all the fears that had been building up in *Commentary* over a decade: homosexuality, appeasement, and Finlandization. *Breaking Ranks* became a keystone text for neoconservatism, one of its most famous and influential books, while *The Present Danger* was simply a statement which merely reiterated the research of the CPD. (Incidentally, at Simon and Schuster, one sales representative accidentally let on that "no one was going to lift a finger" to sell it.) *The Present Danger* was widely read by the Reaganites who loved it. Reagan himself praised the tome, saying it was one of his favorite books, and urged every American to read it. Sidney Hook recommended Podhoretz for a Medal of Freedom.[6]

Commentary created a Reagan in its own image, remaking him as a neoconservative. Like the neocons, they pointed out, Reagan had once been a working-class, left-wing, unionized Democrat. Podhoretz asserted that the Republicans had usurped the abandoned Democratic tradition: not only had Reagan quoted FDR during his acceptance speech at the Republican convention in 1980, but he also offered a program "that echoed in almost every detail the campaign on which John F. Kennedy rode to the

Presidency in 1960." For the first time since Theodore Roosevelt, the GOP under Reagan had become the party of change, acquiring a skilful spokesman, a vast organizational network, a leading position in the pubic-opinion polls, and an alternative vision of what American government and society ought to be like. In contrast, the Democrats were bereft of new ideas. More importantly, Reagan seemed to share the magazine's worldview, advocating the pressing need to counter growing Soviet expansionism and Third World leftism, as well as the virtues of individualism, private enterprise, work ethic, voluntarism, personal freedom, and responsibility. Reagan spoke of "the troubled world" of abortion, quotas, gay rights, feminism, crime and punishment, the family, moral and religious values. Reagan shared *Commentary*'s opposition to big government, legalization of marijuana, abortions, pornography, draft resistance, busing, bans on gun ownership, affirmative action, and quotas. So *Commentary* transformed Reagan into a natural ally.[7]

Not only was this another example of Podhoretz's opportunism, there was also an element of self-deception in his view that the Republican party was committed to his values, deriving from Roosevelt's record of social and political reform, rather than those of big business and suburban ambition. The GOP, with its flavor of small-town Midwestern business America, was seen to be ethnically and cultural uncongenial. Elliot Abrams felt that "Republicans aren't 'our kind of people,' their party holds no comfort for Jews." The neocons, who hailed Moynihan as their hero and the bearer of their political aspirations, were secular, Wilsonian, welfare statist, New Yorkers. They couldn't have been more dissimilar to the already-established coalition of libertarians, traditionalists, the religious right, Cold Warriors, and paleocons largely based in the South and midwest who, in turn, viewed the neocons as impostors and interlopers in the conservative movement. Neocons did not seem to belong to the Right at all, and they didn't (and perhaps never would) feel entirely comfortable in the conservative movement. Nonetheless, ignoring their fears, they joined the Republican Party as their best opportunity for gaining real power and influence.[8]

Furthermore, in order to engineer a Jewish swing toward the Republicans, Podhoretz tried to convince his co-religionists that Reagan was "Good for the Jews?" Consequently, in January 1980 he ran a symposium entitled, "Liberalism and the Jews." Podhoretz's editorial statement, while attempting to lure Jewish votes, was entirely negative, aiming to rupture what he saw as the age-old, "compulsive," and "virtually congenital proclivity" between Jews, liberalism, and the Democratic Party. Rather than promoting Reagan, Podhoretz denigrated liberalism. He questioned the "axiom," taken for granted by most American Jews: that liberalism coincided with and best represented their interests. He raised a litany of emotional issues which he thought might persuade Jews to move to the right in the coming election: the widespread liberal support for affirmative action and quotas, the Left's diminishing enthusiasm for Israel and concomitant growing sympathy for the PLO, as well as its tolerance of the anti-Semitism that surfaced in the wake of Andrew Young's resignation. Together these developments, he argued, had warranted "reconsideration by the Jewish community in general of its traditional commitment to liberalism." Podhoretz even subtly insinuated a comparison between a beleaguered Israel and European Jewry during the Holocaust. Like Podhoretz's editorializing, the overwhelming tone of the symposium was that liberalism and the Democrats had failed the Jews. Former editor Werner Dannhauser wrote, "No 11th—or 614th—commandment exists to the effect that a Jew shall be a liberal." Gertrude Himmelfarb suspected that the "new" liberalism was "inhospitable to us both as individuals and as Jews." Decter added, "Jews are losing their home in the Democratic party" because the "new liberalism is bad for the Jews." "As a social doctrine liberalism has nothing further to teach the Jews," wrote Executive Editor Neal Kozodoy, "and the Jews have nothing further to contribute to it."[9]

Bliss

When Carter conceded in 1976, the feeling of excitement at the magazine was tangible. Decter recalled:

> Nothing in this agenda would in essence have been new to me ... but that the *president of the United States* was asking us to join him in making it national policy ... ! Bliss it was to be alive at that hour—and, even if one was no longer young, very heaven.

Podhoretz was euphoric. He could not restrain himself from an overt shout of joy. Reagan's victory fulfilled his hopes. In an outpouring of happiness, he boasted that Reagan's victory was a vindication of everything he had been arguing for over the last decade and a rejection of all that he had been railing against. Reagan sent out a "powerful positive message," he wrote, "the decline of America, far from being inevitable for the fault of the people themselves, is a consequence of bad policies pursued by government and can therefore be reversed by shifting to other policies." Reagan's economic policy, he hoped, "will unleash the productive energies of an artificially hampered people and thereby foster growth." His program of rearmament "will make our defenses invulnerable and provide us with the power both to contain Soviet expansionism and to protect our vital interests in the Persian Gulf." His legal structure "will encourage the revitalization of the values of 'family, work, and neighborhood.'" Podhoretz expressed a feeling of relief at the thought that "now at least a line will be drawn to keep things from going even further than they already have gone." At last, he felt, "the tidal wave" of hard-core pornography, homosexuality, and abortion, would be prevented. The Reaganite program represented the restoration of patriotism, republicanism, virtue, and permanence in America. Podhoretz could not resist bragging that he had predicted the Reagan landslide from the moment the two candidates were nominated. He saw Reagan's triumph as the completion of bringing together a new Republican majority, a process started by Nixon but hindered by Watergate, which would "freeze the opposition out of power for the next generation or more."[10]

Former contributor Peter Schrag wrote that Podhoretz's article was a great gift to Reagan and the Republicans, a version of history, which brilliantly distorted the facts, and which, would, he predicted have enormous influence. "If there ever is a new period of McCarthyism in America," Schrag opined, "Podhoretz's article will be one of its central texts."[11]

The Norman Invasion

Podhoretz positioned his magazine in close ideological proximity to the new administration, and *Commentary* began to play an increasingly important role in the implementation of public policy. Its essays and polemics were influential among policy makers and politicians, right up to the highest level. It also provided the shock troops for the (so-called) Reagan Revolution. Through the appointment of key individuals to positions in the new administration, *Commentary* was strategically placed to help shape the public policy debate of the early 1980s, as many neocons became either official members or informal adjuncts of the administration, and moved it in directions that propagated their neoconservative agenda. On only Reagan's tenth day in office in January 1981, for example, neocon Michael Novak flew to the Human Rights Commission in Geneva at the president's request, as the first Reagan appointee to speak on any matter of foreign policy at all. He became *Commentary*'s first Reaganaut.

Reagan then appointed Jeane Kirkpatrick as ambassador to the UN. Allegedly an avid reader of *Commentary*, Reagan reported that his selection was largely based on her 1979 *Commentary* essay, "Dictatorships and Double Standards." The Ethics and Public Policy Center had reprinted and distributed her article giving it a wide audience. Richard Allen, a campaign aide on Reagan's attempt for the presidential nomination, brought it to his attention. He was so impressed by the article that he wrote to her and shortly thereafter Kirkpatrick joined Reagan's campaign team as a foreign policy advisor. Kirkpatrick became the second member of the Commentariat to become US ambassador to the UN (ironically, a body the magazine hated). Kirkpatrick may only have served until 1985, but she set the Reaganite foreign policy agenda for the next eight years. All of Reagan's top foreign policy appointees were required to read her article. Then, barely a year after her appointment, many of her ideas had become administration policy, when a policy memorandum codifying a human rights policy clearly based on her article was circulated. Her insistence that totalitarian regimes posed a much greater danger to American interests than did the more authoritarian dictatorships provided an intellectual pillar for the "Reagan Doctrine." Kirkpatrick was seen as Podhoretz's "intellectual protégé." He had raised her, and now she was his representative deep inside the administration.

In addition to Kirkpatrick, other neocons occupied top positions in the Reagan administration. Indeed, stated Murray Friedman, *Commentary* became a "personnel bureau" for major figures in American life under Reagan. Elliot Abrams held three assistant secretary positions in the State Department during 1981–1989 (international organizations, Human Rights division, and inter-America affairs, directing Reagan's Central America policy); Carl Gershman worked for Kirkpatrick at the UN, served as an adviser to the Kissinger Commission on Central America, and was then appointed head of the National Endowment for Democracy; Eugene Rostow served as director of Arms Control and Disarmament Agency; Richard Pipes directed the East European and Soviet Affairs division of the National Security Council (and was influential in helping create the Reagan Doctrine); Chester Finn worked for the Department of Education; Ben Wattenberg received advisory posts in the international communications apparatus; Midge Decter became a member of the Task Force on Food Assistance; Michael Novak led the American delegation at the Bern Conference on Security and Cooperation in Europe; Arch Puddington worked for Radio Free Europe/Radio Liberty; Penn Kemble became director of Prodemca, an organization that mobilized support for Reagan's Central America policy; Gertrude Himmelfarb was appointed to the Council of the National Endowment for the Humanities; Joseph Epstein was appointed to the National Council of the National Endowment for the Arts; and Murray Friedman became vice-chairman of the US Civil Rights Commission. An article in *Commentary*, it seemed, had become the litmus test for entry into the administration. Through such appointments, Reagan rewarded *Commentary* with top policy positions in his Administration.

The President had extended a courtesy to a group that he understood was among his most ardent loyalists.[12]

Nearly thirty of the officials whom Reagan chose for high posts in the first weeks of his administration also belonged to the neocon-dominated CPD. Reagan's views on foreign and defense policies and his ambitious program of defense procurements, found their source in Team B and the CPD, of which many neocons (Podhoretz, Nitze, Pipes, Decter, Kikpatrick, and Rustin) were members. They disapproved of arms control as a political tool, insisted on building up first offensive nuclear forces and then antinuclear defenses, based on the premise that the USSR held a different view of the utility of nuclear weapons from the United States, regarding them as guarantors not of peace but of victory. From their top positions, they encouraged the Reagan administration to view issues such as the Palestinian statehood/nationalism, the Nicaraguan revolution, Third World struggles, and the South African and the Middle East conflicts through the prism of the Cold War, namely international Communism and Soviet expansionism.

Podhoretz became a frequent guest at the White House. He had personal meetings with high Reagan administration officials, including Secretary of State George Shultz and Director of Central Intelligence William Casey. In 1981, he was invited to a White House dinner in honor of the visit of the Chancellor of the Federal Republic of Germany. In the following year Shultz invited him to a meeting reviewing US policy toward the Soviet Union. Podhoretz was appointed to an official position on the US Information Agency (USIA) advisory board, as chair of its New Directions Advisory Committee (other members included fellow neocons Novak, Rustin, Himmelfarb, and Robert Nisbet). Podhoretz even had the ear of the President, as Reagan telephoned him when he had a problem with one of *Commentary*'s more critical articles. Decter, through her work for the Committee for the Free World, was also a frequent guest at the White House, including lunches with the President.

The neocons were in the ascendant and Podhoretz bragged, "Most of those in the Reagan upper echelon are readers of *Commentary*." Podhoretz proudly proclaimed to an audience in the Plaza Hotel in New York City:

> We are the dominant faction within the world of ideas—the most influential—the most powerful . . . By now the liberal culture has to appease us . . . People like us made Reagan's victory, which had been considered unthinkable.

He could rightly claim that *Commentary* had been very successful in altering the terms of the national debate; as a subscription ad for the magazine stated, "Its readers are leaders." Podhoretz's influence even extended beyond America's borders: on a visit to Australia in 1981, then Prime Minister Malcolm Fraser invited him to dinner at The Lodge and acknowledged the influence that Podhoretz's articles in *Commentary* had had on his attitude toward east-west relations. He also met Western Mining's Hugh Morgan and members of the "Quadrant gang"—Leonie Kramer, Richard Krygier, and Paul Johnson in the United Kingdom. When Britain's Channel Four wanted an articulate Jewish defender of Israel for a television discussion of the war by British-Jewish intellectuals, it invited Podhoretz (he insisted on flying Concorde), allegedly because no one else would do the job. In France the magazine *Commentaire* acknowledged the influence of *Commentary* on which it was modeled. In a speech at Eureka College in 1984, Reagan declared his debt to the influence and importance of Podhoretz. Political scientist Seymour Finger observed that "only those of the *Commentary*-Georgetown-neoconservative team are in the inner circle." "Norman and Midge are the golden couple now," remarked Elliot Abrams. "It's strange." Podhoretz's struggle for power had seemingly ended in success.[13]

"Podhoretz as Dr. Strangelove!"

Podhoretz interpreted Reagan's victory and his new intellectual proximity to the White House as a mandate to push his neocon agenda further than he ever had before. At the forefront of his campaign of the 1980s was foreign policy. Podhoretz interpreted Reagan's landslide as the emergence of a "new consensus" to respond more firmly and resolutely to his perceived growth of Soviet power and to arrest and reverse the decline of American power. He championed a US foreign policy dedicated entirely to combating Communism (to the ignoring of other, potentially dangerous threats). Podhoretz's one-dimensional view of the world, single-mindedly focused on the Kremlin and its agents—which he saw everywhere—painted a picture of an aggressive, expansionist enemy. He boiled world conflicts down to a simple East-West divide. In a series of articles—"The Present Danger" (March 1980) and "The Future Danger" (April 1980)—Podhoretz had already exaggerated the extent of Soviet expansionism, and Kristol, Luttwak, Laqueur, Pipes, Gershman, Tucker, Draper, Moynihan, Rustin, and others indulged in gratuitous saber-rattling, presenting apocalyptic scenarios, indiscriminately invoking the fear of "Finlandization." They perceived that American power was weakening and called for the strengthening of US military interests in order to contain the Soviets. They were convinced that the survival of liberty and democracy in the

United States and abroad required the maintenance and exertion of American power.

Commentary may have made a unique contribution to creating "the new consensus" concerning the dangerous growth of Soviet power, the decline of American power, and the urgent need to restore a favorable global balance, as confirmed by Reagan's election, but it did not rest. Despite the vindication he and his allies had now received, Podhoretz warned that the fight was far from over. Still more mopping up had to be done for the universities and the media remained "mired in yesterday's conventional wisdom," having become

> the repository of discredited ideas and shopworn attitudes, a kind of shrine at which the cultists of a dying religion gather to genuflect, changing mindless invocations they imagine arise out of reason to a moribund god they still believe incarnates the living truth.

Though a small minority, these "cultists" remained numerous enough and sufficiently well placed to obstruct or retard the progress of the new consensus.[14]

Podhoretz kept up a persistent drumbeat of warnings that Soviet strength was greater than American and that America was losing the global battle against Communism. *Commentary* maintained the pressure on the new administration to mobilize support for its relaunched policy of containment. Former Marxists and Socialists like Hook, Beichman, Puddington, Rustin, Gershman, Kemble, and Muravchik wrote that the United States was losing the war against Communism. Articles repeatedly called for increased defense spending, arms buildup, both conventional and nuclear, and an enlarged defense program. Podhoretz published alarmist articles stressing US vulnerability to a Soviet counterforce or missile strike, and emphasizing that the Soviets had left America behind in the arms race.

As a corollary, writers argued against arms control and warned that antinuclear agitation had to be dealt with once and for all. They called for a more realistic approach toward nuclear weapons and the achievement of strategic parity at the very least. They dismissed the threat of nuclear war, as quasi-religious fears of the supernatural, asserting that fears of a holocaust have been expressed for more than 5,000 years in religious writings. They felt that the matter of nuclear war should be stripped of its emotionalism. They called for a long-term, patient, approach to defeating the Soviet Union, assisting reformist forces within the Communist orbit rather than by seeking to modify its behavior (which was deemed impossible anyway). They advocated continued political, economic, and military pressure resulting in its collapse, seeing no other solution to a military buildup that included nuclear weapons and antiballistic-missile defense systems, arguing that such military buildup was "morally necessary." The magazine supported and defended Reagan's Star Wars initiative, and often went into excruciating detail concerning ICBM, SS-17, SS-18, SS-19, SS-20, SS-24, SS-25, MX, Midgetman, and Pershing missiles.

Podhoretz challenged the perceived mood of isolationism, neutralism, pacifism, and anti-Americanism. He also attempted to fight off what he saw as the "rising tide of appeasement," which, less than three years after Reagan's election, he felt threatened to overwhelm the new consensus, most urgently in the key areas of defense and Central America. In "Appeasement By Any Other Name," Podhoretz argued that there was a widespread and serious myopia concerning the dangers of totalitarian expansionism, which resulted in *de facto* appeasement. He designated pacifism and isolationism as the most immediate and clearly identifiable sources of such attitudes and policies, which, if left unchecked, would "only give us a world fashioned in the image of the Soviet Union." Furthermore, he for one did not believe that

> the American people will cooperate knowingly in the emergence of such a world. And that is why I think the spirit of appeasement now hovering so heavily over the land can still be blown away by a renewed, persistent, and unembarrassed appeal to the realism, the sense of honor, and the patriotism that erupted after Iran and Afghanistan and then swept Ronald Reagan into office only two-and-a-half years ago.

He argued that the totalitarian drift in Central America had to be stopped and reversed by "whatever may be required, up to and including the dispatch of troops," that democratic government had to be mandated on regimes that had so far resisted such efforts, that a larger defense budget was needed to protect America against Cuba and Nicaragua, and that the eventual war with the Soviet Union could be deterred by being "prepared and willing if necessary to fight."[15]

Podhoretz did not balance out his analysis of US imperial decline against the equivalent reality of Soviet imperial decline. He painted a picture of Soviet expansionism in Afghanistan. It took a reader to presciently point out:

> Events will bear out, I believe, that the Soviet move into Afghanistan will detract from Soviet influence in the Third World. For once Moscow is trying to smash the forces of revolutionary nationalism by

relying on its military prowess. Such an enterprise generally self-destructs in the late 20th century.

Podhoretz was so preoccupied with the Soviet Union that it blinded him to the other dangers to American security. He could not contemplate, for example, the threat posed by Islamic fundamentalism. The Islamic revolution in Iran was simply seen as a prelude to "a Soviet takeover of some kind." Another reader wrote in to respond that he only wished Woody Allen would cast Podhoretz in his next movie:

> Podhoretz as Dr. Strangelove! Podhoretz defoliating the greenery in Vietnam—whoops, I mean Central America! Podhoretz dropping nuclear weapons over Central America! . . . *Star Wars* and *Return of the Jedi*, except Mr. Podhoretz wants to play fatal games with those of us, and the next generation, who inhabit this planet.[16]

Nonetheless, as the mainstream press began to follow *Commentary*'s lead, Podhoretz could not resist boasting. "Suddenly," he bragged,

> somber stories about the Soviet military build-up were appearing in sectors of the media which only yesterday had been notable for ignoring or downplaying or even decrying as hysterical and alarmist the Churchillian warnings of groups like the CPD and individuals like Senator Henry M. Jackson and Governor Ronald Reagan.

Time, *Newsweek*, *The New York Times*, and the commercial and public television network were running stories about the Soviet military build-up, as well as reports on the deplorable state of American military power. This new bipartisan consensus and the change in American political culture it represented was an "immense" achievement, which had taken "years of ferocious struggle" at the "bloody crossroads." Podhoretz felt he had been vindicated.[17]

Abusing Human Rights

As we have seen, *Commentary* had already made up its mind, most notably in the writings of Kirkpatrick, that the Communist threat was so deadly, that the United States must ally itself with anti-Communist regimes, no matter how right-wing, dictatorial, authoritarian, and repressive they were. "Foreign-policy decisions are always exercises in choice," wrote Mark Falcoff, the magazine's expert on Latin America, "usually between unpalatable alternatives." It was precisely to assist in those supposedly difficult choices that *Commentary* formulated in its pages the distinction between two completely different kinds of dictatorship: authoritarian and totalitarian. These distinctions, however, were not fine but broad and basic, creating the belief that authoritarian states were repressive on an *ad hoc* basis and, except for an occasional uprising, would in time moderate into more democratic states. Totalitarianism, on the other hand, was presented as irreversible. There was no suggestion that authoritarian states could also in time become totalitarian. Morally speaking, authoritarian regimes were to be given a benefit of doubt to be denied to totalitarianism. Torturous distinctions between such regimes were devised to bolster this outlook.[18]

The creation of an elaborate theoretical structure based on the distinction between "totalitarian" and "authoritarian" regimes, as *Commentary* attempted to do, therefore, was simply a self-serving attempt to differentiate the Communist from the non-Communist world and to justify strategic, if morally dubious, alliances with the latter against the former. In essence, the magazine advocated alignments with any anti-Communist dictator even if his value system ran contrary to almost everything America stood for. Podhoretz justified such alliances as "an unfortunate political and military necessity" in "holding back the single greatest and most powerful threat to freedom on the face of the earth." Such a foreign policy was dubbed "realistic" and *Commentary* was cynically prepared to abandon the traditional principles of liberal democracy in favor of a policy determined by expediency and self-interest.[19]

Commentary, therefore, dismissed human rights abuses on the part of America's client states. The tortures and murders committed by right-wing armies and death squads were brushed aside, as unavoidable consequences of anti-Communist counterinsurgency warfare. Instead, *Commentary* distracted attention from the central issue, which was that the United States was backing governments that were guilty of perpetrating kidnapping, torturing, and murdering of thousands of innocent and defenseless civilians, by stressing that the United States should remain dispassionate. It assigned all guilt to Communist-affiliated terrorists, omitting to suggest that perhaps the murderous repression of authoritarian regimes might have been the terrorists' inspiration. It was very clear that, when Podhoretz wondered aloud, "What role, if any, should a concern for human rights play in American foreign policy? Is there a conflict between this concern and American national interests?," that he and the magazine had made up their collective mind a long time ago. As Bayard Rustin pointed out, "this is not a question which can be open to discussion." Charles William Maynes, the editor of the highly—influential *Foreign Policy* and a former

Assistant Secretary of State for International Organization Affairs under Carter, wrote further: "the single blinding light of 'the present danger' ... now transfixes many of the contributors to *Commentary* in its high beam." As a prominent supporter of the Reagan administration's human rights policy, Podhoretz led the drive to embrace reaction and condone human-rights abuses so long as American allies committed them in its courting of South Africa and Central America.[20]

He continued to press for support of repressive autocratic governments even when it annoyed the AJC. Hostility to Podhoretz had been seething among its leaders for many months, as Podhoretz's refusal to espouse an all-out human rights position ran counter to the AJC's historic and primary commitment to human rights, rooted in the teachings of the Hebrew prophets and in the Declaration of Independence. Podhoretz's extremist position angered the AJC. It wanted to curb Podhoretz publicly and insisted that he return to a firm human rights position, because failure to do so compromised the very foundation on which the AJC was built. However, it feared that such a course of action risked reprisals from the Reagan administration because Podhoretz had such strong political support. Thus AJC leaders tried to keep the issue from exploding and succeeded for fears of a potential split in its leadership never materialized. Although the AJC denied it, one commentator predicted that, unless Podhoretz returned to an all-out human rights position, his days as *Commentary*'s editor were numbered. But where the AJC had once stated that at the point where it found the editor was inimical to its goals, it would simply replace him, Podhoretz and Kirkpatrick were allowed to continue to advocate support for repressive autocratic regimes both in the magazine and on television with impunity. As one newspaper columnist concluded in puzzlement, "In truth, I, too, am mystified at how an organization can favor human rights in its operating program and oppose them in its major publication."[21]

A Shtetl Mentality

Podhoretz's other major foreign policy concern was Israel. By the early 1980s Podhoretz had retreated to "restrictive, old country attitudes and customs," characteristic of a "shtetl mentality," that asked, "Is it Good for the Jews?" Podhoretz stated that Jews could find salvation for themselves without affording it to others. This was most evident in his coverage of Israel and the Middle East. While *Commentary* wrote about a variety of topics during this decade, its range drastically narrowed. It wrote about none with as regular consistency as foreign affairs, particularly the Middle East. Roughly half of Podhoretz's writings during the 1980s dealt with the threats to Israel.[22]

Commentary called on Reagan to fashion a new Middle East policy in the wake of the unmitigated debacle of the Carter administration. It continued to articulate its "strategic asset" doctrine that Israel was "a unique and impressive ally," an advantage rather than a liability, which often served as a "silent partner" for America in the Middle East. As a free political society, Israel's importance to the United States was invaluable. Furthermore, for Podhoretz, Israel was a country that combated Soviet expansionism by straightforward foreign-policy realism, unregimented by domestic legal constraints. *Commentary* described Israel as "a moral beacon," a "politically righteous society," which "must be permitted its failings without automatically forfeiting its political legitimacy."[23]

Podhoretz and *Commentary* supported the hawkish Israeli PM, Menachem Begin, regardless of his actions. Every excess of the Israeli government was justified, and anyone who publicly criticized it, or who opposed further settlements on the West Bank, was disparaged as either an enemy of the Jews or, if they were Jew, as a self-hater. It was implied that Israel could do no wrong, and thus no self-respecting American Jew could legitimately debate or condemn Israel's actions. Podhoretz published rebuttals of Israel's detractors which often equated Jewish censure of Zionism with Jewish self-hatred. Podhoretz refused to acknowledge the harm of Israel's settlement position and what it might do to US-Israeli relations. Instead, he attacked American critics of Israel, faulting them for exaggerating the importance of the settlements. He sought to smother anything that smacked of criticism of Israel by accusing the critics of being self-hating Jews and debased individuals. He did not believe that open discussion on Israel was important. Rather, the true test of American Jewish self-respect and loyalty, he implied, was how well American Jews tacitly complied with Israel's behavior. Public criticism of Israeli policy by American Jews, on the other hand, exposed Israel to danger at a time when the international community, subservient to Arab economic pressures, had isolated Israel.

Commentary was particularly outraged at the liberal criticism of Israel. The identification of prominent American Jews with a public anti-Israel position was deemed ominous and disconcerting and had broken the unwritten, silent compact that American Jews do not publicly attack Israel. American Jews who criticized Israel, Israeli policy, and Begin were guilty of de-legitimizing the state and were hence giving unpaid assistance to anti-Semitic hostility. It was dangerous because it lent a highly visible measure of added plausibility to the campaign against the legitimacy of Israel. Most disturbing for Podhoretz was that the terms of the American Jewish attack echoed this language of de-legitimation. Leonard Fein of the Jewish magazine *Moment* was singled out as an example of a debased and selfish Jew, who helped to undermine Israel, in his support for a boycott of Israel. (The attack on Fein was also motivated by a call in *Moment* for the silencing of *Commentary*.) *Commentary* particularly despised the Peace Now movement, a leftist Israeli organization opposed to the policies of the Begin government. It excoriated the effort to create an American version and the magazine joined a smear campaign against it. Many *Commentary* readers applauded the exposé—the first in a Jewish magazine—of the harm that Peace Now alleged it was doing to Israel. Apart from its dovish stance, *Commentary* hated it so much because many of the founders of Peace Now had been educated in America during the Vietnam War era, and had created a carbon copy of the Vietnam antiwar movement, even down to taking its slogan. Furthermore, *Commentary*'s longtime rival *Dissent* had begun to favor the movement, too, further de-legitimizing it in Podhoretz's view. But, typically, the issues involved were far more complex than *Commentary*'s reductive, simplistic treatment.

Beginning in the 1970s and continuing well into the 1980s, Podhoretz espoused anti-anti-Zionism and anti-anti-Semitism and the two often merged. *Commentary* continued to warn about threats of anti-Semitism from the Left and ran a number of articles on the roots and practice of anti-Semitism, linking them to critics of Israel. Paul Johnson wrote that anti-Semitism in its new "respectable" form of anti-Zionism is now found predominantly on the Left among intellectuals, because it is "firmly rooted in irrational Marxist conspiracy theory." "The Holocaust's bitter history is now being transformed into a vehicle of anti-Semitism," added Lucy Dawidowicz. "The anti-Semites of the Right, as I have had prior occasion to point out on these pages, deny that there ever was a Holocaust. The anti-Semites of the Left blame it on the Jews."[24]

Podhoretz freely used the charge of anti-Semitism to silence Israel's critics. If those critics were Jewish then they were accused of a "failure of nerve" or self-hatred, as Podhoretz dangerously confused criticism of Israeli government policies with criticism of the state itself. He refused to distinguish between them. "Never, perhaps," he wrote, "has criticism of the state of Israel by American Jews been so open, so widespread, and so bitter as it is today." While Jewish criticism of Israel was nothing new and was rooted in the various traditions of opposition to Zionism from the pre-state era, it had returned "couched in updated forms and espoused by people who may or may not be aware of their provenance." There had been a

> marked change even among American Jews whose commitment to Israel has long been unambiguous and steady. Not only have such Jews become increasingly willing to criticize Israel's policies and even

Israel itself, they have also been more and more disposed to do so in public. Conversely, it is hard to remember a time when favorable comment about Israel has been so muted and so scantly with the American Jewish community.[25]

In trying to understand this state of affairs, Podhoretz typically held a symposium on the issue. His point was that the criticism of Israeli government policies particularly in public constituted attacks on the state, which in turn delegitimized it, and that such actions were illegitimate and should be beyond debate. The overwhelming majority of the forty-nine responses gave him a keen sense of what he wanted to hear. Forty-three of them agreed with him and repeated *Commentary* clichés (democracy worth our support, dependable ally, remarkable achievement, Jewish refuge after the Holocaust, and so on), which, by this point, had become tainted with monotony. Murray Friedman spoke for them all when he wrote:

> The rule to guide us generally, it seems to me, is whether the issue involves the safety and security of the state. Israelis who have to live with the day-to-day results of actions taken by their government to protect them must be left free to make their decision without public pressure from their brethren abroad.

And Gertrude Himmelfarb reiterated the standard *Commentary* line.

> The Law of Return guarantees to every Jew a place in Israel; as Norman Podhoretz has pointed out, if we choose not to avail ourselves of that opportunity, we forfeit the moral right to pass public judgment on matters which for Israelis—but not for us—are questions of life and death.[26]

Commentary highlighted attention on the Holocaust in order to drum up support for Israel, both among Jews and non-Jews. It argued that since the Jews had been abandoned in their hour of need, Jews had no ethical duty to anyone else; since the world was based on selfishness, Jews should learn the lesson of Holocaust and ensure Israel's strength and security. Conversely, *Commentary* tried to make American Christians feel guilty about the Holocaust, in order to manipulate them into supporting the Israeli Right. Such essays stopped when it became apparent that the Religious Right was allied to the Zionist Right but pointed to the extent to which *Commentary* was willing to abandon its earlier fears for expedient gain.

Commentary feared the growth of support for the PLO and tried to marginalize it. It compared European commitment to Palestinian self-determination to Hitler's call for Sudeten self-determination in 1938. It accused the PLO of using terror and intimidation to manipulate the international press. It argued that it was not a representative body and derived far more support from Arab states, merely reflecting their wishes, than the Palestinians themselves whose interests were in turn subordinated to the leaders of those states the PLO served. Israeli writer Menachem Milson argued that Israel must free the West Bank population from PLO domination and create a Palestinian alternative on the ground. As Israeli policy on the West Bank had in the past inadvertently led to the strengthening of the PLO's influence there, he advocated a new policy aimed at weakening the PLO so that the moderate Palestinian "silent majority," who wished to live in peace with Israel, could speak out. Palestinians on the West Bank could then demand that King Hussein repudiate the PLO as "the sole representative of the Palestinian people" and resume his old role as their spokesperson.[27]

As a measure of *Commentary*'s influence, Milson's article was translated into Hebrew and Defense Minister Ariel Sharon appointed Milson, previously a scholar of Arab literature and professor at the Hebrew University of Jerusalem, Head of the Civil Administration of Judea and Samaria from November 1981 to September 1982. During this time, he tried to implement his new and very different policy, which required that Palestinians should and could play a role in the political process. The Israeli Military Government actively attempted to curtail PLO influence, while simultaneously encouraging those Palestinians who openly recognized Israel. The goal was to develop conditions conducive to the emergence of Palestinian leaders ready for peace negotiations. But Milson' plan dismally failed, demonstrating the gap between policy theorizing in the pages of a magazine and the actual implementation of those policies. *Commentary* had gotten ahead of itself. Portentous signs were being ignored.

If, over the past few years, Podhoretz had taken an increasingly rigid position on Israel, Israel's invasion of Lebanon in 1982 illustrated the complete hardening of his stance. He defended the invasion by saying that the Israelis took extraordinary care to minimize civilian casualties, and supported it as an "enormous boon" to Israel and to the strategic interests of the United States. However, the international reaction to the invasion was widespread, hostile, and almost unanimously condemnatory. For Podhoretz it provided proof that the world did not really care about Jews and so Jews should stop thinking about everyone else and start worrying more about themselves. Furthermore, he refused "to stand passively by while dogged attempts are made everywhere to delegitimize the State of Israel or to put unilateral pressure on it, thereby weakening it for an eventual kill." He defined any criticism as anti-Semitic, and took it to be his duty "to denounce anti-Semitism when it makes a public appearance and not to justify it or apologize for it or explain it away." Rather than write an apologetic defense for Israel's actions, Podhoretz wrote a pointed counter-attack against Israel's critics, whom he saw as enemies of Israel. Provocatively titled "J'Accuse," the title was borrowed from Emile Zola's broadside in which the French author charged the persecutors of Dreyfus with using anti-Semitism as a screen for their reactionary political designs. Podhoretz distinguished between "true lovers" of Israel and its "false and misguided" friends. Anyone who criticized the invasion was anti-Semitic, as such criticisms were informed by a double standard; Jews and Israelis who did so were self-haters. Podhoretz stated that the anti-Semitic attacks on Israel in recent weeks were similarly a cover for "a loss of American nerve," for "acquiescence in terrorism," for "the appeasement of totalitarianism."[28]

The response to "J'Accuse" was huge. Twenty letters on a single piece was a heavy response for *Commentary*, but "J'Accuse" provoked more than two hundred. The volume of letters was so heavy that Podhoretz borrowed the space in the December issue normally devoted to book reviews in order to print a small fraction of it. Like Israel's actions, the article split its readers down the middle. Many in the US press denounced him. Even the sympathetic *Wall Street Journal* felt that the article was "written in anger" in which Podhoretz's emotions overcame his "usual good judgment." Podhoretz's critics pointed out that he had refused to acknowledge, even bent over backwards to ignore, the Begin government's reckless disregard of America's interests: Begin's refusal to consider any compromise with its ally, his policies that exacerbated Israel's relations with its neighbors, and caused a huge drop in support for Israel like the refusal to trade land for peace, the insistence that the West Bank was forever Jewish, the use of wild and reckless language, and the willingness to use force. Podhoretz, though, would not accept that anything was wrong with Begin's government. He glossed over Israel's continuing use of the Holocaust to justify its policies. Indeed, he forbade references to Lebanon as an "invasion" and was silent on the civilian casualties in Lebanon, including the mass killings at the Sabra and Shatila refugee camps (although, in his defense, they occurred after his piece had been published). It was easier for Podhoretz to shout anti-Semitism than to consider any of these difficulties. One reader wrote that Podhoretz was guilty of "bullying moralism that has made rational criticism of Israel seem beyond the pale of civilized discourse." Another said that, after thirty years of watching *Commentary* "change from a voice of enlightened humanism to a forum for increasingly narrow and rigid points-of-view," as manifested by Podhoretz's "strained efforts to blunt criticism of Israel's shameful and self-destructive behavior," he knew he'd had enough and cast a vote of no-confidence by canceling his subscription.[29]

Yet, Podhoretz took the many letters of praise, applauding and thanking him for what they felt was his impassioned defense of Israel against its detractors, distorters, and anti-Semites, as vindication. It was a sign for him that the Jewish community overwhelmingly endorsed his thesis that the coverage of and comment of the Israeli invasion of Lebanon "went far beyond unfairness and gave witness to 'an eruption of anti-Semitism.'" Podhoretz estimated that 90 percent of the mail was "enthusiastic, much of it wildly so." He continued by boasting:

> To put it plainly: in thirty years as a professional writer, I have never experienced anything like the response which has greeted this article, nor in twenty-five years as an editor have I seen anything remotely comparable happen to any other piece.

The letters were accompanied by dozens of phone calls. Most of these were from Jews. On this basis, he surmised that

> passions are running very high in the Jewish community, that there is rage—and outrage—at the monstrous unfairness with which Israel has been treated in the media, and that there is a healthy anxiety over the appearance, for the first time since World War II, of brazenly anti-Semitic ideas and attitudes in respectable circles of American opinion.

One of those who responded favorably, although it wasn't published, was President Reagan to whom Podhoretz had sent an advance copy. Reagan thanked Podhoretz and wrote,

> I read it with great interest and, while at times I thought Israel overreacted to P.L.O. forays in West Beirut, like you I was amazed at the one-sided reporting, particularly on television. No attempt was made to differentiate between civilian casualties and those that were P.L.O. fighters. Your article will do much to straighten the record.[30]

Buoyed by his success and the favorable reaction he received to "J'Accuse," Podhoretz continued and widened his attacks on Jewish critics of Israel. His assessments became even more militant in stance, as he felt "driven by conscience," as if on a holy mission, to attack his "fellows Jews who have been attacking Israel." He lumped together any critic of any aspect of Israeli policy in Lebanon, conflating their differences to produce absurd scenarios that grouped the ultra-Orthodox and militantly anti-Zionist Jewish sect *Neturei Karta* with Noam Chomsky. He dismissed them as disloyal "jackals"—a favored term in *Commentary*. He wrote of those Jews who "no longer had the stomach to defend Israel," of public figures who "never called attention to their Jewish origins [yet who were suddenly] willing to make the ultimate sacrifice of identifying themselves in public as Jews in order to lend greater credibility to their attacks on Israel," and of the academic and journalistic "conformity to prevailing opinion." He denounced the Jewish "failure of nerve," particularly when it came to Israel, of Jewish intellectuals. He compared Begin to Nixon, Sabra and Shatila to Watergate and attributed the mass protest against the Israeli government in connection with the massacres simply to the hatred of Begin and his administration. Not content with attacking the legitimacy of Diaspora dissent, Podhoretz had the chutzpah to lecture Israeli dissenters in their political manners, too. He appealed to the Israeli opposition to act with restraint, to refrain from criticizing the government in a way that would assist Israel's adversaries in their effort to "delegitimize" it. He wondered whether Israel, living as it does on so narrow a margin of security, could afford the luxury of an opposition that knew no self-restraint.[31]

Podhoretz repeatedly and approvingly invoked Emil Fackenheim's conception of a "614th Commandment," which mandated Jews to survive, thus thwarting Hitler's planned destruction of the Jews. He warned that Jews who criticized Israel were strengthening the hand of those who have risen up to destroy her and giving "posthumous victories to Hitler." Those who criticized Israel were violating this commandment of Auschwitz. Like Fackenheim, he found in this commandment and warning a mandate for unconditional Jewish support of the State of Israel, regardless of its policies. Podhoretz literally meant it when he wrote, "Jews whose observance of the 613 commandments is likely to be outweighed in the scale of Jewish history by their repudiation of the 614th . . . " He concluded that anti-Zionism had become "so naked and so brazen" that "the overriding order of businesses for any Jew who wants to observe the 614th commandment is to defend Israel against its ideological and political enemies."[32]

Podhoretz's reaction to anti-Zionism had reached a crescendo. The universality that his predecessor Elliot Cohen had worked so hard to achieve for the magazine was gone, as Podhoretz defined American and world Jewry solely in terms of its relationship to the State of Israel. Podhoretz had returned to everything he said he learned as a student at the Jewish

Theological Seminary in the 1950s: "parochialism," "apologetics and defensiveness," "the endless harping on the suffering of the Jews," a "narrow, constricted, provincial" outlook.[33]

In general, the 1980s saw increasing coverage of matters pertaining to Israel in the magazine. Podhoretz became one of Israel's fiercest defenders and among the hardest of hard-liners when it came to issues involving Israel's security. *Commentary* encouraged Washington to view the Arab-Israeli conflict through a Cold War lens, and to identify Palestinian nationalism as an extension of Soviet-induced international terrorism. In that context, Washington could thus view Israel's occupation of Palestinian lands with benevolent disregard. Indeed, *Commentary* saw the Israeli occupation as benign, comparing it with the US occupations of postwar Germany and Japan. It ignored Israel's iron fist approach toward the Palestinians and the consolidation of its hold on the West Bank and Gaza, just as it had earlier sought to whitewash the Israeli invasion of Lebanon. Its dogmatic defense of Israel precluded any consideration of the concept that Israel might also be capable of terror and atrocity. Increasingly, *Commentary*'s analysis began to resemble that of the Likud governments of Begin and Yitzhak Shamir. Both constantly invoked Holocaust imagery to justify the continued Israeli occupation. Both portrayed Jews as embattled people whose very existence would be threatened if Palestinians were given national self-determination. If it weren't for the language difference, it would have been virtually impossible to distinguish between them at times.

Tireless Fanaticism

The magazine was vigilant in exposing "the Left" wherever it detected it. *Commentary*'s tireless fanaticism to sniff out and erase traces of liberal and/or leftist thinking dominated even its movie reviews. Its film critic, Richard Grenier, wrote colorful and provocative reviews, railing against the politicization of American films by which he meant any expression of left-wing sentiment. He attacked what he called the "McGovernization" of Hollywood resulting in a "barrage of films from the Left." While *Gandhi* (1983) was being universally praised, Grenier ripped the film apart for its sanitized, sentimentalized hero who, by his account, was a lecher, racist, hypocrite, fool, and faddist, who wrote less about home rule than about "enemas, and excrement." His review, "The Gandhi Nobody Knows," pointed out the film's conspicuous omissions: Gandhi's cavorting with young girls, the way he could combine a greeting with blunt inquiries about bowel movements, his telling the European Jews that they should not bother resisting Hitler, and the Hindu practice of suttee, banned by the British, of tossing widows onto the funeral pyres of their dead husbands. The whole movie, Grenier asserted, was a pacifist tract, bankrolled by a nation that supported a nuclear freeze, while simultaneously developing nuclear weapons. Grenier also reduced *Another Country* (1984) to being simply "a rhapsody to the beauties of homosexuality." He sentenced the makers of these and similar "left-wing" films to two years in a "Marxist-Leninist country of their choice."[34]

Joseph Epstein complained bitterly against the decline of literary and academic standards. He railed against the "rot" at university literature departments. Radical politics, the compartmentalization of the academy into "feminist and black and other separate studies," and the rise of structuralism, semiotics, and deconstruction, he wrote, had led to a general lowering of standards. As the study of literature in America had become "professionalized" it had also become "parochial." Epstein also blamed the sad condition of artistic criticism and intellectual life in general in America to widespread education, particularly the rise of the middle classes into the higher reaches of education. Other voices joined him in protest. Joseph Adelson bewailed the decline of secondary schooling standards while the academy, in particular its fashion for French thought, was targeted. The academy's fetishization of Continental theory, "of marked-down ideological goods," attributable to the politicization of the campus during the Vietnam era, had destroyed Anglo-American literary criticism. Epstein decried the contemporary literary scene which was "rife with writers whose chief stock in the trade of ideas is a crude anti-Americanism." Robert Coover, Robert Stone, Joseph Heller, EL Doctorow, Ann Beattie, Jill Robinson, and John Updike "do not think well of their country" and are "angry, or soured, or depressed, or outraged, or filled with yearning."[35]

Neo-Puritan Traditionalism

During this time Podhoretz articulated a "traditionalist" approach to morality. It amounted to a stern, repressive Puritanism, which wished to turn back the forces of modernity. He espoused the values (shared by the Christian movement the Moral Majority) of sexual morality, strong family life, and opposition to pornography. Joseph Adelson's "What's Happened to the Schools" in March 1981 concisely presented the values and virtues of Podhoretz's neo-Puritan traditionalism: "merit, accomplishment, competition, and success; self-restraint, self-discipline, and the postponement of gratification; the stability of the family; and a belief in certain moral universals." Religion and tradition underlined these virtues which were portrayed as locked in a fateful struggle with the forces of darkness—the ideology of "modernism—a kind of nihilistic relativism encouraging self-gratification, sensuality, uninhibited self-expression, and topped off by a radical egalitarianism." This perspective was so important to Podhoretz that whenever moral issues were discussed in *Commentary* they were discussed in terms of the list of virtues and vices presented by Adelson.[36]

Podhoretz provided a platform for anyone with the right set of prejudices; he was not interested in exploring, debating, or reasoned exchange among fair-minded people on moral issues. *Commentary* thus reduced moral issues into absolutes and a simple binary opposition between self-restraint supported by tradition and religion on the one hand and self-indulgent nihilism on the other. It blandly oversimplified complex moral issues, resorting to distortion and generalization, presenting its opponents as heartless, insensitive, depersonalized individuals completely detached from reality, when this was probably truer of *Commentary* than of its critics. Podhoretz forsook intelligent investigation of moral issues through critical inquiry in favor of an ideology based on restrictive tradition and religion. Even some conservatives found it to be the "Achilles' heel" of the journal. Indeed, Podhoretz was so "intent" on fighting the perceived absolutism, holism, and extremism of the Left, that he became a victim of such tendencies in his own work and magazine.[37]

Commentary painted a picture of America sliding into moral relativity. In articles on religion, ethics, childbirth, feminists, sex education, education, and even movies, Podhoretz's editorial line boldly asserted itself. Violence and pornography on film and television, in magazines and books and the chic of sexual permissiveness were the cancer causing the "demoralization" that was destroying family values. *Commentary* thus applauded the series of "illiberal" decisions by the conservative-dominated Supreme Court, which had swung to the Right. It praised the Pawtucket, Rhode Island crèche case even though the AJC had joined in an *amicus* brief with the National Council of Churches to challenge it. Where the AJC felt the Burger Court had gone too far in matters of church and state, *Commentary* did not. Murray Friedman blasted Jewish organizations for their support for legal abortion and saw its sharp rise, as well as the growth of violence, the new sexual permissiveness, and family disruption as symptoms of a "breakdown of moral standards." Mary Tedeschi chimed in, unequivocally stating "the killing of unwanted babies is back in fashion."[38]

Podhoretz's opposition to cultural anti-Americanism magnified. He refused to distinguish between justifiable and unjustifiable criticisms of America, between criticism of American domestic inequalities and a hatred of all American institutions, equating criticism of American culture with hatred of America itself. In general, *Commentary* contended, in the words of Joseph Epstein, "that if you are against capitalism, you have also to be, in a spiritual sense, against America, the capitalist country par excellence." *Commentary* became even more affirming under Podhoretz than it had been under Cohen in the 1950s. As he admitted with the title of his latest volume of autobiography—*My Love Affair with America*—Podhoretz was besotted by America. Podhoretz may have felt that dissent was a right, but uncontrolled opposition was a "luxury." He warned that "Even a country as powerful as the United States can hardly afford the unrestrained exercise of this right in the face of an aggressively expansionist Soviet empire," since it "seriously hampers American efforts to resist Soviet expansionism and therefore ultimately endangers our own security."[39]

As *Commentary* sniffed out anti-Americanism in the general culture, Pearl K. Bell and Ruth Wisse looked for anti-Semitism in Jewish culture. Where once essayists like Maurice Samuel, Marie Syrkin, Arthur A. Cohen, and Milton Himmelfarb had offered creative interpretations of Judaism in the face of political and intellectual challenges of America, now *Commentary* became even more negative, attacking any manifestation of American Jewish culture it did not like. While there were articles of Jewish interest, its most "Jewish" column "In the Community" appeared only once during 1980 and, eventually, was quietly dropped thereafter. *Commentary* fulminated against middlebrow, bourgeoisified Jewish culture. Wisse damned *The Jewish Almanac* (1980) for reducing American Judaism to "a folk religion," representing a "soft leftism." She cited Joseph Heller's *Good as Gold* (1979) as a recent example of the Jewish reader's failure to protest certain coarse portrayals of Jews in fiction, which she attributed to the nervous twittering of "the educated and sophisticated Jews . . . about the sanctity of art." Bell considered it to be "deplorable," with its "odious Jewish characters as well as the ineptitude of his style and thought," while Roger Kaplan found it to be a "vicious display of antipathy." Surely, all three had in mind Heller's scathing and thinly-veiled portrait of Podhoretz in the book, even if none of them directly referred to it. It was Podhoretz's rather meek attempt to exact revenge for his former friend's attack on him.[40]

"A Farewell to Civil Rights"

Podhoretz's narrow self-interested arguments effectively killed the magazine's interest in civil rights for blacks, which had distinguished the magazine for its first fifteen years. It turned away from African Americans and looked more and more inward. Because most Jews had made it and no longer personally faced these problems Jews, it argued, should turn away from liberal social programs to eliminate poverty, homelessness, hunger, and unemployment, as well as schemes to improve the worst effects of capitalism: accelerating inequalities of wealth, growing levels of misery, crime, and social deprivation. Indeed, *Commentary* attacked those Jews who continued their involvement in the civil rights movement. It was also quick to point out black anti-Semitism, even though such voices represented a tiny proportion of the total black community, as a further means to attack civil rights for blacks. For example, by exaggerating black leader Jesse Jackson's personal power and influence among African Americans, it argued that his pro-Third World, anti-American, pro-PLO and anti-Israel attitudes were well on the way to becoming "the quasi-official foreign policy of the black community." This had the effect of undermining even more any neocon support for black civil rights. Podhoretz had thus declared "a farewell to Civil Rights."[41]

The magazine supported Reagan's reduction of programs for the poor, which disproportionately hit African Americans the hardest. Rejecting the liberal notion that the state was the "best friend" of blacks, it couched its ideology in the argument that the state was the enemy of black economic advancement and was actually getting in the way of their progress. Local, state, and federal laws had impeded the upward mobility of hardworking blacks, strangling those they were intended to help. Instead, *Commentary* placed its faith in reform generated through the free market rather than legislation imposing equal pay, or making dismissal of an employee costly. It aligned itself with anti-black racism in American society by adopting a "blame-the-victim" ideology. It used black anti-Semitism to justify its support for further cutbacks in taxes and welfare programs. Writing in *Commentary*, neocons like Kristol, Glazer, Podhoretz, Abrams, and Gershman, noted Herbert Hill, "had provided the ideological basis for the civil rights retreat" of the Reagan administration, one of "the most reactionary administrations on civil rights in the twentieth century."[42]

Commentary carried on attacking affirmative action programs. It continued to see affirmative action as an unmitigated evil, despite the fact that Jewish women had been some of its primary beneficiaries, and more relevant than the other pressing issues of the day. If such a pattern continued, warned *Commentary*, the result would be the racial, religious, and ethnic "Balkanization" of America. The magazine reported on a 1980 study of the implementation of affirmative-action admissions policies at Harvard, as its findings allegedly vindicated *Commentary*'s warnings over the years. Tension over admissions policies had produced racial polarization within the student body; the abilities of many black students were doubted leading to a negative experience compounded by insecurity and self-doubt which was particularly high among blacks; racial exclusiveness (black self-segregation) in dining halls and extracurricular organizations. Harvard had carried out affirmative action under optimum circumstances, during a period of calm, and with good resources, and yet it had led to problems. If it can't work at Harvard, the magazine asked, then how will less better off institutions fare? A sensationalist description of the history of discrimination (namely quotas) at Sarah Lawrence College by an ex-professor was published to provide the answer. But the article was "yellow journalism" at its worst, complained its readers: it blended historical fact with inference and innuendo; it was emotional, shallow, inaccurate, outrageously mean-spirited, vengeful, and prone to distortions, exaggerations, and caricatures. And its exposé of the Jewish quotas during the 1930s, 1940s, and 1950s was not news by 1983. Podhoretz published this piece because its author had an ax to grind: she had recently been denied tenure at the college. Sarah Lawrence was also well-known for its liberal policies and thus it provided an excellent opportunity to really "give it to those liberals."[43]

Commentary welcomed black intellectuals who agreed with its civil rights position into its pages. But unlike the Cohen era of the 1940s and 1950s, these writers took a position almost 180-degrees opposite. In his fight against affirmative action, and despite its pseudo-racist tones, Podhoretz eagerly published black intellectuals who advocated his anti-civil-rights establishment line despite the AJC's "mixed reactions" to them. In a steady stream of polemical essays for *Commentary*, black social critics like Thomas Short, Thomas Sowell, Shelby Steele, and Glenn Loury harshly critiqued what they perceived to be the dogmas of the civil rights movement: apologetics, special pleading, and public relations. Instead, they emphasized the internal pathologies of black culture rather than external elements of white attitudes in assessing the condition of the black community. They concluded that matters like family instability, social indiscipline, and educational un-preparedness accounted for the enduring economic plight of poor blacks. They stood against the attitude that white society was completely and exclusively to blame for the black condition and destiny, and was therefore responsible for mending the harm. They argued that no substantial progress could be made until the all-purpose explanatory device of victim status and the perception of unyielding white hostility among blacks were discarded. They called for blacks to abandon the "victim-focused black identity" that may have been necessary in the 1960s, but was a hindrance in the 1980s, preventing them from seizing the opportunities for individual effort and advancement. They ignored the positive results and the affirmative-action objectives based on individual rights. They lumped together all affirmative action policies, even comparing apartheid policies designed to reinforce racial hierarchy in South Africa with those affirmative-action programs designed to eliminate it elsewhere. They argued that whatever gains individual blacks made by taking advantage of racial preferences were far outweighed by the stigma attached to all blacks by affirmative-action, as quotas sent out the destructive message that minorities are losers who will never have anything unless someone gives it to them. They attacked black and minority studies on campus, as special pleading, ethnic celebration, and politicization, leading to a segregated and ghettoized intellectual community within the larger academic world. Their dissections were heavy on analysis but devoid of prescriptive solutions beyond a vague and commitment to the Protestant ideals of self-help, hard work, family values, education, individual initiative, thrift, industry, cleanliness, chastity, orderliness, individual responsibility, personal autonomy, the pursuit of opportunity, private voluntary associations, stable family life and property ownership.

Many blacks labeled these authors as "traitors" to their race and accused them of self-hatred for talking too much about the internal pathologies of the black community. But such criticism only transformed them into the darlings of the neocons. They became their black intellectual heroes, certified scholars whose urban origins often gave them a seemingly bona fide connection to the streets. Invitations to state dinners at the White House soon followed. In March 1987 Loury was chosen to be Deputy Secretary of Education by another member of the Commentariat, Secretary of Education William J. Bennett; he was poised to become the Reagan Administration's second-highest-ranking African American, an appointment he secured through his *Commentary* connections.

When *Commentary* turned against welfare and affirmative action there was a tangible feeling of betrayal among African Americans. The magazine's warnings of black anti-Semitism then became self-fulfilling as the words of black militant Louis Farrakhan and others became more attractive to blacks in the face of growing desperation. In 1984 Kristol wrote "the long alliance between Jewish and black organizations is coming apart . . . polarization between Blacks and Jews is the result." What he neglected to mention was that *Commentary* had played an instrumental part in distancing the two groups, inflicting almost permanent damage on black-Jewish relations. To many African Americans the nation's most prominent Jewish publication, the magazine of a prestigious Jewish organization, was now perceived to be the most important journal of resistance to black progress in America.[44]

Traditional Intellectuals

Podhoretz had established a dynastic empire close to the White House. His influence far exceeded the number of his readers of his magazine. He and his clan were at the height of their institutional power. They held positions extending from the publishing world into government. The connections and power of the neocons created an impressive network of alliances across the American academic, intellectual, and political worlds. Christopher Hitchens referred to it as "a modern medieval family." Indeed, many of the intellectuals in the neocons were tied to one another by kinship and family associations: husbands and wives, fathers and sons. Irving Louis Horowitz felt that there was "the aura of a family affair hanging about this collectivity . . . it harkens back to a shtetl mentality in which trust is vested only in the family and friends of the family . . ."[45]

Podhoretz himself was Chair of the USIA Advisory Committee, a member of the Boards of the CPD, Committee for the Free World (CFW)—established by Decter, who was its executive director, in February 1981 as a revived Congress for Cultural Freedom but without the covert government funding—, and of the Council of Foreign Relations.[46] One their sons-in-law, Steven Munson, served as director of the CFW, edited the influential neocon periodical the *Public Interest*, and worked as a press counselor for Kirkpatrick while she was UN ambassador. His wife, Decter's daughter Naomi, contributed to the CFW's journal *Contentions*. The other son-in-law, Elliot Abrams, held assistant secretary positions within the Reagan administration.

The Podhoretz family also controlled "vast financial and publishing resources." Six of its members were writers: Norman, Midge, Rachel, Naomi, Ruthie, and John. Podhoretz, it was said, could place any younger member of the neocons in any number of conservative journalistic positions. He was able to channel them into other neocon publications, especially *Public Opinion, This World,* and the *Wall Street Journal*, including the children of Ben Wattenberg (Danny) and Irving Kristol and Gertrude Himmelfarb (Liz). As a consequence, many bitter jokes about "min-cons" were heard at the *Washington Times, New York Post*, and other papers following parental attempts to gain them employment on their editorial staff. Podhoretz had helped Hilton Kramer and Samuel Lipman to launch the *New Criterion* in 1982, a journal that expressed *Commentary*'s cultural and political approach to aesthetics, art literature, music, and poetry and included many familiar neocons. Podhoretz had helped to establish his own neocon publishing and reviewing network which had become receptive to the establishment.

This influence of Podhoretz was no more evident than the celebration to mark the twenty-fifth anniversary of his editorship in 1985. Two hundred and fifty guests, including a roll call of some of the most influential and conservative names in America, packed into the splendid Rainbow Grill on the sixty-fifth floor of the Rockefeller Center, New York City, for a black-tie concert and dinner. Fittingly, the toastmaster was the "godfather" of neoconservatism, Irving Kristol, who opened the proceedings with a formal salute of praise from Ronald Reagan. Then, what one correspondent described as "a veritable Podhoretz love-in followed, as guest after guest praised what one called 'the Norman Conquests.'" Even the criticism was jovial. It was a revealing measure of the influence and material success Podhoretz had gained over the last quarter of a century.[47]

As editor of *Commentary*, Podhoretz had finally made it. Under his direction, the magazine had become a leading exponent of neoconservatism: a forceful anti-Communist foreign policy, a strong American defense, and the leading critic of liberal social programs and economic doctrines. The elections of Reagan in 1980 and 1984 had vindicated his view that liberalism had failed. Many of his ideas had been adopted in many Reagan Administration programs like early tax cuts and budget cuts, the drive to deregulate and limit social programs, and foreign policy views. The 1980s were indisputably a triumph for the neocons heralding the "ascendancy of conservatism" and the "transformation of the vocabulary and agenda of the American political economy." As James Nuechterlein put it, "if conservatism is not unambiguously victorious, liberalism has, for the moment and into the foreseeable future, quite definitively lost" because "*no one today calls for the return of the Great Society.*"[48]

Sidney Blumenthal described Podhoretz's neocon empire as the "counter-establishment," and Peter Steinfels described its members as "counterintellectuals." But Podhoretz and *Commentary* were no longer entitled to such a designation. They had joined the majority, the Reaganite conservative coalition, what George Nash called "a conservative ruling class." Nor could they claim the typical mantle of intellectuals. Rather than speaking the truth to power, as intellectuals strive to do, they had been seduced by it. In the words of a 1965 *Commentary* article by Henry Fairlie (a scathing attack on those liberal intellectuals who had been co-opted by the Johnson White House): their vanity, which was "so pathetically flattered by power," had led them into "prostitution." Clearly Podhoretz, who commissioned, edited and published the article, had not heeded Fairlie's advice that: "The intellectual cannot engage in current political discussion and hope, at the same time, to think deeply or precisely." In either supporting the hegemony or being co-opted by it, the neocons became what Antonio Gramsci defined as "traditional" intellectuals. They were the "dominant group's 'deputies,'" who "put themselves forward as autonomous and independent of the dominant social group," but nonetheless seemed to "represent a historical continuity uninterrupted by even the most complicated and radical changes." In fact, in the New York Intellectuals' eyes, they were not really intellectuals at all but "academics" or "high-level technicians" to use Podhoretz's own words.[49]

The clearest example of how power had changed Podhoretz was the reversal of his stance on the Vietnam War in 1982. Where Podhoretz once called for a "complete and immediate withdrawal," he now mirrored Reagan's view of the war as "a noble cause." His book, *Why We Were in Vietnam* (1982), was a defense of the war that strove to provide the intellectual groundwork for Reaganism. Podhoretz wanted to overturn the debate over Vietnam which, he felt, "had already been settled in favor of the moral and political position of the antiwar position." He now disregarded his once blunt resistance to the war and his reinterpretation of it relied almost entirely Guenter Lewy's hawkish interpretation. Podhoretz argued that subsequent events did not prove that the United States was wrong about international Communism. "To interpret Vietnam as 'The War Nobody Won' plays with perfect harmony into the pacifist attitudes that have become so widespread in the past few years." The war was neither a "mistake" nor a "crime." Podhoretz also gave space to others who questioned what he called "The Revised Standard Version" of the war. Several writers recanted their earlier participation in the antiwar movement, as well as their opposition to the war, the Thieu regime in South Vietnam, and their support for the National Liberation Front during the war itself. It was a revealing measure of the intellectual sacrifice Podhoretz had made in struggling for power.[50]

At the same time, the glare of fame and fortune blinded him to the reality that Reagan was no neocon and that Podhoretz's empire was constructed on shaky foundations. The quest for the holy grail of power and influence had produced problems. So enamored with the success of his strategy in the 1980s Podhoretz pushed *Commentary* into an ideological straitjacket in which he found it increasingly difficult to maneuver when events beyond his control occurred. The result was either silence or absurd reasoning that produced contorted outcomes.

Notes

1. Carl Gershman, "The Rise & Fall of the Foreign-Policy Establishment," *Commentary* 70:1 (July 1980), 13–24; Joseph W. Bishop, Jr., "Carter's Last Capitulation,"

Commentary 71:3 (March 1981), 32–5; Daniel Patrick Moynihan, "'Joining the Jackals': The U.S. at the UN 1977–1980," *Commentary* 72:2 (February 1981), 23–31.

2. David Brock, *Blinded by the Right: The Conscience of an Ex-Conservative* (New York: Three Rivers Press, 2002), 5.

3. Ibid., 123–4; Jacob Heilbrunn, *They Knew They Were Right* (London: Doubleday 2008), 154.

4. Brock, *Blinded by the Right*, 123–4; Lee Edwards, *The Conservative Revolution: The Movement that Remade America* (New York: The Free Press, 1999), 248–9.

5. Arnold Beichman, "Liberalism & the Jews: A Symposium," *Commentary* 69:1 (January 1980), 15–82.

6. Rick Perlstein, "He Discovered the Culture Wars, Then Reported Behind the Lines," *Columbia Journalism Review* 43:4 (November 2004/December 2004), 58; Sidney Blumenthal, *The Rise of the Counter-Establishment: From Conservative Ideology to Political Power* (New York: Times Books, 1986), 130, 142; Brock, *Blinded by the Right*, 114.

7. Norman Podhoretz, "The New American Majority," *Commentary* 71:1 (January 1981), 19–28.

8. Elliot Abrams, "Liberalism & the Jews," 17–18.

9. "Liberalism & the Jews," 15–82.

10. Midge Decter, *An Old Wife's Tale: My Seven Decades in Love and War* (New York: Regan Books, 2001) 150–1; Podhoretz, "The New American Majority," 19–28.

11. Peter Schrag, "Rewriting History," *Fresno Bee* (January 14, 1981) [internet version].

12. Murray Friedman, comments at "*Commentary*, the American Jewish Community and American Culture" Conference (The Graduate Center, CUNY, New York), March 10, 2003.

13. Podhoretz quoted in Alfred Kazin, "Saving my Soul at the Plaza," *New York Review of Books* 30:5 (March 31, 1983), 38–42; Seymour Maxwell Finger, "The Reagan-Kirkpatrick Policies and the United Nations," *Foreign Affairs* 62 (Winter 1983–1984), 445; Abrams, quoted in Blumenthal, *The Rise of the Counter-Establishment*, 161.

14. Norman Podhoretz, "The Future Danger," *Commentary* 71:4 (April 1981), 34.

15. Norman Podhoretz, "Appeasement By Any Other Name," *Commentary* 76:1 (July 1983), 38.

16. Letters, *Commentary* 70:3 (September 1980), 4–12; Letters, *Commentary* 76:3 (October 1983), 4–14.

17. Podhoretz, "The Future Danger," 34. Note the use of the term "the bloody crossroads" here which betrays Podhoretz's debt to Lionel Trilling from whom he had learned the phrase.

18. Mark Falcoff, "The Timerman Case," *Commentary* 72:2 (July 1981), 15–23.

19. Norman Podhoretz, *The Present Danger* (New York: Simon and Schuster, 1980), 100.

20. Norman Podhoretz, "Appeasement by Any Other Name," 33–8; Letters, *Commentary* 72:6 (December 1981), 14–23; "Human Rights and American Foreign Policy: A Symposium," *Commentary* 72:5 (November 1981), 25–63.

21. I. D. Robbins, "Jewish Community's Podhoretz Problem," *New York Daily News* (May 21, 1981), 66; Jean Herschaft, "Rumor Podhoretz in Trouble is False," *Jewish Post and Opinion* (July 3, 1981) [internet version].

22. Robbins, "Jewish Community's Podhoretz Problem," 66; Gary Dorrien, *The Neoconservative Mind: Politics, Culture and the War of Ideology* (Philadelphia: Temple University Press, 1993) 184.

23. Steven L. Spiegel, "The Middle East: A Consensus of Error," *Commentary* 73:3 (March 1982), 15–24 and "Israel as a Strategic Asset," *Commentary* 75:6 (June 1983), 51–5; Earl Raab, "Is the Jewish Community Split?" *Commentary* 74:5 (November 1982), 21–5.

24. Paul Johnson, "Marxism vs. the Jews," *Commentary* 77:4 (April 1984), 28–34; Lucy Dawidowicz, "Lies About the Holocaust," *Commentary* 70:6 (December 1980), 31–7 and "Indicting American Jews," *Commentary* 75:6 (June 1983), 36–44.

25. Norman Podhoretz, "American Jews and Israel: A Symposium," *Commentary* 85:2 (February 1988), 21–7.

26. Ibid.

27. Menahem Milson, "How to Make Pace with the Palestinians," *Commentary* 71:5 (May 1981), 25–35 and "How Not to Occupy the West Bank," *Commentary* 81:4 (April 1986), 15–22.

28. Norman Podhoretz, "J'Accuse," *Commentary* 74:3 (September 1982), 21–3; Letters, *Commentary* 74:6 (December 1982), 4–15, 68–80.

29. Vermont Royster to Podhoretz, January 10, 1982, NPLC; Letters, *Commentary* 74:6 (December 1982), 4–15, 68–80.

30. Norman Podhoretz, "What Is Anti-Semitism? An Open Letter to William F. Buckley, Jr.," *Commentary* 93:2 (February 1992), 15–20; Letters, *Commentary* 74:6 (December 1982), 4–15, 68–80; Podhoretz to Reagan, August 23, 1982; Reagan to Podhoretz, September 14, 1982, NPLC.

31. Norman Podhoretz, "The State of the Jews," *Commentary* 76:6 (December 1983), 37–45; Letters, *Commentary* 77:3 (March 1984), 2–17.

32. Podhoretz, "The State of the Jews," 37–45.

33. Norman Podhoretz, *Making It* (New York: Random House, 1967), 43, 44, 45.

34. Dennis Wrong, Letters, *Commentary* 76:2 (February 1983), 6; Joseph Farah, "Columnist Richard Grenier Dies," *WorldNetDaily.com* (January 31, 2002); Richard Grenier, "Bolshevism for the 80's," *Commentary* 73:3 (March 1982), 56–63; "The Gandhi Nobody Knows," *Commentary* 75:3 (March 1983), 59–72; "The Hard Left and the Soft," *Commentary* 77:1 (January 1984), 56–61; and "From Eton to Havana," 7 *Commentary* 8:3 (September 1984), 61–4.

35. Joseph Epstein, "Anti-Americanism & Other Clichés," *Commentary* 75:4 (April 1983), 60–3, "It's Only Culture," *Commentary* 76:5 (November 1983), 56–61; Joseph Adelson, "What's Happened to the Schools?" *Commentary* 71:3 (March 1981), 36–41.

36. Adelson, "What's Happened to the Schools," 36–41; Lee Nisbet, "A Commentary on Norman Podhoretz's Neo-Puritanism," *Free Inquiry* (Spring 1982), 37–9.

37. Nisbet, "A Commentary on Norman Podhoretz's Neo-Puritanism," 37–9.

38. Murray Friedman, "A New Direction for American Jews," *Commentary* 72:6 (December 1981), 37–44; Mary Tedeschi, "Infanticide & Its Apologists," *Commentary* 78:5 (November 1984), 31–5.

39. Joseph Epstein, "The Education of an Anti-Capitalist," *Commentary* 76:2 (August 1983), 51–9; Norman Podhoretz, "The State of World Jewry," *Commentary* 76:6 (December 1983), 37–45.

40. Ruth R. Wisse, "Judaism for the Mass Market," *Commentary* 71:1 (January 1981), 41–5 and "Reading About Jews," *Commentary* 69:3 (March 1980), 41–8; Pearl K. Bell, Letters, *Commentary* 70:2 (August 1980), 15; Fred Kaplan, "Heller's Last Gag," *Commentary* 79:2 (February 1985), 60.

41. Dawidowicz, "Indicting American Jews," *Commentary* 75:6 (June 1983), 36–44; James A. Nuechterlein, "A Farewell to Civil Rights," *Commentary* 84:2 (August 1987), 25–36.

42. Herbert Hill, "Black-Jewish Conflict in the Labor Context: Race, Jobs, and Institutional Power," in *African Americans and Jews in the Twentieth Century: Studies in Convergence and Conflict*, ed. V. P. Franklin, Nancy L. Grant, Harold M. Kletnick, and Genna Rae McNeil (Columbia and London: University of Missouri Press, 1998), 287.

43. Philip Perlmutter, "Balkanizing America," *Commentary* 70:3 (September 1980), 64–6; Peter Skerry, "Race Relations at Harvard," *Commentary* 71:1 (January 1981), 62–4; Louise Blecher Rose, "The Secret Life of Sarah Lawrence," *Commentary* 75:5 (May 1983), 52–6; Letters, *Commentary* 76:2 (August 1983), 4–17.

44. Irving Kristol, "The Political Dilemma of American Jews," *Commentary* 78:1 (July 1984), 23–9.

45. Christopher Hitchens, "A Modern Medieval Family," *Mother Jones* (July–August 1986), 52–6, 74–6; Irving Louis Horowitz, *American Jewish Visions and Israeli Dilemmas: A Commentary on Fifty Commentaries in Commentary* (Middle East Studies Institute, Graduate School of International Studies, University of Miami 1988), 12.

46. Incidentally, in an attempt to forge alliances with the neocons, President Ford's former Secretary of Defense, Donald Rumsfeld, joined the CFW.

47. Elizabeth Mehren, "*Commentary*: High Honors for Editor 25 Years Later," *LA Times* (January 31, 1985), 1.

48. James A. Nuechterlein, "The American 80's: Disaster or Triumph?: A Symposium," *Commentary* 90:3 (September 1990), 40.

49. Peter Steinfels, *The Neoconservatives* (New York: Simon & Schuster, 1979), 189; Blumenthal, *The Rise of the Counter-Establishment*; Henry Fairlie, "Johnson & the Intellectuals: A British View," *Commentary* 40:4 (October 1965), 49–55; see also Letters, *Commentary* 41:1 (January 1966), 4–11; Antonio Gramsci, *Selections from the Prison Notebooks*, ed. and trans. Quentin Hoare and Geoffrey Nowell Smith (London: Lawrence and Wishart, 1971), 6, 7, 12; Podhoretz, *Making It*, 312.

50. Normal Podhoretz, *Why We Were in Vietnam* (New York: Simon & Schuster, 1982), 210, 14, and "Vietnam: The Revised Standard Version," *Commentary* 77:4 (April 1984), 35–41.

6

Decline

Podhoretz's empire shined brightly but it shone briefly. His period of greatest success, influence, and achievement—during Reagan's first administration—was drawing to a close. The 1980s may have been good years for Podhoretz but they also unleashed a series of spectacular blows against him, the neocons, and his magazine such that the foundations of his empire began to crumble. Neoconservatism was falling into growing disarray. It had spent so long in a counter intellectual position railing against the enemy that it was—ironically—uncomfortable with success, with "making it."

Betrayal

Podhoretz never personally got as close to the administration as he would have liked. Years later, in his book *Ex-Friends*, he admitted his influence was "mostly exaggerated." He gestured toward securing the appointment as head of the USIA, but was disappointed when it went to Reagan's old friend Charles Z. Wick, being rewarded only with a red and white band wrapped around copies of his *The Present Danger* on which was printed a directive from the President, "I urge all Americans to read this critically important book." It was only when Midge Decter pulled some strings—she had become a trustee of the Heritage Foundation, whose President, Edwin Feulner, was also chairman of the USIA advisory board—that Podhoretz was appointed to an official position on it.[1]

And Kirkpatrick's departure as UN ambassador signaled a major weakening of Podhoretz's authority inside the White House, as her removal deprived him of his highest level and most influential voice in the administration. When she was fired, Podhoretz announced that "no Jew and no American friend of Israel can feel easy about the Reagan administration."

Although Podhoretz's son-in-law, Elliot Abrams, was still in office, he was no longer a prominent figure. The fight over high-profile neoconservative appointments to the Reagan administration also highlighted the limitations of Podhoretz's power: *Commentary* contributor Carol Iannone was rejected for a position on the National Humanities Council and the failure of the nomination of neocon favorite Robert H. Bork to the Supreme Court was a particularly devastating blow.[2]

The neocons also began to wonder about Reagan's commitment to his own tough rhetoric. "Was Reagan pure enough?" they asked. As early as April 1981, barely three months after Reagan's inauguration, Irving Kristol set the trend by publicly worrying about Reagan's "muddle[d]" foreign policies. In January 1982, Walter Laqueur joined in: at the end of Reagan's first year, he concluded that it had been an *"annus mirabilis."* Evidence for this conclusion, he said, lay all around, in the Middle East and Asia, in Latin America and Africa, but perhaps nowhere as saliently as in the main arena of international affairs, US-Soviet relations, where Laqueur deplored Reagan for his failures in understanding the importance of the political and ideological dimensions of the strategy of containment; in particular, Reagan had inexplicably failed to put Moscow on the ideological defensive over Poland. He complained that just as the Soviets were stressing the primacy of foreign policy, the Reagan administration had opted for the primacy of domestic policy. Max Singer evaluated Reagan's record in Latin America, concluding major opportunities had been missed while important mistakes and failures made. Podhoretz echoed these criticisms, scolding the Reagan administration for its departure from the magazine's recommended course, believing that Reagan had taken "no clearly visible steps to deal with the future danger." Time was running out, warned *Commentary*, as it called for action.[3]

Commentary was particularly stung by Reagan's policies in the Middle East. It called them "a consensus of error" and condemned Reagan for retreating to Carter's policies, brushing the Reagan administration with its worst possible epithets: "Carterism" and "appeasement." It called Reagan's policy in Lebanon an utter failure. But the magazine's pleas fell on increasingly deaf ears. Its appeals to view the Arab-Israeli conflict through a Cold War lens, to identify Palestinian nationalism as an extension of Soviet-induced international terrorism, to place the Palestinian issue on the back burner, to reduce US involvement in schemes intended to produce a solution of the Palestinian problem, and to reject the strategy of "territory-for-peace" in favor of another approach, were all ignored. Furthermore, where the magazine pressed Reagan to treat Israel as a strategic ally and asset (as he had proposed to do during his campaign for presidency) by increasing military and economic assistance and initiating a program of security assistance, as well as the provision of long-term defense contracts for the Israeli defense industry, Reagan seemed to be continuing a policy that many felt had been rejected when he became president. Where the magazine warned that the Arabs were unreliable allies, Reagan allowed his Secretary of State Caspar Weinberger to press for closer relations with pro-American Arab regimes on the theory that this would lead to a more defensible Western position in the Middle East. "King Lear destroyed his life, his family, and his kingdom because he could not judge between friend and foe," warned Steven L. Spiegel. Where the neocons called for a reduction in arms sales to Arab countries, the sale of AWACS jets to Saudi Arabia was upheld by the Senate in October 1981. The arms sales, in particular, were very unpopular: they had raised, wrote Murray Friedman, "the question of the relationship of the Jewish community to American conservatism." "The moral for the US is obvious," Friedman concluded, "The truth is that on Israel, the Jewish community has been badly served by both conservatives and liberals."[4]

In May 1982 Podhoretz capped the complaints with a stinging attack. In spite of his personal proximity to the Reagan administration, Podhoretz had become increasingly disenchanted with Reaganism. Reagan's multiple deviations showed the painful limits of Podhoretz's influence and he did not like it. They also demonstrated that Reagan was not, contrary to Podhoretz's hopes, a neocon. In "The Neoconservative Anguish over Reagan's Foreign Policy," published in the *New York Times Magazine*, Podhoretz complained that Reagan spent more time talking about rolling back Communism than actually doing it and questioned whether Reagan was in fact hard-line enough for him. In a meeting with Secretary of State George P. Shultz in that same year Podhoretz protested that Reagan's policies were not tough enough. Podhoretz felt that the defeat of Communism was not the main and ultimate goal of US foreign policy. Instead, Reagan was a cautious pragmatist who wouldn't risk doing anything unpopular nor in the face of serious opposition. Podhoretz believed that Reagan, like Carter before him, was too lenient towards the Soviet Union, allowing himself to be tempted by détente and trade with Moscow rather than, as he should be, advancing a worldwide campaign against Communism. Even the victory in Grenada in 1983 when US forces deposed a Cuban-backed Marxist regime failed to satisfy Podhoretz. While it may have been a significant blow against Soviet expansionism in the western hemisphere, it was no substitute for direct military action against the Soviet Union and her allies. The supposedly "tough" Reagan administration had conducted a ridiculously weak and inept Lebanon policy in 1982–83 to the great detriment of both America and Israel. In fact, Reagan had changed his strategic position toward the Middle East as presented during his election campaign.[5]

Podhoretz now had "a renewed and very vivid sense of how great are the obstacles that stand in the way of a foreign policy equal to the challenge of Soviet expansionism." He bewailed in mid-1984 that, although Reagan had promised to regenerate the "old conservative dream of going beyond the containment of Communism to the 'rollback' of Communist influence and power and the 'liberation' of the Soviet Empire," in truth "Mr. Reagan as President has never shown the slightest inclination to pursue such an ambitious strategy." Indeed, he accused Reagan of "following a strategy of helping the Soviet Union stabilize its empire, rather than a strategy aimed at encouraging the breakup of that empire from within." In Podhoretz's view, anything less than total victory against Communism was as good as admitting defeat; even those who hinted at the slightest opposition to or even voiced inadequate support for Podhoretz's hard-line stance was an intolerable threat. He turned against Reagan for not committing wholeheartedly to such a strategy, attacking him for what he perceived to be inexcusable compromises. According to John Ehrman, "Podhoretz wrote with the anger of one whose highest hopes had been betrayed." He had truly believed that in Reagan he had found a "champion" who could reverse America's decline. Reagan failed him on this count. Mark Shechner noted that a "crisis mentality" had begun to prevail "in the bunkers of *Commentary*." Things were not going Podhoretz's way: Reaganism had not turned out according to plan. Reagan was neither as tough nor as neoconservative as Podhoretz had initially believed or deceived himself into believing. And to make it worse there was no potential successor in sight to turn things around.[6]

Despair

Reflecting Podhoretz's growing sense of despair, an oversized symposium to mark *Commentary*'s fortieth anniversary special issue in 1985 cast a somber tone. The symposium appraised the record of American behavior since 1945, focusing in particular on the three major issues raised by Elliot Cohen's very first editorial 40 years ago in November 1945: the problems arising from vastly increased productivity and prosperity at home; the ultimate challenge posed by nuclear weapons; and the equally dangerous threat of totalitarianism on the world scene. The 29 leading conservative, neoconservative, and center-left critics and thinkers who contributed were almost unanimous in pointing to the naïve optimism and innocence of Cohen's vision of the postwar world in 1945, as well as to the undoubted social and economic progress America had made since Second World War. The America of 1985, they said, had shaken off the racial and religious bigotry of 1945 and had become a marvel of industrial capitalism. But this emphatic celebration of the success story since 1945 and hymn to contemporary America belied regret about the continued power and oppressive policies of the Soviet Union. "The mood of expectation and hope in which Cohen wrote his prospectus of world concern in 1945," wrote Sidney Hook, had been "replaced by one of disappointment and despair."[7]

As a mark of Podhoretz's growing anguish in the mid- to late 1980s, his attacks on domestic enemies became more hysterical in tone. His return in the mid-1980s to his origins as a literary critic revealed the extent to which his thinking, even his critical vocation, had become consumed by his ideological preoccupation with anti-Communism and the Left. His writing had come to exemplify what Lionel Trilling had once warned against: the lack of political imagination. His reviews (for example, "The Terrible Question of Aleksandr Solzhenitsyn" (February 1985) and "An Open Letter to Milan Kundera" (October 1984)) tended to consider the anti-Communist qualifications of modern novelists, often judging their work in a reductive fashion by analyzing where they stood politically in relation to the Soviet Union. His criticism also addressed the self-imposed task of "speaking as an American in defense of America . . . through the running critique in *Commentary* of the assumptions of the anti-American position in domestic affairs." "Henceforth novelists are not to be judged on any but political standards," commented Thomas Fleming, "and those standards are set by *Commentary*." Fleming concluded that Podhoretz had become the "Mrs. Grundy of the American right."[8]

Podhoretz ran ideologically strident warnings about the ongoing danger of the New Left and anti-Americanism. Typical of this approach were David Horowitz and Peter Collier, two well-known former 1960s leftists who had both come out as Reagan Republicans in a highly controversial *Washington Post* article called "Lefties for Reagan." They typified the "us against them" mentality which *Commentary* had come to exemplify. Liberalism in America was still the target of the magazine's rancor and, as former radicals, Horowitz and Collier were particularly unforgiving in casting their anathemas upon liberals. As Dwight Macdonald had put it in 1956 in reference to *National Review* but which was now just as apt for *Commentary*: "There are so many enemies; the liberal conspiracy is omnipresent." The Commentariat went into battle as if in a civil war, hinting that those who differed were really serving the enemy. Legitimate policy disagreements came to resemble a quasi-religious war, as their attacks on liberals, drugs, pornography, homosexual activism, street crime, decaying educational standards, social erosion, and a growing divorce rate became more strident. Ultimately such pieces harmed the magazine, for one thing distracting it from the budget and trade deficits, the unemployment, bank failures, farm foreclosures, poverty, federal debts, trade and budget deficits, and business bankruptcies which had risen to levels unseen since the Great Depression under Reagan.[9]

Commentary detected anti-Americanism everywhere. It was evident in the politicization of scholarship so Podhoretz published ill-tempered attacks on "Left-inspired literary criticism" (namely structuralism and deconstruction) and "feminist criticism" as adopted by "Literary radicals" to "further the cause of the revolution." Articles, full of contempt for literary and women's studies illustrated what he saw as a problem currently endemic within American higher education: the deformation of traditional canons of teaching and scholarship to suit the purposes of radical activism. Podhoretz feared that, as those students who were absorbed into the political culture of the Left during the 1960s were now coming of age and gaining a considerable hand in the governance of university departments, programs, and institutions, their New Left and countercultural views were decisively shaping the ideological climate on most campuses. With no sense of irony, he was afraid of their allegedly dogmatic adherence to a preconceived set of assumptions. The Campus was characterized as "an island of repression in a sea of freedom."[10]

So-called political correctness (PC) was the main target of attack against Leftist influence in and domination of the university. Yet, in its anti-PC tirades, *Commentary* often resorted to the same excessive rhetoric as it criticized the Left for using. Walter Goodman's criticism of the New Left in *Commentary* in 1970 could equally have been used to criticize *Commentary*'s anti-PC arguments:

> It is a stimulating conceit to think of oneself as holding the line against oppression—"Can we stop 1984." ... The favored tactic ... is to lump events together for maximum impact, leaving to others the work of sorting them out, of going over each change to determine whether indeed there is a pattern of concerted repression here that warrants comparison with Germany in the 1930's.[11]

"Neanderthal[s] in Drag"[12]

The regular rumbling of homophobia in *Commentary* over the last decade developed into a full-blown and steady drumbeat as Podhoretz lashed out. Podhoretz published articles long on subtly propounded homophobia and short on objective and scientific data, in defense of discrimination against and intolerance of homosexuals. *Commentary* supported laws and social attitudes that championed heterosexuality and tainted gay people as socially less valuable. David Robinson deplored and feared the "rising openness and assertiveness among homosexuals and groups representing them, accompanied by attempts to gain and use political power." Decter implied that a Queens, New York elementary school curriculum that taught tolerance of gays, would encourage recruitment of schoolchildren into homosexuality. Other writers didn't think that homosexuals should be adoptive parents or leaders of Boy Scouts.[13]

Commentary writers continued to routinely write about homosexuals in a way that if anyone else did about Jews, it would be up in arms. Podhoretz led the way. In his syndicated newspaper column, Podhoretz callously described AIDS, as "almost entirely a disease caught by men who bugger or are buggered by dozens or even hundreds of other men every year." Questioning the value of a vaccine for AIDS, he wrote that it would permit homosexuals "to resume buggering each other by the hundreds with complete medical impunity." When publicly challenged on this statement by prominent lawyer Alan Dershowitz, Podhoretz responded angrily, "The sentence that Alan Dershowitz quoted from my column on AIDS, which he ridiculed by his tone, was factually correct, and I defy him or anyone else to challenge the truth of that statement." It revealed the strength of Podhoretz's anger, despair, and confusion as he lashed out at his perceived enemies everywhere.[14]

Following Podhoretz's lead, *Commentary* seized upon the AIDS epidemic to promote a return to Puritanism and to assert its high moral fervor. It argued that homosexual promiscuity was fundamental to the AIDS epidemic, urging chastity or monogamy as a means of avoiding the disease. Lawyer Michael A. Fumento—who had written in the *New Republic*, "If AIDS is the plague of the 1980s, then homosexuals are the rats who are the carriers"—wrote numerous articles for *Commentary*. He argued that AIDS was simply a "gay" plague caused by anal sex and needle-sharing. Even though AIDS rates were rising at an alarming rate among the poor and blacks, particularly in Africa, he tried very hard to convince his readers that the heterosexual spread of AIDS was nothing to be worried about and that there was no crisis or epidemic in Africa. Because of who it affected and didn't affect, Fumento did not see AIDS as a sufficiently grave problem in America. His message implied that 200,000 cases of a fatal, sexually-transmitted, incurable viral disease was not an epidemic worthy of attention because the majority of cases occurred in marginalized individuals and not among the white, middle-class, heterosexual population. Indeed, what he called "the AIDS establishment" in America was exaggerating the heterosexual risk in order to spend too much federal funding on AIDS: every dollar spent, every commercial made, every health warning released were "a waste of funds and energy." Cancer and heart disease, he wrote, were far more deadly but, unlike those diseases he suggested that AIDS can be prevented by modified behavior. The editor of *Outweek* vilified Fumento as a "baboon," and a "racist homophobe." A reader of *Bottom Line* was shocked to read *Commentary* described as "the world's leading intellectual publication": "'Among the world's leading neo-fascist publications' would be more like it."[15]

Commentary did not attack the evil of AIDS itself but rather the behavior associated with its transmission. It was not really concerned with homosexuals' welfare so much as stigmatizing them for their "insidious sexual practices." The magazine's central point was that sexually-transmitted AIDS remained primarily a disease of the homosexual community and was chiefly a result of a few particular practices preferred by them. Consequently, its readers were treated to detailed lurid and fascinated accounts of sodomy, copraphilia, analingus, fist fucking, and sadomasochism. There was no suggestion that such things could be practiced safely. Simply, it desired their prohibition. It defended the Supreme Court's 1986 decision to uphold the sodomy laws, suggesting that the court was only trying to protect homosexuals from the fatal consequences of their own, volitional acts. Its desire to see what it considered to be high-risk homosexual activity restricted betrayed an underlying, unstated paternalism. To paraphrase the question asked by one reader: What was "a nice Jewish magazine like *Commentary*" doing publishing homophobic articles like that? The answer was, noted another reader, a clear effort "to impose Old Testament morality on spurious grounds of public health."[16]

The neocons also attacked prominent homosexual writers, both dead and alive. Gertrude Himmelfarb indicted the Bloomsbury Group on the basis of its "queer," "compulsive," "near-incestuous," and "polymorphously promiscuous" homosexuality, bisexuality, and androgyny. E.M. Forster may have been "the novelist *par excellence* of modern liberalism," wrote Joseph Epstein, but his "towering" homosexuality, which was "so central," so "significant," and so "dominant" to his life and work, had rendered his novels "obsolete," as simply "paeans" to such behavior. In *Commentary* and elsewhere, Decter and Podhoretz lambasted the writer Gore Vidal for what they saw as his interlinked political (left wing) and sexual (gay) deviancy. They had both identified Vidal as a chief purveyor of America's moral corruption and ridiculed his ideas about "the American empire."[17]

In doing so, *Commentary* made antigay bigotry publicly respectable beyond the conservative fever swamps because seemingly urbane and sophisticated intellectuals articulated it. But it highlighted the extent of Podhoretz's complexity. For two decades the magazine had railed against gay lib, homosexuality, anal sex, and all manner of related issues. It also targeted individual homosexuals, if they were on the Left. Yet, Podhoretz tolerated homosexual contributors where they furthered his political agenda. He was happy to publish gay writers like David Brock and Bayard Rustin as long as they pushed his right-wing neocon agenda, even though behind their backs Podhoretz's friends and family took great delight in ridiculing homosexuals. It seems that a blind eye was turned to their homosexuality so long as they were useful, but once they had outlived their usefulness the magazine turned upon them. A chastened Brock called it "the bigoted politics and rank hypocrisy of the conservatives."[18]

It was clear that pessimism had replaced optimism among the neocons. Mirroring Podhoretz's feelings, *Commentary*'s tone had become irritated and embattled. It had become a neoconservative pro-authoritarian political magazine. Its positions were dull and repetitive. It chanted the tired litany of familiar topics. In 1956, Dwight Macdonald had reviewed the new conservative magazine, *National Review*, for *Commentary*. In a scathing appraisal he wrote: "Journalistically, the *National Review* actually manages to be duller than the liberal weeklies. It is even more predictable, much more long-winded, and a good deal less competent . . . it is a remarkably amateurish job." A trait of its amateur journalism was the devotion of too "much space in the violent expression of one's opinions and very little in backing them up, or even defining them." Macdonald isolated its four main qualities as "opacity," "brutality," "banality," and "vulgarity," before noting its "mood of helpless isolation." Some thirty years later, precisely the same could be said for *Commentary*, once *National Review*'s opponent, but now its stable partner. (Ironically, Podhoretz had even supplied the title to Macdonald's attack—"Scrambled Eggheads on the Right"). In response, the AJC removed the sentence "Its pages will be hospitable to diverse points of view and beliefs, and it hopes to encourage original creative endeavor in the various fields of culture"—from its "Statement of Aims," which had appeared unchanged in every issue of the magazine since it began in 1945, because the magazine was no longer very diverse and had become a "Johnny one-note." The AJC felt that it would be more accurate if the sentence, which had been in place for 35 years, was deleted.[19]

Ideologue of Zionism

Like in almost every other field, when it came to the subject of Israel Podhoretz ran out of ideas. He was content merely to repeat the Israeli government line. It was no coincidence that his key writer on the Middle

East, David Bar-Ilan, was also a speechwriter for Israeli PM Yitzhak Shamir (he was also editor of the right-wing English-language Israeli daily, the *Jerusalem Post*, for which Podhoretz's daughter, Ruthie Blum, was a regular columnist) and that the then Israeli ambassador (and future Likud PM of Israel), Benjamin Netanyahu, was a fan. Podhoretz lacked political imagination. Typical of his approach was *Commentary*'s complete failure to offer any alternative, constructive or otherwise, to the Israeli occupation of the West Bank and Gaza. Since he felt that Israel could not withdraw successfully from the occupied territories because it was faced with two unpalatable alternatives—annexing the occupied territories or handing them over to the PLO, which was "infinitely more dangerous" and constituted a "mortal threat"—Israel should wait and see what the *intifada*, which had broken out toward the end of 1987, brought next.[20]

In place of formulating concrete policies, all Podhoretz could do was to retreat into a shell, reactively smashing down any ideas counter to his own. He sought to disrupt Palestinian-Israeli dialogue (casting Palestinian moderates like Edward Said as inveterate "ideologues of terrorism" and "professors of terror"). Indeed, *Commentary* denied the very legitimacy of Palestinian claims. A people had been created where there was none, an issue where there was none, a claim where there was none. And now the PLO was seeking to create a state where there already was one. It argued that the Palestinians already had a state in Jordan. Besides, since most Arab leaders used the Palestinians as a screen behind which to pursue their real aims, their rights were less important than appeared. The designs of Arab leaders meant prolonging the conflict for as long as possible. If they and the PLO were to succeed the consequences for Israel, wrote Kirkpatrick, "would be nothing short of catastrophic."[21]

In a morbid nightmarish fantasy, Podhoretz escalated such fears. He looked back at the present from the future, to "predict" the destruction of Israel if a Palestinian state were established on the West Bank and Gaza. The *intifada* was simply "the opening of a third phase in the Arab war against Israel," he wrote, in which young Palestinians armed with stones and Molotov cocktails and sent into the streets against the Israeli Army had replaced the Arab armies and trained terrorists. But he laid some of the blame for his projected annihilation of Israel with Jews themselves. "Looking back at the period between the outbreak of the *intifada* and the birth of the PLO state, many of us have become convinced that dissension among the Jews also played a central part in the destruction of Israel." He wrote of the "burden of shame and self-disgust that is undermining our will to go on as Jews and that is dragging the glorious history of our ancient people to an ignominious end." He lamented the time when most American Jews were once "simply and unconditionally for Israel." Instead, he sought a "unified Jewish front of moral and ideological defense of Israel, and a co-relatively unified front of resistance to the establishment of a PLO state." To do so, he produced a forbidding unreality:

> Looking backward from this grim point in the 21st century, we Jews—the dwindling remnant of a critically wounded people—are still tormented by the memory of the things we did and things we failed to do in the accursed days when Israel was finally lost. After Hitler, we had vowed over and over again that we would never again stand by in helpless passivity and watch a community of our fellow Jews being destroyed for the crime of being Jew. And yet this time it was worse, much worse. This time we were not merely passive. This time we helped the destruction along.

In invoking the analogy of the Holocaust and the "sight of the blood of complicity on our own Jewish hands," Podhoretz contended for public opinion here not by means of reason but by intemperate invective and misrepresentation. It showed how far he had stopped thinking analytically and logically.[22]

It also demonstrated that Podhoretz was never that informed about the internal reality of Israel, except what he learned from his daughter Ruthie who lived there. Indeed, he never really even liked the country. But Podhoretz covered his obstinate refusal to offer solutions with a blanket and facile prescription.

> As I have repeatedly written during the past few years, I believe that any Jew who wants to participate in that debate [on a solution to Israel's security issues] should get on a plane to Tel Aviv and claim Israeli citizenship under the Law of Return; otherwise, by refusing to put his own life on the line, he forfeits the moral standing to advocate a course that could endanger the lives of his fellow Jews in Israel.

Yet, this did not stop him from dismissing the assertion of 1,700 of the highest-ranking Israeli reserve officers, members of the Council on Peace and Security, that giving back the West Bank would not put Israel in fatal danger.[23]

This ideological prescription also meant that Podhoretz had pushed himself and *Commentary* into such an ideological corner that when events confronted him that did not fit he was at a loss to reply. When Jonathan Jay Pollard, a junior civilian intelligence analyst for the Navy was arrested on

November 21, 1985 on charges of spying for Israel, *Commentary* maintained an awkward and embarrassed silence. The news was a shock to Americans and particularly Jews who were astonished that Israel would compromise its relations with America by such actions. Their distress turned to dismay when they realized that Israel had breached an old rule of using a host nation's Jewish community for espionage. The Pollard case presented *Commentary* with some difficulties: it could not be seen to be supporting Israel here, as that would compromise the loyalty of American Jewry and it would be seen to be condoning espionage, but then it would not openly attack Israel either given its stance that such criticism damaged Israel. Podhoretz had to obey his own law and not criticize the Israeli government. So *Commentary* kept quiet for four years on the Pollard case, no doubt because to do so would assist Israel's enemies. Instead it waited until it had blown over. Indicative of *Commentary*'s approach was Eric M. Breindel's "Do Spies Matter?" which, despite its title, failed to mention Pollard in any of its six pages, focusing simply on those who spied for the Soviet Union. In March 1987, Pollard and his wife were sentenced to life imprisonment and five years in jail respectively. When *Commentary* finally commented, it felt Pollard had received peculiarly harsh treatment, incidentally a position it never adopted with the Rosenbergs who had also spied for an ally. At the same time, it contradicted its own long-standing practice of not publicly criticizing the Israeli government, by calling the Pollard case "an act of appalling stupidly." However, it tempered this criticism by saying that both the Israeli and the US governments had acted unwisely.[24]

A False Prophet of Particularism

Podhoretz's despair was manifested as he attacked his coreligionists. In his courting of Reagan, Podhoretz had alienated *Commentary*'s core constituency: American Jews. He was also perturbed by the overwhelmingly Democratic Jewish vote in the 1984 Presidential election. He was infuriated that the Jewish vote for Reagan had declined from 37 percent four years earlier to 30 percent while the rest of the country's support for him increased. The continuing divergence between Jewish voting patterns and those of other white voters embarrassed him. Although he liked to adopt a counterposition as a minority within the intellectual community, frequently resorting to a "populist" tone, as defenders of the common man's values against those of the intellectuals, he had trouble facing the fact that within the Jewish community he was trying to convince, he was the "unpopular" intellectual minority.

So *Commentary* blasted American Jews for failing to grasp new realities and for clinging to outmoded thinking which was no more than "a rehash of the old and now largely discredited liberal agenda." It was annoyed that Jews were "still on the liberal side of the political terrain." Kristol accused American Jews of being "enmeshed in the liberal time warp" and "desperately evading the most obvious of political realities." The world was changing but Jews "stubbornly" stuck their heads in the sand, he wrote, clinging to "anachronistic presuppositions," and "ideological obstinacy" that "beclouded" their thinking. The liberal consensus and the liberal coalition, he raged, were "disintegrating." Liberalism had "remorselessly distanced itself" from the Jews and for "the first time in living memory." Liberalism was synonymous with "evil," as well as a mortal danger to American Jews and Israel.[25]

Jews, the neocons wrote in exasperation, had alienated themselves as a political group from their rightful place in the American consensus. Jewish liberals were guilty of an arrogant elitism, due to the "powerful residual hold" of a "universalist mind-set" that led them to fail to understand their own social and political interests. Since Jewish voting patterns were motivated by a "misguided and ossified universalism," *Commentary* advocated a rejection of this universalism and an adoption of the particularist concept of "Is it good for the Jews?" "They need, in short, to live in this world, not in the world of the politically utopian or the religiously messianic." Milton Himmelfarb wrote of "Jewish dumb smartness" and "the self-righteous hypocrisy of denouncing Reagan voters for pursuing selfish interest." He exclaimed that American Jews must "stop indulging in the luxury of self-delusion" and abandon "old, cozy beliefs and behaviors."[26]

This required breaking the "stubborn" and "obsolete" attachment of Jews to liberalism. *Commentary* sought to discount the idea that liberalism expressed traditional Jewish and biblical values and that it represented the best alternative for representing Jewish interests. A series of articles by Kristol, Glazer, Himmelfarb, and others reiterated this theme. *Commentary* had been telling its readers for some time now that Jewish organizations which continued their allegiance to traditional liberalism not only failed to understand where the Jewish interest lies, but also were out of touch with the majority of American Jews. Jews needed to relinquish their ethical universalism and recognize that they needed to form a specific voting population with specific concerns. Jews must jettison their largely sentimental attachments to racial "goals" and recognize that quotas harm Jewish interests. Kristol ascribed the political position of American Jewish liberals to "cognitive dissonance." He urged Jews to vote with their economic status: that of "white Anglo-Saxon Episcopalians," not like "low-income Hispanics."

He believed American Jews to be knee-jerk liberals, caught in a time warp of Continental "radicalism" that got entangled with prophetic Judaism to produce a "peculiarly intense, Jews, secular humanism" which, rather than being a natural extension of the Jewish moral-religious tradition, was a perversion of it. Podhoretz added:

> Not only is the left bad for the Jews, I believe the left is bad for social justice, for moral values, for the security of Western civilization, for the future of democratic institutions in this country, and on the face of the earth. I now consider it as a community dedicated to bad and immoral values ... Strictly speaking as a Jew, now, I would say that it is virtually suicidal for Jews to go on pretending to themselves that their security rests in a permanent and steady alliance with the liberal community and its characteristic spokesmen and institutions.[27]

Commentary tried to manipulate Jewish fears to persuade them to join the conservative ranks. It even implied that Jews who remained liberal were helping anti-Semitism. Here the magazine was at its most confused and contradictory, revealing the inconsistencies thrown up by Podhoretz's opportunism. Some writers used the Holocaust as a platform for neoconservative polemics, as others admonished that the Shoah should not be made the elemental standard of Jewish values. So, while Robert Alter could write that "serious distortions of the Holocaust itself" occurred when the Holocaust is "politicized," "falsify[ing] our lives as Jews," Podhoretz and Decter invoked Emil Fackenheim's negative conception of a 614th commandment to lecture American Jewry to remember the responsibilities of the Holocaust. The lessons of the Holocaust, they said, conferred on Jews a special obligation to be even more selfish and less compassionate. They pedantically applied the "message of Munich" again and again, exhorting American Jews to remember the Holocaust and back their pro-Republican neoconservative agenda.[28]

Podhoretz wanted to reassure American Jewry that the Right was trustworthy. Jews should swallow their lofty principles and seek new alliances with the Right, in particular Jerry Falwell's Moral Majority, to replace the liberalism of old. *Commentary* sought to allay Jewish fears by defending the Moral Majority against charges of anti-Semitism. It downplayed the threat posed by the Moral Majority to the separation of church and state as "increasingly hysterical and increasingly hollow" "alarmist nonsense" on the part of those who "have fallen victim to polemical heat prostration." It characterized the Moral Majority as simply "the response of anti-modernist Christians to the cultural dislocation of our time," speaking for religious Christians "in their battle against the secularization and debasement of moral values in contemporary life." Anti-Semitism on the Left, the magazine claimed, was worse than that of the Right. "By the standards of Jewish history," Glazer tried to comfort his fellow Jews, "anti-Semitism as a political force has never been so reduced as it is in the US today." And, the "anti-Semitism of the Christian churches has . . . dwindled to a shadow of its past." Podhoretz stated:

> While the tendency on the left has been toward greater unfriendliness towards Jews in the past 15 or so years, the tendency on the right has been in the opposite direction . . . We find a strong pro-Israel [and] a strong anti-quota sentiment. The tendency on the left has been in the opposite direction. I therefore say that whether or not Jews feel comfortable in the right, there seems to me very little question that Jews no longer have a home on the left.

In order to allay Jewish fears further, *Commentary* downplayed the extent to which the Moral Majority dominated Reaganism. It argued that the Moral Majority was pro-Israel and that Jews now had more to fear from anti-Christians than from the Christians themselves. It boldly proposed a Jewish alliance with the Moral Majority. Jews and Christians could effortlessly close ranks, it argued, on all major issues to produce a united front in defense of the free market, the nuclear family, the nuclear deterrent, and the state of Israel, and in determined opposition to homosexuality.[29]

In defending the Moral Majority, the neocons cavalierly dismissed the anti-Semitism of right-wing fundamentalists, accepting their disclaimers without question and ignoring the obvious resolve to create a Christian America. It overlooked anti-Israel Republican stalwarts like Jesse Helms, as well as anti-Jewish elements on the right, such as Pat Buchanan, in order to focus upon Jesse Jackson and black anti-Semitism. It disregarded the fact that Christian fundamentalism rejected the modern liberal tendencies, which had shaped a new understanding of Judaism, of religious conscience, tolerance and pluralism, and that the Moral Majority's religious exclusivism in particular created a climate uncongenial to cultural and religious pluralism, which in turn created an atmosphere hospitable to anti-Semitism. It neglected to mention the embarrassing elements of the Moral Majority's platform: the battles for the teaching of so-called creation science or scientific creationism (the biblical account of creation as set out in Genesis) and to eradicate all teaching of Darwinian evolution from the public schools, on restrictions of civil rights protections, for increased censorship and diminished government aid to the poor, its campaign to elect "good Christians" to public office, to amend the Constitution to abolish all restrictions on prayer in public schools, and enact legislation and constitutional amendments that would bar abortions at any time and under any circumstances despite Jewish law's requirement that the life of the mother takes precedence over that of the fetus. Rabbi Ario S. Hyams described *Commentary*'s efforts in these areas as simply propaganda that "seeks to quiet the alarm many Americans feel over the attempt by fundamentalists to take over the country..."[30]

Podhoretz also presented himself as dispassionate about the movement toward prayer in America's public schools. His need to appease the religious right led to him state he did not feel one way or the other about the issue, because a little bit of Christian prayer didn't hurt him as a student. Instead, he minimized its significance, considering it a screen issue for the flood of pornography and other evils: easy promiscuity, teenage pregnancy, and all of the social pathologies that went with it. Podhoretz was guilty of ignoring that the issue of public prayer in schools was, in the words of Dershowitz,

> part of a conscious two-step process to Christianize America. It is part of a program to get Anne Frank out of the schools, to get creationism into the schools, to get the Bible to become the fundamental vehicle of American literary and political life. It is a screen. But it is not a screen for... pornography. It is a screen for the next step of saying religion is to be preferred over nonreligion. And if religion is to be preferred we have to decide which religion.

In effect, Podhoretz was accepting second-class status as a guest in "Christian America" when he refused to protest Christian prayer in our public schools. It also showed just how far Podhoretz was cynically prepared to abandon or adopt values determined by expediency. It was the same argument that the magazine had used when advocating alignments with any anti-Communist authoritarian regime.[31]

But American Jews were wary of the Moral Majority. The November 1984 election returns demonstrated that American Jews were still suspicious and fearful of the rise of the religious right, in particular the Bible Belt evangelical movement, and anti-Semitism. One of the reasons that the majority of them voted against Reagan was the Moral Majority's support for him. Jewish apprehension about the role of religious fundamentalists in the Reagan administration and the Republican Party led to a Democratic vote against a President who publicly embraced the Moral Majority's vision of a "Christian America" in which prayer and Bible readings would be returned to public schools and in which a battle is waged against "secular humanists," a term broad enough to embrace Jews, even if *Commentary* did not seem to realize this. American Jews refused to break their tenacious loyalty to the politics of American liberalism destroying Podhoretz's own "Grand Design": his dream of arranging a reconciliation between American Jews and neoconservatism.

"All the Rest is Commentary"

Although Jews may have constituted the intellectual leadership of the neoconservative movement in the late 1980s, the neocon Jews had very little impact in persuading Jewish grassroots voters to vote conservative. Voting patterns demonstrated that Jews voted more in accord with their traditional moral principles in support of the oppressed than with the financial principles of self-interest. In 1989, when the *LA Times* asked Jews to identify what feature of their Jewishness was most important to them, twice as many indicated "social justice" than any other feature. *Commentary* had not proved its case. Unlike the magazine, American Jews concluded that Falwell and the Moral Majority, even for all their professions of love for Israel, were potentially more dangerous than Jesse Jackson. If Podhoretz had made any headway in converting the Jews to neoconservatism it was among the older and more financially successful for *Commentary* had provided the wealthier and more established Jews with a rationale to vote with their pocketbooks. The ultraorthodox had been persuaded but they represented a tiny statistical proportion of American Jewry as a whole. What is more, they did not read secular magazines like *Commentary* in the first place. Nevertheless, Podhoretz had succeeded in increasing identification of Jews with neoconservatism to the effect that, as pointed out by Dershowitz, the entire Jewish community was often "blamed" for what a vocal minority promoted.[32]

Commentary had lost touch with American Jewry. Many readers wrote in to complain that the magazine was not reflective of American Jewish opinion. Indeed, this was confirmed by the 1988 election which showed just how distant *Commentary* was from mainstream American Jewry. *Commentary* had made Jesse Jackson the single issue on which Jews should have voted in the election. It believed that Bush should have been the preferred candidate among Jews in 1988 and characterized those who disagreed as "addled," and had "learned nothing and forgotten nothing." It wanted to know how any Jew could logically support a candidate for president whose party had a Jackson in it. But the rest of the Jewish community did not really believe that the Democratic Party shared Jackson's anti-Semitism nor did they feel black anti-Semitism was quite so serious a problem as *Commentary* did. In the end Jews rejected its advice and the Jewish vote for Bush was even lower than it had been for Reagan in 1984. Where *Commentary* pointed out that quotas and reverse discrimination in higher education and employment hurt Jews as a group specifically because they were statistically overrepresented in such institutions, American Jews did not see quotas as a danger to themselves, their group, or America. They saw them as a temporary burden and, indeed acknowledged Jewish women had been some of the primary beneficiaries. *Commentary* even had to backtrack on the issue, and Nathan Glazer rather reluctantly admitted that affirmative action "did not turn out to be that great a threat to Jews" and further that "this particular fear is another one that has not been realized."[33]

Commentary's Jewish neoconservative base was narrow. It ignored whole groups of people, including conservative leaders in Jewish organizations outside the neocons, professional scientists and social scientists, as well as policy personnel. The range of ideological opinion within Judaism was poorly represented, let alone alternative theological or ideological viewpoints from Christians and non-Jews. Instead, teachers in the humanities were overrepresented. Furthermore, a 1984 poll conducted by the AJC revealed the extent of the gap: 70 percent of the Jewish respondents opposed silent meditation in schools, while 87 percent favored gay rights and 80 percent supported federally funded abortions. American Jews were overwhelmingly opposed to every major plank of *Commentary*'s platform. The gap between *Commentary* and the American Jewish community was further illustrated by their respective reactions to Reagan's visit to the Bitburg military cemetery that contained graves of SS members in West Germany in May 1985. While Podhoretz and Decter downplayed its significance as "a rather serious blunder" and a "political embarrassment," but nothing more, American Jewry was "taken by surprise" and its relations with Reagan became prickly as deep resentment and disaffection were stirred. Podhoretz and Decter sought to deflect the issue by claiming that Reagan had been "as staunchly pro-Israel as any President, and, perhaps, more than most." Indeed, they managed to place the blame for the visit with the German Chancellor, Helmut Kohl, exonerating the Teflon President.[34]

For some American Jews, though, *Commentary*'s reaction to the Bitburg disaster was the last straw. It illustrated just how wide the gap between the magazine and the rest of the American Jewish community had become. Rabbi Michael Lerner was worried that the vocal, but minority, Jewish neoconservatism was the most visible representative of the intellectual and cultural voice of Jewishness, at least as far as the media were concerned.

He criticized *Commentary* for "squaloring in a celebration of its own material success, while paying scant attention to the poverty of others and to the spiritual and moral development of its community." He attacked Jews like Podhoretz for "celebrating 'making it' as though this were the goal and destiny of Jewish history." He wrote further:

> All the more unfortunate that in recent decades conservative voices in the Jewish world, claiming to speak for all Jews, have publicly celebrated contemporary America as though it were the embodiment of the messianic age. *Commentary* Magazine, originally a voice of liberals and progressive thinking in the first decades after the Second World War, has become a leading voice of neo-conservative thought. With boring predictability, Norman Podhoretz leads the monthly charge of Jewish intellectuals clamoring for respectability by endorsing every move the Reagan Administration can dream up. Meanwhile, forgetting the deep anti-Semitic meaning of President Reagan's trip to Bitburg and his statement that the SS were victims in the same sense as those they murdered, national leaders of Jewish organizations allow themselves to be used by the President to support foreign policy goals opposed by most Americans.

Commentary's Jewish neoconservatism, vexed Lerner, was congenitally negative. Anti-Semitism had pervaded the consciousness of the neocons to such an extent that they were profoundly pessimistic about any possibility of constructively transforming the world in any positive direction. Worse, they dismissed any advocates of change. Podhoretz had "played a destructive role in moving American Jewry away from Judaism and toward the worship of power and success."[35]

In response, Lerner launched a new rival magazine, *Tikkun*, in 1986. It was conceived as a progressive and liberal alternative to *Commentary* in order to seize the Jewish intellectual leadership from Podhoretz. *Tikkun* emerged and evolved into what Allen Graubard called the "antithesis" of *Commentary*; its "birth document" represented it as the "anti-*Commentary*." Its promotional literature read: "Tikkun" means in Hebrew "to heal, repair and transform the world. All the rest is commentary."[36]

It took three years for *Commentary* to respond to *Tikkun* but even then it never really rose to the challenge. During that time, Podhoretz refused to appear on the same platform as Lerner. Ruth Wisse attempted to insult Lerner in *Commentary*: she described him as Irving Howe's "presumptive heir," but added "nothing is quite so symptomatic of the decline of the intellectual Left as the distance between those two minds." Later on

Cynthia Ozick rather lamely lampooned Lerner in her 1997 novel *The Puttermesser Papers*. It was an attempt to gain revenge for Podhoretz whom she idolized as a "creator of miracles." It was the best the neocons could do to retaliate, and it was a weak response. As a measure of just how far *Commentary* had fallen out of favor with the American Jewish community, only four years after its founding *Tikkun* surpassed *Commentary*, claiming the largest circulation (40 000) of any Jewish journal by 1990. Surveying the Jewish intellectual scene in 1989, Graubard concluded: "If *Commentary* thinks of itself as speaking for most Jewish intellectuals, I doubt that many of those intellectuals would agree."[37]

Twisted Thinking

The quality of *Commentary*'s foreign policy writings, the very area in which the magazine had distinguished itself and made its name, declined sharply, as Podhoretz rigidly stuck to a consistently hard-line anti-Communist and pro-American ideology. The result was that during the mid- to late 1980s *Commentary*'s foreign policy exhibited contradictory, and some might say, mutually exclusive tendencies. For instance, it advocated an aggressive global unilateralism, namely global interventionism combined with unilateral action. This required a total break with US allies and the abandonment by the United States of NATO, the United Nations, and the Organization of American States. It wanted to get rid of allies and entangling treaties and alliances, because they were perceived to be hindrances to American action. Theodore Draper captured it nicely in 1986. "We have had isolationists," he wrote in the NYRB,

> we have had interventionists; we have never had isolationists who were also interventionists. This abnormal crossbreeding of isolationism and interventionism has produced the new species of global unilateralists. They are global in their intervention and unilateral in the way they wish to go about it. In the past, isolationists did not want to intervene and interventionists did not want us to be isolated.

In the service of such an approach, Podhoretz denigrated the alternative of liberal internationalism by resurrecting the 20-year old "Yalta myth." The myth—invented by right-wing opponents of liberal internationalism in the early 1950s to besmirch the reputation of liberal internationalism's greatest exemplar, FDR—held that Roosevelt had been taken in by Stalin and permitted Soviet occupation of Eastern Europe after Second World War, as if there was no alternative, thus betraying it. A systematic assault against FDR was undertaken in a series of articles which put forward the thesis in one form or another. Podhoretz wanted to dispel the kinds of illusions about the Soviet Union that it believed Roosevelt had brought with him to Yalta, and that others, like the NYRB, were seeking, dangerously, to revive.[38]

In another example, *Commentary* adopted a neo-Wilsonian focus in foreign affairs, calling for a policy of vigorous American intervention to export its democratic way of life abroad to produce a global democratic revolution worldwide in which the entire world was brought into line with the American system. Yet, flying in the face of this moralistic focus, the magazine simultaneously recommended that America align itself with some despicable right-wing, authoritarian, dictatorial, and anti-democratic regimes. *Commentary* may have adopted an uber-moralistic approach to domestic matters but when it came to foreign affairs it was guided by naked expediency. While Kirkpatrick's "human rights" theory that distinguished between authoritarian and totalitarian regimes may have provided a moral veneer for supporting authoritarian regimes because they one day might become democratic, *Commentary* clearly and ideologically backed some states that looked far from ever holding free elections, undertaking land reform, and unionization.

A prime case in point was apartheid South Africa, which *Commentary* treated as a valued bulwark against Communism. Because it never said anything to the contrary, *Commentary*, like the United States, was a firm, long-standing supporter of apartheid. It supported the Reagan administration's justification of its unswerving support for apartheid as "constructive engagement." It took ads from South African companies from the late 1960s onwards, despite letters of protest. When it did write on South Africa, it merely reproduced the official governmental political line. Far from subjecting the country to critical scrutiny, it became an apologist for, if not a champion of, apartheid. Indeed, like the Leftists it attacked for praising the Soviet Union, it did not just defend South Africa, it often sympathized with it. Furthermore, it ridiculed the move toward sanctions, arguing against corporate divestment from South Africa. And, rather than attacking apartheid, it railed against liberal hypocrisy. When the battle against sanctions was lost, Podhoretz simply moved the fight to another arena, stepping up the attempts to demonize the ANC, which the magazine accused of having a "totalitarian mindset," and "totalitarian character," crudely and distortedly depicting Nelson Mandela as a relentlessly and dangerously radical Communist.[39]

The twisted logic of *Commentary*'s backing for hard-line authoritarian regimes simply because they were anti-Communist produced particularly bad results in Latin America. That region was a major preoccupation at that time because the Communist threat was felt to be at its deadliest as a result of a deterioration in the United States' position there. Worried about Leftist insurgency and fearing a Soviet takeover in the region, *Commentary* took a benign view of extreme right-wing dictatorships like Pinochet's Chile, Stroessner's Paraguay, and Argentina under the generals. Indeed, it advocated questionable methods in its campaign to "thwart and ultimately reverse the totalitarian advance," recommending "intelligent 'meddling' in the internal affairs of other countries," which, in practice, amounted to secret, counterterrorism activity against "Soviet-sponsored proxies." The magazine also mounted a campaign to garner support for the administration's policies in the area.[40]

Nicaragua was foremost in *Commentary*'s foreign policy attention because of its left-wing Sandanista regime and the magazine backed Reagan's policy of supporting the reactionary "democratic resistance"—the *Contras*. The neocons were among the very small number of Western intellectuals who were willing to identify with the *Contra* cause and in doing so overlooked the atrocities committed by the *Contras* against civilians, including assassination, brutality, and kidnapping. Instead, *Commentary* attempted to coax support for Reagan's policy in Nicaragua by making its case on the dubious question of Sandinista anti-Semitism (even though not one Jew was killed or imprisoned there and all Jews were allowed to emigrate). It painted Nicaragua as a Marxist-Leninist safe house for guerrillas, international terrorists, anti-Semites, racists, and even genocidalists. Several leading neocons even joined forces with the ultraconservative Reverend Sun Myung Moon to raise money for the *Contras*. Podhoretz's "point man" in the administration, Elliot Abrams, one of the last surviving neocons in the State Department, even flew to London under a false name to seek a $10 million donation from the Sultan of Brunei. The sum total of these efforts by the neocons was to help trigger what it called "the bloodiest political battle since Watergate." *Commentary* bore some responsibility for dragging America into the Iran-*Contra* affair—the biggest foreign-policy disaster of the Reagan years.[41]

When, in November 1986, Attorney General Meese announced that profits from secret US-authorized arms sales to the Khomeini regime in Iran were illegally diverted to the *Contras*, *Commentary*'s initial reaction was muted. As Assistant Secretary of State for Latin America, Abrams, Podhoretz's son-in-law and key neocon (described by one disgruntled reader as, "a man with a sociopolitical philosophy two steps to the Right of Hitler"), had carried out the program, assisted by another contributor, Michael Ledeen, who was then serving as an adviser to Oliver North on the

National Security Council. They were simply putting *Commentary* theory into practice in Central America, relentlessly apologizing for and promoting the anti-Communist dictators in the hemisphere, while opposing any Leftist popular movements. Of course, Podhoretz supported such actions, the intellectual foundations of which had originated in Kirkpatrick's 1979 thesis which he had published in the magazine. Podhoretz would not betray his kin and besides he supported the *Contras* anyway. Because he viewed the world through the prism of the Communist threat, he had ruled out Iran as a significant danger; thus, arms sales to it were benign even if they were illegal.[42]

Instead, *Commentary*'s first reaction was to deny that illegal acts had been committed. It chastised as "disastrous" Reagan's decision to appoint a special prosecutor. It then sought to distract attention from the alleged illegality of the affair to the harmful effects of its exposure, ironically using Leonard Garment, a special advisor to Nixon during the Watergate crisis, to write about it. The next step was to hold the Left responsible for steadily undermining the policy of backing the *Contras*. Writer after writer in *Commentary* blamed the affair on a "patchwork of 'human-rights' groups" and "apologists for Communist dictatorships" within the Democratic Party who, by creating a powerful lobby, had exerted enough influence on Congress to cut off US military aid to the *Contras*. Not only was it a betrayal of the *Contras*, it signaled the moment of the Sandinistas' greatest victory and hastened the Soviet achievement of military superiority, they argued. The final step was to bewail the destruction of Reagan's carefully constructed human rights policy in Central America: the "Reagan Doctrine" had been buried and all the good work of the last eight years was undone, representing "a receipt for making the world safe for Communism." The Iran-*Contra* affair, then, was "the first and greatest triumph" by the Left-liberal policy faction in Congress to defeat the Reagan administration's policy in Nicaragua and Central America and replace it with one of nonintervention and withdrawal. Had the United States maintained its support of democracy in Nicaragua, the momentum would have continued and perhaps the political cycle in Latin America might have been broken and democratic regimes might have been firmly established, lamented *Commentary*. The consequences of this failure were likely to haunt the United States well into the future.[43]

The biggest blow came when Abrams was convicted of having lied to and deceived Congress. Ignoring Abrams' lies, *Commentary* accused the Office of Independent Counsel of egregious violations of professional standards, as well as an "outrageous defamation" and "a flat-out, bald-faced lie." When that didn't work, it then sought to explain away Abrams' indictment after the dismissal of the Oliver North and John Pointdexter cases only because independent counsel Lawrence Walsh and his staff "badly needed trophies." Finally, when Abrams admitted he had lied, *Commentary* offered a poor excuse for his behavior: Abrams was forced to plead guilty to charges of withholding evidence from the House committee in order to avoid further legal fees and agony for him and his family, as well as other damaging consequences. It wallowed in sympathy for Abrams and minimized the offenses to which he'd pleaded guilty and then welcomed him back to the magazine with open arms. Abrams showed no remorse and was unrepentant. Indeed, he was proud of his actions, describing himself as a "gladiator" for Reagan's policies in Central America, and arguing that had US support for the *Contras* continued then democratization would have occurred.[44]

As Abrams had been the sole surviving neocon in the administration, his fall signaled the end of Podhoretz's clan within the government and sealed the break with Reagan. Furthermore, all remaining neocons were fired from the NSC as punishment for having yanked the Administration into the Iran-*Contra* affair in the first place. The damage had been done and the fall of the *Commentary*-Reaganaut alliance was complete, further crumbling the Podhoretz Empire.

Confusion

Commentary had become further confused since the succession of Gorbachev as the leader of the Soviet Union in March 1985. Where *Commentary*'s analyses of the Soviet Union had once been lucid, they now increasingly failed to account for new realities and, as would become increasingly evident to everyone but themselves, they got it spectacularly wrong. Soon after Gorbachev came to power he was called a Stalinist in the magazine. Many neocon contributors initially underrated and then tried to brush aside the scale of the subsequent domestic reforms and more conciliatory policy towards the West initiated by Gorbachev. In the autumn of 1985, Walter Laqueur argued that the Soviets had not and would never reform since it was simply not possible under their political system. Eugene Rostow added that Soviet behavior was static. Nick Eberstadt pointed out that hopes of democratization and reform were simply "hardy perennials of hopeful discussion in the West," which had survived 65 years, "and will no doubt last a good many more." "The Soviet Union will not soon collapse from its internal problems, change its view of the world," wrote Donald Kagan "or abandon its ambitions."[45]

Natan Sharansky, a former Soviet Jewish dissident who had spent 9 years in Soviet prisons and labor camps, painted a picture of Gorbachev that likened him to the past Soviet leaders despite his apparent reforms and willingness to change the Soviet system. Gorbachev, he wrote, was simply "the most pragmatic and most realistic of all Soviet dictators . . . Skilful in gauging and manipulating the public mood in the West, he can become more dangerous than his predecessors." It was, therefore, "vitally important to expose his deceptions and demonstrate massive opposition to his policies." French scholar Alain Besançon expressed a similar point of view. When Gorbachev learns that the "marketplace is stronger" than socialism, he guessed that "Gorbachev will choose socialism—which is to say the rule of the party—over the marketplace." "He could introduce no changes, and then philosophically watch over the slow disintegration of the empire, the loss of superpower status, and the final collapse of the system, perhaps within fifteen or twenty years." It was up to the West, not Gorbachev, to choose between the death of Communism in the twentieth century and its survival into the twenty-first he argued.[46]

But when Gorbachev did introduce reforms, *Commentary* sought to explain them away. The reforms were the result of stabilization within the Soviet Empire, it argued, which allowed Gorbachev to strengthen his hold over it by eliminating his political enemies. French political commentator Jean-Francois Revel wrote as late as January 1989 that *Glasnost* was a means by which Gorbachev could "consolidate his own power." Although *Commentary* granted that Gorbachev had introduced certain changes, it argued that he had done so in order to maintain the status of the Soviet Union as a superpower. And therein lay the danger, warned the magazine: the West, galvanized by the spectacle of *Glasnost*, was more than ever eager to do business with a Soviet Union that had still far from given up its goal of building Communism at home and spreading it around the world, too. *Glasnost*, then, had paradoxically strengthened rather than weakened the Soviet threat to the West, for it was not freedom of information but a technique to implant in people's minds the belief that things were really changing, to inspire confidence in the regime, to make people forget its duplicities. Yet another function of *Glasnost* was to turn the Western media and diplomats who, for the most part, accepted unquestioningly the myth that the Soviet Union was a state like any other with which normal peaceful relations could and should be maintained, into an instrument of Soviet propaganda at home where that propaganda was by and large not believed. *Commentary* articles, in contrast, sought to remind readers that *Glasnost* was simply another example of the sophisticated international diplomacy practiced by the USSR since Lenin.[47]

In fact, *Commentary* perceived Soviet reforms not as a sign that it was changing, but rather that it was becoming more invincible. It articulated the case that the Soviet Union was as much of a threat as ever, maybe more so, which by that point had become highly intellectually unfashionable. Its argument rested on three premises: that Soviet actions were in every instance expansionist and indicative of the regime's growing power and strength; that Soviet totalitarianism was irreversible; and, most serious of all, the Soviets would win a nuclear war. Soviet military power relative to that of the United States continued to grow, *Commentary* argued, while Soviet efforts to cushion the consequences of military spending by acquiring Western capital and technology had been more successful than ever. The Soviet Union was now a stronger military power than the United States as a result, and its military strength was growing more rapidly and was on the verge of achieving overwhelming strength, especially in nuclear terms and its control of outer space. The United States was weak in comparison and vulnerable to the Soviet power, as Americans preferred the comforts of pleasure to the challenges of honor and sacrifice, more prone to consume than fight. Podhoretz and the neocons stubbornly refused to acknowledge that the danger from the Soviet Union was declining until the very point that it collapsed. Rather than being close to disintegration, *Commentary* argued, the Soviet Union in mid-1988, was as strong as it had ever been and was not only better suited to fight the Cold War but also that it would actually win it.

Consequently, *Commentary* was suspicious of the Soviet desire for arms-control agreements, arguing that arms control agreements were a means to an end for the Soviets, not an end in themselves. That end was Soviet hegemony—"a true Pax Sovietica." Thus, Reagan's unreserved embrace of arms control in the final months of his administration came as a considerable shock to *Commentary*. Since the Reykjavik summit of October 1986, Reagan had emerged as a champion of radical and sweeping nuclear disarmament measures and the host of assumptions that the neocons held about Reagan was shown to be fundamentally mistaken. In fact, Reagan's sharp shift in foreign policy confused the magazine and Podhoretz was disappointed, even disgusted, with Reagan and what he viewed as Reagan's change of heart. He disputed the consensus that under Reagan relations between the United States and the Soviet Union had become stable, that the Cold War was all but over, that tantalizing prospects existed for negotiations on a whole gamut of issues from arms control to regional conflicts to East-West trade, and that the appropriate catchword for American policy in the new era was cooperation rather than confrontation. Nonetheless, the momentum for an arms control agreement with the Soviets—which *Commentary* opposed—grew steadily. And Reagan continued to cut the military budget in real terms every year from 1985. David Brock summed up the problem as *Commentary* saw it: "In practical terms,

Reagan foreign policy amounted to maintaining the status quo ... we seem to have returned to the détente of the 1970's—a path, it should be noted, that for all his cold-war rhetoric, Reagan had been implicitly following all along." Moreover, Reagan "has not only proved unequal to the challenge, but he has also left a legacy of détente that my turn out to be more dangerous than its precursor of the 1970's." A savage indictment of Reagan's foreign policy in *Commentary* in 1988 concluded that the world was not a safer place than when Reagan took over in 1981.[48]

Commentary feared what it perceived to be Reagan's hasty "rush to disarm." It was irritated by the "startling reversal" in the personal views on the president towards the Soviet Union and felt let down by Reagan. In response, Podhoretz printed articles that readers complained were tantamount to "blatant misinformation," a "form of vituperation and hatred," and "a careless disregard of facts to make a point," and to "discredit the President." Suzanne Garment wrote that Reagan and his administration "have come to look like hypocrites and bumblers, and in most of Reagan's Cabinet departments there is not enough quality or energy or breadth of ideas." The return to arms control was taken as an abrogation, even betrayal, of the magazine's neoconservative ideals. The INF accord, concluded in December 1987, was a particularly unexpected turn of events for the magazine because it signaled the failure of its own agenda and the success of the antinuclear campaign of the early 1980s. Furthermore, the few remaining neocons in Reagan's administration were sidelined in favor of moderates like Shultz as Reagan discarded ideology for politics and believed in the promise of Gorbachev. In return, *Commentary* attacked Reagan from the Right, calling him, in effect, "soft on Communism" for his receptivity to the Soviet reformer's overtures.[49]

In the face of the Soviet threat, *Commentary* continued to insist on the necessity of a missile defense system. In the face of overwhelming scientific and intellectual opinion that it could not be built and even though its scientific basis was far more dubious than conservative journalists and foreign policy experts admitted at the time, *Commentary* stood up for the Strategic Defense Initiative (SDI). It rose to defend the indefensible. In article after article, the magazine argued that since Soviet military power had never been higher relative to that of the United States and was continuing to grow, antimissile defense was strategically rational; in fact, it argued that SDI was never more important. The magazine's expert on this issue, Angelo Codevilla, lamented that Reagan might have bequeathed an emphasis on strategic weapons that defended territory and people rather than destroying them, but unfortunately, he had left merely a low-level research program that was gradually being smothered to death by Congress and bureaucrats within Reagan's own administration. This state of inaction had jeopardized US security and the gap between them and the Soviets was widening he warned. "We find," wrote Podhoretz, "no rational justification for the faith in arms control." Star Wars, however, "really does hold out the rational hope of an eventual escape from the threat of nuclear war."[50]

Podhoretz had been caught out by three unforeseen developments. Reagan's transformation from an advocate of foreign policy realism to one of total nuclear disarmament; Gorbachev's emergence as a Soviet leader capable of making daring and unexpected tactical concessions in the service of broader Soviet global aims; and, the surprising alteration of US proposals for "deep reductions" in nuclear weapons from a widely discounted propaganda initiative into an imminent strategic reality. The third development proved particularly troubling for Podhoretz, since he had traditionally urged realism in matters of defense. He had been cast in an awkward position, forced to choose between preserving his credibility, on the one hand, and stating, on the other, that radical arms cuts would severely damage Western security. So Podhoretz lashed out at Reagan in a steady barrage of columns for the *New York Post*.[51]

Meanwhile, *Commentary* felt uneasy that "some of the most effective opponents of rash and ill-advised arms-control measures had been all but silenced." It called for a "program of delay and reappraisal in arms control," arguing that "A nation that lacks the moral self-confidence to pursue the measures necessary for its defense in the face of criticism from misguided idealists on the one hand and its mortal enemy on the other has lost the capacity to survive." The risk of saying no to the present program of radical arms control is embarrassment but the risk of saying yes is "the loss of our basic security" and ultimately "the relinquishment of freedom itself." Once more *Commentary* rang the alarm bells warning the nation of the continuing "present danger."[52]

Commentary vigorously contested any suggestions that America was in decline and suffering from "imperial overstretch." The magazine argued that America should not retreat, but warned that if America did decline over the next few decades it was because "the American people and their leaders have decided that they want other things more than they want to remain the leading power in the world." It invoked the spirit of Munich to warn of the West's "larger responsibilities": "They made such a choice once before in living memory, when they declined to accept the obligations of leadership after World War I. The results were disastrous." America had to increase its military budget in real terms and spend whatever was needed to deter a war. It should assist those fighting Soviet and Soviet-supported regimes, from Angola to Nicaragua to Poland. The West should cease to finance and build up the Soviet economy and work instead to cut off its access to credit and expertise. Even when it became clear and irrefutable that the Soviet Union's power was waning under Gorbachev, *Commentary* continued to publicize its perceived threat of Soviet expansionism.[53]

The problem was that Podhoretz and *Commentary*'s neoconservative logic was skewed. Kirkpatrick's 1979 article had committed *Commentary* to the ideological straitjacket of "irreversibility"; that once totalitarianism had taken root, it couldn't be turned back or eradicated. This attachment to the analytic logic of totalitarianism, therefore, precluded the possibility of any real change in the Soviet Union. Jean-Francois Revel wrote that

> not a single fully Communist country has been restored or has come on its own to democracy. Despite what so many in the West appear to regard as an extremely easy process, we cannot name a single *completed* instance of Communist reversibility."

As late as 1989, *Commentary* refused to see the writing on the wall: the breakup of a Soviet nuclear submarine beneath the sea, the Chernobyl disaster that spewed radiation for hundreds of miles, the alcoholism and demoralization of Soviet labor, an unpaid military, ethnic unrest in Georgia and elsewhere, the repression of intellectuals and the defection of cultural heroes, and a command economy that refused to obey commands did not sway the magazine one iota. Indeed, the magazine asked, "Can Poland Ever Be Free?"[54]

Commentary refused to join in the widespread conviction that the world was becoming a safer place as a result of the reforms of Gorbachev. Instead, it warned that this conviction was "helping to make the world more dangerous." Where others were optimistic, *Commentary* introduced a pessimistic note by warning of undue optimism. It dismissed it as this "current bout of euphoria," and warned of reproducing the folly of earlier generations by blithely and unguardedly disassembling the structure of containment and Western alliance that had guaranteed the peace for 40 years. Such policies were destined to make the world a more dangerous place. *Commentary* did not agree with those who proclaimed the demise of totalitarianism as a result of the current, unprecedented wave of reform and unrest in the Soviet bloc. Conceding that the supporters of *Glasnost* had achieved an impressive opening up of Soviet society, *Commentary* warned that they had yet to demonstrate the ability to overcome the heavy burden of Russian history, with its "unique tradition of hostility to Western-style freedom."[55]

There were obstacles on the road to democracy which, it predicted, would be long and painful. The nature of the Communist world made the "supposed" victory of democracy and capitalism unpredictable. *Commentary* repeated its mantra that Soviet history had many examples of internal reform and even liberalization going as far back as the accession of Khrushchev in 1953 (which had then heralded optimism but, it said, had proved to be the most dangerous period of the postwar era). For each positive development in the Soviet Union, Poland, and Hungary, *Commentary* produced an example of an equally negative one. The situations there were "ambiguous." Western experts were "out of touch, always assuming that a Communist spring cannot be followed by a Communist winter." It reiterated the point that real change will take a long time; the collapse of Communism will be complex, eventful, and dangerous. Since the Cold War was far from over, optimism "about this uncertain future could be our undoing." Declarations of the end of the Cold War were premature projections of Western wishes and dangerous illusions containing the seeds of Western destruction. *Commentary* even went as far as to suggest they were merely part of a Politburo peace offensive to weaken Western resolve and to lighten the pressures on the Soviet Union. Lulled, the West could well dismantle its military forces and allow NATO to fall apart. This period was as dangerous as the period immediately following Second World War.[56]

Reports of the death of Communist totalitarianism had been greatly exaggerated, shrilled the magazine. Even as Communist ideology everywhere seemed to be disintegrating, *Commentary* merely responded that the Soviet body might be dying, but that the Communist parasite it hosted was still very much alive and well not just in Russia but in the thriving Soviet-backed totalitarian regimes in Rumania, North Korea, Cuba, Ethiopia, Bulgaria, Czechoslovakia, East Germany, South Yemen, Angola, Vietnam, Cambodia, and Nicaragua. What was worse was that the West was providing it with vital transfusions. The West absolutely had to refrain from lending a hand: "What sense does it make for us to keep alive regimes that are permanent sources of misery in the world . . . ?" asked Revel. Concrete issues still existed: Central America, European disarmament, strategic bases in the Philippines and Vietnam, Soviet penetration into the South Pacific, Soviet diplomacy toward post-Khomeini Iran and in Afghanistan after the departure of the Red Army, the bloody Chinese occupation of Tibet, the future of Hong Kong.[57]

The Conservative Crack-Up

In his quest for power, Podhoretz had made opportunistic alliances with the Right. The paleocon-neocon coalition under Reagan had simply been tactical: a means to an and. *Commentary*'s dedicated and running critique of the assumptions of the anti-American position in domestic affairs, combined with its hard-line foreign policy stance, helped forge a strange alliance between the neocons and the Republican businessmen longing to throw off regulation, Christian conservatives and evangelicals, California libertarians, corporate bigwigs, and Rust Belt construction workers all in support of Reagan. They had been joined by a common belief that there had been a failure of will and national purpose in the face of the Soviet geopolitical and ideological threat, that Americans had to be rallied in the fight against Communism, that the isolationist tendencies within American society had to be overcome, and that charges of the American Left that American power would always be used to promote wicked ends must be rebutted. Nonetheless, the neocons had never felt entirely at home in the conservative movement.

For their part, paleocons had always perceived the neocons as latecomers, who had hijacked conservatism and used it to advance a neocon agenda. They complained that the neocons exerted disproportionate influence within the conservative intellectual movement in America, which was now considered synonymous with neoconservatism. They were annoyed that journals like *Commentary* had the effect of helping to push conservatism towards the center such that positions outside of *Commentary*'s parameters and significantly to the right of the magazine were regarded as suspect. Paleocons did not consider neoconservatism as authentic or genuine conservatism because it was insufficiently indistinguishable from welfare-state liberalism and emphasized progress too much. (Where the neocons did not reject modern state planning and still defended the welfare state—albeit with qualifications: they wanted to trim it—the paleocons wanted to dismantle it altogether.) The 1985 symposium, "How Has the US Met Its Major Challenges Since 1945?" was felt to be typical since it included people from the center-Left but, with the exception of Robert Nisbet, ignored everyone to the right of the neocons. And most of the contributors emphasized social progress, while deploring high crime rates and the Soviet military buildup. The symposium elicited stormy responses from the Old Right in the *Intercollegiate Review* and at the annual meeting of the Philadelphia Society in Chicago in April 1986. The debate was raucous and the paleoconservative historian Stephen J. Tonsor expressed dismay that former Marxists had come to play such a dominant role within conservatism, and quipped that had Trotsky not been assassinated he would no doubt be writing articles for *Commentary*. The Old Right felt overrun, usurped by impostors. Southern conservative historian Clyde Wilson summed up the general feeling: "we have simply been crowded out by overwhelming numbers. The offensives of radicalism have driven vast herds of liberals across the borders into our territories. These refugees now speak in our name, but the language they speak is the same one they always spoke."[58]

The battle between the neocons and paleocons for dominance within the conservative movement turned ugly, as the neocons fired back, claiming they were the authentic and genuine voice of American conservatism. *Commentary* waded in by publishing articles denouncing Old Right conservatives as anti-Semites, including some who were Jewish. The neocons were acutely sensitive to any outbreak of anti-Semitism on the Right, as a result of having unavoidably become allies of a political movement that had previously been predominantly Christian. In the summer of 1986, an acrimonious quarrel erupted between Podhoretz, Decter, and Dorothy Rabinowitz and syndicated columnist, commentator on the CBS radio series *Spectrum*, and *National Review* senior editor, Joseph Sobran. For some time, Sobran had been publishing statements critical of the Israeli government, the liberalism of the American Jewish community, the role of Zionists in American political life, and about Jewish hostility toward Christian society. A similar attack was also launched against the author of one of the founding texts of postwar American conservatism *The Conservative Mind* (1953), Russell Kirk, after he made a wisecrack about the pro-Israel neocon stance, remarking in a speech at the Heritage Foundation in 1988 that "not seldom it has seemed as if some eminent neo-conservatives mistook Tel Aviv for the capital of the United States." The neocons were right to be sensitive because some of these comments did indeed suggest inexcusable bigotry, even indefensible anti-Semitism, but then what did the neocons expect to find on the Right? It merely highlighted the extent to which they and Podhoretz were willing to sacrifice integrity for expediency in making alliances with such people in the first place.

Eventually, the uneasy alliance between the different shades of conservatism during the Reagan years, held together by the glue of the Cold War, came unstuck towards the end of the decade, and the alliance fell apart into acrimonious debate. The end of the Cold War had eliminated the great purpose that, more than any other factor, had brought so many disparate groups together into a working coalition. The lines of division—which mirrored those within liberalism of earlier decades out of which *Commentary* and neoconservatism had emerged—were still clearly drawn beneath the façade of consensus. Well-publicized battles erupted over who genuinely represented authentic conservatism: the newcomer neocons or the paleocons. By the late 1980s, the media was referring to "the conservative crackup": the "disunity and disintegration" of the conservative movement, which had been reduced to clashing armies on the Right.[59]

Gloominess

As a result of all these developments, Podhoretz tended to excessively gloomy estimates of his fortunes. He watched in dismay as his empire faltered and foundered in the wake of the Reagan's ideological betrayal, the loss of intellectual leadership to his despised rival Michael Lerner, the collapse of Reagan's neocon-influenced human rights policy, the Iran-*Contra* disaster, the purging of the neocons from the Administration including his son-in law, the accession of Gorbachev and his reforms in the Soviet Union, disarmament, and the loss of political allies and the resulting bitter infighting. Furthermore, conservatism as a whole was faring little better: Republicans lost control of the Senate and, in a particularly huge blow, the Bork nomination crumpled; as David Brock pointed out: "More than any single figure, for the right, Bork's nomination represented the culmination of a strategy put in place at the beginning of the Reagan administration to force a right-wing economic and social agenda on the country by judicial fiat." On so many of the issues that had been central to Podhoretz's neocon program, he had been defeated. *Commentary* even conceded on the issue of affirmative action, having failed "to stem the tide of racial preference that has been engulfing the nation during the past decade." It bemoaned the fact that quotas were no longer referred to as temporary and had become instead, effectively, civil rights themselves. Still, not to be deterred, not least because this would entail a difficult maneuver, Podhoretz carried on his campaign against quotas and affirmative action, spelling out explicit examples of what America had done and what it had cost, as well as questioning their ultimate effectiveness. He worried about what he saw as the administration's excessive eagerness in its declining days to negotiate with the Soviet Union. He wondered uneasily about the future of conservatism once Reagan departed the scene. The "Reagan interlude," wrote David Frum, had misled conservatives into thinking that the American people were with them. But conservatism was really adrift, no longer in control of public opinion, lacking in leadership, internally divided.[60]

Podhoretz's fall from grace was compounded by the election of George H. W. Bush in 1988. Bush was certainly no neocon and it would have taken an ever huger leap of imagination to begin to make him over as one as had been done with Reagan. In a lecture at the Heritage Foundation, Russell Kirk stated (probably not without some glee),

> it appears to me that . . . President Bush will not be eager to obtain the services of this little Sacred Band—which has made itself exclusive, and now finds itself excluded . . . I predict that within a very fear years

we will hear no more of the Neoconservatives: some will have fallen away, and others will have been merged with the main current of America's conservative movement, and yet others' pert loquacity will have been silenced by the tomb.

If any remaining neocons had not already left or been fired, Bush pushed them out. From the position of dominance over foreign policy, defense, and education, Bush steered clear of the neocons of the type that wrote for and read *Commentary*. Some did attain positions under Vice President Dan Quayle, most notably Irving Kristol's son, William, who became Quayle's Chief of Staff. But, in general, Bush carried out a "thorough housecleaning" to purge the last traces of neoconservatism from the White House that had not already been removed under Reagan, sending the neocons back to their think tanks and journals, and those universities that would still take them. There they regrouped, refined their political ideas, if they indeed had any at that point, and disseminated them in position papers, syndicated columns, and new magazines, while building strategic alliances with the New Right. As a result, "Jews in political power are fewer than they were ten years ago; or for that matter, eight years ago at the start of the Reagan administration," observed Irving Louis Horowitz. He continued:

> There has been an erosion of that power, perhaps, on the part of these people, by an over identification with a political philosophy rather than a political theology. The problem that the *Commentary* group has run into is the exhaustion of conservative ideology and rebellion within American life. Just as *Commentary* was part of the vigor of that conservative upswing in the 1970s, so they must bear some of the responsibility for the exhaustion of that vision in the 1980s . . . There is a great deal of doubt within the *Commentary* position. This is reflected in the desperation many of the[m] have.[61]

Commentary had lost its allies and now the hub of the American intelligentsia was also shifting. New York was no longer predominant and Washington, DC was on the rise. On February 13, 1983, speaking at a committee for the Free World conference on "Our Country and Our Culture," Podhoretz reiterated the centrality of politics to intellectual life, calling for the "frank and candid and forthright acceptance of what I would call the duties or responsibilities of partisanship." But, as Tod Lindberg pointed out, "When politics is accorded a position of primacy in the life of the mind, and partisanship no longer conflicts with a commitment to traditional intellectual virtues, then Washington—the city of politics, and of partisanship—is set to become a center of gravity of intellectual matters."

The Heritage Foundation was regarded as the most important think tank in DC; it had the ear and attention of powerful people in the Reagan administration and on Capitol Hill. The *Weekly Standard* and the *National Review*, both DC-based publications surpassed *Commentary*. Power and influence was shifting steadily away from *Commentary* to other magazines and journalists outside the neoconservative orbit, which began to emerge into the limelight. *Commentary* had thus helped to sow the seeds of its own decline by helping to shift the center of political gravity to the right, which DC-based organizations were now beginning to dominate. "From New York's point-of-view, the rise of the Washington intellectual ought to have been a truly alarming sign," wrote Lindberg. And given his linkage with New York, for Podhoretz it was.[62]

Podhoretz himself was distressed as his personal fiefdom collapsed around him. To cap it all, *Commentary*'s circulation had declined to a new low of 40 000 by the end of the decade. A 40-year subscriber cancelled his subscription because he simply could not "stomach any longer" an editorial policy "which recommends courses that, in my opinion, are not only wrong but actually contrary to, as well as damaging to, our country's national interests." He had become disenchanted with the magazine and had had enough of it. *Commentary* was riddled with partisanship. Some of *Commentary*'s most influential and most accomplished contributors such as Daniel Bell, Nathan Glazer, and Daniel Patrick Moynihan stopped writing for the magazine because Podhoretz had personalized their intellectual and political disagreements. They did not share Podhoretz's alarmist views of the dangers of the Soviet Union, the PLO, and what was left of the New Left, and they no longer could work with him. The magazine itself had shrunk in size, and was routinely only about 60–70 pages long (compared to the 100 in previous decades). Fewer books were reviewed (about 4 to 5), and the letters section was shorter, containing few major disagreements but rather clarifications, and arguments over detail rather than principles. Podhoretz returned to publishing fiction and padded out each issue with a short story. And the budget was tight: it had only one word processor in the entire office. The magazine had resorted to bragging: "In the world of ideas, no other magazine comes close." But its claim that it was "the magazine that shapes the minds of the people who shape our world" sounded increasingly hollow.[63]

Notes

1. Norman Podhoretz, *Ex-Friends: Falling Out with Allen Ginsberg, Lionel and Diana Trilling, Lillian Hellman, Hannah Arendt, and Norman Mailer* (New York: Free Press, 1999), 3.

2. Podhoretz, quoted in Murray Kempton, "Kirkpatrick Ire Left to Pygmies," *Newsday* (April 21, 1985), 6, 15.

3. Irving Kristol, "The Muddle in Foreign Policy," *Wall Street Journal* (April 29, 1981), 9; Walter Laqueur, "Reagan and the Russians," *Commentary* 73:1 (January 1982), 19–26; David Singer, "The Record In Latin America," *Commentary* 74:6 (December 1982), 43–9; Norman Podhoretz, "The Future Danger," *Commentary* 71:4 (April 1981), 29–47.

4. Steven L. Spiegel, "The Middle East: A Consensus of Error," *Commentary* 73:3 (March 1982), 15–24 and "Israel as a Strategic Asset," *Commentary* 5:6 (June 1983), 51–5; Murray Friedman, "AWACS and the Jewish Community," *Commentary* 73:4 (April 1982), 29–33.

5. Norman Podhoretz, "The Neo-Conservative Anguish Over Reagan's Foreign Policy," *The New York Times Magazine* (May 1982), 29–31.

6. Norman Podhoretz, "Mistaken Identity," *Commentary* 78:1 (July 1984), 56–60; John Ehrman, *The Rise of Neoconservatism: Intellectuals and Foreign Affairs, 1945-1994* (New Haven and London: Yale University Press, 1996), 146; Mark Shechner, *After the Revolution: Studies in Contemporary Jewish-American Imagination* (Bloomington and Indianapolis: Indiana University Press, 1987), 3. Podhoretz began to doubt the Reagan administration in other areas, too. *Commentary* had attacked the Carter administration for its promotion of affirmative action and quotas, but it didn't find much solace in Reagan's approach to civil rights either. Chester E. Finn, Jr. and Walter Berns examined the record of the administration, concluding its civil-rights program had been "a fitful and uneven process," "clumsy and irresolute" and called for more determined action. Overall, *Commentary* was not impressed with Reagan's civil-rights record. Walter Berns, "Let Me Call You Quota, Sweetheart," *Commentary* 71:5 (May 1981), 48–53 and "Voting Rights and Wrongs," *Commentary* 73:3 (March 1982), 31–6; Chester E. Finn, Jr., "'Affirmative Action' Under Reagan," *Commentary* 73:4 (April 1982), 17–28.

7. "How Has the US Met Its Major Challenges Since 1945? A Symposium," *Commentary* 80:5 (November 1985), 25–107.

8. Norman Podhoretz, *Breaking Ranks: A Political Memoir* (New York: Harper & Row, 1979), 344–5; Thomas Fleming, "The Closing of the Conservative Mind," *Chronicles* 13:9 (September 1989), 12.

9. Dwight Macdonald, "Scrambled Eggheads on the Right: Mr. Buckley's New Weekly," *Commentary* 21:4 (April 1956), 367–73.

10. Elizabeth Lilla, "Who's Afraid of Women's Studies?" *Commentary* 81:2 (February 1986), 53–7; Chester E. Finn, "The Campus: 'An Island of Repression an a Sea of Freedom,'" *Commentary* 88:3 (September 1989), 17–23; Carol Iannone, "The Fiction We Deserve," *Commentary* 83:6 (June 1987), 60–2 and "Feminism vs. Literature," *Commentary* 86:1 (July 1988), 49–53.

11. Walter Goodman, "The Question of Repression," *Commentary* 50:5 (November 1970), 23–38.

12. Matthew Rubenstein, Letters, *Commentary* 103:3 (March 1997), 3–26.

13. David Robinson, Jr., "Sodomy and the Supreme Court," *Commentary* 82:4 (October 1986), 57–61.

14. Podhoretz, quoted in Alan M. Dershowitz, *Chutzpah* (New York and London: Simon and Schuster, 1991), 202–3.

15. Michael A. Fumento, "AIDS: Are Heterosexuals at Risk?" *Commentary* 84:5 (November 1987), 21–7; "Are We Spending Too Much on AIDS?" *Commentary* 90:4 (October 1990), 51–3; and "AIDS So Far," *Commentary* 92:6 (December 1991), 46–9; Harry Stein, *How I Accidentally Joined the Vast Right-Wing Conspiracy (and Found Inner Peace)* (New York: Perennial, 2001), 125; Letter to the Editor, *Bottom Line/Personal* (May 25, 1988) [internet version].

16. Marjorie Rosenberg, "Inventing the Homosexual," *Commentary* 84:6 (December 1987), 36–40; Letters, *Commentary* 85:3 (March 1988), 6–12; Letters, *Commentary* 83:2 (February 1987), 2–6.

17. Gertrude Himmelfarb, "From Clapham to Bloomsbury: A Genealogy of Morals," *Commentary* 79:2 (February 1985), 36–43; Joseph Epstein, "One Cheer for E.M. Forster," *Commentary* 80:3 (September 1985), 48–57. Enraged by their homophobic attacks, Vidal fired a shot back, penning an essay in the March 1986 issue of *The Nation*. Entitled "The Empire Lovers Strike Back" *The Nation* (March 22, 1986), 352–3. Vidal similarly singled out Podhoretz and Decter as an "Israeli fifth column" and Zionist "propagandist[s]." Yet another row flared. Podhoretz planned a "retaliatory strike." He devoted the lead essay of the November 1986 *Commentary* to a response to Vidal. In "The Hate That Dare Not Speaks its Name," (*Commentary* 82:5 (November 1986), 21–32) Podhoretz called Vidal's essay "the most blatantly anti-Semitic outburst to have appeared in a respectable American periodical since World War II." He continued: "His every word drips with contempt and hatred, and underlying it all is a strong note of menace." Vidal replied in kind: "The Podhoretzes are doing more to arouse the essential anti-Semitism of the American people than anyone since Father Coughlin." Meanwhile, Podhoretz then turned this personal spat into a moral litmus test for American liberalism, ordering Managing Editor Marion Magid to write to 29 friends and supporters of *The Nation*, questioning whether such a piece should have even appeared in their magazine in the first place. The storm lasted for two months, during which time approximately thirty pieces had been published about the episode in American and foreign newspapers and magazines, including France, Germany, Australia, England, and Israel. The big US papers looked on with amusement at what to them was an embarrassing private quarrel. *Washington Post* columnist Edwin M. Yoder, Jr. felt that Podhoretz had asked for it by mistaking Vidal's hard-edged teasing for anti-Semitism (Yoder cited in "The Hate That Dare Not Speaks its Name"). *Newsweek* described it as "A Big-League Literary Feud" and licked its lips in anticipation of a "literary quarrel that had everything going for it," with "the prospect of more vitriolic prose, more character assassinations, and, in all likelihood, more broken friendships." *The Washington Post* further described it as the "dirty little war of words" which had gone "nuclear": "Long bombarding each other with verbal abuse, Vidal and Podhoretz have now engaged in a exchange that is by all accounts ugly, burying the issues in an atomic barrage of name-calling." *The L.A. Times*' Jody Powell wrote: "What we have here is a trio of aging, self-righteous ideologues bent on exposing the absurdities of their intellectual configuration to all who can stomach the spectacle. What emerges is that they are more alike than different" (Powell cited in "The Hate That Dare Not Speaks its Name"). The glee was generally shared outside of the neocons. One prominent Jewish leader went around saying that Podhoretz and Vidal deserved each other. Even the AJC did not bother to come to Podhoretz's defense because it was felt Podhoretz could take care of himself.

Podhoretz himself was hurt that what he saw as a blatant example of anti-Semitism was being trivialized as an individual squabble between him and his wife and Vidal. But Podhoretz had cried wolf too often and many within the Jewish community were sick and tired of Podhoretz calling anti-Semitism any time Israel was criticized.

18. Brock, *Blinded by the Right: The Conscience of an Ex-Conservative* (New York: Three Rivers Press, 2002), 191. Brock, who was gay, was a darling of the right for his scandalous exposés of Anita Hall and Troopergate. Nonetheless, he was subject to nasty gossip about his private life behind his back. But once Brock came out and refused to write a damning exposé of Hillary Clinton, the neocons turned on him. Decter wrote a particularly sardonic, damning, and homophobic review in the *Weekly Standard* ("Brock Loves Hillary"). Elliot Abrams, perhaps less hypocritical than the others, could not bring himself to join in a standing ovation at the annual *American Spectator* dinner in February 1994 and sat on his hands rather than give an open homosexual such a rousing reception. Brock, Blinded by the Right, 190, 68, 191, 113, 45, 46.

19. Macdonald, "Scrambled Eggheads on the Right," 367–73; Bertram Gold, telephone interview with author, September 6, 2002; I. D. Robbins, "Jewish community's Podhoretz problem," *New York Daily News* (May 21, 1981) 66.

20. Richard N. Haass, "Paying Less Attention to the Middle East," *Commentary* 82:2 (August 1986), 22–6; David Bar-Ilan "Can Israel Withdraw?" *Commentary* 85:4 (April 1988), 27–38; Daniel Pipes and Adam Garfinkle, "Is Jordan Palestine?" *Commentary* 86:4 (October 1988), 35–42.

21. Norman Podhoretz, Letters, *Commentary* 88:1 (July 1989), 4–16; Edward Alexander, "Professor of Terror," *Commentary* 88:2 (August 1989), 49–50; Daniel Pipes, "Arab vs. Arab Over Palestine," *Commentary* 84:1 (July 1987), 17–25; Jeane J. Kirkpatrick, "How the PLO Was Legitimized," *Commentary* 88:1 (July 1989), 21–8.

22. Norman Podhoretz, "Israel: A Lamentation From the Future," *Commentary* 87:3 (March 1989), 15–21; Letters, *Commentary* 88:1 (July 1989), 4–16.

23. Norman Podhoretz, Letters, *Commentary* 88:1 (July 1989), 4–16.

24. Eliot A. Cohen, "The Pollard Case," *Commentary* 88:2 (August 1989), 51–6.

25. Milton Himmelfarb, "No Hitler, No Holocaust," *Commentary* 77:3 (March 1984), 37–43 and "Are Jews Becoming Republican?" *Commentary* 72:2 (August 1981), 27–30; S. M. Lipset and Earl Raab, "The Election & the Evangelicals," *Commentary* 71:3 (March 1981), 25–31; Irving Kristol, "The Political Dilemma of American Jews," 23–9; Murray Friedman, "A New Direction for American Jews," *Commentary* 72:6 (December 1981), 37–44.

26. Milton Himmelfarb, "Another Look at the Jewish Vote," *Commentary* 80:6 (December 1985), 39–44.

27. Jerold S. Auerbach, "Liberalism & the Hebrew Prophets," *Commentary* 84:2 (August 1987), 58–60; Irving Kristol, "Liberalism & American Jews," *Commentary* 86:4 (October 1988), 19–23; Letters, *Commentary* 87:1 (January 1989), 2–11; Podhoretz, quoted in Dershowitz, Chutzpah, 205.

28. Robert Alter, "The Deformations of the Holocaust," *Commentary* 71:2 (February 1981), 48–54.

29. Nathan Glazer, "On Jewish Forebodings," *Commentary* 80:2 (August 1985), 32–6; Richard John Neuhaus, "What the Fundamentalists Want," *Commentary* 79:5 (May 1985),

41–6; Lucy Dawidowicz, "Politics, the Jews & the '84 Election," *Commentary* 79:2 (February 1985) 25–30; Brigitte Berger and Peter L. Berger, "Our Conservatism and Theirs," *Commentary* 82:4 (October 1986), 62–7; Podhoretz, quoted in Dershowitz, Chutzpah, 202–3.

30. Rabbi Ario S. Hyams, Letters, *Commentary* 80:2 (August 1985), 12–15.

31. Dershowitz Chutzpah, 203, 204.

32. Michael Lerner, *Jewish Renewal: A Path to Healing and Transformation* (New York: HarperPerennial, 1994), 210, 213; Dershowitz, Chutzpah, 201.

33. Milton Himmelfarb, "American Jews: Diehard Conservatives," *Commentary* 87:4 (April 1989), 44–9; Dawidowicz, "Politics, the Jews & the '84 Election," 25–30; Letters, *Commentary* 79:5 (May 1985), 6–20; Nathan Glazer, "On Jewish Forebodings," *Commentary* 80:2 (August 1985), 32–6.

34. Louis Horowitz, *American Jewish Visions and Israeli Dilemmas: A Commentary on Fifty Commentaries in Commentary* (Middle East Studies Institute, Graduate School of International Studies, University of Miami 1988), 12; Paul Gottfried, *The Conservative Movement* (revised edn. New York: Twayne, 1993), 81; Susan Rosenbluth, "Podhoretz: Exclusive Interview," *The Jewish Standard* (May 17, 1985), 10–11; Midge Decter, "Bitburg: Who Forgot What," *Commentary* 80:2 (August 1985), 21–7.

35. Michael Lerner, "The Founding Editorial Statement," *Tikkun* 1 (1986), 3, 4, 5, 7, 9; Jewish Renewal, 19, 205 and quoted in David Twersky, "Left, right, Left Right: After half a century, *Commentary* remains defiantly out of step," *Moment* 20:3 (June 1995) 59.

36. Allen Graubard, "From *Commentary* to Tikkun: The Past and Future of 'Progressive Jewish Intellectuals,'" *Middle East Report* (May–June 1989), 17. *Tikkun*'s founding editorial statement highlighted what *Commentary* stood for (or against):

> *Tikkun Magazine* hopes to provide a voice for those who still dare to hope, for those who are not embarrassed to dream, for those Jews and non-Jews alike who are still moved by the radical spirit of the Prophets and who insist on keeping their message alive. *Tikkun* hopes to articulate strongly the needs and interests of Jewish women, the insights of Jewish feminism. *Tikkun* will support the oppressed rather than dictators and oppressive regimes of the left or right. It seeks to win back the language of community and family, religion and spirituality, ethics and traditional values from the Right.

37. Ruth R. Wisse, "Jewish Guilt and Israeli Writers," *Commentary* 87:1 (January 1989), 25–31; Graubard, "From *Commentary* to *Tikkun*," 20.

38. Theodore H. Draper, "Neoconservative History," NYRB (January 16, 1986) [internet version].

39. Paul Johnson, "The Race for South Africa," *Commentary* 80:3 (September 1985), 27–32; Peter L. Berger and Bobby Godsell, "Fantasies About South Africa," *Commentary* 84:1 (July 1987), 35–40; David Roberts, Jr., "The ANC in Its Own Words," *Commentary* 86:1 (July 1988), 31–7.

40. Jeane Kirkpatrick, "U.S. Security & Latin America," *Commentary* 71:1 (January 1981), 29–40.

41. L. Gordon Crovitz, "Crime, the Constitution, And the Iran-Contra Affair," *Commentary* 84:4 (October 1987), 23–30.

42. J. W. Barchfield, Letters, *Commentary* 88:3 (September 1989), 8–9.

43. Peter Collier and David Horowitz, "McCarthyism: The Last Refuge of the Left," *Commentary* 85:1 (January 1988), 36–41; Mark Falcoff, "Making Central America Safe for Communism," *Commentary* 85:6 (June 1988), 17–24; Robert Kagan, "Losing in Latin America," *Commentary* 86:5 (November 1988), 45–51.

44. Terry Eastland, "Above the Constitution?" *Commentary* 91:5 (May 1991), 60–2; Robert H. Bork, "Against the Independent Counsel," *Commentary* 95:2 (February 1993), 21–6; Elliot Abrams, quoted in *The Observer* (August 19, 2001) [internet version].

45. Walter Laqueur, "Is There Now, or Has There Ever Been Such a Thing as Totalitarianism?" *Commentary* 80:4 (October 1985), 29–35; Eugene V. Rostow, "Why the Soviets Want an Arms-Control Agreement, And Why They Want It Now," *Commentary* 83:2 (February 1987) 19–26; Nick Eberstadt, "The Latest Myths About the Soviet Union," *Commentary* 83:5 (May 1987), 17–27; Donald Kagan, "World War I, World War II, World War III," *Commentary* 83:3 (March 1987), 21–40.

46. Natan Sharansky, "As I see Gorbachev," *Commentary* 85:3 (March 1988), 34; Alain Besançon, "Gorbachev Without Illusions," *Commentary* 85:4 (April 1988), 47–57.

47. Jean-Francois Revel, "Is Communism Reversible?" *Commentary* 87:1 (January 1989), 19.

48. John Patrick Diggins, "*Commentary*'s Cold War on Liberalism," paper delivered at the "Commentary Magazine in the American Jewish Community and American Culture" conference, March 11, 2003, 17; Rostow, "Why the Soviets Want An Arms-Control Agreement," 19–26; David Brock, "What the Kill-and-Tell Books Tell," *Commentary* 86:2 (August 1988), 26, 27; Mary Tedeschi Eberstadt "Arms Control & Its Casualties," *Commentary* 85:4 (April 1988), 39–46.

49. Letters, *Commentary* 86:1 (July 1988), 2–10; Suzanne Garment, "The Eureka Treatment," *Commentary* 83:5 (May 1987), 64–8.

50. Podhoretz, quoted in the *New York Times* (January 24, 1985), 25. Sidney Blumenthal suggested that Podhoretz embraced Reagan's vision of SDI as "a way to compensate" for his failure to "broker the Jewish vote for Reagan" in 1984:

> Now Star Wars offered a fresh opportunity for them to rehabilitate their standing within the [conservative] movement by demonstrating their famous skills as publicists and debaters. They marked out a position to Reagan's right, more Catholic than the Pope, supportive of Star Wars but critical of any arms-control negotiations.

(Sidney Blumenthal, *The Rise of the Counter-Establishment: From Conservative Ideology to Political Power* (New York: Times Books, 1986, 308).

51. Podhoretz, "Reagan's Forbidden Truths," *New York Post* (October 29, 1985); "How Reagan Succeeds as a Carter Clone," *New York Post* (October 7, 1985); "Nixon, The Ghost of Détente Past," *New York Post* (November 5, 1985); "Reagan—The Crippled Hawk," *New York Post* (June 25, 1985); "The Madness of Arms Control," *New York Post* (October 1, 1985); "Reagan: A Case of Mistaken Identity," *New York Post* (August 6, 1985); "The Courage of Reagan's Convictions," *New York Post* (June 3, 1986); "Gorbachev's Salami Tactics," *New York Post* (October 20, 1987); "Moscow's Double Missile Trap," *New York Post* (September 22, 1987); "What the Soviets Really Want," *New York Post* (November 19, 1985); "The Danger is Greater Than Ever," *New York Post* (December 1, 1987); "Reagan's Reverse

Rollback," *New York Post* (November 10, 1987); "The Myth of Our Military Buildup," *New York Post* (September 30, 1986); "Propping Up the Soviet Empire," *New York Post* (July 15, 1986); "From Containment to Appeasement," *New York Post* (June 18, 1985); "Peace, Peace, When There Is No Peace," *New York Post* (February 16, 1988); "Reagan Was Right the First Time," *New York Post* (June 7, 1988); "Gorbachev Wins One for Lenin," *New York Post* (December 13, 1988); "Munich and Gorbachev: The Lesson Is Still Valid," *New York Post* (October 4 1988); "Now for the Left-Wing Dictators," *New York Post* (March 4, 1986).

52. Patrick Glynn, "Reagan's Rush to Disarm," *Commentary* 85:3 (March 1988), 19–28; Ronald Brown, Letters, *Commentary* 86:1 (July 1986), 8; Richard Pipes, "Team B: The Reality Behind the Myth," *Commentary* 82:4 (October 1986), 25–40; Rostow, "Why the Soviets Want an Arms-Control Agreement," 19–26.

53. Williamson Murray, "Munich at Fifty," *Commentary* 86:1 (July 1988), 25–30; Owen Harries, "The Rise of American Decline," *Commentary* 85:5 (May 1988), 32–6.

54. Revel, "Is Communism Reversible?" 17–24; Alain Besançon, "Can Poland Ever Be Free?" *Commentary* 87:4 (April 1989), 15–20.

55. Arch Puddington, "The Future of the USSR," *Commentary* 88:3 (September 1989), 60–3.

56. Stephen Miller, "Totalitarianism, Dead and Alive," *Commentary* 88:2 (August 1989), 28–32; Patrick Glynn, "The Dangers Beyond Containment," *Commentary* 88:2 (August 1989), 15–22; Charles H. Fairbanks, Jr., "Gorbachev's Cultural Revolution," *Commentary* 88:2 (August 1989), 23–7.

57. Jean-Francois Revel, "Hastening the Death of Communism," *Commentary* 88:4 (October 1989), 19–23.

58. Stephen J. Tonsor, "Why I Too Am Not A Neoconservative," *National Review* (June 20, 1986), 55; Clyde Wilson, "The Conservative Identity," *Intercollegiate Review* 21 (Spring 1986), 6–8;.

59. John B. Judis, "The Conservative Crackup," *American Prospect* 3 (Fall 1990), 41.

60. Brock, Blinded by the Right, 49; Terry Eastland, "Racial Preference in Court (Again)," *Commentary* 87:1 (January 1989), 32–8; David Frum, *Dead Right* (New York: Basic Books, 1994), 204.

61. Russell Kirk, "The Neoconservatives: An Endangered Species," Heritage Lecture 178 (Washington, DC: The Heritage Foundation, 1988), 3, 4; Horowitz, *American Jewish Visions and Israeli Dilemmas*, 17.

62. Tod Lindberg, "New York Down, Washington Up," *Commentary* 81:1 (January 1986), 36–42.

63. Walter A. Sheldon to Norman Podhoretz, October 27 and November 17, 1986; Norman Podhoretz to Ira Silverman, June 7, 1988, Norman Podhoretz Papers, Manuscript Division, Library of Congress, Washington, DC (NPLC).

7

Fall

If the series of blows the neocons and *Commentary* received over the last few years were not fatal enough to finish them off, they certainly left them gasping for breath. There was no let up in the next decade either, as Podhoretz gained further injuries, and his magazine and neocon empire drastically declined. All he could do in the face of this collapse was to retreat into the past and cling to his old rhetoric while producing distorted ideological analyses that either revised the past or toed the conservative line. It was a period in which *Commentary*'s neoconservative analysis turned out to be wrong in almost every area.

Intellectual Sacrifice

In his greatest act of opportunism in pursuit of material success, Podhoretz sacrificed his magazine in return for a healthy financial state. It was a return to the Cultural Cold War of the 1950s but rather than accepting money from the government, Podhoretz took it from right-wing foundations. At the end of 1989, the AJC went through a financial crisis, leading to "draconian cuts" across the board, including a 15 percent decrease of its overall staff. In 1990 it took the decision to end its responsibility for subsidizing *Commentary*'s entire budget and informed Podhoretz that from then on it would pay only for the magazine's overhead and rent, but could not absorb any debt beyond income—at that time, *Commentary*'s annual deficit ran to about $300,000. Furthermore, like many other magazines, *Commentary*, took a hit in advertising pages in the 1990s and advertising revenues had dropped about $100,000 per year from their peak in the late 1980s.

In place of AJC largesse, *Commentary* received its most significant source of income from a small number of conservative foundations. These included the Lynde and Harry Bradley Foundation, the John M. Olin

Foundation, the Carthage Foundation, the J. Howard Pew Freedom Trust/Pew Charitable Trusts, the Smith-Richardson Foundation, and the Sarah Scaife Foundation. Like every leading conservative publication, think tank, and individual scholar at that time, *Commentary* came to depend on money from these foundations, whose war-chests were vast, seemingly bottomless, to the extent that they still dole out the money today. In the period 1990–2005, for example, *Commentary* received $2,342,000 million from the Bradley, Brady Education, Olin, Carthage, Hickory, and Gilder Foundations.

Podhoretz personally received $818,857 from the conservative foundation backed Hudson Institute. As Scott McConnell put it, *Commentary*'s AJC support was replaced by "a publication committee of formidably wealthy people." *Commentary* no longer had to worry financially for the major foundations helped to keep it financially stable.[1]

Podhoretz was well placed to take advantage of foundation philanthropic generosity. The links between the various conservative foundations and neocon publications and individuals are well documented and neocons certainly dominated the key foundations which doled out millions of dollars. Midge Decter, for example, sat on the boards of the Smith-Richardson and the Heritage Foundations. She acted as a mediator, helping to set up allocations to other magazines, for example, a great deal of grant money had gone to her Committee for the Free World. Eric Breindel noted the suspicion (in his opinion, unjustified) that a "collective of enormously wealthy foundations was financing a highly organized ideological struggle led by Decter's Committee and the various little magazines." Another important neocon instrumental in fund-raising was neocon Leslie Lenkowski, who headed the Philanthropic Roundtable.[2]

This funding was not purely altruistic. It was part of a wider conservative project spanning three decades to reshape politics, public, and elite opinion, and public policy priorities at the national, state, and local levels. Right-wing foundations had provided millions of dollars in grants to develop a vast and interconnected institutional web of conservative media outlets—publishing houses, magazines, journals, research institutes, think tanks, public affairs programming on public television and radio, radio and television talk shows, media critics—designed to influence public debate by infiltrating the media in order to spread a singular and disciplined conservative agenda. Ironically, this conservative apparatus discharged the very same functions that the Communist Party had done in an earlier generation. In the words of Stephen Longstaff,

> They registered concerns, spoke up for its accomplishments, regulated entry and standing within its orbit, saw to the recruitment and

training of its newest voices, provided its members with a passport to the outside centers of power and creativity, and generally served as an emblem of their collective standing in the wider world.[3]

According to an insider, Michael Lind,

> the neocon network orchestrated by the foundations resembled an old-fashioned political patronage machine, or perhaps one of the party writers' or scholars' guilds in communist countries. A shared pool of right-wing writers and scholars in receipt of foundation grants from the same program officers was established into which conservative journals like *Commentary*, *American Spectator*, *Policy Review*, *Public Interest*, *National Interest*, *New Criterion*, and *Wall Street Journal* regularly dipped.

He continued:

> Washington had come to resemble Hollywood, with the foundations playing the role of the big studios, the program officers acting as producers, editors playing directors, and the talent —policy wonks, publicists—divided between a few well-paid superstars and legions of poorly paid wannabes.

While foundation funding was nothing new (liberals had been doing it for years), the scale of that of the right-wing foundations dwarfed anything that had preceded it. The multimillion dollar annual operating budget of any one of the big conservative thinks such as the American Enterprise Institute, the Hoover Institution, and the Heritage Foundation, exceeded the combined budgets of all left-of-center think tanks. John B. Judis characterized the period as one of competing Washington hustlers looking for money and not being overly scrupulous about where they found it and moderate Republican author John Saloma described as the "new conservative labyrinth." The conservative foundations' funding of *Commentary* was part of this strategy.[4]

The money came at a heavy price, however; one that Podhoretz would not be openly willing to admit he had paid. In return for foundation money, he had to adhere to the foundations' right-wing agenda. *Commentary* essays were required to attack liberals and support official Republican Party positions. It was to undertake to provide scholarly sounding rationalizations for the conservative Republican line once it had been agreed upon. It had to discredit the political adversaries of pro-Republican pressure groups like the Christian Coalition and the NRA. Debate was to be stifled and was acceptable only where the official Republican Party position had not yet been decided. Public dissent on matters of concern, most notably, the reduction of public spending and taxation on the rich, deregulation of business, the strict anti-abortion line, and gun control was not permitted. It had to refrain from criticizing other conservatives in receipt of the same foundation funds. It frequently had to feature the work of foundation-funded authors. Grant recipients were kept on a short leash and those that disobeyed would have their funding cut off.[5]

Podhoretz had sacrificed his intellectual independence and editorial freedom. But he would deny this since he agreed with most of the right-wing agenda anyway. As Lind put it, "It was not so much a matter of external censorship as of reflexive self-censorship." It was not, then, such a stretch for Podhoretz. Besides, he attended the periodic "conservative summits" at which the party line was determined by leading conservative editors, journalists, politicians, and foundation executives. As one reader wrote to Podhoretz,

> Commentary is serving well the most reactionary circles in the US, and they normally pay well. Neither should you have to pay the writers in Commentary. They too work for the most reactionary institutions and foundations in the country, and they are probably paid well by them, using the prestigious collaboration in your journal as a good introduction.

Podhoretz had replaced the editorial freedom of the AJC with the ideological straitjacket of the conservative foundations. In doing so, that which had made Commentary historically unique among English-language publications had disappeared, as it merged into and became almost indistinguishable from the morass of the right-wing press in America. Ironically, in swapping one sponsor for others, Podhoretz became much more subservient to his new ones than he had ever been to the AJC. And the demands of the new sponsor were much greater. In return for large sums of money, Podhoretz had rendered his magazine impotent.[6]

The Gospel of American Conservatism

A host of issues highlighted the extent of Podhoretz's sacrifice. He was prepared to say what the Right wanted him to say regardless of the costs in terms of intellectual independence. The anti-PC campaign, for example, was originated and well-funded by the conservative foundations. In 1984,

Roderic R. Richardson wrote a memo for the right-wing Smith-Richardson Foundation in which he argued that to facilitate its educational agenda the right needed to aim for the rhetorical high ground. Decter, a member of the Smith-Richardson Foundation, reaffirmed this "high-ground" strategy in a 1985 *New York Times* op-ed piece. One year later, Stephen H. Balch and Herbert I London published "The Tenured Left," in *Commentary*. Balch and London deplored the rapid diffusion of "peace studies" programs at primary, secondary, and higher-education levels, as "emotionally loaded and propagandistic," which represented "a comprehensive effort at radical indoctrination." They hated what they saw as the grotesque, self-righteous political posturing of left-wing academics. It was one of the first-anti-PC articles in the media and predated the mass media's picking up of the issue by some half decade. Although prompted by the conservative foundations, Podhoretz was nevertheless proud of earning the opprobrium of the politically correct.[7]

Similarly, the steady stream of homophobia in *Commentary* had grown into a concerted strategy not just because it reflected the bigotry of Podhoretz and the neocons, but also because it suited the political realities of the era. In their embrace of Pat Robertson and Pat Buchanan, Republican leaders revealed that bashing gays was now an explicit party strategy. To justify the Republican Party's antigay stance, respected conservative voices argued that homosexuality was a "learned behavior," as George Bush's vice president Dan Quayle had put it. Thus, in the magazine Harvard psychologist, E. L. Patullo, advocated legal and social discrimination against gays on the dubious theory that most young homosexuals were actually what he called "waverers"—they could go either way—and thus could be coerced by social disapproval into leading heterosexual lives.[8]

Likewise, the neocons knew that the arguments for SDI were deliberate "half-truths and falsehoods," wrote Lind, but supported it anyway rather than jeopardize a potential source of cash and its alliance with "the foundation-subsidized conservative intelligentsia."[9]

Furthermore, as dictated by the conservative foundations, Podhoretz now openly preached the gospel of American conservatism. Supply-side economics and free-market radicalism had become the right-wing orthodoxy, reflecting what political scientist Walter Dean Burnham called the "hegemony of market theology." If capitalism became a political religion, then Podhoretz was ultraorthodox not least because it helped to vindicate his personal quest for material success over the last 30 years. He fully embraced unrestrained, free-market capitalism, allowing explicit apologetics for its excesses to appear in *Commentary*'s pages. The magazine championed the conservative economic orthodoxy as the panacea for society's evils. Its vision of the future of American capitalism was the same low-wage, low-tax, low public-service, low-investment anti-government policies that, it argued, had produced the "great Reagan boom of the 1980's." Indeed, its idealization and adoption of the free-market bordered on fundamentalism.[10]

In line with mainstream conservative thinking but in contradiction to neocon thought, Podhoretz also published articles attacking the welfare state. He wished to reduce the range of government intervention and to cede greater authority to individuals and families, as well as to average Americans and entrepreneurs, believing that certain problems could be most effectively dealt with at the local level and by individuals and families and churches and neighborhood groups. Charles Murray proposed restructuring the entire system of welfare benefits. He argued that the welfare system so encouraged dependency that only by scrapping it can the necessary incentives to get poor people into the workplace and to stop single teenage mothers from having babies out of wedlock be provided. He asserted that excessively generous welfare was a contributing factor to, if not the primary cause of, a dramatic increase in illegitimacy among poor blacks in the inner cities. He even proposed a negative income tax, as advocated by Milton Friedman, as the "cleanest of systems for eradicating poverty." *Commentary* had become an advocate for the rich and the privileged, and insensitive, even hostile, to the needs and circumstances of the poor. Its economic policies justified tax cuts for the former and increasing poverty for the latter.[11]

If the magazine disagreed over anything here, it was how best to phase out a particular feature of the welfare state rather than over the harm it had done and the desirability of working to get rid of it. David Frum blamed the welfare state as the real villain responsible for the decline of traditional values. Above all, he wanted conservatives to repudiate Big Government, root and branch. This was a new departure for *Commentary*, which had previously rarely included an appreciation for limited government, marking the start of a new trend in this direction. Newt Gingrich wrote in to approve. Not everyone was happy, though. This shift to a free-market theology alienated more than one contributor and reader. Richard Schifter, who had been reading *Commentary* since the 1940s felt the magazine "has become an echo, or more appropriately, a cheering section for the nihilism of the New Right. And so, until a new common cause unites us again, Farewell."[12]

Podhoretz justified his defense of the free market by narrow self-interest: it was good for the Jews. Since most Jews in America had made it, he reasoned, they no longer needed the protection afforded by the welfare state and would do very well from the unrestricted and ruthless operation of capitalism. *Commentary* even drew upon Judaism to provide a theological and spiritual rationalization for participating in capitalism. It argued that Jewish sources supported private property and free enterprise, as well as justified self-interest as a Judaic conduct. It went further to deny that Judaism preached concern for the poor and the oppressed. In "Blessing Capitalism," Paul Johnson argued capitalism was "the best way we have yet devised" to "enjoy the fruits of the earth" as envisaged in the "divine plan" and "God's promises to Moses." He quoted Michael Novak approvingly: "in a godly society . . . one where the Judeo-Christian ethic finds strong public and private expression—capitalism is a wonderfully creative force." Here *Commentary* had some influence: it offered a rationalization for those American Jews drawn to ideology of self-interest; as Alan Dershowitz pointed out how, when "Jews become wealthier and more established, some look for rationales to vote with their pocketbooks, and the neocons provide such a rationale." In this way, the magazine had become no different from mainstream conservatives who, since the 1970s, had been claiming, with escalating blatancy, that their package of pro-business measures was the natural outgrowth of the Judeo-Christian tradition.[13]

The Wrong Side of History

Podhoretz was exhilarated by the collapse of Communism in Eastern Europe. The "Evil Empire" was in dissolution. The Berlin Wall had been torn down and East Germans were voting with their feet. Poland, Hungary, and Czechoslovakia replaced years of Communist rule with new democratic institutions and were moving toward replacing centralized economies with the free market. And, even the Soviet Union was headed down the path of political and economic reform in the direction of capitalism and democracy. The neocons erupted into an orgy of victorious outpourings. "The recent events there have surpassed the wildest fantasies," Richard Pipes gushed. The magazine rejoiced in victory and in the West's success over the Soviet Union. It charmed itself with stories of its success and basked in its own glory and sense of having been proven right.[14]

But the neocons had been dramatically mistaken in their assessment of the Soviet threat. Basing their analyses on the belief that totalitarianism as a system was incapable of evolution to democracy they could not or refused to understand the changes taking place before their very eyes. They were too wedded to the belief that totalitarianism could not shed its police-state characteristics; that it died only when power was wrenched from its hands. This doctrine of irreversibility, most notably associated with Jeane Kirkpatrick and popularized by *Commentary*, was thoroughly discredited, as change came from within the Soviet Union itself. For ten years, the magazine had doggedly insisted that totalitarian regimes could never change internally. It willfully ignored Gorbachev's accession to power, his reforms, and the dismantling of the Communist system by the Russian people themselves without any outside military intervention, no doubt because of the intellectual consternation and confusion these developments provoked and because so much intellectual capital was tied up in its dogma.

Other scholars had predicted the Soviet Union's collapse by emphasizing the changes occurring there, but as a result of its Cold Warrior ideological blinders, *Commentary* and the neocons' general tendency was to ignore any internal Soviet change, unless it was for the worse. They overestimated the extent and durability of Soviet power and the threat it represented and was late in realizing that the Soviet Union was in a state of serious crisis. Pipes, for example, may have realized that there was a serious crisis under way within the Soviet Union, but he was wrong in thinking that the West could not bring about any change there because of its inability to stand united and firm. As late as 1990, he still had difficulty telling whether the Soviet Union was breaking up or cracking down. Merely repeating an extreme version of the "present danger" thesis, Pipes gave no sense whatsoever that the Soviet Union was in serious internal crisis. Either he did not know or did not wish to know. Chernobyl, military, ethnic unrest, repression of intellectuals, labor unrest, the breaking apart of the Soviet submarine were all clues that he (and *Commentary*) ignored. The neocons remained blinkered by their own rhetoric to the very end.

Consequently, journalists, historians, intellectuals, and readers began to tear down the walls of Podhoretz's intellectual empire and to indict the neocon foreign policy record. Michael Kinsley mocked the omniscient pretensions of the neocons in the *New Republic* in December 1989. He pointed out how, having said the collapse of Communism would not happen, *Commentary* now claimed credit for it. In the only book addressing neocon foreign policy of that time, John Ehrman showed how, in the mid-1980s, *Commentary* grossly misread the nature and pace of developments in the Soviet Union, and downplayed the significance of Gorbachev's reforms.[15]

In response, Podhoretz sought to defend his neocon record of hawkish analysis from charges that it had been erroneous. Consequently *Commentary* made its case one of conservative success versus liberal failure.

The Left, it argued, was consistently wrong about the Soviet Union. As John Patrick Diggins, pointed out,

> *Commentary* celebrated the end of the cold war almost as though it were a victory over American liberalism as much as Soviet communism. Presumably America had won the long protracted struggle and had done so because the country finally came around to listening to conservatives teach us how to think about communism.

Indeed, *Commentary* suggested that many self-proclaimed liberals should atone for their moral and intellectual obtuseness during the Cold War; "cleansing" and purging themselves through a five-year period of repentant silence.[16]

Containment, stated the magazine, had been spectacularly vindicated. "In reality, it is the doves, not the hawks, who assumed the stability of Communist regimes," wrote Pipes. "The hard-liners believed that firmness on the part of the West would not only contain but in time fundamentally alter the Communist system: the harder they were, the more confident they felt of democracy's eventual triumph over totalitarianism." He continued:

> Even if one admits that the conservatives, along with everyone else, saw the Communists as more solidly entrenched than they turned out to be, the conservatives at least correctly diagnosed totalitarian regimes to be suffering from an incurable disease. It was their opponents on the Left who insisted that the patient was in good health.

Sam Tanenhaus added that Gorbachev's "Western well-wishers, should have known better. That revolt was long in preparation, as the anti-Communist writers—often to the jeers, and worse, of their fellow writers—foresaw so many years ago." Had the free world permitted the "anti-cold war brigade's prescriptions to take root," wrote Arch Puddington, "The cold war would almost certainly still be on, and the collapse of Communist totalitarianism would have been delayed instead of being hastened."[17]

Commentary produced a sympathetic neocon revisionist interpretation of history that credited the Reagan administration, as championed by *Commentary* and the neocons, for winning the Cold War. This became a vitally important means of trying to salvage their reputations. Over the last decade, Podhoretz had done much to build up the reputation of neocon analysis; indeed, he had converted his magazine into a platform for its views. If such analysis were wrong, then the authority of his movement, his magazine, and most importantly, himself, would also decrease. *Commentary* consequently resorted to oversimplification in its anxiousness to prove its ideological thesis that Reagan's visionary leadership (ably assisted by that of Margaret Thatcher) was the *sine qua non* for victory. The elections of both leaders had ushered in a new spirit, "a return to the traditions of genuine liberalism," which, in turn, helped spark the seminal revolt in Poland, where "Solidarity espoused the very ideals that the left-wing intellectuals in the West labeled neoconservative" and whose "heroes were Thatcher and Reagan."[18]

Reagan and Thatcher were glorified as "apostles of victory" over Communism and enshrined in the *Commentary* pantheon. All of the neocon contributors to the 1990 *Commentary* symposium, "The American 80's: Disaster or Triumph," considered it a self-evident truth that Reagan's application of the traditional policy of containment, the Reagan doctrine, the deployment of Euromissiles, SDI, the massive arms build-up that bankrupted Moscow, the refusal to deal with the Soviet Union as a "normal" country, the unbending rhetoric condemning the "evil empire"— all ideas advocated in *Commentary*—led directly to the collapse of the Communist empire, with which only the most unrepentant leftists would disagree. As James Nuechterlain wrote, "those who believe that the revolution in Eastern Europe had little or nothing to do with the policies of the Reagan administration might as readily believe in the ministrations of the tooth fairy." Podhoretz was perhaps the loudest proponent of the neocon tendency to give Reagan's policies massive credit for causing the Soviet collapse. As late as December 1999, he wrote that Reagan's SDI plan prompted Gorbachev's regime to begin massive reforms which "blew their whole system apart."[19]

Commentary indulged in chanting reprises of this neocon litany that became increasingly tiresome as the decade wore on. Others credited high-profile neocon Reaganauts with helping to win the Cold War. Jay Winik congratulated Jeane Kirkpatrick and Elliot Abrams, while Richard Gid Powers assigned Podhoretz a notable role in the final stages of the Cold War drama in his 1995 book *Not Without Honor*. Neocons won the Cold War by virtue of their character, wrote Owen Harries: "stubbornness, perseverance, endurance, and a simple uncomplicated sense of right and wrong. To stay the course while being deeply pessimistic about the outcome is, after all, a very conservative way of achieving victory." Such laudatory comments contributed to the neocon revisionism that somehow history had either stopped or was permanently on their side, and all that was left on the agenda was to bask in the roseate glow cast by the Reagan presidency.[20]

Commentary's efforts to give principal credit for the collapse of Communism to the Reagan administration, though, were unconvincing. As John Patrick Diggins pointed out, Powers' *Not Without Honor*, was simply an endorsement of Podhoretz's "Present Danger" thesis, and thus should be regarded "as the academic historian's counterpart to *Commentary*." The reality was that neocons within the Reagan administration had been sidelined. As a measure of this, Paul Nitze, one of the most hard-line of the founding Cold Warriors who headed up "Team B," wound up having to disavow what he saw as extremist neocons. Some went further to argue that had Reagan listened to the neocons back then, a nuclear war might have resulted. Others believed that neocon "indiscriminate bellicosity on a global scale succeeded mainly in provoking a dangerous arms race, needlessly exacerbating and prolonging conflicts with adversaries, alienating friends, and sowing the seeds of future mistrust of American intentions." Dana H. Allin, for example, contended that far from winning the Cold War, the neocons' hard-line policies and aggressive polemics against détente, actually prolonged it—by greatly augmenting its costs and risks by means of confrontational rhetoric and a relentless military buildup—because they were blind to the fact that by the time Reagan took office in 1980, the Cold War was all but won. Allin was particularly critical of neocon warnings about the ease with which western Europe might be intimated by Soviet pressure, that is, "Finlandized." Allin concluded: "Neoconservatism was, above all, a critique of détente, that supposed snare and delusion that rationalized American appeasement and Western Europe's Finlandization. In terms of the actual American policy, debate, this is what neoconservatism was about. It was wrong."[21]

The inaccuracies multiplied as *Commentary* desperately defended its neocon record. No evidence was proffered that Reagan's policies—arms buildup, SDI, aid to Afghanistan, and denunciation of the Soviet system—were anything other than a continuation of similar policies of all previous administrations since 1947. Its analysis failed to explain why there was no positive change when Reagan confronted Brezhnev, Andropov, and Chernenko, nor why Reagan could move Gorbachev but not them. It found no room to mention the Soviet military debacle in Afghanistan as the decisive factor in destroying the Soviet Union since this glaring omission fit so poorly with the ideological thesis it was so anxious to prove. *Commentary* was reluctant to acknowledge the forces of freedom that courageously took to the streets in Eastern Europe. William Stern pointed out in the Letters pages:

> There was nothing imaginative, resourceful, or courageous that Reagan did that can possibly be compared with what Gorbachev did, and to interpret this most edifying historical happening of our

century as an achievement of Ronald Reagan is a distortion which no amount of fancy rhetoric ... can disguise.

Walter C. Uhler added:

The publication of Solzhenitsyn's *One Day in the Life of Ivan Denisovich* (1962) in the Soviet Union and the publication abroad of *The Gulag Archipelago* (1973) did more to undermine the Stalinist system both inside and outside Russia than all the blustering and weapons of our cold warriors in the years 1945–1985. Yet one searches in vain for mention of Solzhenitsyn's role. One suspects a willful ignorance is at work here, one which hesitates to credit Solzhenitsyn (normally the darling of the conservatives) not only for fear of minimizing Reagan's role, but also for fear of revealing how abysmally the cold warriors failed to recognize the possibility of change under Communism.[22]

Podhoretz and the neocons also ignored the fact that Reagan's victory over Communism was ultimately brought about not simply by his posture of strength but by his willingness not to be blinkered by own rhetoric. They brushed aside the effects of forty-four years of consistently anti-Communist American foreign policy. They did not discuss the impact of cultural and technological factors on the decline of Communism. And they took little note of significant internal developments in the Soviet bloc. They overlooked the students and young people behind the Iron Curtain and the fact that the United States did nothing in Czechoslovakia and Romania, as well as China, where thousands of students were killed. In doing so, they even ignored their own writings which had deplored the Reagan administration's lack of foreign policy success, its disastrous Middle East program, and its embarrassing Central America policy. Their own statements attacking him were on record but they now claimed Reagan's legacy as their own. Writers like Pipes, Puddington, and Charles Horner, complained readers, sought "to deflect scrutiny by claiming victory, and muddying the waters through tendentious essays."[23]

Podhoretz and the neocons downplayed the importance of any positive change in the Soviet Union and certainly did not attribute it to Gorbachev. They described Gorbachev's reforms as "cosmetic." Indeed, they continued to do so well into the late 1990s, praising Reagan (and to a lesser extent, Thatcher) for the demise of Communism, when it became abundantly clear that Gorbachev was the major catalyst of change. Instead, they argued that by sponsoring and endorsing the idea that Gorbachev did it all, liberals were simply trying to cast doubt on conservative claims. All in all, it amounted to an ignoble distortion of the past.

Commentary also sought to defend Reagan's domestic record. Journalists, historians, and intellectuals increasingly characterized the 1980s as a costly if not disastrous decade for America. Yet, despite the current US economic difficulties, mass homelessness, increasing income inequalities, post-industrialism, tax cuts, deregulation, decline of national productivity, federal deficits, savings and loans swindles, racial discord, an expanding gap between rich and poor, the rise in violent crime, the decline of key industrial sectors, the drop in savings, and the fall in labor productivity, *Commentary* not only championed Reaganomics but glorified Reaganite conservatism to produce twisted and torturous defenses of Reagan's performance on social and economic issues. This was also partly motivated by the need to vindicate an economic strategy that *Commentary* was currently pushing.

Podhoretz initiated a symposium, "The American 80's: Disaster or Triumph?" to counter the charges that

> the economic and social policies of the Reagan administration stimulated greed on Wall Street and in the business community, encouraged a general mood of selfishness, and were responsible for an actual increase of poverty (as symbolized in particular by the plight of the homeless).

He could not comprehend that, despite "the worldwide triumph by the end of the decade of the prevailing ideas and policies of the American 80's," "the fact that so many people in America itself have been condemning those ideas and policies." The failings of America during the 1980s were thus presented as a debatable point ("Do you accept these characterizations?").[24]

Instead, Podhoretz spoke of the "worldwide triumph" of the "prevailing ideas and policies" of that decade as an undisputable reality. As was to be expected from a magazine that provided some of the intellectual underpinnings of the Reagan Revolution, the responses were primarily eulogies to the Reagan administration, positively assessing Reagan's domestic and foreign policies (albeit with some minor qualifications). They found the 1980s wonderful: they celebrated the revolution in human rights, the building up of democracy around the world and, of course, the collapse of the "Evil Empire." Against critics who argued that the United States was on the way to becoming a third-world country or was suffering from "imperial overstretch," *Commentary* countered with the view that, far from being in a state of decline, the United States was still the wealthiest and most influential society in the world and was, moreover, heading toward even greater achievements in every sphere. Every sentence was informed with blinkered Panglossian optimism that was typical of *Commentary* at that time and which fondly recalled eight years of Reaganism. Since *Commentary* "presented an exaggerated premise," noted *Newsweek* columnist Gregg Easterbrook, "many commentators responded with exaggerated visions."[25]

These responses proved just how deep Podhoretz's refusal to face facts head-on really was. He ignored the very real problems that Reagan had left behind like homelessness, which was a key symbolic issue of the 1980s. He also failed to deal with the legitimate indictment of 1980s greed-and-selfishness. Indeed, *Commentary* spent more time attacking the Left, betraying nostalgia for the days when everything could be blamed on Carter. Kirkpatrick even managed to blame the homeless problem on Reagan's failure to solve the problem of "liberal" extremism. Likewise, *Commentary* had no credible responses to repeated liberal charges of 12 years of Republican neglect of civil rights under Reagan and Bush. Arch Puddington conceded that these administrations had given "every sign of obliviousness to the racial problem and in the process reinforced the impression that conservatives simply do not care much whether blacks succeed or not." But *Commentary* denied Republican responsibility and instead blamed the Great Society reforms of 25 years ago, the internal pathologies of the black community, and liberal white racism. It insisted that "black racism, anti-Semitism, and lawlessness" had been tolerated for too long, "justified by the mindless application of a false paradigm of black victimization." "This reversing of the debatable with and the factual is an example of the habit," observed Paul Berman, "of dousing ourselves with celebratory champagne in order not to notice the evidence of capitalist horrors that sprawls nightly across our own doorsteps." It reflected the poverty of the conservative movement of which *Commentary* was now indisputably a part, and this was reflected in the election 1992 presidential campaign. Readers predicted conservatism's decline if it didn't root its political thinking into a sense of reality, what was actually going on than what their favored theories said ought to be going on.[26]

Similarly, when Nelson Mandela was released to a hero's welcome in 1990 after several decades in prison, Podhoretz was in a tight spot and found himself in the strange place of being on the losing side of history. Kirkpatrick's distinction between "traditional" and "revolutionary" regimes meant that *Commentary* backed the apartheid-regime in South Africa as an anti-Communist proxy. If it did not directly support apartheid, then its deafening silence on the topic was shameful. Between 1957 and 1985 no article on that topic appeared. When apartheid collapsed, there were no signs of remorse about this significant political and moral failure. In fact, the magazine's tone on South Africa may have become somewhat more equivocal, but the sniping did not stop thereafter. It continued to regard Mandela with suspicion. It wrote that Mandela's radical beliefs would lead his people to ruin. He would emerge to become an embittered, authoritarian tyrant intent on settling scores with the minority white populations. But when Mandela proved to be a magnanimous leader and statesman, presiding over a peaceful transition of power to the black majority, an embarrassing silence prevailed. *Commentary*'s predictions of doom had not been borne out. It had been wrong about black self-rule, the ANC, and Mandela. South Africa became a parliamentary democracy no longer based on the racist regime of apartheid. Every argument made by *Commentary* concerning apartheid was proven wrong and that seldom had there been a more decisive repudiation of conservative dogma than in the case of South Africa. Far from being a failure, sanctions had worked. *Commentary*'s defense of and complicity with white-ruled South Africa was dishonorable. Its case for apartheid, wrote Jacob Heilbrunn, "was not just morally reprehensible—it was also false."[27]

Identity Crisis

Podhoretz and the neocons had clearly lost their way. Celebrations of the end of the Cold War could not hide this salient fact. "The events of the recent past in Central and Eastern Europe unfolded so swiftly and with such cinematic surrealism as to have left, amid the celebration, a good deal of intellectual confusion," noted Sam Tanenhaus. Seemingly 40 years of history had been "erased overnight, repudiated as if by reflex." Podhoretz had a special difficulty in moving out too smartly to claim credit for the Soviet collapse because, to do so, would also mean admitting that he had been wrong. Podhoretz had become such a Cold War ideologue that he would not or could not admit that the world was improving. There was an element of calculation about this, too. Podhoretz had built himself up on the back of the Cold War, without it, he and his magazine would become useless and would lose their *raison d'être*. He had too much intellectual and moral capital invested in the Cold War: he was shaped by it, most of his contributors and editors had lived their entire adult lives against the backdrop of the conflict, they had spent a great deal of time reading, thinking, writing, and arguing about it, they had been engaged in it to an exceptional extent. They could not simply write off the Cold War as an episode that was no longer relevant, or dismiss it as something that was not only over but done with and did not need to be thought seriously about again.[28]

So, fearing that in the face of a diminishing danger Podhoretz would lose his influence, he maintained a hard-line and printed articles about Soviet atrocities and Communist "totalitarian oppression" as reminders of what Stalinism and Communism were all about. He ex-communicated—as apostates—those who suggested that the threat had disappeared. *Commentary* warned that Communism was not yet finished and pessimistically predicted that "the specter of Den Xiaoping" may well be likely "to haunt the world." Military readiness, therefore, was still necessary, as was Star Wars. There was "no strong argument against SDI in the post-Soviet era," wrote Joshua Muravchik and Podhoretz rather the lack of missile defense was "militarily and morally outrageous," as well as "positive madness" because it left the United States "at the mercy of the worst elements of mankind."[29]

Podhoretz was suffering from an identity crisis. Gary Dorrien astutely observed, "the loss of a defining foreign demon would prove difficult to absorb" as the "certainties that had fueled Podhoretz's writing for the past twenty years were swept way." His posture had been overwhelmingly geared to the Soviet threat. William Phillips once remarked that it appeared that Podhoretz had been created by the Left, suggesting that Podhoretz would have nothing to write about "if left-liberals did not feed him with their illusions about Soviet communism, the Third World, or the P.L.O." Once that threat subsided, as the very idea of totalitarianism collapsed, Podhoretz was bewildered by his new surroundings in which he had lost his bearings. He surely had nightmares of being left without a mission and a job to do. His anti-Communism was a "crippling rigidity." Everything had become viewed through the distorting lens of the Cold War and now that had been taken away. But Podhoretz could not disentangle himself from the language of the Cold War, finding it increasingly hard to abandon his familiar if gloomy notions of the Cold War struggle. He was anxious about the future, unable to hide his bitterness that his comfortable Cold War axioms had lost their potency and ability to terrify. So Podhoretz simply stopped writing, leaving his major planned articles unwritten. In 1989, Owen Harries, the editor of the *National Interest* invited Podhoretz to contribute to a series of articles he was planning on the role of America in a post-Cold War world. After thinking about it long and hard, he declined, because he had been unable to make up his mind as to what he thought America's purpose should be "now that the threat of Communism, which had supplied the organizing principle of our foreign policy for more than four decades, had been decisively eliminated." "The implosion of the Soviet bloc," suggests Dorrien, "sealed Podhoretz's silence." "The prospect of writing literary criticism or anything else without the devouring Soviet threat to confer seriousness on his work was a deflating turn."[30]

Similarly, in 1990 Decter shut down her Committee for the Free World for the same reasons. It had been

> so much focused on Soviet Communism—both its power in the world and the culture in the United States to which a great fear of that power had given rise—that I wasn't sure what we should or could be doing now,

she recalled. "I had found the prospect of grinding on—for without the Soviet Union, that's how our work would have felt to us—too depressing."[31]

Neoconservatism took its lead from its general. The greatest prop underlining it—the Communist threat—which had dominated its entire existence, had been removed. Unless, it adapted to the new realities, the movement was bound to lose ground and influence. It failed to do so. It had great difficulty in adjusting to the end of the Cold War for which it was poorly equipped. The world might have changed since the fall of the Berlin Wall but any reader of *Commentary* of during the late 1980s and early 1990s onwards would not have known that. It had become boringly predictable. Its inflexible ideology and hostility to any form of compromise meant that the deterioration of the Soviet Union left the magazine directionless and irrelevant in the field of foreign affairs. Paradoxically, while all of *Commentary*'s neocon foreign policy was directed at destroying the Soviet empire, it could not see its collapse coming. And when it did fall, the magazine and movement was left floundering, rudderless, without an enemy to drive its animus. While it had been vindicated to a certain extent (the West triumphed), this came at a heavy price: Podhoretz, the neocons, and *Commentary* were now increasingly marginalized in American foreign policy debates. Their conspicuous failure to grasp the magnitude of change in the Soviet Union led to the end of the halcyon era, when *Commentary* dictated the parameters of intellectual debate, provided public policy for the presidency, and got its neocon writers appointed to high-profile positions. Irving Kristol's *National Interest* overtook *Commentary* and usurped its intellectual dominance in foreign affairs. This was illustrated by the publication of Francis Fukuyama's "The End of History?" in the summer of 1989 in *National Interest* rather than *Commentary*. For Ehrman, a sympathetic voice, it showed that the *National Interest* was simply a more consistently exciting and relevant magazine. "Suddenly, *Commentary* appeared not only to be providing old answers to old questions, but it no longer seemed even to be making the right inquires," he wrote.[32]

For the neocons, the new world it had entered in 1990 seemed more turbulent than it actually was. The events of 1989 had knocked the wind out of *Commentary*'s sails. In the first year of the new decade, there were far fewer pieces on foreign policy (only two in January and none in February 1990). Instead there was a focus on *internal* issues: the election of the first black mayor, David Dinkins, in New York City; the Act for Better Child Care Services, controversial art; the battle over Robert Bork's Supreme Court nomination; legalization of drugs; and bilingual education.

The Culture Wars

With the Cold War over, Podhoretz declared a "culture war" in its place. The collapse of his primary foe—the Soviet Union—left Podhoretz eager to channel the magazine's energies in a different direction. So, mirroring his declaration of war against "The Movement" in 1970, he called for an exaggerated culture war on every front, from crime to poverty, from the schools and universities to religion and the arts, even international relations. A culture war also had the added bonus that it served the conservative foundations' agenda and furthermore deflected attention from their economic program, which *Commentary* had also adopted, that favored big business and the elites over the less well-off sections of US society (both middle and working class alike). Besides, it was much easier to blame the Left and their allies on the university campus than to address the problems that Reagan, with the neocons' help, had bequeathed America.[33]

Comparing America to Yugoslavia, Podhoretz argued that the common culture was Balkanizing, breaking down even, under the weight of pressure from multiculturalism, racial polarization, distrust of authority, dissolution of shared moral and religious values. Podhoretz's own confidence in the moral and cultural spheres of American life had been "very severely shaken," because America had become "two nations"—the "traditionalists" vs. the "liberationists"—in "a state of war" with each other. He regarded the realm of morality and culture as "the life blood" of the nation, so the division into two nations was by far the most threatening development of the 1990s. At one end, were those like the neocons, "mostly middle-class people still bound by the traditional norms," while on the other, were those who had "been liberated from those traditional norms" by aggressively imposing affirmative action, feminism, gay rights, and multiculturalism. Passions on both sides ran high, with enough hatred and enough fear in each camp to fuel not just a metaphoric civil war but a real one, so much so, that Podhoretz could not envisage "the terms of a treaty that would usher in an era of harmonious coexistence."[34]

Podhoretz and the neocons positioned themselves as the defenders of the values of Western civilization against the multicultural, deconstructionist, homosexual, and feminist onslaught. As they had done in the 1970s, Podhoretz and the neocons declared war. Francis Fukuyama stated that "a culture war is upon us, and that this fight will be a central American preoccupation now that the cold war is over." He predicted it would be fought "block-by-block," not against foreigners but against those among us. Midge Decter announced that it would be a "long and bloody" fight, "a war to the death." She intended to carry the fight "to every inch of ground, private as well as public, on which Americans live with one another, and collectively in the world at large." The enemy HQ, they said, was located in the heart of the American academy, which had been completely overrun by the forces of political correctness and the "nihilist onslaught of deconstruction." *Commentary* painted this war as a *Kulturkampf* between "the overwhelming majority of Americans" and the "the enemies of culture" entrenched in the universities. The politicization of teaching and scholarship had transformed the universities from places of learning to arenas contaminated with foreign and "totalitarian modes of thinking," antithetical to the Western tradition. The only place where Marxism still survived in America was on the campuses and there free speech was dead. These "faculty ideologues" and "radicals" were dug in deeply, particularly in departments such as ethnic and women's studies. They maintained their position through institutionalized racial preference and by hiring only like-minded people. They limited the range of views to "a diversity of radical positions" and they spread their insidious message through political correctness.[35]

Podhoretz was at the forefront of the fight against what he saw as the new barbarism that went under the name of PC, ever since his wife had initiated the first strike in this foundation-generated strategy back in 1985. PC was represented as the greatest intellectual and ethical test for American civilization now that the Cold War was over. Just as it had detected Leftism and McGovenism ubiquitously in the 1970s, *Commentary* found their modern incarnations in PC everywhere, not just on the university campus. Clint Eastwood, once "the enforcer of law and justice," had "gone soft" because of PC. Even America's "greatest journalistic institution" could not escape the ravages of PC: radicalized, jazzed up, and dumbed down, the *New York Times* had surrendered to the wave of the present "degradation."[36]

The neocons prepared themselves for a concentrated effort on defending its social and moral issues, the civilizational values of the West, those same values that had triumphed in the Cold War, against the so-called academic activists. Podhoretz brought in the heavy guns, providing a platform for completely conservative-foundation-constructed and financed, conservative mercenary "radicals," the most prominent of whom was Dinesh D'Souza, who had earned the nickname "Distort D'Newsa." They were obsessed with the contemporary movements of environmentalism, sexual liberation, anti-capitalism, and multiculturalism. An advert in the magazine highlighted such fears.

> Appalled by the arts?
> Afraid for our children?
> Nervous about Russia?
> Shocked by our schools?
> Distressed about welfare?
> Bewildered by foreign policy?
> Disgusted by the universities?
> Incensed by affirmative action?
> Uneasy about national defense?
> Infuriated about rampant crime?
> Worried for the Western world?

The neocons argued that America was failing at every level to educate its young people properly. America's system of public education was one of the worst in the industrialized world and the signs of failure were everywhere. The public school was threatening the democratic culture by fostering divisiveness. Feminists had distorted textbooks into nonfictional examples of what George Orwell (now transformed into a neocon hero) had once referred to as Newspeak. Public-school children were being "indoctrinated into a state-approved sexual ethic." The public school had been altered from a place dedicated to the transmission of the common culture and of the skills necessary to understand an to extend it, to an agency of social change, replacing competition with "cooperative learning" and helping students "feel good about themselves" by doing away with objective measures of achievement and passing everyone along through the system. The result was a corruption of the system itself; no longer an educational enterprise but an increasingly political one with social work and therapy replacing teaching and learning.[37]

The neocons desired to preserve the stability of traditional political institutions and to preserve and transmit the great traditions of the common cultural and artistic inheritance and learning and the values they embodied. They argued that "the ideas and ideals expressed in the great works of Western civilization, and the custom and ceremony that have grown up around them, needed defending from the ideologues, whether in

Hollywood or at Harvard." They understood themselves to represent "the guardian of culture, of the historically transmitted, of the 'givens' of how we order our life together." They returned to the markings of the cultural barometer of the 1950s: highbrow, middlebrow, and lowbrow, which Clement Greenberg had outlined in his June 1953 *Commentary* article, "The Plight of Our Culture." They narrow-mindedly assumed that the 1990s were an age of mediocrity and worried that its artistic products would achieve museum and canonical status.[38]

The neocons decried the wreckage of American family life, brought about, as they saw it, by the social policies of the 1960s and 1970s. Indeed, the prospect of undoing some of the damage had been one of the main appeals of Reaganism, and "strengthening the family" became a rhetorical catchword for the Right. The "real political issue," wrote Joshua Muravchik, was "the progressive dilution of moral standards, expressed in rising rates of divorce, illegitimacy, and venereal disease" and "clamorous 'liberation' groups that seem to deny the inherent differences between men and women, and between heterosexual unions and homosexual ones." The traditional two-parent family and its values, which needed to be encouraged and supported, had broken under radical feminism's assault over the last two decades. Now, *Commentary* stated, illegitimacy was the central social problem of the 1990s. Family, schools, and religious institutions were tragically demising. There was a clear-cut deterioration in moral life, drug abuse, secularization of religion, and moral skepticism. Life was no longer held as sacred and had become cheap. The taboos against abortion, homicide, suicide, and euthanasia were breaking down, if they hadn't already done so. *Roe v. Wade* had given approval to destructive attitudes towards pregnancy and the 1.5 million annual abortions were "a national catastrophe" which, undoubtedly, had a "coarsening effect" on adults' attitude towards children. Romance and courtship had been lost, sex had become too casual, language had become crude and explicit, and dancing obscene. "Sexual commissars" had taken over sex education and produced a "date-rape/sexual-harassment hysteria." The antiharassment and date-rape campaigns represented a triumph for "man-hating lesbian" feminists. Men were bullied into becoming "wimps." Podhoretz's personal rhetoric reached excessive levels of priapism, misogyny, chauvinism, and "neo-Neanderthal" ideology complained readers.[39]

Podhoretz published many articles in line with conservative foundation thinking. They urged sexual restraint, opposed the legalization of drugs, but saw the new antismoking campaign as a pious return of the "insidious" and "frightening" New Class agenda (which the neocons despised) that suppressed rugged individualism in the name of the collective good. No doubt because of Big Tobacco, they even made tortuous distinctions between nicotine and cocaine and heroin, in order to justify the Right's pro-smoking agenda. The neocons had subscribed to the bleating of smokers, tobacco growers, and tobacco companies that this was a civil rights issue and that curtailment of smoking in public spaces represented a form of dictatorship. Ironically, the neocons preached and pontificated on every other issue (drugs, abortion, families, values, etc.) but somehow stated smoking should be left untouched. It was no doubt for this reason that Philip Morris Companies ran an advert flattering Podhoretz on the occasion of his retirement. In thrall to the conservative pro-business, antienvironmentalist stance, Podhoretz failed to publish a single serious article on the environment, relegating the depletion of the ozone layer and Amazon forests to the margins. And when *Commentary* finally did take notice, it did so to debunk it as environmental alarmism. Jeffrey Salmon called the Greenhouse effect a "global-warming scare." He argued that many scientists wildly exaggerated the threat posed by global warming, thereby stirring disproportionate concern among policy-makers and providing fodder for environmentalists who are supposedly hell-bent on slashing fossil fuel use at any cost. His article was typical of *Commentary*'s dismissive attitude toward what it called the "eco-awareness" movement, the "eco-lobbies," "eco-professionals," "eco-enlightened," "eco-funds" and of the wisdom of actions to mitigate greenhouse-gas emissions and of the need to lessen human-induced climate change. *Commentary* also attacked the standard conservative targets: blacks, secularists, and homosexuals (although it drew the line at attacking Jews and immigrants).[40]

Social Darwinist Laissez-Faire Racism

Perhaps the most alarming effect of the conservative funding was the complete abandonment of any civil rights policy. *Commentary* resorted to a form of social Darwinist laissez-faire racism. It gave up proposing serious alternatives to the current system of affirmative action and nowhere developed policies to reduce racial inequities. The formula offered by Thomas Sowell, "No one who extinguishes a forest fire or removes a cancer has to 'replace' it with anything," was repeated in the magazine. It advocated a hands-off policy, letting African Americans sink or swim, as there was nothing else, it said, that could be done. It was time to leave it to inner-city blacks to take responsibility for their own lives, urging self-help. And worse, it was expressed in racist terms, that black men were animalistic (Decter even used the term "sire"). Even former *Commentary* stalwart and fellow neocon Daniel Patrick Moynihan found such statements "depraved."[41]

The nadir of *Commentary*'s approach to civil rights came in 1994 when neocons Charles Murray and Richard Herrnstein published their book,

The Bell Curve. They linked intelligence, genetics, and race to argue that blacks, Hispanics, and lower-income whites were genetically predisposed toward lower IQs and lesser achievement-than upper-income white Americans. It was widely seen as a piece of profoundly racist and classist pseudo-science, methodologically flimsy, and a screed designed to promote a radical political agenda, which had relied heavily on studies financed by the Pioneer Fund, a neo-Nazi organization that promoted eugenicist research. The American Psychological Association denounced it. Although there was an almost near-universal attempt to discredit its findings, *Commentary* gave the book a largely approving although by no means uncritical review which found it to be "a work of great value." Not only did *Commentary* favorably review the book when almost no one else had done (most of the comment was hostile), Podhoretz even gave Murray space in the magazine to defend his book against the fierce avalanche of justified criticism aimed at it. In "rallying to the defense of Murray and Herrnstein," wrote Lind, Podhoretz did much here to counterbalance the avalanche of opprobrium heaped upon the book and its authors, and "gave the appearance of credibility to claims that opponents of pseudo-scientific racism [were] nothing more than liberals frightened of daring scholarship." Decades of white Jewish liberal support for the civil rights struggle had been completely wiped out, as the magazine fell for a classically racist position. It called into question whether Podhoretz had ever been truly committed to the cause of civil rights in the first place, or, as one reader put it, was simply content with displaying dirty laundry before a national audience.[42]

Biblical Morality

As it had done in an earlier Cold War era, *Commentary* frequently appealed to biblical and religious authority in service of the culture wars. Judaism and the Hebrew Bible were used to articulate its deeply conservative morality and sociopolitical ideology. The magazine focused on moral questions in attempt to restore them to the analysis of American politics. It moralized about abortion, out-of-wedlock-parenting, homosexuality, recreational drug use, obscene art, and social obligations to the poor. Chicago philosopher Leon Kass, who some have called "the Religious Right's favorite intellectual," wrote angry, disgusted polemics, opposing or at least vexing over virtually every new reproductive technology, from in vitro fertilization to cloning and referred to abortion as "feticide." He treated *Commentary*'s readers to soapbox sermonizing, Bible lessons on euthanasia, the sexual revolution, in particular the pill. He used the dietary laws to articulate a call for self-restraint and denial. "Canaan will still—and again—be cursed to live like a pagan," he wrote. Only through abstention could America's "rapid slide toward Shechem" be reversed. *Commentary* increasingly sounded like a fundamentalist preacher in what it called a "new religious war" between "those who affirm the classical Jewish and Christian notion of an objective moral order" and "the encroachments of neopagan." This was a war to be fought over the state schools and what was permitted within them, the use of taxpayers' money; the interpretation of the Constitution by the courts; the enactment of congressional and state legislation on private and public morals; the selection of candidates for public office; and, above all, abortion. As *Commentary* once warned against the dangers of Communism, it now admonished against the dangers of secularism, paganism, and "anti-biblical barbarism." It was a battle between "Sodom and Gomorrah and Middletown," between "the values of the Bible and the values of the mass media," the greatest challenge to the unity and conscience of the American people since the Civil War itself."[43]

Podhoretz fell back on old, comfortable, and reassuring shibboleths. He clung to the exhausted Left-Right, liberal-conservative paradigm. In the search for a post-Communist demon, he resurrected the fight against the New Left and anti-anti-Communism even though they had far exceeded their relevance. The 1960s might have been over but *Commentary* kept them—or its version of them—alive and well. It defined itself against the "moral decay" of that decade, cataloguing with great care all its many "grotesqueries," and immersing itself in the task of hauling away its last rusted-out ideas. In *Commentary*'s world, sixties radicals and their descendents were still dangerous individuals and there was an unmistakable *frisson* and a delicious adrenalin rush at their mention. It painted a picture of an America that was utterly unreal and inaccurate as Podhoretz hysterically exaggerated liberalism and absurdly underestimated the social conservatism of American society, fantasizing about New Class crusades.[44]

Podhoretz expressed a deeply conservative morality, pushing his culture war arguments to extremes. He used the same rhetoric of the Cold War to fight the culture wars. As with all neocon cultural criticism, he painted the forces of PC, deconstruction, and the forms of academic Leftism associated with it as totalitarian modes of thinking, while the Right were the defenders of liberty. He often presented the neocons as victims of the forces of the liberal establishment and campus PC. In *Commentary*'s self-proclaimed fight against PC, noted its long-suffering readers,

> its misrepresentations repeated, again and again, followed a formula: some ill-considered and inaccurate history, a rehash of selected

(and dated) campus atrocity stories, a recitation of accounts from the popular press, all adding up to proof of a grand radical conspiracy that PC was threatening the very lifeblood of American democracy.

Commentary substituted "hyperbole" for "serious scholarship" and "reasoned analysis" in which it "conjure[d] up frightening scenarios of campus Reds run amok and the terminal decline of time tested standards." Its writers displayed "a chutzpah in their claims to be defending intellectual standards against vulgar Leftists while their own careers consisted mainly of vulgarizing the complex ideas of Left scholars at the level of tabloid journalism." Podhoretz, *Commentary*, and the neocons were too blinded by dogma to get their criticisms right and so resorted to misrepresentation and oversimplification, as a means of evading the substantive issues raised by the Left.[45]

Podhoretz deployed the language of civil war (for example, its comparisons between America and Yugoslavia), helping to destroy the linguistic ground necessary for reasoned debate. He resorted to a discourse of an increasingly narrow "us" versus an increasingly alien "them," and helped to transform the universities into arenas of political confrontation. He crowed about being the unique defender of disinterested critical values, never once dropping his pretense of nonpartisanship (for, in his own mind "conservative" was synonymous with "non-political") nor openly arguing for the superiority of right-wing over left-wing cultural politics. Podhoretz was guilty of what he attacked Leftists for, of making the same reductive and ideologically driven points over and over again. These assaults became tiresome after a while and readers began to complain. Where *Commentary* referred to the ease with which it was possible to predict any *New York Times* editorial position, the magazine's own "editorial predictability," noted one reader, was "granite compared with the *New York Times*' clay." A chronic narrowness of purpose and literalness of mind dogged its conservatism. "[I]f you wanted to read an ideological tract," wrote Andrew Sullivan, editor of the *New Republic*, "you could read the *Nation*. Or *Commentary*. To me, they already read like documents from an earlier era."[46]

Entering the Fever Swamps

In his continued search for power, Podhoretz took an even sharper turn to the right and formed an alliance not with his (now) natural moderate allies in the Republican Party, but with the Christian fundamentalists of the Religious Right. Only a few years earlier, the neocons had been denouncing them as coming from "the fever swamps," in the words of Decter.

Podhoretz's move was a tactical one for he calculated that, following the 1992 presidential campaign, Pat Robertson and his Christian Coalition were key power brokers in the conservative movement and the GOP. To reject the Religious Right would be not only to marginalize his own influence but would also endanger the foundation funding on which *Commentary* was now so dependent. So, Podhoretz embraced right-wing religious fundamentalism, rationalizing this new alliance on the grounds that only religion of any kind could halt what he perceived as the moral deterioration of the time, as well as the growth of left-wing anti-Semitism, anti-Americanism, and anti-Zionism.[47]

Podhoretz argued that he had come to see the Religious Right as a valuable ally in the effort to halt and perhaps even reverse the moral decline of American society. He adopted the attitude that his enemy's enemy was his friend and the support of fundamentalist groups for Israel (albeit for their own peculiar chiliastic reasons) was not to be lightly dismissed. The Zionist Right was politically allied to the Religious Right and in any case Christians were necessary to deal with the new Muslim threat. Views inconsistent with those of his new-found friends began to disappear from the magazine as Podhoretz stopped publishing the denunciations of Christianity that had appeared in *Commentary* in earlier years and dropped any contributor who wrote them. Hyam Maccoby ceased writing for *Commentary* because he was known to regard medieval Christianity as chiefly responsible for the demonization of the Jews which had persisted under various forms into modern times. Indeed, over the years *Commentary* had featured many articles, which traced the roots of modern persecution to Christian anti-Semitism, for example, those by Norman Ravitch. But now, *Commentary*'s pages were closed to such pieces. Instead, Podhoretz published pieces cheering the influence of the fundamentalist Christians in the Republican Party. Irving Kristol often wrote them, out of genuine sympathy for the movement's cultural conservatism.

Podhoretz embarked on a campaign to convince Jews that fundamentalist Christians were pro-Israel and therefore friendly. He pointed out that while Jews correctly recognized anti-Semitism in resurgent black nationalism and the rhetoric of Jesse Jackson, they erroneously saw in it Christian evangelism. He urged Jews to work together with Christians to restore American civilization. He sought to prove that conservatism was compatible with the deepest ideals of Judaism. He equated Margaret Thatcher's notion of "Victorian values"—hard work, diligence, thrift, responsibility, civility, devotion to family, and respect for law and order—with Judaism. He argued that Judaism was a conservative, not liberal, religion. He complained about the Left-liberal agenda of the official American Jewish community, which it called, "out of sync with the mood of the country." In a provocative article entitled, "Why Religion is Good for the Jews," Kristol likewise urged his coreligionists to abandon its erstwhile faith—liberalism—in favor of an even older one: Judaism. Welfare-state liberalism was "anachronistic," he said. To bolster its efforts, Kristol tried to scare the Jewish community. He raised the twin fears of intermarriage and anti-Semitism. In order to ensure demographic survival the Jewish community must purge itself of the prevailing "liberal ethos," which, he charged, had spawned not only a religious malaise, but was also responsible for "the most blatant and vicious form of anti-Semitism in this country emanat[ing] from the black community." And while liberalism had prepared Jews to fight the traditional foe of anti-Semitism, it had blinded them to their new enemy: intermarriage. The new challenge facing Jews was "how to live as equals in American society without committing demographic suicide."[48]

Podhoretz painted a picture that the tragic demise of the family, schools, and religious institutions during the last 30 years had had a profoundly damaging impact upon American Jewry. The erosion of society's support for the traditional values that were deemed central to Judaism like marriage and the family, nurturing children, moral values including the sanctity of life, and personal sacrifices and service had contributed monumentally to shaping a younger generation that was largely alienated from its Jewish roots and values, and, therefore, very prone to assimilation into the decadent culture that typified secular America. Jews must look inward and educate their children about Jewish religious traditions and practices. To this end, *Commentary* recommended a greater knowledge and cultural literacy of Hebrew, in the service of its message. It was attempting to inspire nothing less than a Jewish religious revival. But its prescriptions for the future were naïve and unrealistic, believing that if only rabbis and communal leaders loudly proclaimed their commitment to traditional values, Jewish behavior would change. It also represented a nostalgic yearning for the romanticized "simplicities of an earlier era," noted readers, "a return to the Orthodoxy of the *shtetl*."[49]

Commentary's prescription for Jewish public policy was the same as that of the conservative foundations. Abandon support for church-state separation; suspend concern for the disadvantaged; withdraw from the struggle for adequate health-care coverage; end support for public education, protection of the environment, and a woman's right to choose; and stop wasting time in joining coalitions with minorities and other groups of Americans—except, of course, with conservative Republicans. In particular, the continuing, "inflexible," and "obsessive" commitment of Jewish communal agencies to the "impermeable" separation of church and state distressed *Commentary*. It was felt likely to increase the level of tension between Jews and other Americans. It called this "separationist faith" a "sin" and opposed the Jewish call to lead the campaign against a constitutional amendment permitting school prayer. It also tried to break "the stubborn Jewish attachment to secularism" out of which derived the American Jewish dichotomy of private religion/public secularism. Here *Commentary* was simply reiterating ideas from the past; 40 years ago, theologian Will Herberg had advanced such ideas in the magazine but they had been ridiculed by his fellow intellectuals. Now the dust was blown off and they were revived again as the magazine moved away from the doctrine of strict separationism which it had once promoted.[50]

Podhoretz and the neocons leapt to the defense of the Religious Right no matter what its offence. When an ADL report of 1994 accused Robertson and other Religious Right leaders of anti-Semitic tendencies, Midge Decter savaged it in the magazine. She also gathered 75 signatures for a full-page ad in the *New York Times*, accusing the ADL of slighting the conservative Christian movement. On her authority William Buckley also absolved Robertson of the charge of anti-Semitism. "Who's Afraid of the Religious Right?" "Not I," her husband went on to write in the *National Review*. And when Robertson published his book *The New World Order* in 1991, which, among other things, accused George Bush and the Council on Foreign Relations of being a Judeo-Masonic-Satanic conspiracy, Podhoretz produced a circuitous vindication of Robertson in order to exonerate him from the charges of anti-Semitism. Jacob Helibrunn called them "contortions."[51]

Although, Podhoretz argued, it was beyond dispute that Robertson had "purveyed ideas that have an old and well-established anti-Semitic pedigree,"—Robertson proposed that modern world history has been largely determined by a two-centuries-old conspiracy by Bavarian Illuminati, Freemasons, Communists, and Wall Street financiers; central to the conspiracy had been a succession of Jews, ranging from eighteenth-century Rothschilds in Frankfurt to Moses Hess and the American banker Paul Warburg—it was unfair to charge him with being an anti-Semite. At any rate, in light of the ancient rabbinical rule of *batel b'shishim*, Roberton's pro-Israel statements and deeds outweighed his anti-Semitic propaganda, rendering him kosher: "if the contaminant has slipped in accidentally or unintentionally, and is no more than one-sixtieth of the whole, it is neutralized and the food can be lawfully eaten." Indeed, by this reasoning, not only was Robertson kosher, according to Rabbi Podhoretz, but he deserved a Jewish *hechsher* because he was a Zionist. "For Podhoretz," therefore, observed Lind, "it seems practically any lunacy can be forgiven the conspiracy-mongering leader of a mass movement, as long as he supports Israel."[52]

In volunteering to act as a spin-doctor for Robertson, Podhoretz conveniently ignored the fact that Christian-Zionism was not rooted in any concern for Jews. Indeed, most of the Christian Right believed that a strong Israel hastened the millennial End Times in which all except the true followers of Christ would be destroyed. Robertson's support for Israel was likewise contingent and equivocal, because he saw Zionism as a fulfillment of a prophecy: the prelude to Rapture, the mass conversion and slaughter of the Jews, and ultimately the return of Christ. Podhoretz overlooked these uncomfortable facts, leading to conjecture whether Podhoretz would back Farrakhan, if the Nation of Islam supported Israel. Podhoretz's circumlocutions didn't wash. One Jewish reader warned: "History will show that the company you are in is no friend to Jews. They may be using you know, but eventually they will spit you out, when their aim achieved." A 20-year subscriber, who for the most part agreed with *Commentary*'s overall stance, was "flabbergasted" by the exculpatory piece which "attempted to cleanse Robertson by an apology to dietary laws. Here he is the kind of rabbi that will apply the *batel b'shishim* rule to a sausage made from one ritually slaughtered chicken and one porkbelly." Another regular subscriber to *Commentary* since it began was dismayed by the disgustingly "obsequious tone" of the article. "I have not objected as *Commentary* became conservative even faster than I did over the years, though it has been troubling that its conservatism has been so rigidly doctrinaire." One former contributor summarized their feelings. "Finding the good side of Pat Robertson is not something that should be in the ken of an American Jewish magazine."[53]

Who's Afraid of the Religious Right?

The neocons, though, made very little headway among Jews. Jewish neocons may have dominated the conservative movement, but they had little impact on their own religious community. Their defense of the Christian Right merely took them further away from Jewish voters, for whom the threat from the Religious Right was more menacing than that from the Left. For years *Commentary* had been trying to understand why American Jews were so intransigently committed to liberalism in general and the Democratic Party in particular. A succession of articles over the last decade (by Kristol in particular) had addressed the drift towards liberalism—religious and political—within the American Jewish community, and about what might be done to change its course. But the magazine had singularly failed to help crack the secret to winning the allegiance of American Jewry because Podhoretz simply did not recognize that it was in fact he and *Commentary* that were increasingly out of touch. They had failed in his attempt to convert the majority of American Jews to conservatism. Jewish voting patterns indicated that grass-roots Jews voted more in accord with their traditional moral principles in support of the downtrodden than with the financial principles of supporting "number one," noted Alan Dershowitz. American Jews had not only refused to become more conservative but actually became more liberal in their thinking about social issues. On the issue of abortion, for example, Jews remained overwhelmingly the single most pro-choice group within the electorate. Indeed, the vote for Bush was lower in 1992 than in the previous two elections. The predominant shift among Jews from the Democratic to the Republican Party had occurred among the older and more financially successful Jews—who would naturally stray towards neoconservatism anyway—and among the ultraorthodox who generally did not read secular magazines like *Commentary*. Thus, *Commentary* could not even take credit for the only Jewish groups who had responded positively to the neoconservative message.[54]

If they achieved anything, the neocons had normalized conservatism within the American Jewish community so that it was hardly considered worthy of comment to be both Jewish and conservative. Jews anyway also saw through Podhoretz's belated attempts to reconvert to Judaism. Although *Commentary* seemed to have gotten more Jewish in the 1990s, following the end of the Cold War, it was much too little and much too late. In 1990, for example, only twenty-four out of roughly seventy articles focused on something specifically related to Judaism or things Jewish: thirteen dealt directly with subjects relating to Jewish religion, history, or identity; six with anti-Semitism; three with Israel; and two with Jews in the arts. Indeed, there was a great deal of chutzpah in Podhoretz telling Jews to be more Jewish and in his attempt to create a conservative Jewish-Christian alliance, Podhoretz had been courting the very people American Jewry feared most.[55]

"Saddam-is-Hitler"

The collapse of the Soviet Union and the end of the Cold War left a foreign-policy vacuum and in its place Podhoretz groped around for a new enemy. The answer was soon provided by the 1990–91 Persian Gulf crisis, which, coming as it did while *Commentary* was in the midst of searching for its new role, was a godsend for Podhoretz. The entrance of the Middle Eastern bogeyman in the form of Saddam Hussein (the arming of whom by the

United States Podhoretz had conveniently overlooked for the last decade) confirmed the existence of the new species of rogue threats and justified the maintenance of the same military structure of the last 40 years used in defending against the Soviet threat (sizable ground and armored forces equipped with advanced technology and heavy firepower and SDI). Podhoretz sought to replace the old Soviet threat with a new foe, the Arab world, and to set in motion a collision course between the West and Islam. He painted the Middle East conflict in ur-Cold War terms as a moral struggle between Arab despotism and hatred and Western (and Israeli) democracy, tolerance, and pluralism.

Such a course justified the continued strategic alliance between America and Israel that some felt was beginning to look obsolete in the wake of the Soviet Union's collapse. With an Arab enemy the value of the special relationship between the United States and Israel suddenly increased, since the military strength of the latter could serve as a deterrent to radical Arab regimes and help shore up shaky ones. By this vision, Israel was to be the stronghold of the West in the Middle East. A War in the Gulf, it was hoped, would also help to distract attention from the Palestinian *intifada* and relieve the pressure on the Israeli government to make concessions. Although Israel would benefit from a weakened Iraq, the neocons opposed any linkage of the Persian Gulf crisis with the Palestinian problem, determined to prevent the decisive efforts of the Bush administration to follow up the rollback of Saddam with an Israeli-Palestinian settlement based upon land for peace.

Podhoretz vigorously threw himself into pushing for war against Saddam because he represented a "mortal threat" (a favorite Podhoretz phrase during this period) to Israel, as well as to vital American interests in the region. Podhoretz wanted more than just the liberation of Kuwait and the deterrence of an Iraqi invasion of Saudi Arabia; he also desired the destruction of Saddam's military machine ("crush" and "batter" him, Podhoretz wrote), specifically his chemical, biological, and nuclear warfare capabilities. He argued that the stakes were high: politically unimpeded access to oil, an independent Kuwait, the stability of the global economy, and the very nature of the world in the future. The reasons for undertaking military action were "politically and morally compelling," as well as "favorable." Furthermore, the Persian Gulf crisis could determine whether anything had really changed since Vietnam, or whether defeat in that war had left America "capable only of fly-swatting operations like Grenada and Panama but otherwise permanently debellicized and forever unmanned by the idea (which Nietzsche saw as the mark of a slave) that nothing is worth fighting and dying for." Podhoretz supplied the same ideological rhetorical formula that helped to push for an attack against Iraq, as *Commentary* had once done in pushing a hard-line anti-Communist stance: "Saddam-is-Hitler." Saddam was "a ruthless aggressor" who threatened "a more peaceful order in the post cold-war world." Saddam posed the same danger to Israel, as Hitler had posed to European Jewry. Failure to take action, he warned, would lead to "incalculable damage" to America, Israel, and the world.[56]

There were benefits to go to war, too. Not only would a "quick and decisive" American-led victory be "personally gratifying" by discrediting those who warned that a war would result in thousands of casualties and vindicating those who suspected otherwise and had supported the military buildup during the Reagan years, but it would also "remoralize our whole country":

> Everyone would experience a new surge of confidence in America—in American technology, so triumphantly on display in our planes and smart munitions; in American wisdom and courage, so vividly manifest in the very act of going to war; in American leadership, so brilliantly exhibited in the coalition politics through which George Bush has brought us to this pint. Goodbye to the decline-of-America theories; goodbye to the idea that Japan and Germany are outstripping us; goodbye to the isolationists of Left and Right who have come out of the woodwork since the end of the cold war; goodbye to all that. And goodbye, at long last, to Vietnam.

The neocon vision would be fulfilled as America could finally return to its role as a global interventionist, making the world safe for democracy.[57]

A foreign policy based on democratic internationalism, however, was now in the minority intellectually and politically. There was a growing trend toward retrenchment and traditional isolationism long associated with the paleo–Old Right, and the neo-isolationism of the Vietnam-era New Left. Realism of the classic European/*Realipolitik* form had also emerged. Altogether there was cynicism about the prospects for democracy abroad, the capacity of American power to foster it, and the interest the United States had on its behalf. Podhoretz, though, was once again able to adopt a counterposition of sorts (after all he was supporting the administration), as he railed against those who were antiwar. He warned that a post–Cold War foreign policy based on realism rather than idealism bode ill for the future. In foreign policy terms, he stood *Commentary* in a counterposition within his own movement: against the majority of conservatives who had reverted to neo-isolationism, skepticism, and realism. He decided to mount a "visible challenge" to his neo-isolationist enemies on "the hard Right," the most visible example of whom was former Nixon speechwriter Pat Buchanan. He referred to them as "the new peace party, with its constant harping on "body-bags."" His nephew, Joshua Muravchik, accused them of anti-Semitism. "Is Buchanan attacking Jews, then, because they happen to be neocons, or is he attacking neocons because they happen to be Jews?"[58]

As the first scenes from the Gulf War were broadcast on American television, Podhoretz was cheered. "I can't remember when I tasted such exhilaration," he gushed. There was a sense of triumph and celebration. The war signaled the success of the coordinated effort to push for war with Iraq. Neocon influence had returned and Podhoretz was fighting once again, the place where he liked to be best. A sense of satisfaction was reflected in the pages of *Commentary*, as it celebrated the war. It welcomed the possibility of an American-Arab war which would turn the Palestinian *intifada* into a sideshow. The Iraqi missile attacks on Israel, and the Palestinian support for them, vindicated Israel's refusal to recognize their national aspirations. It hoped that the war would revive the "strategic asset" concept, which had seemed doomed by the changing relationship in the post–Cold War world.[59]

But Podhoretz's joy soon turned sour when the limits of American policy in the Gulf became clearer. His hopes were dashed by President's Bush's obvious desire for Israel to stay on the sidelines, and the effectiveness with which such Arab countries as Egypt and Saudi Arabia cooperated, both militarily and economically. His initial celebrations were further tempered by the reservation that Israel would be coerced into conciliating the Palestinians once the war was over. His euphoria rapidly changed to disgust as the war was mysteriously and fatally, in his opinion, stopped before Baghdad had asked to surrender and Saddam removed from power. He had been suspicious that Bush and his Secretary of State James Baker would in the end make a deal that got Saddam out of Kuwait but left his military machine intact and this "nightmare scenario," soon came true as Operation Desert Storm ended abruptly. Vladimir Bukovsky wrote:

> After faithfully following the Gulf War for 44 days and nights, I must have fallen asleep in front of my television set at the crucial moment. For when I awoke on the morning of February 28, I could not understand what had happened.[60]

Bukovsky's bewilderment was a typical neocon response. Desert Storm was "one of the most brilliant military operations in U.S. history," wrote Laurie Mylroie, but the aftermath was "dismal" producing "a human catastrophe carried out under the watch of the US military in what should have been its moment of undiluted triumph." Indeed, *Commentary* felt that, US "acts of commission and omission" had not only helped Saddam to survive but had also strengthened his rule. "Saddam now seemed to be about the only person in Iraq who had not suffered as a result of the war." Elie Kedourie asked:

> Who says that an Iraq which has preserved its integrity is less of a menace than one in which Baghdad's despotic and terrorizing rule has been dismantled? In such a grisly cost-benefit analysis, the cost is heavy and visible, the benefit shadowy and illusory.

Angelo Codevilla summed up the overall feeling, "Operation Desert Storm might well have lived up to its name—a disturbance that blows the sand dunes around, but changes nothing."[61]

The neocons attacked Bush's policies as half-hearted and ineffective, particularly his failure to destroy Saddam's regime. Bush had violated Clausewitz's basic rule, "No one" ought to start a war "without first being clear in his mind what he intends to achieve by that war and how he intends to conduct it." They remained frustrated because Bush's objectives were not as extended as they had wished. They had imagined an even greater and total victory had Bush not stopped US troops, assuming that the Iraqi military would have dissolved and that the Iraqi people would have risen up to overthrow Saddam. Bush's talk of a "new world order" was shown to be a "meatless bone." "Far from trying to create a new political system in the Middle East, the Bush administration set its face even against any change of regime," moaned Podhoretz. In fact, the United States was guilty of "complicity" with Saddam in quelling the Kurd and Shiite uprisings.

> The war, it turns out, was fought merely to get Saddam Hussein out of Kuwait and to "defang" him—not, in other words, to establish a new order in the Middle East (except on the West Bank!) but precisely to restore the old one and to make sure it would remain secure from any further disruption by Iraq or any other ambitious local ruler.

Rather than producing the desired stability, it had left Iraq in "murderous turmoil." Consequently, America could not fully enjoy the fruits of peace.[62]

With few exceptions, the neocons were frustrated, pessimistic, and disappointed with the Bush administration. Bush had brought America back from idealism to realism. He had been guided by political expediency, guilty in their eyes of embracing the same type of "amoral, cold-blooded *Realpolitik*," which had proved so disastrous in the 1930s. *Commentary* reckoned that if Reagan or Thatcher were still in power, neither would have let the Iraqi dictator of the hook so lightly after the success of Desert Storm. Increasingly unhappy with the Bush administration, *Commentary* vented its spleen. Podhoretz described Bush's presidency as "a kind of *coitus interruptus*": "nothing completed, nothing consummated." As Reagan's successor, Bush represented a watered-down conservatism that would doom his reelection chances. Decter bewailed the fact that "there was no Ronald Reagan, not even the skeleton of one to hang in Bush's closet."[63]

Podhoretz was also extremely critical of the Bush administration's policy towards Israel. He blasted Bush for what he perceived as his obsessive and irrational Middle East policy, his "hostility" toward Israel and begged the United States to refrain from pursuing policies which could lead to the destruction of Israel. He was furious with Bush for withholding vitally needed (and previously promised) American loan guarantees when the Likud government would not agree to a freeze on the building of Jewish settlements on the West Bank; he described it as "attempted rape." Likewise, the neocons were particularly hostile towards Baker and described the four Jews centrally involved in the making of policy toward Israel in the Bush administration as "the Four Jewish Horsemen of the Apocalypse." Martin Peretz argued that the Jewish perception of hostility on the part of Bush and Baker towards Israel was fully justified by their pro-Syrian, pro-Saudi, anti-Israel record. In place of Bush, they looked forward to the nomination of Vice President Dan Quayle as the Republican candidate, even though for many he was a national joke, because he was a pro-Israel conservative in the Reagan mold. He also had the only remaining White House neocon or minicon (William Kristol) on staff.[64]

Some of the neocons were so disillusioned with Bush that in the run-up to the 1992 election there was much talk of a possible move back to supporting the Democrats. Although disappointed with Bush, Podhoretz still could not personally commit to supporting Clinton. No doubt there was an element of political calculation as Bush might still win the election and Podhoretz did not want to jeopardize conservative foundation funding by switching sides so suddenly. True to form, Podhoretz equivocated, awaiting the outcome before stating his position, writing that both presidential candidates were unsatisfactory and that neither inspired much confidence. Indeed, he later wrote an article entitled, "Why I thought Perot Would Win." These were tough times for Podhoretz and the neocons as neither candidate was really acceptable and no clear choice for them emerged: Bush was no neocon and a realist to boot, while Clinton was a Democrat. Although Podhoretz did allow so-called New Democrats like Joshua Muravchik and Richard Schifter to outline Clinton's merits (pro-Israel, anti-McGovernite, centrist), he tempered their praise by publishing others like David Twersky, Thomas Sowell, and Daniel Pipes who were skeptical that the Democratic Party had "really freed itself from the Leftist forces whose accession to power in 1972 drove them out in the first place" and questioned what Clinton meant exactly when he described himself as "a new kind of Democrat." Nonetheless, that there were even "new Democrats" highlighted the neocons' opportunism as they tried to court the new President. Copying his uncle's expediency, Muravchik even sought a position in the new administration.[65]

"Jimmy Clinton"

Despite having mixed feelings for Bush, the election of Clinton was a further blow to Podhoretz and the neocons. Post-1960s liberalism, they feared, was dominant and now governed America; Clinton's election was "the capstone in the arch." Clinton was a "counterculture McGovernik." His foreign policy "betrayed the earmarks" of the "left-over liberalism" of the 1970s. "Jimmy Clinton" showed irresolution, "weakness and appeasement" in foreign policy and a "lack of sympathy for the military", which had weakened its structure, and damaged its morale, "diminished America's military strength and damaged its credibility." Clinton was simply a modern reincarnation of Carter. Irwin Stelzer called Clintonism a "counterrevolution," which signaled that conservatives had lost the culture war: the children of the radical 1960s had already captured the academy and the media and now they had captured the White House, too. Now they were there,

> Their goal is to consolidate the victory they have won, and to extend and institutionalize the great change in social attitudes that grew out of the radical movement of the 60's by placing the state with all its resources and coercive power on the side of feminists, homosexuals, minorities, and the various beneficiaries of the welfare state.

It was now the hard and immediate task to resist these changes and to contain liberalism and its depredations. Only a religious revival and a "bold new conservatism" would prevent a takeover. He warned, "For the serious conservative opposition, it will be a tough four years."[66]

Stelzer was right, for under Clinton, Podhoretz and the neocons felt their influence wane even more. Their prestige and power had weakened further, even after the series of blows they had suffered in the late 1980s and early 1990s. *Commentary*'s rival *Tikkun* had supplanted it both in terms of readership and influence. Podhoretz's nemesis Michael Lerner now had the ear of the White House that Podhoretz had enjoyed during the 1980s. Podhoretz's sense of impotence was communicated by David Frum: "Sooner or later, the conservative put down his copy of *Tikkun*, or stepped out of the theater from whose stage some actor had been hectoring him, and then his cultural powerlessness smacked him in the face." Podhoretz had been knocked off his pedestal.[67]

Clinton's election and presidency simply drove the neocons further into the arms of the conservative Right, allying themselves with traditional Republicans who defined themselves in opposition to everything favored by Clinton. This shift was no doubt assisted by one of *Commentary*'s benefactors, the Scaife Foundation, which was notorious in liberal circles for bankrolling anti-Clinton organizations. The White House pointed to Richard Mellon Scaife as a major force behind what Hillary Clinton called a "right-wing conspiracy" against her husband. Indeed, the reclusive right-wing billionaire was funding the "Arkansas Project," a campaign run by a group of conservatives to bring down the Clintons by smear and scandal.

A Hero at a Safe Distance

A further blow to Podhoretz's self-esteem was Likud's defeat in the 1992 Israeli election. By this point Podhoretz was utterly obsessed with Israel. He had become much more aggressive in defense of Jewish interests in general and of Israel in particular. At a dinner party he wouldn't even shake the hand of a former contributor who had written a negative piece on Israel. Podhoretz's distaste was palpable, "I always liked you . . . But you wrote an anti-Israel piece, and I'm very ideological on that subject." In his own words, Podhoretz was "a frighteningly effective propagandist for Jewish hawkishness" and he vilified anyone who dared to express a view deviating from what he deemed "politically correct" on matters pertaining to Israel. He positioned *Commentary* as the antidote to what he saw as the incessant and blatantly one-sided coverage of the American media. In June 1992, he introduced a new department (the first in years), "Israel Watch," to detect the "egregious anti-Israel bias" of the US media and to counter it. Although the Israeli Right had lost, it allowed him to resume his favorite counterposture once again.[68]

Podhoretz mourned the loss of Begin ("the most democratic and law-respecting of all Israeli leaders to date") and aimed his fire at the victorious Labor leader Yitzhak Rabin, particularly his policy of "trading land for peace." Podhoretz opposed a Palestinian state. He believed that "far from being a formula for peace and stability," it "would lead in very short order to instability and war." He doubted the Palestinians were capable of making peace. Arafat could not ensure security, and would only exacerbate the likelihood of further war in the region. A better interlocutor would be a constitutionally reformed, parliamentary Jordan, which he believed was already the Palestinian state. He argued that progress in the Middle East was now contingent on keeping the Palestinians away from the peace process. Only with a change in the Arab world comparable to the one that had occurred in the former Soviet Union, could Israel withdraw from the occupied territories. But that meant unconditional recognition of Israel on the part of each and every Arab country; immediate cessation of the economic boycott; an end to all propaganda against the Jewish state and against its Jewish supporters; adherence by Egypt to all the terms of the Camp David agreement; regional cooperation on the water supply and other ecological issues; and a pan-Arab fund and political program for the resettlement of Arab refugees, including educational and cultural facilities. Of course, Podhoretz said nothing of what Israel had to do.[69]

Since Podhoretz emphatically believed that a Palestinian state posed a mortal threat to the survival of Israel, he felt it was his overriding duty to resist any peace process that might lead to such an outcome. In fact, from 1992 onwards, that was pretty much the sum total of *Commentary*'s stance on Israel. Podhoretz led the fight against the Rabin administration. He devoted his energies to attacking Rabin's "land for peace" program, which he felt looked increasingly unrealistic, dangerous, and reckless. He argued against the peace process because it would bring about the establishment of an independent Palestinian state which in turn would endanger Israel's existence. Podhoretz believed that only a miracle akin to the collapse of Communism could make the Arab world trustworthy. In line with its leader, *Commentary* characterized Rabin's enthusiastic policy of cooperation as too flexible, wrongheaded, and defeatist; it would make Israel more vulnerable to attack because the PLO and the Arabs would perceive it as sign of "growing Israeli political weakness."[70]

Having watched from the sidelines for long enough, Podhoretz decided "to speak out as a Jew against the course Israel is now taking." In a signed and impassioned editorial, "A Statement on the Peace Process," in the April 1993 issue of *Commentary*, Podhoretz took Rabin to task for accepting Arafat as a negotiating partner, warning that the peace talks would in fact lead to war. The very *popularity* of Israel's policies worried him: "if those policies are meeting with so much approval in certain quarters, it *must* mean that they are not good for Israel." He rejected outright the notion that Israel's policies were meeting with general approval because they made sense. He could not help suspecting that "the enemies of Israel know something about these policies that the friends of Israel are failing to see." He concluded by "praying with all my heart and all my soul and all my might that my apprehensions about the negotiations now going on are ill-founded," and that he will turn out to be a false prophet. Typically, though, Podhoretz offered no alternative to the present peace process he was so busy criticizing. He preferred the pre-peace process position. He concluded that the only alternative was to do nothing or to stall by going through the charade of engaging in a peace process in order to keep America off Israel's back. The real objective, then, was to maintain the status quo that did not relinquish any territory in the West Bank and Gaza: to adopt a wait-and-see policy, that gave up time, not territory, for as long as it took for the Arab world to undergo "revolutionary" change.[71]

Powerless to stop the Oslo agreement of August 1993, Podhoretz attacked that, too, as the "first step" in the phased destruction of Israel. Not only would partition make Israel more vulnerable inside redrawn borders, but also it would lead to "a dictatorship run by Hamas or the PLO." Jerusalem would be divided again, despite spurious Palestinian claims to the Holy City, creating another Danzig, as well as a rationale for a corridor that would split Israel. Podhoretz disapproved of Rabin's policy of unilateral withdrawal and could only foresee disaster. Article after article criticizing the Rabin government appeared in *Commentary* reflecting Podhoretz's own obsession. It rejected the idea of compensating Israel with American money and technology in return for a withdrawal from the Golan, as unsound and unrealistic. In a rare move, Podhoretz published a special report, produced by the Center for Security Policy in Washington, DC, conducted by eleven experts, on the idea of stationing US forces on the Golan Heights as an element of a peace agreement between Israel and Syria. It set forth a detailed argument for the continuing importance of territorial buffers in the age of missiles, therefore opposing Israeli withdrawal and deployment of US military forces. Podhoretz found its analysis "so thorough and definitive" that he departed from his normal editorial practice and reproduced it in its original form. Not content with criticizing the Rabin government, *Commentary* attacked what it alleged to be the leftist excesses in Israeli political thought. It sought to discredit the "new historians," who were rewriting the history of the state. It chastised Israeli apologies and self-recrimination (what *Commentary*'s editors called "self-flagellation") for Jewish excesses, as "self-hatred." Scott McConnell summed up the situation:

> Norman Podhoretz's *Commentary* had been waging a lonely battle against the Oslo peace process (a track leading to a Palestinian state in Gaza and the West Bank), but its position was very much in the minority among both foreign-affairs experts and American Jews.[72]

Podhoretz's attitude smacked of complexity and inconsistency. He had made a 180-degree turn in his long-standing position that it was wrong for American Jews to criticize Israel's security policies, because they lacked the "moral standing" bestowed only by residence there, that Diaspora Jews could not participate in a debate where their lives were not on the line. After years of having told American Jews that they had "no moral right to criticize Israel's security policies" because their words provided ammunition for anti-Semitic inspired criticism of Israel by non-Jews, Podhoretz had done just that. He had transgressed one of the very commandments he had set forth. He joined the public debate on the direction of Israeli policy, a discussion which he had insisted on condemning for years (unless of course it was conducted in his magazine). Now that the Israeli government had changed, and it was his turn to take the counter intellectual role once again, Podhoretz changed the rules to suit him. From 1977 to 1992 when the hard-line Likud government, whose policies Podhoretz approved, was in power he had maintained that no Jew should criticize Israel. But as soon as the Rabin government made moves toward conciliation, Podhoretz had no moral problems in speaking out. As Richard Cohen, in the *Washington Post* wrote, "he has crossed a line he himself drew, erasing it to suit his intellectual convenience."[73]

Podhoretz then attempted to justify his U-turn. He went through contortions to legitimize his kind of criticism while continuing to vilify that of others. He said it was legitimate for him to criticize Israeli policy because *he* was speaking in defense of Israel's interests and his doubts communicated support rather than providing cover for anti-Semitic and ideological enemies of Israel. He distinguished between "leftist" critiques of Israel, which were determined to delegitimize the state by vilifying it as immoral and criminal, and his own position which was merely an expression of doubts and anxieties over the prudence of policies pursued by the Israeli government. Unlike those critics on the Left who accused Israel of all sorts of heinous crimes, he was simply "questioning the prudential wisdom of its policies." Besides, the "new circumstances" of 1993 warranted such criticism: the political dangers involved in Jewish criticism, he said, had for the moment faded and the United States was no longer trying to force Israel into taking steps which were threatening to its security. Furthermore, he was attacking Israel at a time when its policies were meeting with general approval. Indeed, it was the very *popularity* of Israel's policies that worried him.[74]

Podhoretz's position on Israel had put him back where he preferred to belong: in a counter position. Articles, editorials, opinion pieces, and letters pillorying him appeared in international and US press. The major Jewish organizations (including the AJC) attacked him. Even the Israeli government issued a rejoinder to try to blunt his criticism. Podhoretz was being listened to once again, not despite the hypocrisy and inconsistency, but because of it. Podhoretz was uncomfortable intellectually with being part of the establishment, an inevitable result. Furthermore, he had found it increasingly hard to adopt a position outside the conservative mainstream over the last few years because of his act in selling out in exchange for right-wing foundation funding. He had spent a lifetime seeking material success, and he did not want to abandon by forsaking his current and generous sponsors by speaking out on issues dear to them. However, Israel allowed him his cake and to eat it. It afforded him that opportunity to speak out because it would not alienate his sponsors. Indeed, a pro-Israel stance was a key part of the Religious Right's platform.

One year on from the Oslo agreement, Podhoretz's outlook was gloomy, pessimistic, and apocalyptic. He found the new situation uncomfortable. In face of the progress the peace process had made over the past twelve months, he still warned that it was more likely to end in a "nightmare." The Israeli government was still ignoring his pleas. And his highly critical stance toward the peace process over which Rabin presided caused a personal rupture between him and the Israeli PM. Podhoretz first met Rabin in 1967 in Israel, right after the Six Day War, when he was still chief of staff of the IDF. About a year or so later, on his way to Washington to take over as the newly appointed ambassador to the United States, he stopped at Podhoretz's apartment in New York where, at the request of the Israeli consul-general, Podhoretz had arranged for him to meet a group of prominent American intellectuals. They met many times, although they never became close friends, and their relations were relatively cordial. But, when Podhoretz began publicly voicing his misgivings over the changes in Rabin's thinking that led to the handshake with Arafat on the White House lawn, Rabin understandably grew cold and, after a very tense accidental encounter in Jerusalem, they never met again. It did not help that Podhoretz was lauding hard-line Benjamin Netanyahu, the newly elected head of Likud, for his JFK-like qualities of youth, courage, and communication. Podhoretz had now marginalized himself in Israel, too.[75]

A "Counterrevolution" of the Right?

Podhoretz desperately tried to prevent the hemorrhaging of *Commentary* readers and contributors in the 1990s. In 1994, in an attempt to reenergize the magazine, he introduced two new departments. The first, "Contentions," was written by Decter to replace her CFW magazine (from which it took its name and which had ceased publication in 1990). It was devoted to the critical examination of a significant recently published article or report which was representative of an important tendency in contemporary American thought and culture. But in December 1994, only eight months after it was introduced, the column was quietly dropped. Obviously, it had not made the anticipated impact. At around the same time, Podhoretz broke with a major tendency and began to start proposing concrete solutions rather than simply attacking existing ideas, in a second new series, "What To Do About." Up to that point, *Commentary* did not say how to make things right in America, how it would handle the "new and serous challenges," it offered no prescriptions to its prognoses. Each piece in the series began with a reexamination of a particular issue by an expert. For the first time since the 1960s, *Commentary*, at last, started proposing solutions for creating the kind of world it sought but it was too little, too late. Readership had dropped to 27,000.

Nonetheless, displaying the blindness that had become the hallmark of his magazine in the 1990s, Podhoretz felt that things were looking up by 1994. He described the results of the midterms as "a spectacular political vindication" and interpreted them as a mandate for his particular brand of conservatism. Caught by surprise by the suddenness of this "so great a conservative victory," Podhoretz argued that the Republican success represented a decisive repudiation of contemporary liberalism, a "counterrevolution" and a "coming-to-power of [a] new breed of Republican counterrevolutionaries" led by Newt Gingrich. Podhoretz supported Gringrich, approving of his "aggressive candor," as well as his twin assaults on the "entrenched institutions of the welfare state and the moral legacy of the counterculture." Of course, Podhoretz supported the Republican Congress's "Contract with America" in 1994 because, as David Twersky pointed out, it had taken its intellectual firepower from *Commentary*'s pages: "rejecting affirmative action, over-hauling welfare, and in general trying to return America to more 'traditional values.'"[76]

Podhoretz hoped that what he called the "counterrevolution" of the Right in 1994 would settle the culture war decisively in its favor. He was caught in conservative self-congratulation that America was in the midst of a conservative social, cultural, and political resurgence. He jubilantly declared that the Republican Party had successfully converted America to its views. And he felt that "the Clinton administration would get weaker and weaker as a result." But he could not have been more wrong. Twelve years of Republican rule had misled Podhoretz and the neocons into thinking that most Americans sided with conservatism, but most Americans still disagreed with conservative views on social issues and the economy and it would take another six years for a Republican to be elected President, and even then in dubious circumstances.[77]

Notes

1. Scott McConnell, "The Weekly Standard's War," *The American Conservative* (November 21, 2005) [internet version]. About $635,000 (including $60,000 alone in 1998) came from the philanthropist Richard Mellon Scaife, via the Carthage Foundation, one of the Scaife family's four charitable trusts. In 1995, the Olin Foundation gave $60 000 in support of the magazine so that it could continue "to make a vital contribution to our nation's discourse." The funds offset circulation and publication expenses as well as unspecified special project costs. These figures have been taken from Media Transparency, http://www.mediatransparency.org/storedsearchresults.php?storedSearchID=2 and http://www.mediatransparency.org/recipientgrants.php?recipientID=4658. Last accessed in February 2008.

2. Eric Breindel, "Mission Accomplished," *New York Post* (January 10, 1991), 31.

3. Stephen A. Longstaff, "The New York Family," *Queen's Quarterly* 83 (1976), 561.

4. Michael Lind, *Up From Conservatism: Why the Right is Wrong for America* (New York: The Free Press, 1996), 85–9, 94; John Saloma, quoted at "The Strategic Philanthropy of Conservative Foundations," http://www.mediatransparency.org/conservativephilanthropy.php [last consulted in February 2008]; John B. Judis, "The Conservative Crackup," *American Prospect* 3 (Fall 1990), 41.

5. See Lind, Up From Conservatism, 85–9, 94; Gottfried, The Conservative Movement, 120.

6. Lind, *Up From Conservatism*, 85; Walter Saltzman to Podhoretz, March 10, 1995, Norman Podhoretz Papers, Manuscript Division, Library of Congress, Washington, DC (NPLC).

7. Midge Decter, 'More Bullying on Campus,' *New York Times* (December 10, 1985), A31; Stephen H. Balch and Herbert I. London, "The Tenured Left," *Commentary* 82:4 (October 1986), 41–51. Meanwhile, Balch and London, as well as other regular members of the Commentariat such as Peter Shaw, Carol Iannone, and Michael Levin, had been meeting regularly in Manhattan during the 1980s to discuss what they perceived to be disturbing leftist intolerance on campus. This group was later incorporated as the National Association of Scholars in 1985, with its own journal (*Academic Questions*) and a yearly budget, supplied by right-wing foundations, of a quarter of a million dollars, and Balch and London became, respectively, the chair of the board and president. Within 6 years it had 2,300 members across 27 states. See Jim Neilson, "The Great PC Scare: Tyrannies of the Left, Rhetoric of the Right," in *PC Wars: Politics and Theory in the Academy*, ed. Jeffrey Williams (New York and London: Routledge, 1995): 60–89.

8. E. L. Patullo, "Straight Talk About Gays," *Commentary* 94:6 (December 1992), 21–4; Letters, *Commentary* 95:3 (March 1993), 2–17.

9. Lind, *Up From Conservatism*, 178.

10. Walter Dean Burnham, quoted at www.transparency.org. Last consulted in December 2008.

11. Charles Murray, "What To Do About Welfare," *Commentary* 98:6 (December 1994), 26–34 and "Helping the Poor: A Few Modest Proposals," *Commentary* 79:5 (May 1985), 27–34.

12. David Frum, "It's Big Government, Stupid," *Commentary* 27–31; Schifter to Podhoretz, April 17, 1995, NPLC.

13. Paul Johnson, "Blessing Capitalism," *Commentary* 95:5 (May 1993), 33–6; Alan M. Dershowitz, *Chutzpah* (New York and London: Simon and Schuster, 1991), 201.

14. Richard Pipes, "Gorbachev's Russia: Breakdown or Crackdown?" *Commentary* 89:3 (March 1990), 13–25.

15. Michael Kinsley "Who Killed Communism?" *New Republic* (December 4, 1989), 4; John Ehrman, *The Rise of Neoconservatism: Intellectuals and Foreign Affairs, 1945–1994* (New Haven and London: Yale University Press, 1996).

16. John Patrick Diggins, "*Commentary*'s Cold War on Liberalism," paper delivered at the "*Commentary* Magazine in the American Jewish Community and American Culture" conference, March 11, 2003, 16–17; George Weigel, "Their Lustration—and Ours," *Commentary* 94:4 (October 1992), 34–9.

17. Pipes, "Gorbachev's Russia," 13–25; Sam Tanenhaus, "What the Anti-Communists Knew," *Commentary* 90:1 (July 1990), 32–6; Arch Puddington, "The Anti-Cold War Brigade," *Commentary* 90:2 (August 1990), 30–8.

18. Paul Johnson, "Leading Lady," *Commentary* 97:1 (January 1994), 56–8; Pipes, "Gorbachev's Russia," 13–25; Letters, *Commentary* 90:1 (July 1990), 3; George Weigel, "Shultz, Reagan, and the Revisionists," *Commentary* 96:2 (August 1993), 50–3.

19. James A. Nuechterlein, "The American 80s: Disaster or Triumph?" *Commentary* 90:3 (September 1980), 41; Norman Podhoretz, "Strange Bedfellows: A Guide to the New Foreign-Policy Debates," *Commentary* 108:5 (December 1999), 19–31.

20. Jay Winik, *On the Brink: The Dramatic, Behind-The-Scenes Saga of the Reagan Era and the Men and Women Who Won the Cold War* (New York: Simon & Schuster, 1996); Richard Gid Powers, *Not Without Honor: The History of American Anticommunism* (New Haven and London: Yale University Press, 1995). Powers wrote, "During the bleakest winter days of American anticommunism, there was, however, the first faint stirring of new life, of rebirth, a sign of vigor at odds with the uncertainty and pessimism that pervaded the tired veterans of the old cause. One man summoned the will, the strength, and the imagination to commence the giant task of rebuilding the anti-communist coalition. This was Norman Podhoretz, editor of the American Jewish Committee's *Commentary*" (Richard Gid Powers, *Not Without Honor: The History of American Anticommunism* (New Haven, CT and London: Yale University Press, 1995), 341–2); Owen Harries, "The Cold War & the Intellectuals," *Commentary* 92:4 (October 1991), 13–20.

21. Diggins, "*Commentary*'s Cold War on Liberalism," 21; Wesley Yang, message posted to H-DIPLO, June 23, 2003; "The American 80's: Disaster or Triumph?: A Symposium," *Commentary* 90:3 (September 1990), 13; Dana H. Allin, *Cold War Illusions: America, Europe, and Soviet Power, 1969–89* (London: St Martin's, 1994), 164, 178.

22. William Stern, Letters, *Commentary* 93:2 (February 1992), 2–8.

23. Wesley Yang, H-Diplo, June 23 and 25, 2003; Letters, *Commentary* 90:6 (December 1990), 8-10.

24. "The American 80's," 13.

25. "The American 80's," 13-52; Gregg Easterbrook, "The View from Both Sides," *Newsweek* (September 10, 1990), 65.

26. Arch Puddington, "Is White Racism the Problem?" *Commentary* 94:1 (July 1992), 31-6; Philip Gourevitch, "The Crown Heights Riot & Its Aftermath," *Commentary* 95:1 (January 1993), 29-34; Paul Berman, "The American 80's," 21; Letters, *Commentary* 94:2 (August 1992), 2-21.

27. Jacob Heilbrunn, "Apologists Without Remorse," *The American Prospect* 9:36 (January 1-February 1, 1998) [internet version].

28. Tanenhaus, "What the Anti-Communists Knew," 32-6.

29. Angelo M. Codevilla, "Is Olof Palme the Wave of the Future?" *Commentary* 89:3 (March 1990), 26-32; Joshua Muravchik, "Clintonism Abroad," *Commentary* 99:2 (February 1995), 36-40; Norman Podhoretz, "Book TV," C-SPAN 2 (July 1, 2001).

30. Gary Dorrien, *The Neoconservative Mind: Politics, Culture and the War of Ideology* (Philadelphia: Temple University Press, 1993), 134, 201, 324, 206; William Phillips, "The World According to Norman," *Partisan Review* 47:3 (1980), 336; Norman Podhoretz, "After the Cold War," *Commentary* 92:1 (July 1991), 55-6.

31. Midge Decter, *An Old Wife's Tale: My Seven Decades in Love and War* (New York: Regan Books, 2001), 172, 173.

32. Ehrman, *The Rise of Neoconservatism*, 177, 171-172, 173, 179-180.

33. Lind, *Up From Conservatism*, 136-7; Dorrien, *The Neoconservative Mind*, 386.

34. Norman Podhoretz, contribution to "The National Prospect: A Symposium," *Commentary* 100:5 (November 1995), 23-116; see also Heather MacDonald, "Toward Yugoslavia?" *Commentary* 93:6 (June 1992), 61-3.

35. Francis Fukuyama, "Immigrants and Family Values," *Commentary* 95:5 (May 1993), 26-32; Midge Decter, "Ronald Reagan & the Culture War," *Commentary* 91:3 (March 1991), 43-6; Peter Shaw, "The Rise & Fall of Deconstruction," *Commentary* 92:6 (December 1991), 50-3; George Weigel, "The New Anti-Catholicism," *Commentary* 93:6 (June 1992), 25-31; Anita Susan Grossman, "Enemies of Culture," *Commentary* 89:6 (June 1990), 60-2; Harries, "The Cold War & the Intellectuals," 13-20.

36. Richard Grenier, "Clint Eastwood Goes PC," *Commentary* 97:3 (March 1994), 51-3; Joseph Epstein, "The Degradation of the 'New York Times,'" *Commentary* 97:5 (May 1994), 34-9.

37. Weigel, "The New Anti-Catholicism," 25-31; Rita Kramer, "War Diary," *Commentary* 93:5 (May 1992), 62-4.

38. Kramer, "War Diary," 62-4; Novak, "The American 80's," 48.

39. Joshua Muravchik, "Why the Democrats Finally Won," *Commentary* 95:1 (January 1993), 17-22; William J. Bennett, "What To Do About the Children," *Commentary* 99:3 (March 1995), 23-8; Norman Podhoretz, "Rape in Feminist Eyes," *Commentary* 92:4 (October 1991), 29-35; Letters, *Commentary* 93:3 (March 1992), 2-8.

40. James Q Wilson, "Against the Legalization of Drugs," *Commentary* 89:2 (February 1990), 21-8; Peter L. Berger, "Furtive Smokers—and What They Tell Us About America,"

Commentary 97:6 (June 1994), 21–6; Jeffrey Salmon, "Greenhouse Anxiety," *Commentary* 96:1 (July 1993), 25–8.

41. Timothy Maguire, "My Bout with Affirmative Action," *Commentary* 93:4 (April 1992), 50–2; Midge Decter, "How the Rioters Won," *Commentary* 94:1 (July 1992) 17–22; Moynihan, quoted in Charles Murray, "The Legacy of the 60's," *Commentary* 94:1 (July 1992), 23–30.

42. Chester E. Finn, "For Whom It Tolls," *Commentary* 99:1 (January 1995), 76–80; Lind, *Up From Conservatism*, 207; Letters, *Commentary* 94:3 (September 1992), 21.

43. Leon R. Kass, "Death With Dignity and the Sanctity of Life," *Commentary* 89:3 (March 1990), 33–43; "Seeing the Nakedness of His Father," *Commentary* 93:6 (June 1992), 41–7; and "Regarding Daughters and Sisters: *The Rape of Dinah*," *Commentary* 93:4 (April 1992), 29–38; Paul Johnson, "God and the Americans," *Commentary* 99:1 (January 1995), 25–45; Irving Kristol, "The Future of American Jewry," *Commentary* 92:2 (August 1991), 21–6.

44. Jean Bethke Elshtain, "A New Covenant?" *Commentary* 99:4 (April 1995), 70–2; David Bromwich, Ellen Willis, and Phyllis Franklin, Letters, *Commentary* 99:6 (June 1995), 12–14.

45. David Merkowitz, Letters, *Commentary* 93:2 (February 1992), 11–13; David Bromwich, Ellen Willis, and Phyllis Franklin, Letters, *Commentary* 96:4 (October 1993), 13–18.

46. Michael Halpern, Letters, 96:4 (October 1993), *Commentary* 13–18; Letters, *Commentary* 98:2 (August 1994), 11–12; Andrew Sullivan, Letters, *Commentary* 100:1 (July 1995), 7.

47. Decter, quoted in Lind, *Up From Conservatism*, 98.

48. Jack Wertheimer, "A Jewish Contract With America," *Commentary* 99:5 (May 1995), 31–5; Gertrude Himmelfarb, "Victorian Values/Jewish Values," *Commentary* 87:2 (February 1989), 23–31; Linda S. Lichter, "Home Truths," *Commentary* 97:6 (June 1994), 49–52; Irving Kristol, "Why Religion Is Good for the Jews," *Commentary* 98:2 (August 1994), 19–21.

49. Jack Wertheimer, "Family Values & the Jews," *Commentary* 97:1 (January 1994), 30–4; Letters, *Commentary* 98:5 (November 1994), 10.

50. Wertheimer, "A Jewish Contract With America," 31–5; Robert M. Seltzer, "American Jews & Their Judaism," *Commentary* 97:3 (March 1994), 47–50. For *Commentary*'s separationist stance see, for example, Leonard Levy's "School Prayers & the Founding Fathers" in September 1962. The magazine's changed position brought it into conflict with the AJC which disagreed with *Commentary*'s attempt to infuse the "naked public square" with a hefty dose of morality via religion. The former AJC Vice President, Jordan C. Band wrote in, as did the current president, Robert S. Rifkind, to reiterate the Committee's commitment to preserving the separation of church and state. The Committee felt that if the constitutional principle of the separation of church and state was to have any meaning at all, it should mean at the very least that a state cannot confer its governmental powers on a religious body. The AJC believed deeply in reasonable religious accommodation for people of all faiths and had so contended in numerous cases before the Supreme Court. Robert S. Rifkind, Jordan C. Band, Jack Wertheimer, Letters, *Commentary* 100:2 (August 1995), 2–8; Samuel Rabinove, Letters, *Commentary* 99:2 (February 1995), 10–11; Samuel Rabinove, Letters, *Commentary* 99:5 (May 1995), 7–10.

51. Midge Decter, "The ADL vs. the Religious Right," *Commentary* 98:3 (September 1994), 45–7; Podhoretz, "The Christian Right and Its Demonizers," *National Review* (April 3, 2000) [internet version]; Jacob Heilbrunn, *They Knew They Were Right*, (London: Doubleday 2008), 20.

52. Norman Podhoretz, "In the Matter of Pat Robertson," *Commentary* 100:2 (August 1995), 27–32; Lind, "Rev. Robertson's Grand International Conspiracy Theory," NYRB (February 2, 1995) [internet version] and "On Pat Robertson and His Defenders," NYRB (April 20, 1995) [internet version]. It was not the first time that this had happened either. Kristol set the standard back in 1984 when he excused an evangelical Protestant leader who had remarked that God does not hear the prayers of Jews, with the words: "Why should Jews care about the theology of a fundamentalist preacher?... What do such theological abstractions matter as against the mundane fact that this same preacher is vigorously pro-Israel?" He did so to argue that Jews should swallow their lofty principles and seek new alliances with the Christian Right. Irving Kristol, "The Political Dilemma of American Jews," *Commentary* 78:1 (July 1984), 23–9.

53. Lind, *Up From Conservatism*, 112, 119; Moderchai Shelef to Podhoretz, n.d., NPLC; Jacob Weissman to Podhoretz, August 8, 1995, NPLC; Anonymous interview by author, September 2, 2002.

54. Dershowitz, *Chutzpah*, 201.

55. I am grateful to George D. Gittleman for these figures. See his, "An Analysis of *Commentary*: Ideas, Trends and Attitudes toward Jews and Judaism for the year 1990" (Term paper, HUC-IJR, Cincinnati, OH, 1994), 3.

56. Norman Podhoretz, "A Statement on the Persian Gulf Crisis," *Commentary* 90:5 (November 1990), 17–20 and "Enter the Peace Party," *Commentary* 91:1 (January 1991), 17–21.

57. Norman Podhoretz, "In Israel, With Scuds and Patriots," *Commentary* 91:4 (April 1991), 19–26.

58. Podhoretz, "In Israel, With Scuds and Patriots," 19–26; Joshua Muravchik, "Patrick J. Buchanan and the Jews," *Commentary* 91:1 (January 1991), 29–37. *Commentary* had been attacking Buchanan as far back as 1987. In a scorching review of Pat Buchanan's memoirs, *Right from the Beginning*, self-styled "rightwing hitman" David Brock had warned of the corrosive dangers to the Republican Party of a divisive right-wing holy war that aimed to fan the flames of nativism, bigotry, and social intolerance. "Buchanan's language of 'religious war,' leaving as it does no room for compromise or diversity," he wrote, "threatens the new conservative coalition and could yet trigger a corrosive and ultimately self-defeating battle with the Republican Party." His prophecy was self-fulfilling, as Podhoretz declared Buchanan's candidacy for president in 1992 as the "fight now beginning for the soul of the conservative movement." Podhoretz cautioned that if Buchanan, "the darling of the paleos and other troglodytic yearners for the dark ages of American conservatism," was allowed to succeed, then the conservative movement would be "dragged back into a marginal sectarian status with very little appeal to anyone outside its own fever swamps." David Brock, "Street-Corner Conservative," *Commentary* 85:6 (June 1988) 62–4; Norman Podhoretz, "Buchanan and the Conservative Crackup," *Commentary* 93:5 (May 1992), 30–4; and Letters, *Commentary* 94:3 (September 1992), 2–12.

59. Podhoretz, "In Israel, With Scuds and Patriots," 20.

60. Podhoretz, "In Israel, With Scuds and Patriots," 19; Vladimir Bukovsky, "What to Do About the Soviet Collapse," *Commentary* 92:3 (September 1991), 19–24.

61. Laurie Mylroie, "How We Helped Saddam Survive," *Commentary* 92:1 (July 1991), 15–19; Bukovsky, "What to Do About the Soviet Collapse," 19–24; Elie Kedourie, "Iraq: The Mystery of American Policy," *Commentary* 91:6 (June 1991), 15–19; Angelo Codevilla, "War and Warriors," *Commentary* 92:2 (August 1991), 60–2.

62. Codevilla, "Magnificent, But Was it War?" *Commentary* 93:4 (April 1992), 15–20; Podhoretz, "After the Cold War," *Commentary* 92:1 (July 1991), 55–6.

63. David Bar Ilan, Letters, *Commentary* 94:3 (September 1992), 2–12; Norman Podhoretz, "Why I Thought Perot Would Win," *Commentary* 94:3 (September 1992), 33; Decter, "Ronald Reagan & the Culture War," 43–6.

64. Norman Podhoretz, "A Statement on the Peace Process," *Commentary* 95:4 (April 1993), 20; Ruth R. Wisse, "A Purim Homily," *Commentary* 93:5 (May 1992), 53; Martin Peretz, "Bush, Clinton & the Jews: *A Debate*," *Commentary* 94:4 (October 1992), 15–23.

65. Peretz "Bush, Clinton & the Jews," 15–23; David Twersky, "A New Kind of Democrat?" *Commentary* 95:2 (February 1993), 51–3.

66. William Kristol, "A Conservative Looks at Liberalism," *Commentary* 96:3 (September 1993), 33; Norman Podhoretz, "Comes the Counterrevolution," *Commentary* 99:1 (January 1995), 49; Muravchik, "Clintonism Abroad," *Commentary* 99:2 (February 1995), 36–40 and "How the Cold War Really Ended," *Commentary* 98:5 (November 1994), 40–5; Irwin Stelzer, "Clintonism Unmasked," *Commentary* 95:5 (May 1993), 21–5; William Kristol, "A Conservative Looks at Liberalism," *Commentary* 96:3 (September 1993), 33–6.

67. David Frum, *Dead Right*, (New York: Basic Books, 1994), 56–7.

68. Scott McConnell, "Right Is Still Right," *The New York Press* (October 16–22, 2002) [internet version]; Norman Podhoretz, "America and Israel: An Ominous Change," *Commentary* 93:1 (January 1992), 21–5 and Letters, *Commentary* 93:5 (May 1992), 4–8; Editorial Note, *Commentary* 93:6 (June 1992), 21.

69. Podhoretz, "America and Israel," 21–5; Letters, *Commentary* 93:5 (May 1992), 4–8.

70. Ruth R. Wisse, "The Might and the Right," *Commentary* 94:3 (September 1992), 50.

71. Podhoretz, "A Statement on the Peace Process," 19–23; "Another Statement on the Peace Process," *Commentary* 95:6 (June 1993), 25–30; and Letters, *Commentary* 96:3 (September 1983), 2–20.

72. David Bar-Ilan, "Next Year in (a Divided?) Jerusalem," *Commentary* 98:3 (September 1994), 35–9 and "Israel: Guilt & Politics," *Commentary* 97:5 (May 1994), 25–8; Podhoretz, "U.S. Forces on the Golan Heights?: A Special Report," *Commentary* 98:6 (December 1994), 73; Hillel Halkin "Israel Against Itself," *Commentary* 98:5 (November 1994), 33–9; McConnell, "The Weekly Standard's War."

73. Cohen, quoted in Podhoretz, "Another Statement on the Peace Process," 25.

74. Podhoretz, "A Statement on the Peace Process," 19–23.

75. Norman Podhoretz, "The Peace Process So Far," *Commentary* 98:6 (December 1994), 21–5; Letters, *Commentary* 99:4 (April 1995), 20; and "Israel—With Grandchildren," *Commentary* 100:6 (December 1995), 38–47.

76. David Twersky, "Left right, Left Right," *Moment* 20:3 (June 1995), 57.

77. Norman Podhoretz, "The National Prospect," 100; "In the Matter of Pat Robertson," 27–32; "Comes the Counterrevolution," 46–50; and "Introduction," in *What to Do About . . . A Collection of Essays from* Commentary *Magazine*, ed. Neal Kozodoy (New York: Regan Books, 1995), xi, xii, xiii.

8

After the Fall

The Death of Neoconservatism

By the mid-1990s, once neoconservatism had served its purpose, and when it not only no longer ceased to be useful but also was a liability, it was discarded. Podhoretz had moved too far to the right. In becoming neoconservative, he had pushed himself and his magazine into an ideological corner from which he could not escape. He had two choices: renege on his conservatism, or push the envelope further. He opted for the latter course. The other major conservative magazines had upped the ante and *Commentary* had to become even more extreme to try to mark itself apart. The "neo" parts of Podhoretz's conservatism for all intents and purposes ceased to exist. By this point, *Commentary* had rejected any semblance of support for moderate liberalism and became simply a mainstream conservative magazine. The magazine dropped any lingering attachments to the welfare state, support for a strong federal government, New Deal social market capitalism, commitment to secular, scientific modernity, trade unionism, and social democratic anti-Communism. The abandonment of these things no longer distinguished its neoconservatism from traditional conservatism. Compared to those neocons who had stayed loyal to the Democratic Party and had remained committed to the welfare state of FDR, Truman, and LBJ and to the civil rights tradition of King—like Daniel Patrick Moynihan, and Daniel Bell—Podhoretz had abandoned all of the positions that tied him with liberalism in economic and civil rights measures and which had once distinguished him from the Old Right. Russell Kirk had prophetically put it back in 1988 as, "Neoconservatives . . . will have been merged with the main current of America's conservative movement."

Podhoretz's neoconservatism, in its original form as the continuation of the New Deal and vital center liberalism, was dead. As he wrote in 1999:

> the "neo" (meaning of course "new") has no longer seemed applicable to those of us who broke ranks with the Left a quarter of a century ago or more. For another thing, the distinctive characteristics that originally distinguished us from the old Right (as represented, say, by William F. Buckley, Jr.) faded as we gradually moved farther to the Right than at the start, while the conservatism of the Old Right became less radical than it had been in the 50's. At some juncture—it is hard to fix a precise date—we met somewhere to the right of center. Differences have remained, but they are matters more of emphasis and tone than of substance.

Its abandonment was manifested in Podhoretz's support for Newt Gingrich, Dick Armey, and Phil Gramm in their efforts to enact the antiregulatory and antilabor agenda of corporate America. He adopted an agenda that was markedly paleo: free-market capitalism, supply-side tax cuts, pro-life, the erosion of the wall separating church and state, the promotion of school prayers and creationism in public schools, support for the Religious Right, and the dismantling of the New Deal. His claim that the neocons had remained true to the liberal principles of their past was belied by their contribution to the defeat of universal health care, a key element of the reform programs of both Truman and Johnson. Podhoretz had therefore completely repudiated *Commentary*'s earlier centrist liberal views and had surrendered to the economic and social orthodoxy of the Right. Instead of converting the Republican Party, as they had hoped to do, the neocons were taken over by the Republican Party. As a result, neoconservatism was transmuted into just another mild variant of the more orthodox and familiar conservative mainstream.[1]

Experts queued up to testify to the death of the movement for which *Commentary* was the standard-bearer. The "godfather" of neoconservatism, Irving Kristol, stated that neoconservatism had had its own distinctive qualities in its early years, but by now had been absorbed into the mainstream of American conservatism. John Ehrman, the first scholar to write a book about the neocon influence on foreign policy, retracted his statement (written in 1995) that neocon thinking would undergo a resurgence in the latter part of the 1990s. He came around to the view that the neocons were becoming indistinguishable from mainline conservatives and would gradually disappear as a separate group. In a speech during a conference at

Harvard to celebrate *Commentary*'s fiftieth anniversary in February 1995, even Podhoretz announced that the last difference separating conservatives and neoconservatives—the latter's attachment to the welfare state—had disappeared. Since *Commentary* had simply become conservative during the 1990s he wondered aloud out if it was in fact time to retire the "neo" permanently. Writing in *Commentary* he argued that neoconservatism no longer could or should be distinguished from American conservatism. Glenn Loury confronted Podhoretz on this point, "Norman, you say there are no more neoconservatives, because no conservatives believe that the welfare state is worth salvaging. But I still believe in the welfare state, so what does that make me?" "Well, Glenn," Podhoretz replied, "you may be the last neoconservative in America." In the following year, neocon historian Mark Gerson declared: "Neoconservatism is now coming to an end." As a mark of this *Commentary* is now listed in *The Conservative Press in Twentieth Century America*, its liberal and neo roots having been discarded. The very movement it had helped to nurture and which precipitated its finest hour was now deceased.[2]

Sickness

At the time of the demise of neoconservatism, those who were still labeled neocons lost their influence. Podhoretz had severely disabled *Commentary*, a hub of the neocon imperium. Its circulation figures dropped from 40,000 in 1990 to 27,000 in 1995. In late 1994, a new department had been introduced and, in a drastic measure, the magazine had a complete makeover towards the end of 1995. But these strategies did not work and by 1998 circulation had dropped to a new low of 25,000, at which it has stayed by the time of writing. Podhoretz saw the writing on the wall and jumped ship, retiring in June 1995, 35 years after taking over as editor of *Commentary*. He took up a position as a Senior Fellow at the Hudson Institute and accepted generous grants from the Lynde and Harry Bradley, Carthage, and John M. Olin Foundations, as his reward for faithfully promoting their conservative goals, writers, and agenda over the previous decade.

After a lifetime spent at the magazine, Podhoretz handed the reins over to his protégé and successor, Neal Kozodoy, who took over as Editor-in-Chief. With the one hundredth issue, in July 1995, Kozodoy assumed control of the magazine to become only its third chief editor in the magazine's half-century of its existence. There was no major disruption, however, since Kozodoy had been at *Commentary* since 1966 and had been schooled in its catechism. As a sign of this, Podhoretz was very proud of Kozodoy, having dedicated his book *The Present Danger* to him; as Podhoretz wrote:

> I know from having worked closely with Neal Kozodoy for a very long time now that he feels much as I do about these matters. I also know that, while setting his own distinctive stamp on *Commentary* as he leads it into what I am certain will be a brilliant new period of its history, he will continue defending the dual heritage by which he too has been formed.

He added, almost as an order, "I expect the magazine to continue with the same point of view." In turn, as the chosen heir, Kozodoy promised to faithfully maintain the Podhoretz tradition. And, although Podhoretz retired as Editor-in-Chief, there was not a complete break, as Podhoretz did not let go entirely: he still retained the position of "Editor-at-Large," serving in an advisory capacity, and he still contributes frequently.[3]

On the occasion of Podhoretz's departure from the magazine, Kozodoy observed, "This is a moment of transition for *Commentary*, a tricky moment." It was a statement of euphemism; Podhoretz had left the magazine in a sickly state. He bequeathed Kozodoy an ailing magazine, as well as the onerous task of breathing life into it. Surely it is no coincidence that neoconservatism died coterminously with the decline of *Commentary*.[4]

If, as I have suggested, Podhoretz held the views he did, not because he considered them to be correct but for the reason that they enabled him to attain political power, then in his thirst for success he had made a Faustian pact. In this quest for power and influence, Podhoretz had sacrificed the magazine that Elliot Cohen had created. Podhoretz may have achieved a higher circulation, a greater profile, and more influence than Cohen might have done, but he did so at the exorbitant price of surrendering *Commentary*'s quality and critical intellectual independence. His compromises dropped the magazine's long-held standards that had originated under Cohen in return for conservative foundation largesse. The principles of serious journalism, policy, and scholarship had been abandoned, as *Commentary* became a spokes-journal for the Right. *Commentary* had become something quite different from what it was originally conceived to be (and originally was), shifting from a journal of cultural and political life to a policy platform for increasingly strident and rigid conservative policymakers and would-be policymakers. This was clearly indicated by the fact that, as time went on, the AJC distanced itself further and further from the magazine, paying less and less attention to it, and ultimately setting up rivals to provide the sort of cultural and Jewish ideas that it had originally wanted to see in *Commentary*. Ultimately, in January 2007, the AJC and

Commentary split and, for the first time in its history, the magazine became fully independent. The upshot is that surely the large donors will have even more say on how their money is spent.[5]

Since Podhoretz had enlisted the magazine in a conservative campaign, this cause, the holy war, had simply overridden more objective judgments of quality. Where the contradictory elements of the 1960s had led to the magazine's highest ever readership—its capacity to blend vastly opposing elements had made it attractive to an ever-wider circle of readers—the drastic narrowing of magazine into an undebated dogma accelerated its decline. Podhoretz could have sprinkled in articles from a different point of view but this would simply have undermined the crusade, even more so if the pieces were really good. So it was a choice of priorities, and the political cause became the dominant imperative. Just as Elliot Cohen had purged the magazine of any writers who could not contribute to the hard-line anti-Communist/pro-American stance of the late 1940s, so Podhoretz refused to publish anyone that detracted from his line. Podhoretz felt sure that eventually he could develop first-rate writers who would pursue this point of view. But eventually the truth was clear: only substandard, mediocre writers were reliable enough to stick to the *Commentary* line. The magazine was unintentionally scuttled as the best writers were replaced by the most reliable writers, even if they were second- and third-rate. The perceptive pieces and serious argument of an earlier era were discarded and replaced with those written in anger.

Podhoretz set the tone. There was a sense of extremism that ran through his more political and social pieces. His energies were reduced into attacks on feminists, anti-Semites, Leftists, multiculturalists, environmentalists, and anti-Zionists. He vented his wrath by pushing his culture war to extremes. His conservatism became increasingly neurotic, rooted in fear, aggression, and dogmatism. It was intolerant of ambiguity. It preferred moral certainty and frequently expressed its dislike of nuance and shades of grey. He clung to the familiar, arriving at premature conclusions, and simplistic clichés and stereotypes. He preached a return to an idealized past and condoned inequality. He had a tendency to characterize the ideas that he opposed in their most extreme form. He resorted to familiar targets, voicing his antigay obsessions, lamenting the fact that the culture no longer regarded homosexuality as a "perversion or even a mental illness," and warning of a new wave of young boys being "encouraged and seduced" into homosexuality because "feminism" had made "young girls more formidably intimidating."[6]

Nowhere was there any chastening influence to soften Podhoretz's fits of delirium. Debate was excised as dissenting views disappeared from *Commentary*'s pages. It didn't help that *Commentary*'s tone was self-congratulatory and self-important and that Podhoretz cultivated anger in his writers. Podhoretz himself had a preaching, self-righteous, rabbinic insinuation, as if pontificating from the pulpit. The magazine offered an insufficient variety of style, as if written by the same hand. In 1981, Podhoretz had written of how the universities and the media were "mired in yesterday's conventional wisdom," having become "the repository of discredited ideas and shopworn attitudes, a kind of shrine at which the cultists of a dying religion gather to genuflect, changing mindless invocations they imagine arise out of reason to a moribund god they still believe incarnates the living truth." His magazine had now come to fit that apt description. Podhoretz suffered from what he himself had diagnosed in 1967 as "the intellectual rigidity to which the human mind is prone in politics." The unprecedented attention and success of the Reaganites belied the stark poverty of *Commentary*'s thought which became all too clear once Reagan had gone. The ravages of the anti-PC scorched earth campaign had taken its toll. It not only made no attempt to be PC but rather it delighted in printing exactly the opposite. Nuance and subtlety were lost as a deliberately flagrant racism, sexism, and classism took their place.[7]

Over the years, Podhoretz had been responsible for the driving away of many promising contributors, much to the magazine's and neoconservatism's detriment. He closed his magazine to unwelcome guests, even those who had once been his closest comrades. The list is long and includes Hannah Arendt, Joseph Heller, Norman Mailer, Philip Roth, and Lionel and Diana Trilling. Podhoretz had never been known for his profound fidelity to his friends. This is a point unintentionally emphasized by Joseph Epstein when he quoted from Noel Annan's book *The Dons*, in which Annan observed that intellectuals, "vacillate and move gingerly to judgments about people, slide away at first hint of trouble, ... and then decamp when their friend is in trouble, or worse, when he is in disgrace." As a *Commentary* reader, paraphrasing what George Bernard Shaw said of his fellow Irishmen, stated, "Put a *Commentary* writer on a spit, and you can always get another *Commentary* writer to turn it ..." In words that were meant for Cohen but are just as apt for Podhoretz, "he had many enemies. Editors always have enemies, but he had more than anyone ever needed to have. Everybody hated him at least once a year for something" and "no man ever earned bitterer enemies." Podhoretz was seemingly proud of this fact, naming the third installment of his autobiography, *Ex-Friends*. While the title comes as no surprise, it could have been an even larger book because this tendency worsened towards the end of his editorship.[8]

Indeed, Podhoretz even managed to alienate his own neoconservative constituency. Long-time ally, Daniel Patrick Moynihan, was *persona non grata* after his "betrayal" (by the mid-1980s Moynihan had become a more traditional Democratic party partisan; he became interested in international law and criticized Reagan's intervention in Grenada). Besides, Moynihan had drifted away because Podhoretz had taken the magazine too far to the right. Jeane Kirkpatrick wrote a single, insignificant contribution after she left the UN. Robert Tucker, Nathan Glazer, Daniel Bell, and S. M. Lipset no longer contributed. They had split from Podhoretz when his uncritical support of Israel's actions began to anger them. Glenn Loury felt betrayed when Podhoretz refused to allow him to rebut *The Bell Curve*. Hyam Maccoby, Bruce Bawer, Jeffrey Herf, Jacob Heilbrunn, and Michael Lind left the fold as a result of *Commentary*'s excruciating circumlocutions in order to justify its continued alliance with the religious right—for example, its whitewash of the anti-Semitic theories purveyed by Pat Robertson and the Christian Coalition, and its questioning of evolution—as they would not write articles to support such fundamentalist positions. Lind in particular had been one of the great hopes of the next generation of formerly neoconservative intellectuals. They were replaced by less impressive and less perceptive writers.

Podhoretz had also begun to split from other long-term allies, the *theoconservatives*. While superficially resembling the neocons, this group of religious, predominantly Catholic, and conservative intellectuals displayed significant ideological divergences. Nonetheless, up until the mid-1990s the two blocs had forged a tactical political alliance in furtherance of shared conservative goals. Midge Decter had acted as an uncredited editor of the theocon journal *First Things* (established in 1990, it quickly grew to rival *Commentary*), and Gertrude Himmelfarb, Peter Berger, and Walter Berns served on the editorial board. Toward the end of 1996, however, all three had resigned and Podhoretz wrote to its editor to accuse the journal of "extremist hysteria" which gave "aid and comfort" to the "bomb-throwers among us." Decter add that the theocons had thus succeeded in "strengthening the Devil's hand."[9]

Another of Podhoretz's great faults was that he failed to nurture a new generation of younger neocon intellectuals to take the place of the one he had helped to push away. As he grew older, younger contributors grew more distant from him, and he scared away those young authors who might have led *Commentary* and neoconservatism into the twenty-first century. The younger generation of neocons that he did nurture, however, produced no great thinkers or writers, no classic books or landmark articles, no successors to their elders. Even the offspring of the neocons (William Kristol, John Podhoretz) are referred to, only half-jokingly, as "minicons." The most successful of them did not end up in *Commentary*, as they did a generation ago, but rather as top functionaries in right-wing Australian tycoon Rupert Murdoch's media empire, or as hosts of cable TV chat shows. Others still would give up intellectual pretensions altogether and go straight into politics. One of their former comrades, David Brock felt that, "There was something ersatz about this Third Generation of conservatives."[10]

With little new blood, Podhoretz relied on a tired-sounding roster of increasingly wearisome names. Podhoretz depended heavily on a reliable stable of youthful and abrasive pro-Zionist, pro-immigration, and anti-isolationist polemicists (like Daniel Pipes, Joshua Muravchik, and David Frum), who routinely leveled charges of racism and anti-Semitism against any heretics and dissenters. At a conference on *Commentary* in March 2003, very few new and young intellectuals could be rustled up; instead it fell back on the tried and trusted like Murray Friedman, Nathan Glazer, Ruth Wisse, Muravchik, and Cynthia Ozick. Irving Kristol and Jeane Kirkpatrick were invited but in a sign of the times they didn't show up. Nepotism replaced critical selection and *Commentary* increasingly took on the look of an inbred and incestuous family enterprise—the connections were everywhere.

A week after the November election in 1994, David Brooks published a short essay titled "Meet the New Establishment," on the *Wall Street Journal*'s editorial page. In it, he heralded the ascent of a "new generation" of 30- and 40-something conservative opinion-makers: journalists, columnists, policy intellectuals, and assorted other media and political types. In February 1995, James Atlas followed up in the *New York Times Magazine* with a cover story headlined, "Look Who's the 'Opinion Elite' Now." The tag line read: "They're young, brainy, and ambitious—and adversarial band of conservatives winning the war against liberalism and having a grand old time." Atlas pointed out that these young men and women, who were the architects of last November 1994 Republican triumph, were "a new conservative opinion elite, a counter-counterculture." On the cover appeared Brock, Adam Bellow, Lisa Schiffren, James Golden, and Laura Ingraham. Other members of this New Establishment included the editors of *The American Spectator*; William Kristol, Myron Magnet, Roger Kimball, Dinesh D'Souza, Cathy Danielle Crittenden, David Frum, Betsy Hart, and David Brooks. These "Brash Conservatives" were the new "counter-intelligentsia" who had made Gingrich's electoral triumph possible. And where was *Commentary* in all of this? It was mentioned only in connection with John Podhoretz. By and large, these were not *Commentary* writers, even if they had occasionally contributed to the magazine. *Commentary* had been usurped within its own movement.[11]

Because there was no young blood to flow through *Commentary*'s veins, there were no new or refreshing insights to be made. After all, it had taken the illness and death of Cohen to blow away the cobwebs of hard-line anti-Communism in the late 1950s when Podhoretz succeeded him and injected a new, radical life force into the magazine. A similar occurrence did not seem in sight at this time, even when Podhoretz retired and Kozodoy took over. Like the wider neocon movement of which it was a part, *Commentary* was empty of vision. If *Commentary* had any ideas by then, it was an unshakeable belief in Israel on which it was urgent and strident. Since the 1970s, Podhoretz's view of the world had been defined more by what he opposed than by what he favored. He had become too extreme and too predictable, reducing every question to the issue of conservatism versus liberalism. When that great threat of Soviet totalitarianism collapsed, like many of the neocons, he was ill-prepared for the altered reality that would emerge. As a result, *Commentary* had little to say about the kind of new world it sought in the post-Cold War era. Podhoretz was so far wedded to the Cold War that he could not bring him to admit that, once it was over, the direct military threat to America had subsided. Instead *Commentary* saw new threats in "a new generation of doomsday theoreticians" who advocated other causes like ecology, animal rights, a ban on atomic energy, drugs and the drugs trade, AIDS, criminals, terrorism, and terrorist states.

Intellectually lost in a world in which the old Left-Right categories did not serve very well, Podhoretz clung to internationalism like a life preserver. Together with his suspicions of the motives of Old Right/paleo, liberal, and radical calls for isolationism, these were his sure principles. In September 1993, for example, Podhoretz signed an open letter to Clinton, "What the West Must Do in Bosnia," published in the *Wall Street Journal* in which he called for US military intervention in Bosnia-Herzegovina and Serbia. He also advocated the effective use of American power, intervention in the interests of preserving peace, encouraging humane order, and preventing the emergence of a hostile imperium. As the United States had a duty to people in other countries, the danger lay in an American "abdication of power" not an "arrogance of power." He aggressively criticized the US government and military, the UN and the American public for resisting US military intervention. Yet here Podhoretz entered into a strange and opportunistic alliance with the overwhelming liberal calls for American military intervention in the post-Gulf War era. Because Podhoretz lived in a Manichean world, divided between Left and Right, liberals and conservatives, this stance confused him. Podhoretz desperately tried to make a distinction between them, arguing that he stressed both interests *and* values. What he did not realize was that the distinctions between them after the polarizing 1960s and 1970s were breaking down and new alliances forming. The clash between ethnic particularism and democratic universalism was replacing the old Left-Right and class polarities and now *Commentary*'s democratic internationalism pushed it nearer to the liberal camp, just as the hard right's neo-isolationism drove it closer to the far Left.[12]

It was vexing for Podhoretz, his magazine, and the former neocons to come up with any issues or original thoughts of their own. Clinton had stolen their ideas. Following the brief Republican success and takeover of Congress in 1995 (which had led to a party atmosphere among the conservatives), Clinton had adopted a policy of "triangulation"—occupying a middle position between the Gingrich revolutionaries on the right, and the Congressional Democratic leadership on the left. He signed a balanced budget, and turned historic deficits into surpluses, co-opting the Republican Wall Street constituency. In his 1996 State of Union address, he declared the age of big government was over. A few months later, he ended welfare as a federal entitlement. In his speeches, noted Mark Gerson, there was "far more than an echo of old articles sitting in bound volumes of *Commentary* ... Current debates over a panoply of issues, from the welfare state to religion in the public square, are conducted with the ideas and sometimes the very language employed by contributors to *Commentary* ... two and three decades ago."[13]

While *Commentary* could pat itself on the back for the acceptance of its ideas, it was a victim of its own success. It helped to shift the national consensus to the right on the key subject of taxation and welfare, altering the terms of political debate in America, and convincing many Americans, including neoliberals and centrists, that excessive taxation has burdened the American economy, producing a favoring of supply-side economics. It was so successful that Clinton had to stand as the most conservative Democrat ever. But, having helped to nudge Clinton to the political center, the magazine did not reap the credit for doing so, or for popular initiatives like the balanced budget and welfare reform. By successfully triangulating, Clinton left the Republicans and the former neocons clinging to a cluster of unpopular right-wing social issues.[14]

Podhoretz's Protégé

Since taking over, Kozodoy has maintained Podhoretz's mainstream American conservative political line with extraordinary consistency. Under Kozodoy, *Commentary* has consistently criticized political correctness, homosexuality, and other manifestations of what it views as the ill-effects of the intellectual elite on American culture; advocated free market policies; supported Israel; and urged strong defense and foreign policies. A familiar checklist of targets with tired-sounding titles has remained. If there's been a change, then perhaps the Jewish content under Kozodoy has grown stronger. And its clear pro-immigration stance has shown some slight signs of wavering such that at the time of writing it hadn't treated it at all. Yet Kozodoy has failed to heed Podhoretz's diagnosis of where *Commentary* had (he said) gone wrong in the late 1950s. "What did concern me was to get the family reading it and writing for it again, most of them having fallen or been driven away during the years of trouble." Kozodoy hasn't, it seems, found a way of attracting those of similar intellectual capacity to recapture the prestige that *Commentary* has lost.[15]

Podhoretz, *Commentary*, and the former neocons seemed to have no program and no vision for the country after liberalism was reined in. They were so frustrated that they instead "practised a brand of attack politics that required no alternative vision to Clintonism," recalled Brock. The only thing holding the Right together was the anti-Clinton investigations and a common loathing of the Clintons, which persisted and intensified as Clinton adopted the most appealing parts of their agenda. Clinton's reelection in 1996—the first Democratic president to win re-election since FDR—compounded the misery and bitterness hung over the conservatives. They were adrift, bereft of ideas, as never before. Their policy examinations had become increasingly more prescribed. On some matters, such as Israel, global democracy, immigration, and the appropriateness of using public education to instill "democratic values," they were tiresomely predictable and establishment-sounding. George Nash summarized the type of conservatism Podhoretz, *Commentary*, and the former neocons had come to espouse as "bourgeois democratic order."[16]

Commentary was now just one more conservative magazine on a shelf full of them. The rot had set in back during the 1980s when, according to David Frum, editors lost their best writers to administration jobs, talent was spread thinly as new journal after journal opened, and "the natural savagery of journalists was thwarted by their responsibility to defend their allies in the administration. As Reaganite opinions lost their power to shock, conservative journalism lost its verve." And, with no new ideas or policies, little distinguished *Commentary* from *National Review*, the *Weekly Standard*, and the *American Spectator*. They were all critical of Clinton and his brand of liberalism, they all advocated strong foreign and defense policies, they all defended the policies of the Christian Right, they all opposed affirmative action, and they were all skeptical of religious liberalism. And these other magazines had stolen *Commentary*'s thunder. Kristol's *The Weekly Standard*, a new conservative magazine funded by Murdoch in September 17, 1995, produced even more vituperative attacks on typical *Commentary* targets like gays, abortion, and feminists. *The American*

Spectator had a circulation of 340 000—over twelve-and-a-half times that of *Commentary*. The *Spectator* scored all the big scoops like Brock's expose of Anita Hill and Whitewater. Unlike *Commentary*, the *Spectator* could claim with perhaps a tiny bit more justification: "We're saying what the American people are thinking." As the meager attendance at the March 2003 conference confirmed, conservatives in America are inspired by other magazines. On the morning of the conference's second day, someone handed John Podhoretz a section from that day's *New York Times*. There, on the cover, was an article about *The Weekly Standard*, entitled "White House Listens When Weekly Speaks." The center of conservative journalism had shifted from New York City to Washington and *Commentary* was out of the loop.[17]

Even Podhoretz's continued prestige among the conservative movement, intellectuals, and media could not hide the grim reality. As much as he wanted to shield himself from the horrible truth by surrounding himself with sycophants and by basking in long-gone successes, Podhoretz could not ignore the fact that his influence—that is, his ability to see his ideas translated into action—had declined. Podhoretz had reached the zenith of political influence and power during the Reagan years and was now on the wane. Under Clinton Podhoretz and the neocons discovered what twelve years of Republican rule blinded them into not seeing: "the uncomfortable fact" that most Americans were not really with them. Conservative social and cultural ideas and values had lost much ground in Clinton's America. Eventually, and as a result, Podhoretz, *Commentary*, and the former neocons were marginalized. They spoke only for a splinter group. They had even lost and alienated their core Jewish constituency. The years had taken its toll and American Jews were simply not prepared to read a magazine that consistently articulated positions contrary to their own. Podhoretz had singularly failed to break the paradigm whereby the vast majority of American Jews remain liberal Democrats and regard the neocons as, at best, an eccentric minority. To put it mildly, things weren't looking too good in the late 1990s. In 1999 Podhoretz admitted that although *Commentary* (and by extension neocon ideas) might still exist, it no longer comprised an intellectual focus in the way it once did. It had aged and was suffering from, as one former editor put it, "a slight arterial sclerosis."[18]

Reviving Reagan

With neoconservatism dead and his empire in decline, Podhoretz and his now former-neocon allies retreated under Clinton and bunkered down in the think tanks and institutes and those universities that would still have them. They reorganized and refined their political vision. They reinvented themselves, realizing, in the words of Gary Dorrien, "the foreign policy issue was the key to their identity and political future." They forged alliances with Old Right conservatives like Dick Cheney and Donald Rumsfeld. The result was yet another organization, the Project for a New American Century (PNAC), formed in June 1997, and dedicated to promoting American global hegemony. Podhoretz and many other prominent neocons like Elliott Abrams, William J. Bennett, Eliot A. Cohen, Midge Decter, Donald Kagan, Peter W. Rodman, and George Weigel signed its "Statement of Principles." Significantly, in addition to Cheney and Rumsfeld, the group included new allies like Jeb Bush, I. Lewis Libby, and Paul Wolfowitz. PNAC's aim was to revive, in its own words, "a Reaganite policy of military strength and moral clarity" by increasing defense spending, strengthening ties with democratic allies and challenging regimes hostile to US interests and values, promoting the cause of political and economic freedom abroad, and taking responsibility for preserving and extending an international order friendly to US security, prosperity, and principles. It was yet another harking back to the past but conveniently PNAC overlooked the former neocons' own misgivings about Reagan and the fact that Reagan ultimately won the Cold War not by force but by negotiation and patience.[19]

As for Podhoretz, between August 1997 and July 2000, practically all of his articles looked back at the past. His essay in *Commentary* in December 1999 was typical, calling for "post-Reagan Reaganism." He also continued to pursue a checklist of familiar targets (homosexuality, the peace process) with articles entitled "How the Gay-Rights Movement Won" and "The Tragic Predicament of Benjamin Netanyahu."[20]

Life After Death?

Yet, seven years after Podhoretz—whom Joshua Muravchik described as "the conductor of the neocon orchestra"—pronounced the death of neoconservatism in *Commentary* the former neocons were accused of wielding more influence than ever before. Since the election of George W. Bush in 2000, neoconservatism seemingly experienced a new lease of life. Bush resuscitated those erstwhile former neocons that had been dormant under eight years of Clintonism. Like zombies, they were resurrected from the dead, from the graves of various foundations and institutes, and restored once again to the center of government.

Those former neocons who were appointed by the Bush administration to prominent positions included Richard Perle, chairman of the Defense

Policy Board, an advisory panel to the Pentagon; Deputy Secretary of Defense Paul Wolfowitz; and Douglas J. Feith, Under Secretary of Defense for Policy. John DiIulio and David Frum served on the senior White House staff in the Office of Faith-Based Initiatives and as a speechwriter respectively, while David Horowitz emerged as an influential Bush supporter. Frum even helped to coin the phrase "axis of evil." Elliot Abrams was selected by Bush to be director of the National Security Council's office for democracy, human rights, and international operations (despite his previous conviction). Murray Friedman was one of only two Jewish officials invited to a meeting of religious leaders to discuss the president-elect's plan for faith-based initiatives. Leslie Lenkowsky became Chief Executive Officer of the Corporation for National and Community Service. Leon Kass was appointed to run the new President's Council on Bioethics. In turn, Kass selected James Q. Wilson to sit on its board. Kass was a central figure in Bush's morality-driven administration, being one of two men (the other was Karl Rove) who had most influence on Bush's approaches to bioethics and stem-cell research. Together with Rove, Kass was responsible for one of the most radical science policy changes to emerge from the Bush White House: the clampdown on human cloning, as Bush announced in 2001 that he would end government funding for the cultivation of new cell lines, forcing scientists to find private funding or rely on exiting, often contaminated lines. "As a result," Kristol stated while looking around him, "neoconservatism began enjoying a second life, at a time when its obituaries were still being published."[21]

In accepting these appointments, however, Podhoretz's cohort of former neocons displayed a tendency toward short memories or simply it was another manifestation of their opportunism. Initially, they were not pro-Bush. As with LBJ before him, the former neocons were wary of the Texan. They had supported the candidacy of Bush's primary opponent Senator John McCain prior to the 2000 election. In the *New York Post*, Podhoretz cheered McCain for "upending the old coalition." Midge Decter added, "We decided that we liked McCain, then we came up with our justifications." Podhoretz even went as far to write a neoconservative defense of the Clinton Administration.[22]

As a result of their support for McCain, the former neocons "had to battle for access to Bush" as he was not automatically predisposed toward their agenda. Even once Bush was in power, John Micklethwait and Adrian Wooldridge remind us that, "until September 11, the neoconservatives were the junior members of the Bush team. Only about twenty of them found their way into the administration in 2001." Gerard Baker and Stephen Fidler pointed out that "they are not as numerous as often depicted and are often defeated by internal opponents." It was the Old Right conservatism of Vice President Dick Cheney and Secretary of Defense Donald Rumsfeld, as well as the conservatism of National Security Advisor Condoleezza Rice, Secretary of State Colin Powell (a particularly prominent opponent of neocon foreign policy ideas), and Karl Rove that trumped the neocons; and Bush was certainly no neocon. "We were really ticked off with the direction the administration was taking," said Gary Schmitt executive director of PNAC. Bush's lack of support for Israel and his nonconfrontational policy toward Russia and China particularly disturbed them. As James Mann put it, "The neocons did not control the Bush administration's first-term policy toward China or Russia, which conformed to the classic realist principles of former Secretary of State Henry Kissinger and former National Security Advisor Brent Scowcroft." In early 2001, Cheney dismissed the former neocons in a TV interview, saying: "Oh, they have to sell magazines; we have to govern."[23]

In turn, despite their dislike of Bush, the former neocons saw his administration and particularly September 11 as another opportunity which they grabbed eagerly with both hands. It was the continuation of the strategy of courting power that Podhoretz had initiated since the 1960s. Daniel Pipes, Charles Horner, Samuel Huntington, Bernard Lewis, and Robert Kagan stepped forward to advise America on its duties in its time of crisis. Stephen Schwartz, a historian, whose book *The Two Faces of Islam* became a key text for those who wanted the United States to sever its ties with Saudi Arabia, was increasingly influential. Michael Ledeen called for "a war to remake the world." Middle East expert and director of the Philadelphia-based Middle East Forum, Pipes was a leading voice in US public debates over terrorism and the Middle East, warning of the danger posed by fundamentalist Islam. Rewarding him for his outspoken views in 2003, Bush nominated Pipes to the board of directors at the US Institute of Peace, a federally funded think tank.

As a result, the 2002 National Security Strategy of the United States reflected *Commentary*'s neocon thinking since it built on previous neocon premises about the scale of US power and responsibility and outlined measures the United States would take to preserve its position and counterthreats of the sort suggested by the 9/11 attack.

Commentary's sponsor, the American Jewish Committee was one of the few Jewish organizations favored by the Bush administration. In fact, the AJC received more attention from the Bush White House than from previous administrations. Its increased access came from a mix of favorable policy and politics, as the AJC has adopted a pose of not trying to irritate the administration. Above all, the AJC's president, Los Angeles lawyer Bruce

Ramer, was one of Bush's most prominent supporters in the Jewish community. One of the only speeches Bush gave to a Jewish audience was at the AJC's annual dinner in May 2001. And his first-term national security adviser, Condoleezza Rice, and White House Chief of Staff Andrew Card addressed the organization the following two years.

Podhoretz Returns

The September 11 attacks reenergized the 74-year-old Podhoretz, causing him to return to writing about contemporary issues. In January 2001, for example, Podhoretz had the feeling "something that will surprise everyone will erupt. You just never know." In the wake of the terrorist attacks, Podhoretz transferred his allegiances and became a strong supporter of Bush. Justifying his U-turn, he wrote that September 11 had transformed the president from a leader without an apparent vision to one who could realistically claim to be "following in the footsteps of Ronald Reagan." Just as Podhoretz had conveniently forgotten his own misgivings about Reagan, so he ignored those he had about Bush. In "Oslo: The Peacemongers Return," he approved of Bush's "disinclination to follow Bill Clinton's example of stationing himself between the Israelis and the Palestinians." Although he felt that Bush's attempt to round up a coalition before invading Afghanistan was absurd, in general Podhoretz commended Bush with the greatest compliment he felt he could pay: "It has been said—by me, among others—that George W. Bush bears a closer political resemblance to Ronald Reagan than to his father," conveniently forgetting that even the neocons didn't feel that Reagan was tough enough. Similarly, Midge Decter contributed a paean to Donald Rumsfeld. And to cap it all, their son wrote a book in praise of the president. Old allegiances and animosities were forgotten as a new love affair was kindled.[24]

Shortly after September 11, Podhoretz, along with Decter and other former neocons, joined the CPD, that Cold War relic which was revived but now directed towards fighting the threat of what they called "radical Islamists." Decter enlisted in the Independent Women's Forum, a group contributing to the Iraq war effort by using $10 million of State Department funds to prepare Iraqi women for participation in democratic life.

Podhoretz sought to influence the administration's direction. Only ten days after September 11, Podhoretz signed an open letter to the White House, calling on the president, among other things, to make "a determined effort to remove Saddam Hussein from power in Iraq." In February of 2002, he gave a major speech in Washington. He spoke of the "new patriotic mood" that had emerged after the terrorist attacks. But from the beginning, he "could not fully share the heady confidence of some of my political friends that this was a permanent and not an ephemeral change." He recalled the Vietnam period, in which "elite opinion trumped popular opinion." Would such opinion work its will again? It would depend, said Podhoretz, on the progress of the war. "Of one thing we can be sure: As the war widens, opposition will widen along with it." And conservatives, among others, should "mobilize" to "fight off . . . appeasement and defeatism." In April, he signed a PNAC letter urging Bush to reinforce America's obligations to Israel. Finally, just as he had produced a textbook for the Reagan administration (*The Present Danger*), Podhoretz wrote a 30,000-word article in the September issue of *Commentary* in support of the Bush Doctrine, entitled, "World War IV: How It Started, What It Means, and Why We Have to Win." Changes in regime in the Middle East, Podhoretz proclaimed, were "the *sine qua non* throughout the region," as they might "clear a path to the long-overdue internal reform and modernization of Islam." Podhoretz had set out the road to war, according to David Hirst, "in its most comprehensive, well-nigh megalomaniac form" (a form which was reportedly read by policy-makers).[25]

In that same year, Podhoretz published another book, *The Prophets: Who They Were, What They Are*. Initially, the book seemed a strange return to a subject that Podhoretz had studied over fifty years ago while an undergraduate at Columbia: the Hebrew prophets. However, old habits die hard and this purportedly scholarly analysis was interwoven with many references to himself, as well as an attempt to remake the prophets over as proto-neocons. Early on in the book, for instance, Podhoretz stated that the prophets were fighting an "enemy they knew as idolatry," which "keeps coming back under different names and in mutated forms that are not always easy to recognize." He went to argue that the weapons that had defeated that enemy two thousand years ago "are ready to hand in the Bible" and "may still be sharp enough to cut him [the enemy] down again today." Podhoretz compared the prophets' views and fight for monotheism and against paganism to his own outlook, and in his final chapter, "The Prophets and Us," he pursued a familiar checklist of targets condemning the Movement, relativism, the counterculture, political correctness, feminism, gay rights, deconstructionism, multiculturalism, environmentalism, appeasement, anal sex, and Norman Mailer. At one point, he even used the language of one prophet to rail against the peace process:

> Jeremiah's words blazingly articulated the dangers posed under any circumstances by the pursuit of peace when the reality is that peace is *not* at hand, and when the conditions for it are *not* present. It was

a warning that would be ignored by his descendants in the modern state of Israel who—misunderstanding the nature of the prophetic utopianism subliminally egging on their conscious calculations—tried prematurely and unilaterally to make pace with an enemy who had not the slightest desire to make peace with them.

Writing in the *New York Times*, Judith Shulevitz explained the message of Podhoretz's prophets as "to vote Republican and back the war against Iraq."[26]

Indeed, Podhoretz was at the forefront of support for the Iraq War. Furthermore, not only did he defend the American invasion of Iraq, but he also stated that the United States should help liberate other Middle Eastern countries to destroy the seedbed of Islamic radicalism. He told the *New York Times*, "I am not advocating the invasion of Iran at this moment although I wouldn't be heartbroken if it happened." He later wrote "wholeheartedly" that America "ought to 'kill' the regimes in Iraq, Syria, and the PLO, which together 'are the effective cause of global terrorism.'" He also added Iran, Lebanon, Saudi Arabia, and Egypt to his wish list of regimes that America "should destroy . . . 'as quickly as possible' by capturing their leaders and then subjecting them to punishments ranging from execution to imprisonment to banishment from public life—just as we did with the Nazis." But as the last quote reveals, Podhoretz is stuck in the past, re-fighting earlier wars, not realizing that September 11 had "changed everything." He was still out of touch. Nonetheless, he had struck a chord with the White House, and in 2004 his efforts were recognized by the Bush administration when he was awarded the Presidential Medal of Freedom.[27]

Mere Posturing

But the extent of the influence of former neocons has been grossly exaggerated. Concomitantly, rumors of the death of neoconservatism as a movement have not. Even Muravchik describes those claims that former neocons—in the words of Steven Halper and Jonathan Clarke—"primed with a far-reaching agenda to be put in action at the first opportunity," have transformed George W. Bush beyond all recognition by "hijacking" his administration's foreign policy, as potent fiction. No former neocon, he points out, was elevated in office after September 11.[28]

If the Bush administration followed the *Commentary* neocon line, it is because those ideas had become those of mainstream conservatism. In July 2002, "the neocons are no longer a wing of the conservative movement," reported *The New Republic*, "they *are* the conservative movement.

Supply-side economics, Israel, welfare reform, vouchers—all the old neocon pet causes have become enshrined in conservative conventional wisdom." If neoconservatism survives it is because it is perceived to exert a disproportionate influence within the conservative movement in America so that American conservatism is now considered synonymous with neoconservatism. To paraphrase *Commentary* of the 1950s, neoconservatism was kept alive and well in the fascinated fears of the media and intelligentsia. Its enemies kept it breathing because it served an extremely valuable partisan center-right purpose: to defend the Bush administration from attacks warranted by its egregious mistakes since 2001. Arguing that neo-cons "hijacked" US foreign policy made them a convenient scapegoat. Veteran conservative activists increasingly blamed neoconservatives for placing Iraq at the center of the war on terrorism. An example of this was articulated by Halper and Clarke who claim that the misperceptions which arose over Iraq were the fault of the neocons exploiting the opportunities presented by 9/11. And there also is little doubt that the term neocon is used as a polite synonym where Jew or Zionist is actually intended. As Irwin Stelzer has pointed out, "con" stands for conservative and "neo" for Jew.[29]

In reality, apart from a pro-Israel and a Wilsonian foreign policy, the traces of the "neo" are long gone. And if neocon foreign policy thinking is just selective interventionism based on the principles of realism, there's nothing inherently neo about it. What the so-called (but in reality, ex-) neocons won't admit to is that they are basically conservatives who have been taken over by the Old Right paleoconservatives and the Religious Right. The actuality is that 9/11 revived a neocon foreign-policy *posture* but the new species of neocon that exists today differs from that which existed in the 1970s and 1980s (which is probably more accurately labeled as "paleoneoconservative"); the neoconservatism that is trumpeted in the media today is not the same now as it was then. While once receptive to large-scale welfare programs, those today labeled as neocons now share the general conservative hostility toward the welfare state and its assumptions about social engineering. Even in foreign policy, where neocon opinion is thought to be uniform, in the late 1990s a split developed between the Wilsonians and the realists, a fight that assumed greater prominence after American actions in Iraq and Afghanistan. Genuine neoconservatism, in its original form, is dead, and a new ideological variant, one of moralist, post-utopian, post-modern, puritan social engineering, has emerged over the last ten years. It has been given names such as "neo-imperialism," "Pax Americanism," "unipolarism," "neo-Reaganism," "neo-Manifest Destinarianism," and "liberal imperialism." This new post- or ersatz neoconservatism is being pushed by a second younger generation, people like Elliott Abrams,

Richard Perle, Frank Gaffney, Joshua Muravchik, and Michael Ledeen. In contrast to their forebears, who were primarily men of letters, this new generation is one composed of politicians, and predominantly foreign-policy-oriented ones at that.

Myth-Making

However, the former neocons willingly participated in the deception by developing their own legends. They produced a mythology which tended to elide their differences with the past while wildly inflating their own importance in the present. They have certainly been partly responsible for writing what Lind called "its own triumphalist" and "sanitized version of history" which "grossly overemphasizes the importance of intellectuals in politics." On a BBC TV documentary broadcast in 2003, for example, former neocon after former neocon was paraded to attest to the strength of their influence. Even Muravchik, who derided the BBC's claims as pure fiction, boasted:

> On September 11, we learned in the most dreadful way that terrorists would not be appeased by our diffidence; quite the contrary. We saw—they themselves told us—that they intended to go on murdering us in ever larger numbers as long as they could. A sharp change of course was required, and the neoconservatives, who had been warning for years that terror must not be appeased, stood vindicated—much as, more grandly, Churchill was vindicated by Hitler's depredations after Munich.

Not only did the neocons have an analysis of what had gone wrong in American policy, they also stood ready with proposals for what to do now: to wage war on the terror groups and to seek to end or transform governments that supported them, especially those possessing the means to furnish terrorists with the wherewithal to kill even more Americans than on September 11. Neocons also offered a long-term strategy for making the Middle East less of a hotbed of terrorism: implanting democracy in the region and thereby helping to foment a less violent approach to politics. Tod Lindberg added: "Once again, neoconservatives were at the forefront of the new thinking. They shouldn't shrink from this fact. They should be proud of it." He continued to say:

> But win or lose, the vindication of neoconservatism has already taken place, in that the Democratic candidate in 2004 has found it

impossible to run for the Oval Office on a platform of its repudiation, but rather has embraced its central strategic insights.

Neocons couldn't resist bragging, which is why Irving Kristol helped keep neoconservatism alive and well, via some rhetorical manipulation, by simply renaming it a "persuasion" rather than a "movement" so he could claim credit for much Bush administration policy. At the same time, former neocons also attempted to protect their legacy against claims that they got it wrong by denying the extent of their influence.[30]

This mythology has grown to such an extent that it must be reevaluated. The neocons' record, to say the least, is mixed. In many areas they simply got it wrong. John Patrick Diggins has pointed out that *Commentary*

> did much to help create the perilous post-cold war situation in which America now finds itself. *Kapital* is gone but the *Koran* has taken its place ... twenty years ago, *Commentary* dismissed "the Islamic revolution" as little more than "a side show" concealing the movement of the Soviet Union into the Mid East and hence saw nothing wrong with America arming Saddam Hussein and Osama Bin Laden in America's Cold War struggle against the Soviet Union. Its moral and inflexible anti-Communism, which worked hard to legitimate concepts of "good" and "evil" as organizing categories of public discourse, policy and belief, diverted it and America from other more dangerous threats like Saddam and Islamic fundamentalism. Its misjudgments led to consequences which we are suffering with today, for the State Department was listening to *Commentary* and its author-advisors as it carried out a foreign policy that can only be called, in all honesty, "Dictatorships and No Standards."

Commentary was never critical of America's support for Saddam in the 1980s, it all but ignored Donald Rumsfeld's visit to Iraq. Rather it deflected attention onto West Germany's contribution to the development of Iraq's weaponry, alleging that its government played a substantial and deliberate part in helping Iraq build up its chemical-weapons programs. It spent a decade ignoring the threat of Islamic fundamentalism and terrorism.[31]

Similarly, in its uncritical support for the Likud Administration in Israel, *Commentary* forgot its own prophetic words, written back in 1989.

> It is undoubtedly Sharon's ambition to become Prime Minister of Israel. That will probably not happen, save in one circumstance. In the highly unlikely event that the country were to find itself facing

catastrophe, Israelis might turn to a man with the hard will, hot patriotism, and cold intelligence (one should not call it wisdom) of Ariel Sharon. There are many reasons for hoping that hour will not arrive.

The neocons, alas, have short memories.[32]

Two prominent neocons resigned from the Bush administration: David Frum and John DiIulio. Afterwards, the latter said,

> There is no precedent in any modern White House for what is going on in this one: a complete lack of a policy apparatus. What you've got is everything—and I mean everything—being run by the political arm. It's the reign of the Mayberry Machiavellis.

As I mentioned above, early in the administration, the former neocons were disturbed by Bush's lack of support for Israel and his nonconfrontational policy toward Russia and China. While some former neocons certainly played a role in the formulation of America's Iraq policy, perhaps going as far as converting Cheney and Bush to their cause, the prime movers were Cheney, Rumsfeld, and Rice. The United States' reversal of policy in turning to the UN for help with the reconstruction of Iraq and refusal to pacify Iraq with greater armed force was a further blow to neocon dreams of American imperial unilateralism. The former neocons also faced one of their biggest challenges in trying to persuade the Bush administration to adopt their regime-change policy toward Iran, Syria, the PLO, Lebanon, Saudi Arabia, and Egypt, even while their regime-change policy in Iraq appears to be crumbling.[33]

That Bush was seemingly serious about pushing the Middle East Road Map—he told European leaders that he would make a serious effort to try to resolve the conflict—also indicated the limits of neocon influence since this was never a part of their agenda. As an illustration of this, when the president addressed the neocon think tank the American Enterprise Institute in 2003, his speech outlining the case for a viable Palestinian state was greeted with stony silence. And, if anything, Bush's foreign policy, particularly in the Middle East, was driven more by the demands of the Religious Right, in particular evangelical Protestantism, than the neocons. Hiding behind accusations of a "Jewish lobby" or an "Israel lobby," the neocons' detractors (and others) often fail to spot what Martin Durham observed: "Recent events have seen the development of a crucial relationship between evangelicalism and foreign policy in the United States . . . with the election of George W. Bush, it is evangelical Protestantism that has had the greatest impact."[34]

"America's Gay Summer" of 2003 also indicated the limited power of the reactionary neocon "vision." In the face of conservative outrage, gay rights advanced at an amazing speed, including the landmark Supreme Court decision to throw out a Texan law forbidding gay sex, the appointment of an openly gay bishop in the Episcopalian Church, the moves to legalize gay marriages, and the creation of a specifically gay public secondary school in New York. To cap it all off, homosexuality is even more present in mainstream entertainment, bringing gay characters into the living rooms of every television-owning household in America. The Court's ruling on sodomy (*Lawrence v. Texas*) and to uphold affirmative action, in 2003, was another blow to the conservative reaction against civil rights. They led *Commentary* to ask in October of that year, "Has the Supreme Court Gone Too Far?" Conservatives appear to have lost the battle on homosexual rights.

In November 2004, the American people delivered their verdict on neo-conservatism. It was decisively rejected by the "blue" states who voted for John Kerry as well as by the "red" states who embraced wholesale the mainstream values-based conservatism represented by Bush, Cheney, and Rove. Iraq and the economy—two of the voters' major concerns—and the very policies underpinned by neocon thinking, were rejected.

The neocons were reeling, in particular taken aback by events in Iraq. Podhoretz lamented the darkening mood of "gloom and doom," in particular the "newborn pessimism among supporters" of the Iraq war. "Things have gone not badly, not disastrously, but triumphantly," he declared in September 2004. But, as ex-neocon Scott McConnell remarked of his former colleagues, "And yet they don't breathe easily . . . All betray the same anxiety: that despite their wealth and position, the neoconservatives sense that they are no longer gaining adherents and now are losing them." The power of the neocons inside the administration was diminished during Bush's second term as the neocon architects of the Iraq policy, who were perceived to have got Bush into the mess, lost influence. As James Mann put it, "the impact of the Iraq war has served to reduce further the neocons' clout. The war they so strongly favored has lasted vastly longer than they predicted. It took more US troops and cost much more money than they led the nation to believe." In fact, experts again queued up to testify to the demise of the neocons: Mann dismissed neocon doctrine as a "spent force" and wrote that the foreign policy realism of Henry Kissinger is "again ascendant." The editor of *Foreign Policy* magazine, Moises Naim, scoffed that neoconservative ideas "lie buried in the sands of Iraq." While Patrick J. Buchanan gloated that the "salad days" of the neocons were over, Robert Kuttner was even more forthright in another article: "Because Iraq has gone badly, Bush [will] waste [...] no time in dispatching Jewish neoconservative advisers like Douglas Feith and Paul Wolfowitz."[35]

Indeed, the first to go was Deputy Secretary, Paul Wolfowitz, who was nominated to the Presidency of the World Bank, possibly as a reward for services rendered, or as a means to advance neocon aims without going to war. Ultimately, after a brief spell at the World Bank, Wolfowitz was forced to resign following a corruption scandal. Neocon John Bolton was appointed as US ambassador to the UN, a position which had been held by prominent neocons in the past. Martin Jacques suggested that both appointments demonstrated "a determination to place the cadres of the neocon revolution in key positions of power and influence and thereby create the conditions for its continuation and expansion." However, the lengthy ratification of Bolton by the Senate, ultimately overcome only by a presidential recess appointment which was only temporary, indicated the amount of dissatisfaction with neoconservatism. Then, towards the end of 2006, Rumsfeld, a key neocon ally, stepped down. John Micklethwait and Adrian Wooldridge concluded, "the neo-conservative dream at its most fanciful is surely over."[36] The final nail in the coffin was delivered in November 2008 with the election of Barack Obama as president, a campaign in which the neocons played little overt part, particularly since the departure of Rudy Giuliani from the race.

Nonetheless, Podhoretz displayed a remarkable ability to bounce back and keep himself in the limelight. In the late spring of 2007, he met with Bush and Karl Rove to urge Bush to bomb Iran after which he published "The Case for Bombing Iran" in *Commentary* in June. He was then appointed senior foreign policy adviser to Republican presidential candidate Giuliani, joining other neocon consultants such as Daniel Pipes and Peter Berkowitz. Podhoretz stated, "I decided to join Giuliani's team because his view of the war—what I call World War IV—is very close to my own." In deciding to back Giuliani, Podhoretz turned his back on Senator John McCain, another candidate in the race for the Republican nomination, even though he had supported him in 2000 when he ran against George W. Bush. Interestingly, in his most recent book, Podhoretz could find no foreign policy differences between them, writing "if either one of them should win in 2008, chances are that the Bush Doctrine will remain our guiding strategy." This begs the question of whether Podhoretz opted for Giuliani simply because he was asked, or because he saw Giuliani as ideologically akin, or because at that point in the race McCain's chances and campaign funds were seemingly spent. Yet, in doing so, Podhoretz allied himself with a candidate whose stance on domestic issues, like abortion and gay marriage, are far from his own. Furthermore, it was questionable how far Giuliani's foreign policy views matched Podhoretz's ardent support of the Bush doctrine's emphasis on unilateral action, preemptive war, and the exportation of democracy to the Middle East. Podhoretz was certainly more optimistic about the war in Iraq than Giuliani. Why, one wonders, therefore did he turn his back on McCain?[37]

During this period, Podhoretz republished his long article in *Commentary* as a book entitled *World War IV: The Long Struggle against Islamofascism* which Podhoretz followed up with numerous media appearances reiterating his desire to see Iran bombed. The almost uniformly hostile reaction to Podhoretz's article and book from liberals, traditional conservatives, and even former neocons like Francis Fukuyama indicated how far out of step he was with American thinking. Summarizing the reaction, the *New York Times* described the book as

> a hectoring, often illogical screed based on cherry-picking facts and blustering assertions (often made without any supporting evidence), a book that furiously hurls accusations of cowardice, anti-Americanism and sheer venality at any and all opponents of the Bush doctrine, be they on the right or on the left.[38]

In the meantime, it was announced that John Podhoretz was to be the next editor of *Commentary* when Neal Kozodoy retired. Unable to find, or even willing to look for new blood (there was no search process as there was when Norman Podhoretz was appointed in 1959), the magazine, like the now-defunct neocon movement of which it was a part, resorted to nepotism and bestowed a position upon an individual whom, even among conservatives, is not regarded as an intellectual heavyweight. Yet, those who support the appointment argue that the family connection is merely coincidental; but there are those who contribute to the Commentary Fund who are troubled by the appointment. With John Podhoretz's appointment, a generational dynasty has been secured with Norman as editor at large and his grandson Sam Munson as online editor. As Adam Bellow remarked, "There's a family business aspect to the neoconservative enterprise," but this is surprising given their outward commitment to meritocracy. It is a mark of how *Commentary* has come full circle.

Notes

1. Norman Podhoretz, "Strange Bedfellows: A Guide to the New Foreign-Policy Debates," *Commentary* 108:5 (December 1999), 29, 19–31; Michael Lind, *Up From Conservatism: Why the Right is Wrong for America* (New York: The Free Press, 1996), 61, 46, 62.

2. John Ehrman, message posted on H-DIPLO, November 22, 2002; Podhoretz, quoted in Robert S. Boynton, "Loury's Exodus," *New Yorker* (May 1, 1995) [internet version]; Mark

Gerson, "Introduction," in *The Essential Neoconservative Reader*, ed. Mark Gerson (Reading, MA: Addison-Wesley Publishing Co., 1996), xvi.

3. Norman Podhoretz, "Editing *Commentary*: A Valedictory," *Commentary* 99:6 (June 1995), 19–20 and quoted in Deirdre Carmody, "Critic of the Left Ready to Step Aside," *New York Times* (January 19, 1995) [internet version].

4. Kozodoy, comments made on the occasion of Norman Podhoretz's retirement, May 25, 1995.

5. *New York Sun*, December 21, 2006, 3.

6. John Ehrman, "*Commentary*, the *Public Interest*, and the Problem of American Jewish Conservatism," *American Jewish History* 87: 2&3 (June & September 1999), 174; Norman Podhoretz, *Ex-Friends: Falling Out with Allen Ginsberg, Lionel and Diana Trilling, Lillian Hellman, Hannah Arendt, and Norman Mailer* (New York: Free Press, 1999), 221.

7. Norman Podhoretz, "The Future Danger," *Commentary* 71:4 (April 1981), 34 and *Making It*, (New York: Random House, 1967), 293.

8. Joseph Epstein, "Intellectuals—Public and Otherwise," *Commentary* 109:5 (May 2000), 49; Letters, *Commentary* 60:5 (November 1975), 4–15.

9. Damon Linker, *The Theocons: Secular America Under Siege* (New York: Doubleday, 2006), 102, 103.

10. David Brock, *Blinded by the Right: The Conscience of an Ex-Conservative* (New York: Three Rivers Press, 2002), 35.

11. James Atlas, "The Counter Counterculture," *The New York Times Magazine* (February 12, 1995) [internet version]; Brock, *Blinded by the Right*, 251–2.

12. Podhoretz, "Strange Bedfellows," 19–31.

13. Gerson, *The Neoconservative Vision: From the Cold War to the Culture Wars* (Lanham, MD: Madison Books, 1997), 350, 356; Paul Gottfried, *The Conservative Movement*, Revised edn. (New York: Twayne, 1993), 95–6.

14. See Lind, *Up From Conservatism*, 157.

15. John Ehrman, "*Commentary*," in e Conservative Press in Twentieth Century America, (ed.) Ronald Lora and William Henry Longton (Westport, CT and London: Greenwood Press, 1999), 620; Podhoretz, *Making It*, 286.

16. Brock, *Blinded by the Right*, 252, 298–300, 311; George Nash, "*Commentary* and Conservatism," Paper delivered at the *Commentary*, the American Jewish Community and American Culture Conference, The Graduate Center, CUNY, New York, March 11, 2003.

17. David Frum, *Dead Right* (New York: Basic Books, 1994), 134; Ehrman, "*Commentary*, the *Public Interest*, and the Problem of American Jewish Conservatism," 174; Alana Newhouse, "When 'All the Rest' Was the Rage: *Commentary* Looks Back in Pride," *Forward* (March 21, 2003) [internet version].

18. Podhoretz, *Ex-Friends*, 221; Dannhauser, interview by author, August 22, 2003.

19. Gary Dorrien, *Imperial Designs: Neoconservatism and the New Pax Americana* (New York and London: Routledge, 2004), 2; for PNAC, see http://www.newamericancentury.org/statementofprinciples.htm.

20. Norman Podhoretz, "Bellow at 85, Roth at 67," *Commentary* 110:1 (July/August 2000), 35–43; "Looking Back at 'Catch-22,'" *Commentary,* 109:2 (February 2000), 32–7; "What Happened to Ralph Ellison," 108:1 (July/August 1999), 46–58; "A dissent on Isaiah Berlin," *Commentary* 107:2 (February 1999), 25–37; "The adventures of Philip Roth,"

Commentary 106:4 (October 1998), 25–36; "Israel and the United States: A Complex history," *Commentary* 105:5 (May 1998), 28–43; "My War with Allen Ginsberg," *Commentary* 104:2 (August 1997), 27–40.

21. Norman Podhoretz, "World War IV: How It Started, What It Means, and Why We Have to Win," *Commentary* 118:2 (September 2004), 17–54.

22. Podhoretz and Decter, quoted in Franklin Foer, "Arguing the GOP," *The New Republic* (March 20, 2000), 13.

23. Foer, "Arguing the GOP,"13; John Micklethwait and Adrian Wooldridge, *The Right Nation: Why America is Different* (London: Penguin, 2005), 200; Gerard Baker and Stephen Fidler, "America's democratic imperialists," *Financial Times* (March 6, 2003), 17; James Mann, "Four More Years," *Foreign Policy* (November 2004) [internet version].

24. Susanne Klingenstein, "It's Splendid When the Town Whore Gets Religion and Joins the Church: The Rise of the Jewish Neoconservatives as Observed by the Paleoconservatives in the 1980S," *Shofar*, 21:3 (Spring 2003), 85; Norman Podhoretz, "Oslo: The Peacemongers Return," *Commentary* 112:3 (October 2001), 21–33 and "In Praise of the Bush Doctrine," *Commentary* 114:2 (September 2002), 19.

25. *The Washington Times* (September 21, 2001), A27; David Hirst, "The war game," *The Observer* (September 21, 2003), 31; Podhoretz, "In Praise of the Bush Doctrine," 19–28; Podhoretz, "World War IV," 17–54.

26. Norman Podhoretz, *The Prophets: Who They Were, What They Are* (New York: The Free Press, 2002), 2, 327; *New York Times* (November 3, 2002), 31; Steven Menashi, "The Word is Nigh," *The Claremont Institute* (August 27, 2003) [internet version].

27. Podhoretz, quoted in *New York Times*, August 22, 2004; Norman Podhoretz, "The Path to Victory: A Symposium on the War," *The Claremont Review of Books* II: 4 (Fall 2002), 11–12; Jay Nordlinger, "All Spelled Out," *National Review* (October 25, 2004) [internet version].

28. Stefan Halper and Jonathan Clarke, *America Alone: The Neo-Conservatives and the Global Order* (Cambridge: Cambridge University Press, 2004), 73; Joshua Muravchik, "The Neoconservative Cabal," *Commentary* 116:2 (September 2003), 33.

29. Franklin Foer, *The New Republic* (July 11, 2002) [internet version].

30. Muravchik, "The Neoconservative Cabal," 33; Tod Lindberg, "The Referendum on Neoconservatism," *The Weekly Standard* (November 1–8, 2004) [internet version]; Lind, *Up From Conservatism*, 130.

31. Diggins, "*Commentary*'s Cold War on Liberalism," 1, 29.

32. Eliot A. Cohen, "Arik," *Commentary* 88:6 (December 1989), 64.

33. Baker and Fidler, "America's democratic imperialists," 17; Halper and Clarke, *America Alone*, 112; John DiIulio, quoted in Sidney Blumenthal, "The Cracks in Bush's Crown," Salon.com (October 14, 2004).

34. Martin Durham, "Evangelical Protestantism and foreign policy in the United States after September 11," *Patterns of Prejudice* 38:2 (2004), 145.

35. Robert Kuttner, "What Would Jefferson Do?" *The American Prospect* (November 2004), 31; Laura Rozen and Jason Vest, "Cloak and Swagger," *The American Prospect* (November 2004), 21; Thomas Omestad, "Fixin' for a fight," *U.S. News & World Report* (October 25, 2004), 51; Scott McConnell, "Among the Neocons," *The American Conservative* (April 21, 2003) [internet version]; Mann, "Four More Years"; Jacob Heilbrunn, "The

Neocons Last Gasp? Not So Fast," *Los Angeles Times* (November 17, 2004), B13; Robert Kuttner, "Next: Exiting Iraq," *The Boston Globe* (November 3, 2004), A27 and "What Would Jefferson Do?" 31.

36. Martin Jacques, "The Neocon Revolution," *The Guardian* (March 31, 2005), 23; John Micklethwait and Adrian Wooldridge, "A conservative make-over," *The Australian* (November 3, 2004), 15.

37. *New York Times* (October 26, 2007) [internet version]; Podhoretz, "World War IV," 206.

38. *New York Times* (October 26, 2007).

Conclusion

On the surface, understanding Norman Podhoretz has been a seemingly simple task because he has been so prolific. In addition to his numerous books, he has penned countless articles, speeches, and other writings. While they have provided the basis for beginning the process of comprehending Podhoretz, these texts are often self-serving and highly subjective, operating as a form of "discursive self-fashioning." Although Podhoretz once said, "I will leave it to others to decide what *Commentary* did or did not accomplish during my tenure," he has left his own record of events that, almost inevitably, will color any such attempts. Taken together the Podhoretz *oeuvre* constitutes a form of hagiography in which Podhoretz has enshrined himself in what has been noted by others as a most self-congratulatory and pietistic tone. His memoirs are littered throughout with references to his achievements: he can't resist pointing to his success in a succession of superlatives. John Ehrman, for example, put it rather tamely when he noted, "Podhoretz undoubtedly has a talent for self-promotion." Another, an anonymous reader on the Amazon.com website, opined: "The Podhoretz clan has come to be synonymous with gushing hyperbole." Podhoretz has spent his lifetime constantly trying to prove himself, loudly blowing his own trumpet. After almost fifty years since he became editor of *Commentary*, he is still doing so even though his own intellectual abilities and considerable achievements as editor of *Commentary* are beyond doubt and even when he has a considerable cohort of fellow neoconservatives who would happily do it for him.[1]

As a result, a mythology has grown up, as some historians of intellectual life in twentieth-century America have largely been content to take Podhoretz at his word. Such writing has become worshipping, often smacking of sycophancy, as echoed in titles like *The Conservative Revolution* or *The Neoconservative Vision*. Such laudatory perspectives have little direct (but much other) value. Surprisingly, though, no one has yet undertaken the task of writing Podhoretz's biography (although there have been brief biographical sketches of him). In contrast, it has been this book's aim to puncture, where necessary, the mythology that surrounds Podhoretz.

As James Bowman wrote, "Sometimes the cruelest thing you can do to an author is to make him appear as he really is." It is this that I hoped to accomplish here and, in doing so, to reveal the nature of man who was the driving force of the neocons. As Jacob Heilbrunn has put it, "he offers a fascinating study in the psychology of the neoconservative movement, with its fevered intellectualism, its immigrant class anxieties, and its intense father-son dynamics."[2]

Podhoretz was driven by a panoply of personal demons. The desire to prove himself—as a real American, as a Jew, as a critic, and as an editor—was paramount. Another was the impulse to shed his lower-class origins and to make it in the face of class antagonism. Heilbrunn refers to Podhoretz's ethnic antipathies, "longed for acceptance and inclusion," and that he "never tried to mask his immigrant background or resentment of the WASP establishment and of the assimilated Jews who sought to emulate it." Furthermore, Podhoretz was "an obvious and self-confessed social climber." As we have seen, he was quite open about his "self-acknowledged, unashamed, and altogether uninhibited" ambitions. He prefaced his 1967 autobiography *Making It* with the revelation,

> Money I now saw . . . was important: it was better to be rich than to be poor. Power, I now saw . . . was desirable: it was better to give orders than to take them. Fame, I now saw . . . was unqualifiedly delicious: it was better to be recognized than to be anonymous.

He called it the "'dirty little secret' of the age": a "lust for success which . . . had replaced sexual lust." In fact, *Making It* (perhaps the most honest of all his memoirs) is littered with references to success (the title itself notwithstanding). This explains his reluctance to join fully the New Left in the early 1960s. Such a person as he, infatuated with materialistic and bourgeois achievement, and incessantly compelled to seek it, could never really be sympathetic to leftism or even gentle bohemianism.[3]

Although Podhoretz said it took him until the age of 35 to realize this fact, his vanity, his ambition, and his yearning for money, power, and fame have driven him *throughout* his career. As early as 1953, in one of his first pieces for *Commentary*, he celebrated the virtues of a bourgeois lifestyle, praising the virtues of television shows which championed "the values and aspirations of the newly emerged middle class." Podhoretz's former friend, Joseph Heller, in his fictionalized portrait of Podhoretz (as Lieberman) in his 1979 novel *Good as Gold*, imaginatively put it in these terms,

> All through college Lieberman's dearest wish for the future had been to manage a small intellectual magazine. Now he had his magazine, and

it wasn't enough. Envy, ambition, and dejection were still ravaging what few invisible good qualities he might have been born with . . .[4]

Furthermore, Podhoretz was disingenuous about the means by which he achieved his goals: tactical ideological opportunism. Podhoretz's real, but as yet unadmitted "dirty little secret," is that he was not always a man of principle. At times he clearly acted like an opportunist. Some of his opinions were dictated only by his desire to "make it" and to build a successful and provocative journal and career. As Heller put it, "Listen," he [Lieberman] once boasted,

> I got invited to the White House for dinner once, just for supporting a war. I would support a war every day in the week if I knew I could eat at the White House again . . . I don't think they appreciate how loyal I can be. I can switch positions overnight on any issue they want me to.

Podhoretz's choice of heroes is revealing on this front. In 1983, writing in *Harper's*, Podhoretz claimed that if George Orwell "were alive today, he'd be a neo-conservative." Orwell indeed provided the perfect model for Podhoretz. As Scott Lucas has shown, Orwell flip-flopped ideologically: "he was neither consistent nor complete"; his "'negative' attacks on the Left and Socialism had no 'positive' alternative"; and, once he "had established his own position, he associated any possible challengers with the broadest of injustices." This comparison between Orwell and Podhoretz was (unintentionally) reinforced most recently by Paul Johnson when he introduced the latest collection of Podhoretz's writings.[5]

Unlike Elliot Cohen who had convictions so strong that they eventually killed him, Podhoretz was not always a man of principle. As Philip Rahv and the Greenberg brothers had worked out back in the 1950s, Podhoretz was an opportunist. After all, this was the man who wrote *Making It*, in which he revealed his "dirty little secret": the incessant compulsion for materialistic and bourgeois achievement. Arthur Miller who met Podhoretz in 1965 recalled, "I recognized the symptoms and he had them really bad, as he was all but admitting to me himself." According to Michael Wyschogrod, Podhoretz had never forgotten the shame of his Brownsville origins, always seeing himself as Mrs. Haft saw him: *Slum child, filthy little slum child.* "Those words . . . are burned into his consciousness," wrote Michael Wyschogrod.

> He knows that he is not class, that life is a fight in which only a few get to the top. The desperate search for recognition, for being in the limelight and talked about, is the search for a slave that will numb the pain

of a desperately ugly self-image ... it is controlling. It robs the man of the slightest modicum of serenity, and therefore, of affection for his origins ... for Podhoretz, his proletarian origins gnaw at his innards as he passes through Columbia and Cambridge, and thus, though this is what he wishes least, a lower-class identity becomes fixed which he cannot erase.[6]

Podhoretz's pursuit of power and influence required many hypocrisies and compromises to achieve his dream. He often changed his opinions (it seemed almost at will at times), to suit the tastes of those in power or who he felt would one day be powerful. He saw which way the wind was blowing and shifted accordingly. When he couldn't accurately predict it, he vacillated, as in 1960 when the election between Nixon and Kennedy was too close to call. On both occasions, as the elections drew nearer, he could not make up its mind which candidate to support. Podhoretz's indecision was reflected in the magazine. Even after the emergence of a Republican majority in 1968, Podhoretz was tempted by the other side as indicated by his willingness to meet with Carter in 1980 even though Podhoretz had been constantly attacking his administration since 1977. Some of his cohort flirted with Clinton in 1992 and even though Podhoretz opted for McCain in 2000, he switched to Bush following the terrorist attacks of 2001, and joined Giuliani's team in 2007.

At the same time, Podhoretz loved to resist. In many ways it is entirely apt that Podhoretz wrote a book about the prophets, as he surely perceived himself as a lonely prophet haranguing his fellow Israelites for their ungodly ways. Heilbrunn uses the metaphor of Sinai but while Podhoretz may have appeared as a Mosaic figure to his fellow neocons, comparisons to Job or others seem more apt. For unlike the biblical prophets, he preferred to voice his jeremiads at other intellectuals more consistently than he did at power (unless it suited him). As an intellectual, he typically adopted an oppositional position. He was thus a "counter intellectual," someone who opposed the adversary stance toward the general culture that intellectuals typically adopt.[7]

Podhoretz possessed a vindictive streak. It really seemed at times that he was driven more by a desire for partisan revenge than any interest in principle. As a public intellectual, he was described variously as "vigorous," "irascible," "pugnacious," "combative," "hard-nosed," "a stubborn defender of his opinions," "quick to take offense at perceived slights," and "tended to personalize intellectual differences." In words that were used to describe his predecessor at *Commentary*, Elliot Cohen, but which I feel are just as apt for him, he "was a bully who dressed up his personal ideas as though they were a holy mission." Podhoretz has been called "perhaps the most hated editor in America," "the most bloodthirsty intellectual since Tamberlane...," "an argumentative, even 'Bolshevik' temperament; and [with] a coarse streak to boot."[8]

Podhoretz, it appeared, had learned a valuable lesson which he carried with him for the rest of his career.

> Since... I took a highly irreverent stance toward several inflated literary reputations which had bullied large numbers of these people into worrying over the soundness of their taste, I came to be held by some in almost priestly regard. By the same token, I had made enemies, but enemies are all to the good at an early stage of a critic's career, helping as they do to spread his name around.

Podhoretz credo, in his own words, was: "My enemies, I expect them to hit me as hard as they can. That's the way it should be." He styled himself as a so-called tough Jew: "Like me, and practically every Brooklyn boy I had known, he was direct and pugnacious and immensely preoccupied with the issue of manly courage." As a member of a street gang called Club Cherokee, he recalled in a 1999 television interview, "the main desideratum was to be tough and not to back down from a fight. And to be a sissy, as people used to say, or a coward was probably the worst possible condition into which you could fall." Podhoretz was in a class of his own when it came to intellectual brawling. He was the pugilist par excellence, and he has spent a lifetime demonstrating it by fighting. It was if he had swallowed Tacitus' observation that, "It is so much easier to repay injury than to reward kindness, for gratitude is regarded as a burden, revenge as a gain." At a cocktail party for *Encounter* magazine in 1985, for example, friends who saw them talking thought that Podhoretz was about to hit *Spectator* diarist Peregrine Worsthorne. Never before in his entire professional life, Worsthorne recalled, had he endured such personal and vituperative abuse.[9]

Podhoretz was therefore a complicated and in many ways a contradictory figure. He wanted to be street tough, resembling those African Americans he so envied as a youngster but in a professional world that was cerebral and for some effete. Consequently, he took, what seemed at times, an often paradoxical stance. He blended opportunism with oppositionalism and ideology all at the same time. He courted power but despite himself often did things which didn't seem to position him well for it (such as alienating the wrong people). He tried to anticipate and blow with the wind but also stood himself against it. He had certain deeply held beliefs, but he was also an opportunist who desired political power and influence and who became increasingly ideological as he grew older.

Podhoretz stood out for being willing to accept and acknowledge a close linkage of power and intellectual life that ultimately compromised and corrupted the intellectual calling. He was far too ready to swap intellectual influence for political power when the chance offered itself. He blurred the distinction between critical thought and policymaking. He was intent on seeking power and boasting of it. He wanted to be a policymaker. With power came riches, and he became part of the complacent middle classes who had reached settlement with America. His magazine "became the sort of thing you'd find on the coffee table of a very good Long Island gynecologist, to show they were serious people," observed one famous writer and former contributor who requested to stay anonymous. Rather than disturb and sow some unease into the ambient contentment of the last twenty odd years, *Commentary* fed it. Podhoretz, therefore, stands as an exemplar for the sad decline of the public intellectual in American life. In tracing the history of neoconservatism in general and Podhoretz's particular role in it, it is a story of the transformation of a cadre of intellectuals from the type that "spoke to power" to those who spoke for it.

Podhoretz was also a tragic figure. During his early days as editor of *Commentary*, Podhoretz was more interesting, more willing to experiment and be inclusive, something that he clearly wasn't in his later renditions. He was a young intellectual who went from promise to ideological rigidity. He was schizophrenic and narcissistic—he recoiled at his lack of power yet hungered for it at the same time. The more he failed, the more he grew depressed and melancholic.

How does this connect to neoconservatism? Since he was one of its leading thinkers and intellectuals, its tactician, general, and "conductor" even, Podhoretz imbued that part of the movement that followed him with his personal style of politics and selected recruits who acted obediently to his will. His followers copied his example. The propensity to distortion and exaggeration, vindictiveness, the ideological opportunism, oppositionalism, and flip-flopping, the lust for material success and search for money, fame, power, and influence, the pugnacity were all elements of Podhoretzian neoconservatism (as distinct from the Kristol, Moynihan, and Bell strands). As a consequence, the neocon empire that Podhoretz built up around him was constructed on the sham of self-seeking material success, opportunism, and vengeance. Its ideological foundations were flimsy and diluted and ultimately discarded when they no longer suited.

The next installment is to appear soon when John Podhoretz takes over where his father left off.

Notes

1. Norman Podhoretz, "Editing *Commentary*: A Valedictory," *Commentary* 99:6 (June 1995)," *Commentary* 99:6 (June 1995), 19. I have taken the phrase "self-fashioning" from David Savran, *Communists, Cowboys, and Queers: The Politics of Masculinity in the Work of Arthur Miller and Tennessee Williams* (Minneapolis and London: University of Minnesota Press, 1992), 9; John Ehrman, *The Rise of Neoconservatism: Intellectuals and Foreign Affairs, 1945-1994* (New Haven and London: Yale University Press, 1996), 42; "Bagels and Cream Cheese," Amazon.com (March 26, 2004).

2. James Bowman, "A Sharp Eye and a Sharp Tongue," *Wall Street Journal* (January 15, 2004), D8; *Heilbrunn, They Knew They Were Right,* 71.

3. Heilbrunn, *They Knew They Were Right,* 71; Norman Podhoretz, *Making It,* (New York: Random House, 1967) xi, 55, 243.

4. Norman Podhoretz, "Our Changing Ideals, as Seen on TV," *Commentary* 16 (1953), 534–40; Joseph Heller, *Good as Gold* (New York: Simon & Schuster, 1979) 12.

5. Heller, *Good as Gold*; Scott Lucas, *The Betrayal of Dissent: Beyond Orwell, Hitchens and The New American Century* (London: Pluto Press, 2004), 11, 29, 19; Paul Johnson, "Introduction," in *The Norman Podhoretz Reader: A Selection of His Writings from the 1950s through the 1990s,* ed. Thomas L. Jeffers (New York: Free Press, 2004), xii, xiii.

6. Podhoretz, *Making It,* 10; Arthur Miller, *Timebends: A Life* (New York, Grove Press, 1987), 575; Michael Wyschogrod, "My *Commentary* Problem,—And Ours," *Judaism* 17:2 (Spring 1968), 161.

7. I have taken this notion from Peter Steinfels, *The Neoconservatives* (New York: Simon & Schuster, 1979), 189.

8. Martin Greenberg, interview by Bill Novak, May 1, 1974; Michael Novak, "The Enduring Importance of Norman Podhoretz," *LA Herald Examiner* (February 10, 1985), E5; Jack Newfield, "War Wimps: The Sequel," *The Village Voice* (July 23, 1985), 15.

9. Podhoretz, *Making It,* 242; Podhoretz, quoted in Jacob Heilbrunn, "Norman's Conquest: Why Rudy Giuliani loves Norman Podhoretz," *Washington Monthly* (December 1, 2007) [internet version]; Peregrine Worsthorne, "Diary," *The Spectator* (December 14, 1985), 7.

Bibliography

Interviews/Correspondence

Sherry Abel, Tamara Adler, Edward Alexander, Robert Alter, Al Alvarez, Noel Anderson, Andrew J. Bacevich, Daniel Bell, Saul Bellow, Christopher Bright, Douglas Charles, Noam Chomsky, Arthur A. Cohen, Sylvia Cohen, Werner J. Dannhauser, Hannah Desser, Harris Dienstfrey, Morris Dickstein, Emil Fackenheim, Leslie Fiedler, Morris Fine, Michael Fixler, Seth Forman, Herbert J. Gans, Carl Gershman, Mark Gerson, Nathan Glazer, Ben Zion Gold, Paul Gottfried, Frances Green, Clement Greenberg, Martin Greenberg, Dennis Gura, Arthur Hertzberg, Milton Himmelfarb, Irving Howe, Tamar Jacoby, George Kateb, Neal Kozodoy, Benny Kraut, Irving Kristol, Walter Laqueur, Alan Levine, Tod Lindberg, SM Lipset, Staughton Lynd, Hyam Maccoby, Scott McConnell, Alan Mintz, Alan W. Miller, Tom Montgomery, Joshua Muravchik, Charles Murray, Michael Meyer, Brian Noel, Jacob Neusner, Marc Plattner, Steven Plaut, Norman Podhoretz, Nelson Polsby, David Pryce-Jones, Jerry Ravetz, Norman Ravitch, Sylvia Rothchild, Stanley Rothman, Jonathan Sarna, Peter Schrag, Mary Lea Schieman, Seymour Siegel, Marshall Sklare, John Slawson, Ted Solotaroff, Rob Toren, Lionel Trilling, David Vital, George Weigel, Elie Wiesel, Herbert Weiner, Ruth Wisse, Dennis Wrong.

Archival Materials

American Jewish Committee Records, Record Group 347, GEN-12 and GEN 10, YIVO Institute for Jewish Research, New York.

Hannah Arendt Papers, Manuscript Division, Library of Congress, Washington, DC.

Jessie Bloom Papers, American Jewish Archives, HUC-JIR, Cincinnati, Ohio.

Kenneth B. Clark Papers, Manuscript Division, Library of Congress, Washington, DC.

The *Contemporary Jewish Record* Archive, American Jewish Archives, HUC-JIR, Cincinnati, Ohio.

Herbert B. Ehrmann Papers, American Jewish Archives, HUC-JIR, Cincinnati, Ohio.

Solomon Andhil Fineberg Papers, American Jewish Archives, HUC-JIR, Cincinnati, Ohio.

Henry Hurwitz and the Menorah Association Papers, American Jewish Archives, HUC-JIR, Cincinnati, Ohio.

Dan Jacobson Papers, Harry Ransom Humanities Research Center, University of Texas at Austin, Austin, Texas.

Michael Josselson Papers, Harry Ransom Humanities Research Center, University of Texas at Austin, Austin, Texas.

Alfred A. Knopf Archive, Harry Ransom Humanities Research Center, University of Texas at Austin, Austin, Texas.

Dwight Macdonald Papers, Sterling Library, Yale University, New Haven, Connecticut.

Bernard Malamud Papers, Harry Ransom Humanities Research Center, University of Texas at Austin, Austin, Texas.

Julian Morgenstern Papers, American Jewish Archives, HUC-JIR, Cincinnati, Ohio.

Oral History Research Office, Columbia University, New York.

Norman Podhoretz Papers, Manuscript Division, Library of Congress, Washington, DC.

Steven S. Schwarzschild Papers, American Jewish Archives, HUC-JIR, Cincinnati, Ohio.

John Slawson Papers, YIVO Institute for Jewish Research, New York.

C. P. Snow Papers, Harry Ransom Humanities Research Center, University of Texas at Austin, Austin, Texas.

Lionel Trilling Papers, Columbia University Rare Book and Manuscript Library, Columbia University, New York.

Harry S. Truman Papers, Harry S. Truman Library, Independence, Missouri.

Morris D. Waldman Papers, American Jewish Archives, HUC-JIR, Cincinnati, Ohio.

William E. Weiner Oral History Library of the American Jewish Committee, Jewish Division, New York Public Library, New York.

Trude Weiss-Rosmarin Papers, American Jewish Archives, HUC-JIR, Cincinnati, Ohio.

Books

Abrams, Nathan. *Commentary Magazine 1945–1959: "A journal of significant thought and opinion."* London and Portland, OR: Vallentine Mitchell, 2006.

Adler, Renata. *Gone: The Last Days of the New Yorker*. New York: Simon & Schuster, 1999.

Alexander, Edward. *Irving Howe: Socialist, Critic, Jew*. Bloomington and Indianapolis: Indiana University Press, 1998.

Allin, Dana H. *Cold War Illusions: America, Europe, and Soviet Power, 1969–89*. London: St Martin's, 1994.

Arendt, Hannah. *Eichmann in Jerusalem: A Report on the Banality of Evil*. London: Penguin, 1994.

Atlas, James. *Delmore Schwartz: The Life of an American Poet*. New York: Farrar Straus Giroux, 1977.

— *Bellow: A Biography*. London: Faber and Faber, 2000.

Baldwin, James. *The Fire Next Time*. The Dial Press: New York, 1963.

Bar-Ilan, David. *Eye on the Media*. Jerusalem: The Jerusalem Post, 1993.

Barrett, William. *The Truants: Adventures Among the Intellectuals*. New York: Doubleday, 1982.

Bloom, Alexander. *Prodigal Sons: The New York Intellectuals and Their World*. New York and Oxford: Oxford University Press, 1986.

Blumenthal, Sidney. *The Rise of the Counter-Establishment: From Conservative Ideology to Political Power*. New York: Times Books, 1986.

Brock, David. *Blinded by the Right: The Conscience of an Ex-Conservative*. New York: Three Rivers Press, 2002.

Brightman, Carol. *Writing Dangerously: Mary McCarthy and Her World*. London: Lime Tree, 1993.

Brightman, Carol (ed.). *Between Friends: The Correspondence of Hannah Arendt and Mary McCarthy, 1949-1975*. New York: Harcourt Brace & Co., 1995.

Buckley, William F., Jr. *In Search of Anti-Semitism*. New York: Continuum, 1992.

Budick, Emily Miller. *Blacks and Jews in Literary Conversation*. Cambridge: Cambridge University Press, 1998.

Busch, Noel F. *Briton Hadden: A Biography of the Co-Founder of Time*. New York: Farrar, Straus & Co., 1949.

Campbell, James. *Talking at the Gates*. New York: Penguin, 1991.

Cohen, Naomi W. *Not Free to Desist: The American Jewish Committee 1906-1966*. Philadelphia: The Jewish Publication Society of America, 1972.

The Condition of Jewish Belief: A Symposium Compiled by the Editors of *Commentary* Magazine. Northvale, NJ and London: Jason Aaronson, 1995.

Corey, Mary F. *The World through a Monocle: The New Yorker*. Cambridge, MA: Harvard University Press, 1999.

Cruse, Harold. *The Crisis of the Negro Intellectual*. New York: William Morrow, 1967.

Decter, Midge. *The Liberated Woman and Other Americans*. New York: Coward, McCann & Geoghegan, 1971.

— *Liberal Parents, Radical Children*. New York: Coward, McCann & Geoghegan, 1975.

— *An Old Wife's Tale: My Seven Decades in Love and War*. New York: Regan Books, 2001.

Dershowitz, Alan M. *Chutzpah*. New York and London: Simon and Schuster, 1991.

Dollinger, Marc. *Quest for Inclusion: Jews and Liberalism in Modern America*. Princeton and Oxford: Princeton University Press, 2000.

Dorman, Joseph. *Arguing the World: The New York Intellectuals in Their Own Words*. New York: The Free Press, 2000.

Dorrien, Gary. *The Neoconservative Mind: Politics, Culture and the War of Ideology*. Philadelphia: Temple University Press, 1993.

— *Imperial Designs: Neoconservatism and the New Pax Americana*. New York and London: Routledge, 2004.

Edwards, Lee. *The Conservative Revolution: The Movement that Remade America*. New York: The Free Press, 1999.

Ehrman, John. *The Rise of Neoconservatism: Intellectuals and Foreign Affairs, 1945-1994*. New Haven, CT and London: Yale University Press, 1996.

Evory, Ann, (ed.). *Contemporary Authors, New Revision Series*. Detroit, MI: Gale Research Co., 1982.

Farell, James T. *Sam Holman*. Buffalo, NY: Prometheus Books, 1983.

Forman, Seth. *Blacks in the Jewish Mind: A Crisis of Liberalism*. New York: New York University Press, 1998.

Franklin, V. P., Grant, Nancy L., Kletnick, Harold M., and McNeil, Genna Rae (eds.). *African Americans and Jews in the Twentieth Century: Studies in Convergence and Conflict*. Columbia and London: University of Missouri Press, 1998.

Friedman, Murray (ed.). *Commentary in American Life*. Philadelphia: Temple University Press, 2005.

Friedman, Murray, *What Went Wrong? The Creation and Collapse of the Black-Jewish Alliance*. New York: Free, 1995.

Frum, David. *Dead Right*. New York: Basic Books, 1994.

Gerson, Mark (ed.). *The Essential Neoconservative Reader*. Reading, MA: Addison-Wesley Publishing Co., 1996.

Gerson, Mark. *The Neoconservative Vision: From the Cold War to the Culture Wars*. Lanham, MD: Madison Books, 1997.

Gid Powers, Richard. *Not Without Honor: The History of American Anticommunism*. New Haven and London: Yale University Press, 1995.

Ginsberg, Benjamin. *The Fatal Embrace: Jews and the State*. Chicago and London: The University of Chicago Press, 1993.

Glazer, Nathan. *American Judaism*. Chicago: The University of Chicago Press, 1957.

Goffman, Ethan and Morris, Daniel (eds.). *The New York Intellectuals and Beyond: Exploring Liberal Humanism, Jewish Identity, and the American Protestant Tradition*. West Lafayette, IN: Purdue University Press, 2009.

Goldberg, J. J. *Jewish Power: Inside the American Jewish Establishment*. Reading, MA: Addison-Wesley Publishing Co., 1996.

Goren, Arthur A. *The Politics and Public Culture of American Jews*. Bloomington and Indianapolis: Indiana University Press, 1999.

Gottfried, Paul. *The Conservative Movement*. Revised edn. New York: Twayne, 1993.

Gramsci, Antonio. *Selections from the Prison Notebooks*, ed. and trans. Quentin Hoare and Geoffrey Nowell Smith. London: Lawrence and Wishart, 1971.

Graver, Lawrence. *An Obsession with Anne Frank: Meyer Levin and the* Diary. Berkeley: University of California Press, 1995.

Guttenplan, D. D. *The Holocaust on Trial: History, Justice and the David Irving Libel Case*. London: Granta, 2001.

Hacker, Louis M. and Hirsch, Mark D. *Proskauer: His Life and Times*. Tuscaloosa: The University of Alabama Press, 1978.

Halper, Albert. *Goodbye Union Square*. Chicago: Quadrangle, 1970.

Halper, Stefan and Clarke, Jonathan. *America Alone: The Neo-Conservatives and the Global Order*. Cambridge: Cambridge University Press, 2004.

Harap, Louis. *In the Mainstream: The Jewish Presence in Twentieth-Century American Literature, 1950s-1980s*. Westport, CT: Greenwood Press, 1987.

Harris, David A. *In the Trenches: Selected Speeches and Writings of an American Jewish Activist 1979-1999*. Hoboken, NJ: Ktav Publishing House, 2000.

Heilbrunn, Jacob. *They Knew They Were Right*. London: Doubleday 2008.

Heineman, Kenneth J. *God is a Conservative: Religion, Politics, and Morality in Contemporary America*. New York: NYU Press, 1998.

Heller, Joseph. *Good as Gold*. New York: Simon & Schuster, 1979.

Hellman, Lillian. *Scoundrel Time*. New York: Bantam, 1977.

Hertzberg, Arthur. *The Jews in America: Four Centuries of an Uneasy Encounter*. New York: Touchstone, 1989.

Hodgson, Godfrey. *The World Turned Right Side Up: A History of the Conservative Ascendancy in America*. Boston and New York: Houghton Mifflin, 1996.

Hoeveler, J. David, Jr. *Watch on the Right*. Madison: University of Wisconsin Press, 1991.

Hook, Sidney. *Out of Step*. New York: Carroll & Graf, 1987.

Horowitz, Irving Louis. *American Jewish Visions and Israeli Dilemmas: A Commentary on Fifty Commentaries in* Commentary. Middle East Studies Institute, Graduate School of International Studies, University of Miami 1988.

Howe, Irving. *Celebrations and Attacks: Thirty Years of Literary and Cultural Commentary*. New York: Harcourt Brace Jovanovich, 1979.

— *A Margin of Hope: An Intellectual Autobiography*. London: Secker & Warburg, 1982.

Isserman, Maurice. *If I Had a Hammer: The Death of the Old Left and the Birth of the New Left*. Urbana and Chicago: University of Illinois Press, 1987.

Jacoby, Russell. *The Last Intellectuals: American Culture in the Age of Academe*. New York: Basic Books, 2000.

Jay, Martin. *Permanent Exiles: Essays on the Intellectual Migration from Germany to America*. New York: Columbia University Press, 1985.

Jeffers, Thomas L. (ed.). *The Norman Podhoretz Reader: A Selection of His Writings from the 1950s through the 1990s*. New York: Free Press, 2004.

Jumonville, Neil. *Critical Crossings: The New York Intellectuals in Postwar America*. Berkeley: University of California Press, 1991.

Kadushin, Charles. *The American Intellectual Elite*. Boston: Little, Brown, 1974.

Kaplan, Fred. *Gore Vidal*. London: Bloomsbury, 2000.

Kaufman, Jonathan. *Broken Alliance: The Turbulent Times Between Blacks and Jews in America*. New York: Scribner's, 1988.

Kaufman, Menahem. *An Ambiguous Partnership: Non-Zionists and Zionists in America 1939-1948*. Jerusalem: The Magnes Press, The Hebrew University of Jerusalem, 1991.

Kazin, Alfred. *A Lifetime Burning in Every Moment: From the Journals of Alfred Kazin*. New York: HarperCollins, 1996.

Kohler, Lotte and Saner, Hans, (eds.). *Hannah Arendt/Karl Jaspers Correspondence, 1926-1969*. San Diego: Harvest Book/Harcourt Brace, 1993.

Kozodoy, Neal (ed.). *What to Do About . . . A Collection of Essays from* Commentary *Magazine*. New York: ReganBooks, 1995.

Kramer, Hilton. *The Twilight of the Intellectuals: Culture and Politics in the Era of the Cold War*. Chicago: Ivan R. Dee, 1999.

Kristol, Irving. *On the Democratic Idea in America*. New York: Harper & Row, 1972.

— *Reflections of a Neoconservative: Looking Back, Looking Ahead*. New York: Basic Books, 1983.

— *Neoconservatism: The Autobiography of an Idea*. New York: Ivan R. Dee, 1995.

Laskin, David. *Partisans: Marriage, Politics, and Betrayal Among the New York Intellectuals*. New York: Simon and Schuster, 2000.

Lerner, Michael. *Jewish Renewal: A Path to Healing and Transformation*. New York: HarperPerennial, 1994.

Levin, Meyer. *In Search: An Autobiography*. New York: Pocket – Simon & Schuster, 1973.

Lind Michael. *The Next American Nation: The New Nationalism and the Fourth American Revolution*. New York: Free Press, 1995.

— *Up From Conservatism: Why the Right is Wrong for America*. New York: The Free Press, 1996.

Linker, Damon. *The Theocons: Secular America Under Siege*. New York: Doubleday, 2006.

Lora, Ronald and Longton, William Henry (eds.). *The Conservative Press in Twentieth Century America*. Westport, CT and London: Greenwood Press, 1999.

Lucas, Scott. *The Betrayal of Dissent: Beyond Orwell, Hitchens and the New American Century*. London: Pluto Press, 2004.

Maisel, L Sandy and Forman, Ira N. (eds.). *Jews in American Politics*. Lanham, MD: Rowman & Littlefield, 2001.

Marty, Martin E., Deedy, John G., Jr., and Lekachman, Robert. *The Religious Press in America*. New York: Holt, Rinehart and Winston, 1963.

Micklethwait, John and Wooldridge, Adrian. *The Right Nation: Why America is Different*. London: Penguin, 2005.

Miller, Arthur. *Timebends: A Life*. New York: Grove Press, 1987.

Miller, Sally M. (ed.). *The Ethnic Press in the United States: A Historical Analysis and Handbook*. Westport, CT: Greenwood Press, 1987.

Mills, Hilary. *Mailer: A Biography*. London: New English Library, 1985.

Moynihan, Daniel Patrick. *Maximum Feasible Misunderstanding*. New York: The Free Press, 1969.

— *A Dangerous Place*. Boston: Little Brown, 1978.

Nash, George H. *The Conservative Intellectual Movement in America since 1945*. New York: Basic Books, 1976.

Nobile, Philip. *Intellectual Skywriting: Literary Politics and the New York Review of Books*. New York: Charterhouse, 1974.

Noveck, Simon. *Milton Steinberg: Portrait of a Rabbi*. New York: Ktav Publishing House, Inc., 1978.

Novick, Peter. *The Holocaust in American Life*. Boston and New York: Houghton Mifflin Co., 1999.

Omi, Michael and Winant, Howard. *Racial Formation in the United States*. New York: Routledge, 1994.

Oren, Dan A. *Joining the Club: A History of Jews and Yale*, 2nd edn. New Haven: Yale University Press, 2000.

Ozick, Cynthia. *The Puttermesser Papers*. New York: Alfred A. Knopf, 1997.

Pells, Richard. *The Liberal Mind in a Conservative Age: American Intellectuals in the 1940s and 1950s*. New York: Harper & Row, 1985.

Phillips, William. *A Partisan View: Five Decades of the Literary Life*. New York: Stein & Day, 1983.

Pipes, Richard. *Vixi: Memoirs of a Non-Belonger*. New Haven & London: Yale University Press, 2004.

Podhoretz, Norman. (ed.). *The Commentary Reader: Two Decades of Articles and Stories*. New York: Atheneum, 1966.

Podhoretz, Norman. *Doings and Undoings: The Fifties and After in American Writing*. London: Rupert Hart-Davis, 1965.

— *Making It*. New York: Random House, 1967.

— *Breaking Ranks: A Political Memoir*. New York: Harper & Row, 1979.

— *The Present Danger*. New York. Simon and Schuster, 1980.

— *Why We were in Vietnam*. New York. Simon and Schuster, 1982.

— *The Bloody Crossroads: Where Literature and Politics Meet*. Simon and Schuster, 1986.

— *Ex-Friends: Falling Out with Allen Ginsberg, Lionel and Diana Trilling, Lillian Hellman, Hannah Arendt, and Norman Mailer*. New York: Free Press, 1999.

— *My Love Affair with America: The Cautionary Tale of a Cheerful Conservative*. New York: Free Press, 2000.

— *The Prophets: Who They Were, What They Are*. New York: The Free Press, 2002.

— *World War IV: The Long Struggle against Islamofascism*. New York: Doubleday, 2007.

Polsgrove, Carol. *Divided Minds: Intellectuals and the Civil Rights Movement*. New York and London: W.W. Norton & Co., 2001.

Porter, Jack Nusan and Dreier, Peter (eds.). *Jewish Radicalism: A Selected Anthology*. New York: Grove Press, 1973.

Proskauer, Joseph. *A Segment of My Time*. New York: Farrar, Straus, 1950.

Richler, Mordecai. *This Year in Jerusalem*. London: Chatto & Windus, 1994.

Rogin, Michael. *Blackface, White Noise: Jewish Immigrants in the Hollywood Melting Pot*. Berkeley and Los Angeles: University of California Press, 1996.

Rosenberg, Bernard and Goldstein, Ernest (eds.). *Creators and Disturbers: Reminiscences by Jewish Intellectuals of New York*. New York: Columbia University Press, 1982.

Roth, Philip. *The Anatomy Lesson*. London: Penguin, 1986 .

Rothman, Stanley and Lichter, S. Robert. *Roots of Radicalism: Jews, Christians, and the Left*. New Brunswick and London: Transaction Publishers, 1996.

Said, Edward W. *Representations of the Intellectual*. London: Vintage, 1994.

Savran, David. *Communists, Cowboys, and Queers: The Politics of Masculinity in the Work of Arthur Miller and Tennessee Williams*. Minneapolis and London: University of Minnesota Press, 1992.

Seabrook, John. *Nobrow: The Culture of Marketing and the Marketing of Culture*. London: Methuen, 2000.

Shafir, Shlomo. *Ambiguous Relations: The American Jewish Community and Germany Since 1945*. Detroit: Wayne State University Press, 1999.

Shandler, Jeffrey. *While America Watches: Televising the Holocaust*. New York and Oxford: Oxford University Press, 1999.

Shapiro, Edward S. A. *Time for Healing: American Jewry since World War II*. Baltimore: Johns Hopkins University Press, 1992.

Shechner, Mark. *After the Revolution: Studies in Contemporary Jewish-American Imagination*. Bloomington and Indianapolis: Indiana University Press, 1987.

Sherry, Michael S. *In the Shadow of War: the United States since the 1930s*. New Haven and London: Yale University Press, 1995.

Singerman, Robert. *Jewish Serials of the World. A Research Bibliography of Secondary Sources*. Compiled by Robert Singerman. Foreword by Zvulun Rarid. New York and London: Greenwood, 1986.

Sklare, Marshall. *Observing America's Jews*, ed. Jonathan D. Sarna. Hanover and London: Brandeis University Press, 1993.

Slesinger, Tess. *The Unpossessed: A Novel of the Thirties*. New York: The Feminist Press, 1984.

Solotaroff, Ted. *First Loves: A Memoir*. New York: Seven Stories Press, 2003.

Staub, Michael E. *Torn at the Roots: The Crisis of Jewish Liberalism in Postwar America*. New York: Columbia University Press, 2002.

Stein, Harry. *How I Accidentally Joined the Vast Right-Wing Conspiracy (and Found Inner Peace)*. New York: Perennial, 2001.

Steinfels, Peter. *The Neoconservatives*. New York: Simon & Schuster, 1979.

Svonkin, Stuart. *Jews Against Prejudice: American Jews and the Fight for Civil Liberties*. New York: Columbia University Press, 1997.

Teres, Harvey. *Renewing the Left: Politics, Imagination, and the New York Intellectuals*. New York and Oxford: Oxford University Press, 1986.

Tomes, Robert R. *Apocalypse Then: American Intellectuals and the Vietnam War, 1954–1975*. New York: New York University Press, 1998.

Trilling, Diana. *The Beginning of the Journey: The Marriage of Diana and Lionel Trilling*. New York and London: Harcourt, Brace & Co., 1993.

Wald, Alan. *The New York Intellectuals: The Rise and Decline of the Anti-Stalinist Left from the 1930s to the 1980s*. Chapel Hill and London: The University of North Carolina Press, 1987.

Warshow, Robert. *The Immediate Experience: Movies, Comics, Theatre and Other Aspects of Popular Culture*. Enlarged edn. Cambridge, MA: Harvard University Press, 2001.

Webb, Clive. *Fight Against Fear: Southern Jews and Black Civil Rights*. Athens and London: The University of Georgia Press, 2001.

Weisbord, Robert G. and Stein, Arthur. *Bittersweet Encounter: The Afro-American and the American Jew*. Westport, CT: Negro Universities Press, 1970.

Wilford, Hugh. *The New York Intellectuals: From Vanguard to Institution*. Manchester and New York: Manchester University Press, 1995.

— *The CIA, the British Left and the Cold War: Calling the Tune?* London: Frank Cass, 2003.

Wills, Garry. *Reagan's America: Innocents at Home*. London: Heinemann, 1988.

Winchell, Mark Royden. *"Too Good to Be True": The Life and Work of Leslie Fiedler*. Columbia and London: University of Missouri Press, 2002.

Winik, Jay. *On the Brink: The Dramatic, Behind-The-Scenes Saga of the Reagan Era and the Men and Women Who Won the Cold War*. New York: Simon & Schuster, 1996.

Wisse, Ruth. *If I Am Not for Myself: The Liberal Betrayal of the Jews*. New York: Free Press, 1993.

Wreszin, Michael. *A Rebel in Defense of Tradition: The Life and Politics of Dwight Macdonald*. New York: Basic Books, 1994.

Yagoda, Ben. *About Town: The New Yorker and the World It Made*. London: Duckworth, 2000.

Young-Bruehl, Elisabeth. *Hannah Arendt: For Love of the World*. New Haven and London: Yale University Press, 1982.

Articles

Abrams, Nathan. "Review of Norman Podhoretz, *Ex-Friends: Falling Out with Allen Ginsberg, Lionel and Diana Trilling, Lillian Hellman, Hannah Arendt, and Norman Mailer*," H-Ideas, H-Net Reviews (January 2001).

——"'A Profoundly Hegemonic Moment': De-Mythologizing the Cold War New York Jewish Intellectuals,' *Shofar: An Interdisciplinary Journal of Jewish Studies* 21:3 (Spring 2003): 64–89.

——"Consistently Controversial: *Commentary* Magazine, 1945 to the Present," *Reconstruction* 8.4 (2008). [Online].

——"A Profoundly Hegemonic Moment': De-Mythologizing the Cold War New York Jewish Intellectuals," in *The New York Intellectuals and Beyond: Exploring Liberal Humanism, Jewish Identity, and the American Protestant Tradition*, ed. Ethan Goffman and Daniel Morris (West Lafayette, IN: Purdue University Press, 2009): 17–34.

Atlas, James. "The Counter Counterculture," *New York Times Magazine* (February 12, 1995) [internet version].

Avishai, Bernard. "Breaking Faith: *Commentary* and the American Jews," *Dissent* 28:2 (Spring 1981): 236–56.

Baker, Gerard and Fidler, Stephen. "America's democratic imperialists," *Financial Times* (March 6, 2003): 17.

Bartley, Robert L. "A Most Improbable 'Conservative,'" *Wall Street Journal* (November 10, 1970): 18.

——"Split in the Family?" *National Review* (December 15, 1970): 1335.

Berman, Paul. "Allen Ginsberg's Secret: What He did with Norman Podhoretz at Columbia," Slate.com (June 5, 1997).

Blumenthal, Sidney. "The Cracks in Bush's Crown," Salon.com (October 14, 2004).

Bowman, James. "A Sharp Eye and a Sharp Tongue," *Wall Street Journal* (January 15, 2004): D8.

Boynton, Robert S. "Loury's Exodus," *New Yorker* (May 1, 1995) [internet version].

Breindel, Eric. "Mission Accomplished," *New York Post* (January 10, 1991): 31.

Bright, Christopher. "The Neoconservatives and the Reagan Administration," *World Affairs* 153:2 (Fall 1990): 51–80.

Brustein, Robert. "Who's Killing the Novel?" *The New Republic* 153:17 (October 23, 1965), 22–4.

Carmody, Deirdre. "Critic of the Left Ready to Step Aside," *New York Times* (January 19, 1995) [internet version].

Cohen, Nick. "Pink Power Sinks the Tories," *The Observer* (November 10, 2002) [internet version].

Dannhauser, Werner J. "Review of *Cornell '69: Liberalism and the Crisis of the American University*, by Donald Alexander Downs," *Academic Questions* 12:4 (Fall 1999): 87–9.

Decter, Midge. "More Bullying on Campus," *New York Times* (December 10, 1985): A31.

Denby, David. "Robert Warshow: Life and Works," in Robert Warshow, *The Immediate Experience: Movies, Comics, Theatre and Other Aspects of Popular Culture* (enlarged edn. Cambridge, MA: Harvard University Press, 2001): i–xii.

Draper, Theodore H. "Neoconservative History," *The New York Review of Books* (January 16, 1986) [internet version].

Durham, Martin. "Evangelical Protestantism and Foreign Policy in the United States after September 11," *Patterns of Prejudice* 38:2 (2004): 145–58.

Easterbrook, Gregg. "The View from Both Sides," *Newsweek* (September 10, 1990): 65.

—"Ideas Move Nations," *Atlantic Monthly* (January 1986): 66–88.

Ehrman, John. "Commentary," in *The Conservative Press in Twentieth Century America*, (ed.) Ronald Lora and William Henry Longton (Westport, CT and London: Greenwood Press, 1999), 620.

—"*Commentary*, the *Public Interest*, and the Problem of American Jewish Conservatism," *American Jewish History* 87:2&3 (June and September 1999): 159–81.

Elkoff, Marvin. "Everybody Knows His Name," *Esquire* 62:2 (August 1964): 120–1.

Encyclopedia Judaica (Jerusalem: Keter Publishing, 1971), 792.

Epstein, Joseph. "The New Conservatives: Intellectuals in Retreat," *Dissent* (Spring 1973): 151–62.

Farah, Joseph. "Columnist Richard Grenier Dies," *WorldNetDaily.com* (January 31, 2002).

Fein, Leonard J. "Liberalism and American Jews," *Midstream* 19:8 (October 1973): 3–18.

Fiedler, Leslie. "'A Very Stern Discipline': An Interview with Ralph Ellison," *Harper's* 234 (March 1967): 76–95.

Finger, Seymour Maxwell. "The Reagan-Kirkpatrick Policies and the United Nations," *Foreign Affairs* 62 (Winter 1983–1984): 436–57.

Fleming, Thomas. "The Closing of the Conservative Mind," *Chronicles* 13:9 (September 1989): 12.

Foer, Franklin. "Arguing the GOP," *The New Republic* (March 20, 2000): 13.

Frauenglas, Robert. "Norman Podhoretz: A Great Intellectual Who Has the President's Ear . . . Still a Mensch after All These Years!", *Good Fortune* (June 1985): 70–5.

Fried, Lewis. "The *Menorah Journal*: Yavneh in America, 1945–50," *American Jewish Archives* (1998): 77–108.

Friedenberg, Edward Z. "Du côté de chez Podhoretz," *New York Review of Books* 10:2 (February 1, 1968): 11–13.

Friedman, Murray (ed.). "American Jewish Political Conservatism," special issue of *American Jewish History* 87:2 & 3 (June and September 1999).

—"*Commentary*, the American Jewish Community and American Culture," Conference (The Graduate Center, CUNY, New York), March 10, 2003.

Gerson, Mark. "Et Tu Moynihan," *National Review* (August 5, 1983) [internet version].

—"Norman's Conquest: A Commentary on the Podhoretz Legacy," *Policy Review* 74 (Fall 1995): 64–8.

Glazer, Nathan. "Art, Culture and Conservatism: A Symposium," *Partisan Review* (Summer 1972): 440–3.

—"The New Left and the Jews," *The Jewish Journal of Sociology* 11:2 (December 1969): 121–31.

Goldberg, Jonah. "The Neoconservative Invention," *National Review* (May 20, 2003) [internet version].

Goodheart, Eugene. "The Deradicalized Intellectuals," *The Nation* (February 8, 1971): 177–80.

Goodman, Walter, "Irving Kristol: Patron Saint of the New Right," *New York Times Magazine* (December 6, 1981): 90, 190–3.

Graubard, Allen. "From *Commentary* to *Tikkun*: The Past and Future of 'Progressive Jewish Intellectuals,'" *Middle East Report* (May–June 1989): 17–23.

Grubisich, Thomas. "Norman Podhoretz: New Left's Enemy From Within," *Washington Post*, Style Section (April 11, 1971): G1–9.

Grumet, Elinor. "Elliot Cohen: The Vocation of a Jewish Literary Mentor," in *Studies in the American Jewish Experience*, ed. Jacob R. Marcus and Abraham J. Peck (Cincinnati: American Jewish Archives, 1981): 8–25.

Hadar, Leon T. "The 'Neocons': From the Cold War to the 'Global Intifada,'" *Washington Report on Middle East Affairs* (April 1991) [internet version].

Harap, Louis. "X-Ray on Commentary," *Jewish Life* 1:9 (July 1947): 19–24.

—"*Commentary* Moves to the Right," *Jewish Currents* 25:11 (December 1971): 4-9, 27-30.

Heilbrunn, Jacob. "Norman's conquest: why Rudy Giuliani loves Norman Podhoretz," *Washington Monthly* (December 1, 2007) [internet version].

—"Apologists Without Remorse," *The American Prospect* 9:36 (January 1–February 1, 1998) [internet version].

—"The Neocons Last Gasp? Not So Fast," *Los Angeles Times* (November 17, 2004): B13.

Hentoff, Nat. "Cool, Like Blocked," *The Nation* 198:13 (March 23, 1964): 298–300.

Herschaft, Jean. "Rumor Podhoretz in trouble is false," *Jewish Post and Opinion* (July 3, 1981) [internet version].

Hill, Herbert. "Black-Jewish Conflict in the Labor Context: Race, Jobs, and Institutional Power," in *African Americans and Jews in the Twentieth Century: Studies in Convergence and Conflict*, ed. V. P. Franklin, Nancy L. Grant, Harold M. Kletnick, and Genna Rae McNeil. Columbia and London: University of Missouri Press, 1998: 264–92.

Hirst, David. "The war game," *The Observer* (September 21, 2003): 31.

Hitchens, Christopher. "A Modern Medieval Family," *Mother Jones* (July–August 1986): 52-6, 74-6.

—"Unmaking Friends: Norman Podhoretz as Crumb," *Harper's* (June 1, 1999): 73–6.

Hollinger, David. "Ethnic Diversity, Cosmopolitanism and the Emergence of the American Liberal Intelligentsia," *American Quarterly* 27 (May 1975): 131–51.

Hover, Julie and Kadushin, Charles. "Influential Intellectual Journals: A Very Private Club," *Change Magazine* (March 1972): 38–47.

Jacques, Martin. "The neocon revolution," *The Guardian* (March 31, 2005): 23.

Jeffers, Thomas L. "Norman Podhoretz's Discourses on America," *The Hudson Review* 54:2 (Summer 2001): 202–28.

Judis, John B. "The Conservative Crackup," *American Prospect* 3 (Fall 1990): 41.

Katz, Milton S. "*Commentary* and the American Jewish Intellectual Experience," *Journal of American Culture* 3:1 (Spring 1980): 155–66.

Kazin, Alfred. "Saving my Soul at the Plaza," *New York Review of Books* 30:5 (March 31, 1983): 38–42.

Kempton, Murray. "Kirkpatrick Ire Left to Pygmies," *Newsday* (April 21, 1985): 6 and 15.

King, Richard H. "American Dilemmas, European Experiences," *The Arkansas Historical Quarterly* 56:3 (Autumn 1997): 314–33.

Kinsley, Michael. "Who Killed Communism?", *The New Republic* (December 4, 1989): 4.

Kirk, Russell. "The Neoconservatives: An Endangered Species," *Heritage Lecture* 178. Washington: The Heritage Foundation, 1988.

Klingenstein, Susanne. "'It's Splendid When the Town Whore Gets Religion and Joins the Church': The Rise of the Jewish Neoconservatives as Observed by the Paleoconservatives in the 1980s," *Shofar: An Interdisciplinary Journal of Jewish Studies* 21:3 (Spring 2003): 83–98.

Kristol, Irving. "Memoirs of a 'Cold Warrior,'" *New York Times Magazine* (11 February 1968): 457–68.

—"Looking Back on Neoconservatism: Notes and Reflections," *The American Spectator* (November 1977): 6–7.

—"The Muddle in Foreign Policy," *Wall Street Journal* (April 29, 1981): 9.

Krug, Mark M. "*Commentary*'s Subtle Zion-baiting," *The Reconstructionist* (7 February 1947): 13–17.

Krupnick, Mark. "Jewish Intellectuals and the 'Deep Places of the Imagination,'" *Shofar: An Interdisciplinary Journal of Jewish Studies* 21:3 (Spring 2003): 29–47.

Kuttner, Robert. "Next: Exiting Iraq," *The Boston Globe* (November 3, 2004): A27.

—What Would Jefferson Do?" *The American Prospect* (November 2004): 31.

Lekachman, Robert. "Mean to Me," *The Nation* (10 November 1979): 469–70.

Lerner, Michael. "The Founding Editorial Statement," *Tikkun* 1 (1986): 3–12.

Lind, Michael. "On Pat Robertson and His Defenders," *New York Review of Books* (April 20, 1995) [internet version].

—"Rev. Robertson's Grand International Conspiracy Theory," *New York Review of Books* (February 2, 1995) [internet version]

Lindberg, Tod. "The Referendum on Neoconservatism," *The Weekly Standard* (November 1–8, 2004) [internet version].

Longstaff, Stephen A. "The New York Family," *Queen's Quarterly* 83 (1976): 556–73.

Lyons, Matthew. "Deportations Not Bombs: Conservatives Split over War," *Z Magazine* 16:1 (January 2003): 36–40.

"Magazine of Quality," *Time* (January 29, 1951) [internet edition].

Maitre, H. Joachim. "Mit *Commentary* gegen die Kentauren" ("With *Commentary* against the Centaurs"), *Die Welt* (December 14, 1979): 27.

Mann, James. "Four More Years," *Foreign Policy* (November 2004) [internet version].

Marja, Fern. "*Commentary*'s Number One," *New York Post Home News Magazine* (February 17, 1949): 1.

McConnell, Scott. "*The Weekly Standard*'s War," *The American Conservative* (November 21, 2005) [internet version].

—"Right Is Still Right," *New York Press* (October 16–22, 2002) [internet version].

—"Among the Neocons," *The American Conservative* (April 21, 2003) [internet version].

Mehren, Elizabeth. "*Commentary*: High Honors for Editor 25 Years Later," *LA Times* (January 31, 1985): 1.

Menashi, Steven. "The Word is Nigh," *The Claremont Institute* (August 27, 2003) [internet version].

Micklethwait, John and Wooldridge, Adrian. "A conservative make-over," *The Australian* (November 3, 2004): 15.

Miller, Merle. "Why Norman and Jason Aren't Talking," *New York Times Magazine* (March 26, 1972): 34–5, 104–11.

Neilson, Jim. "The Great PC Scare: Tyrannies of the Left, Rhetoric of the Right," in *PC Wars: Politics and Theory in the Academy*, ed. Jeffrey Williams (New York and London: Routledge, 1995): 60–89.

Newfield, Jack. "War Wimps: The Sequel," *The Village Voice* (July 23, 1985): 15.

Newhouse, Alana. "When 'All the Rest' Was the Rage: *Commentary* Looks Back in Pride," *Forward* (March 21, 2003) [internet version].

Nisbet, Lee. "A Commentary on Norman Podhoretz's Neo-Puritanism," *Free Inquiry* (Spring 1982): 37–9.

Nobile, Philip. "A Review of the *New York Review of Books*," *Esquire* (April 1972): 103–26.

Nordlinger, Jay. "All Spelled Out," *The National Review* (October 25, 2004) [internet version].

Novak, Bill. "Philip Roth and the Jews," *Response* 5:2 (Fall 1971): 71–86.

Novak, Michael. "The enduring importance of Norman Podhoretz," *LA Herald Examiner* (February 10, 1985): E5.

Novak, William. "*Commentary* and the Jewish Community: the Record Since 1960," *Response* 7:3 (Fall 1973): 49–66.

—"This Quarter: The Jewish Press, Present and Future," *Response* 8:1 (Spring 1974): 7–11.

—"Commentary: The Good, the Bad, and the Ugly," *InterChange* 3 (September 1977) [internet version].

Nuechterlein, James A. "This Time," *First Things* 68 (December 1996): 3–4.

—"Life at the Intellectual Barricades," *First Things* 46 (October 1994): 12–13.

Omestad, Thomas. "'Fixin' for a fight," *U.S. News & World Report* (October 25, 2004): 51.

Patterson, John. "The Great Defender," *The Guardian* G2 (May 31, 2002): 5.

Paul, Notley. "*New Criterion*," in *The Conservative Press in Twentieth Century America*, ed. Ronald Lora and William Henry Longton (Westport, CT and London: Greenwood Press, 1999), 608.

Pawel, Ernst. "Smugness in Eden, Is it Good for the Jews? *Commentary* on the Jewish Scene," *Response* 7:3 (Fall 1973): 39–49.

Perlstein, Rick. "He Discovered the Culture Wars, Then Reported Behind the Lines," *Columbia Journalism Review* 43:4 (November 2004/December 2004): 58.

Phillips, William. "The World According to Norman," *Partisan Review* 47:3 (1980): 336–40.

Podhoretz, Norman. "The Path to Victory: A Symposium on the War," *The Claremont Review of Books* II: 4 (Fall 2002): 11–12.

—"The Christian Right and Its Demonizers," *The National Review* (April 3, 2000) [internet version].

—"Ideas, Influence and American Politics: The Case of *Commentary*," *Survey* 29:3 (Autumn 1985): 20–6.

—"The Neo-Conservative Anguish Over Reagan's Foreign Policy," *The New York Times Magazine* (May 1982), 29–31.

—"The Culture of Appeasement," *Harper's* (October 1977): 25–32.

—"The Know Nothing Bohemians," *Partisan Review* 25 (Spring 1958): 305–18.

—"The Beat Generation," *Partisan Review* 25 (Summer 1958): 472–9.

Ravenal, Earl. "Fear of Force in the Middle East: The Oil Grab Scenario," *The New Republic* (January 18, 1975) [internet version].

Robbins, I. D. "Jewish community's Podhoretz problem," *New York Daily News* (May 21, 1981): 66.

Rosenbluth, Susan. "Podhoretz: Exclusive Interview," *The Jewish Standard* (May 17, 1985): 10–11.

Rothstein, Richard. "*Tikkun* Conundrum," *LA Weekly* (February 2–8, 1990): 12.

Rozen, Laura and Vest, Jason. "Cloak and Swagger," *The American Prospect* (November, 2004): 21.

Schaeffer, Howard. "Eastsider Norman Podhoretz: Editor of *Commentary*," *The East Side TV Shopper and Restaurant Guide*, n.d.: 25.

Schrag, Peter. "Rewriting History," *Fresno Bee* (January 14, 1981) [internet version].

Schwarzschild, Steven S. "The *Commentary-Monat* Axis," *Menorah Journal* 41 (1953): 87–105.

Shenker, Israel. "Ideological Labels Changing Along With the Label-Makers," *New York Times* (November 12, 1970): 45.

Simes, Dimitri. "The Anti-Soviet Brigade," *Foreign Policy* 37 (Winter 1979/80), 28–42.

Singer, David. "Reflections on *Commentary*: Foreword," *Jewish Social Studies* 3:2 (Winter 1997): 17.

Solomon, Deborah. "The Legacy," *New York Times* (December 9, 2007) [internet version].

Solotaroff, Theodore. "The New York Publishing World," in *Creators and Disturbers: Reminiscences by Jewish Intellectuals of New York*, ed. Bernard Rosenberg and Ernest Goldstein (New York: Columbia University Press, 1982): 412–15.

Staub, Michael E. "'Negroes are not Jews': Race, Holocaust Consciousness, and the Rise of Jewish Neoconservatism," *Radical History Review* 75 (Fall 1999): 3–27.

Steinberg, Milton. "*Commentary* Magazine," in his *A Believing Jew: The Selected Writing of Milton Steinberg* (New York: Harcourt, Brace, 1951): 136–65.

Steinfels, Peter. "The Cooling of the Intellectuals," *Commonweal* (May 21, 1971): 255–61.

Stern, Sol. "My Jewish Problem – And Ours: Israel, the Left, and the Jewish Establishment," *Ramparts* (August 1971): 38–40.

Stone, I. F. "War for Oil?" *New York Review of Books* (February 6, 1975) [internet version].

Strauss, Lauren B. "Staying Afloat in the Melting Pot: Constructing an American Jewish Identity in the *Menorah Journal* of the 1920s," *American Jewish History* 84:4 (December 1996): 315–31.

Tonsor, Stephen J. "Why I Too Am Not A Neoconservative," *The National Review* (June 20, 1986): 54–6.

Traub, James. "Norman Podhoretz: Leaving It," *New Yorker* 70:48 (February 6, 1995): 30.

Twersky, David. "Left Right, Left Right: After half a century, *Commentary* remains defiantly out of step," *Moment* 20:3 (June 1995): 40–5, 57–9.

Vidal, Gore. "The Empire Lovers Strike Back" *The Nation* (March 22, 1986): 352–3.

Waskow, Arthur I. "Malkhut Zadon M'herah T'aker," *Judaism* 20:4 (Fall 1971): 404–15.

Weiss-Rosmarin, Trude. "*Commentary* and *Midstream*," *Jewish Spectator* 23:10 (December 1958): 3–6.

Williamson, Clinton. Jr. "Norman Podhoretz: The Universal Man," *The World & I* (September 1988): 669–79.

Wilson, Clyde. "The Conservative Identity," *Intercollegiate Review* 21 (Spring 1986): 6–8.

Wisse, Ruth R. "The Making of *Commentary* and of the Jewish Intellectual," *Jewish Social Studies* 3:2 (Winter 1997): 29–41.

Worsthorne, Peregrine. "Diary," *The Spectator* (December 14, 1985): 7.

Wyschogrod, Michael. "My *Commentary* Problem – And Ours," *Judaism* 17:2 (Spring 1968): 148–61.

Zipperstein, Steven J. "*Commentary* and American Jewish Culture in the 1940s and 1950s," *Jewish Social Studies* 3:2 (Winter 1997): 18–28.

Unpublished Research

Abrams, Nathan D. "Struggling for Freedom: Arthur Miller, the *Commentary* Community, and the Cultural Cold War." PhD dissertation, University of Birmingham, 1998.

Berkson, Marc E. "The Case of Ethel and Julius Rosenberg: Jewish Responses to Period of Stress." Rabbinic dissertation, HUC-IJR, Cincinnati, OH, 1978.

Diggins, John Patrick. "*Commentary*'s Cold War on Liberalism." Paper delivered at the "*Commentary*, the American Jewish Community and American Culture" Conference, The Graduate Center, CUNY, New York, March 11, 2003.

Gittleman, George D. "An Analysis of *Commentary*: Ideas, Trends and Attitudes toward Jews and Judaism for the Year 1990." Term paper, HUC-IJR, Cincinnati, OH, 1994.

Grumet, Elinor Joan. "The Menorah Idea and the Apprenticeship of Lionel Trilling." PhD dissertation, University of Iowa, 1979.

Hukari, Harvey H. "Attitudes Towards Race in *Commentary* Magazine, 1963 through 1972." Graduate seminar paper, School of Journalism, Stanford University, 1973.

Leder, Steven. "*Commentary* Magazine, Its Form and Content." Term paper, HUC-JIR, Cincinnati, OH, 1985.

Liebschutz, Thomas P. "How Jewish is *Commentary*: A Study of the Jewish Articles in *Commentary* Magazine." Term paper, HUC-JIR, Cincinnati, OH, 1963.

Nash, George. "*Commentary* and Conservatism," Paper delivered at the *Commentary*, the American Jewish Community and American Culture Conference, The Graduate Center, CUNY, New York, March 11, 2003.

Novak, William. "*Commentary*'s Treatment of American Jewish Affairs, 1960-1972." MA thesis, Brandeis University, 1973.

Commentary Articles

Abrams, Elliot. "The Quota Commission," *Commentary* 54:4 (October 1972): 54-7.
Adelson, Joseph. "What's Happened to the Schools?" *Commentary* 71:3 (March 1981): 36-41.
Aldridge, John W. "Literary Onanism," *Commentary* 58:3 (September 1974): 82-6.
Alexander, Edward. "Professor of Terror," *Commentary* 88:2 (August 1989): 49-50.
Alter, Robert. "Sentimentalizing the Jews," *Commentary* 40:3 (September 1965): 71-5.
—"Israel & The Intellectuals," *Commentary* 44:4 (October 1967): 46-52.
—"Appropriating the Religious Tradition," *Commentary* 51:2 (February 1971): 47-54.
—"Defaming the Jews," *Commentary* 55:1 (January 1973): 77-82.
—"The Deformations of the Holocaust," *Commentary* 71:2 (February 1981): 48-54.
Ario, Rabbi S. Hyams, Letters, *Commentary* 80:2 (August 1985): 12-15.
Auerbach, Jerold S. "Liberalism & the Hebrew Prophets," *Commentary* 84:2 (August 1987): 58-60.
Bacevich, A. J. "Learning from Aidid," *Commentary* 96:6 (December 1993): 30-3.
Balch, Stephen H. and London, Herbert I. "The Tenured Left," *Commentary* 82:4 (October 1986): 41-51.
Bar-Ilan, David "Can Israel Withdraw?" *Commentary* 85:4 (April 1988): 27-38.
—"Israel: Guilt & Politics," *Commentary* 97:5 (May 1994): 25-8.
—"Next Year in (a Divided?) Jerusalem," *Commentary* 98:3 (September 1994): 35-9.
Beichman, Arnold. "Liberalism & the Jews: A Symposium,"*Commentary* 69:1 (January 1980): 15-82.
Bennett, William J. "What To Do About the Children," *Commentary* 99:3 (March 1995): 23-8.
Berg, Louis. "McCarthy as Buccaneer," *Commentary* 56:2 (August 1973): 82.
Berger, Brigitte and Peter L. Berger, "Our Conservatism and Theirs," *Commentary* 82:4 (October 1986): 62-7.
Berger, Peter L. "The Greening of American Foreign Policy," *Commentary* 61:3 (March 1976): 23-7.
—"Furtive Smokers – and What They Tell Us About America," *Commentary* 97:6 (June 1994): 21-6.
Berger, Peter L. and Bobby Godsell, "Fantasies About South Africa," *Commentary* 84:1 (July 1987): 35-40.
Berns, Walter. "Let Me Call You Quota, Sweetheart," *Commentary* 71:5 (May 1981): 48-53.
—"Voting Rights and Wrongs," *Commentary* 73:3 (March 1982): 31-6.
Besançon, Alain. "Can Poland Ever Be Free?" *Commentary* 87:4 (April 1989): 15-20.
—"Gorbachev Without Illusions," *Commentary* 85:4 (April 1988): 47-57.
Bickel, Alexander M. "Judging the Chicago Trial," *Commentary* 51:1 (January 1971): 31-40.
Bishop, Joseph W. Jr. "Carter's Last Capitulation," *Commentary* 71:3 (March 1981): 32-5.
Bloom, Harold. "Kabbalah," *Commentary* 59:3 (March 1975): 65.

Bork, Robert H. "Against the Independent Counsel," *Commentary* 95:2 (February 1993): 21-6.

Breindel, Eric M. "The Communists & the Committees," *Commentary* 71:1 (January 1981): 46-52.

—"Progressives' Progress," *Commentary* 75:3 (March 1983): 81-4.

Brock, David."Street-Corner Conservative," *Commentary* 85:6 (June 1988): 62-4.

—"What the Kill-and-Tell Books Tell," *Commentary* 86:2 (August 1988): 21-7.

Codevilla, Angelo M. "Is Olof Palme the Wave of the Future?" *Commentary* 89:3 (March 1990): 26-32.

—"War and Warriors," *Commentary* 92:2 (August 1991): 60-2.

—"Magnificent, But Was it War?" *Commentary* 93:4 (April 1992): 15-20.

Coffy, Warren. "Faith and the Issues," *Commentary* 37:3 (March 1964): 82-5.

Cohen, Eliot A. "The Pollard Case," *Commentary* 88:2 (August 1989): 51-6.

—"Arik," *Commentary* 88:6 (December 1989): 60-4.

Collier, Peter. and Horowitz, David. "McCarthyism: The Last Refuge of the Left," *Commentary* 85:1 (January 1988): 36-41.

Crain, Jane Larkin. "Feminist Fiction," *Commentary* 58:6 (December 1974): 58-62.

Crovitz, Gordon, L. "Crime, the Constitution, And the Iran-Contra Affair," *Commentary* 84:4 (October 1987): 23-30.

Dawidowicz, Lucy S. "Middle-Class Judaism: A Case Study," *Commentary* 29:6 (June 1960): 492-503.

—"Lies About the Holocaust," *Commentary* 70:6 (December 1980): 31-7.

—"Politics, the Jews & the '84 Election," *Commentary* 79:2 (February 1985): 25-30.

Decter, Midge. "Popular Jews," *Commentary* 32:4 (October 1961): 358-60.

—"The Liberated Woman," *Commentary* 50:4 (October 1970): 33-44.

—"The Boys on the Beach," *Commentary* 70:3 (September 1980): 35-48.

—"Socialism and Its Irresponsibilities: The Case of Irving Howe," *Commentary* 74:6 (December 1982): 25-32.

—"Bitburg: Who Forgot What," *Commentary* 80:2 (August 1985): 21-7.

—"Ronald Reagan & the Culture War," *Commentary* 91:3 (March 1991): 43-6.

—"How the Rioters Won" *Commentary* 94:1 (July 1992): 17-22.

—"The ADL vs. the Religious Right," *Commentary* 98:3 (September 1994): 45-7.

—"Remembering Robert Warshow," *Commentary* 113:4 (April 2002): 45-51.

Decter, Moshe. "The Origins of the Cold War: An Exchange," *Commentary* 31:2 (February 1961): 142-59.

Denes, Magda. "Performing Abortions," *Commentary* 62:4 (October 1976): 33-7.

Dienstfrey, Ted. "A Conference on the Sit-ins," *Commentary* 29:6 (June 1960): 524-8.

Draper, Theodore. "Appeasement & Détente," *Commentary* 61:2 (February 1976): 27-38.

—"Beyond Berlin," *Commentary* 32:5 (November 1961): 302-10.

—"Five Years of Castro's Cuba," *Commentary* 37:1 (January 1964): 25-37.

—"Israel and World Politics," *Commentary* 44:2 (August 1967): 19-48.

Eastland, Terry. "Racial Preference in Court (Again)," *Commentary* 87:1 (January 1989): 32-8.

—"Above the Constitution?" *Commentary* 91:5 (May 1991): 60-2.

Eberstadt, Mary Tedeschi. "Arms Control & Its Casualties," *Commentary* 85:4 (April 1988): 39–46.

Eberstadt, Nick. "The Latest Myths About the Soviet Union," *Commentary* 83:5 (May 1987): 17–27.

Elon, Amos. "Letter from the Sinai Front," *Commentary* 44:2 (August 1967): 60–8.

Elshtain, Jean Bethke. "A New Covenant?" *Commentary* 99:4 (April 1995): 70–2.

Epstein, Joseph. "What Makes Vidal Run," *Commentary* 63:6 (June 1977): 72–5.

—"Paul Goodman in Retrospect," *Commentary* 65:2 (February 1978): 70–3.

—"Anti-Americanism & Other Clichés," *Commentary* 75:4 (April 1983): 60–3.

—"It's Only Culture," *Commentary* 76:5 (November 1983): 56–61.

—"Mailer Hits Bottom," *Commentary* 76:1 (July 1983): 62–8.

—"The Education of an Anti-Capitalist," *Commentary* 76:2 (August 1983): 51–9.

—"It's Only Culture," *Commentary* 76:5 (November 1983): 56–61.

—"What Does Philip Roth Want?" *Commentary* 77:1 (January 1984): 62–7.

—"Sex and Euphemism," *Commentary* 77:4 (April 1984): 55–60.

—"The Degradation of the 'New York Times,'" *Commentary* 97:5 (May 1994): 34–9.

—"Intellectuals – Public and Otherwise," *Commentary* 109:5 (May 2000): 46–51.

Evelyn N. Rossman. "A Fund-Raiser Comes to Northrup" *Commentary* 33:3 (March 1962): 218–25.

Fackenheim, Emil L. "The Dilemma of Liberal Judaism," *Commentary* 30:4 (October 1960): 301–10.

—"Apologia for a Confirmation Text," *Commentary* 31:5 (May 1961): 401–10.

—"Jewish Faith and the Holocaust," *Commentary* 46:2 (August 1968): 30–6.

Fairbanks, Charles H. Jr., "Gorbachev's Cultural Revolution," *Commentary* 88:2 (August 1989): 23–7.

Fairlie, Henry. "Johnson & the Intellectuals: A British View," *Commentary* 40:4 (October 1965): 49–55.

Falcoff, Mark. "The Timerman Case," *Commentary* 72:2 (July 1981): 15–23.

—"Making Central America Safe for Communism," *Commentary* 85:6 (June 1988): 17–24.

Farber, Leslie H. "'I'm Sorry, Dear,'" *Commentary* 38:5 (November 1964): 47–54.

Finn, Chester E. Jr., "'Affirmative Action' Under Reagan," *Commentary* 73:4 (April 1982): 17–28.

—"For Whom It Tolls," *Commentary* 99:1 (January 1995): 76–80.

Friedman, Murray. "Black Anti-Semitism on the Rise," *Commentary* 68:4 (October 1979): 31–5.

—"A New Direction for American Jews," *Commentary* 72:6 (December 1981): 37–44.

—"AWACS and the Jewish Community," *Commentary* 73:4 (April 1982): 29–33.

Frum, David. "It's Big Government, Stupid," *Commentary* 97:6 (June): 27–31.

Fukuyama, Francis."Immigrants and Family Values," *Commentary* 95:5 (May 1993): 26–32.

Fumento, Michael A. "AIDS: Are Heterosexuals at Risk?" *Commentary* 84:5 (November 1987): 21–7.

—"Are We Spending Too Much on AIDS?" *Commentary* 90:4 (October 1990): 51–3.

—"AIDS So Far," *Commentary* 92:6 (December 1991): 46–9.

Galbraith, J. K. "An Agenda for American Liberals," *Commentary* 41:6 (June 1966): 29–34.

Garment, Suzanne. "The Eureka Treatment," *Commentary* 83:5 (May 1987): 64–8.

Gass, Oscar. "The World Politics of Responsibility," *Commentary* 40:6 (December 1965): 85–90.

Gershman, Carl. "After the Dominoes Fell," *Commentary* 65:5 (May 1978): 47–54.

—"The Rise & Fall of the Foreign-Policy Establishment," *Commentary* 70:1 (July 1980): 13–24.

Glazer, Nathan. "Liberalism and the Negro: A Round-Table Discussion," *Commentary* 37:3 (March 1964): 25–42.

—"Negroes and Jews: The New Challenge to Pluralism," *Commentary* 38:6 (December 1964): 29–34.

—"The New Left and Its Limits," *Commentary* 46:1 (July 1968): 31–9.

—"Blacks, Jews and the Intellectuals," *Commentary* 47:4 (April 1969): 33–9.

—"On Being Deradicalized," *Commentary* 50:4 (October, 1970): 74–80.

—"The Role of the Intellectuals," *Commentary* 51:2 (February 1971): 55–61.

—"The Limits of Social Policy," *Commentary* 52:3 (September 1971): 51–8.

—"Is Busing Necessary?" *Commentary* 53:3 (March 1972): 39–52.

—"The Exposed American Jew," *Commentary* 59:6 (June 1975): 25–30.

—"An Answer to Lillian Hellman," *Commentary* 62:6 (June 1976): 36–9.

—"American Values and American Foreign Policy," *Commentary* 62:1 (July 1976): 32–7.

—"Verdicts of History," *Commentary* 76:3 (October 1983): 66–70.

—"On Jewish Forebodings," *Commentary* 80:2 (August 1985): 32–6.

Glynn, Patrick. "Reagan's Rush to Disarm," *Commentary* 85:3 (March 1988): 19–28.

—"The Dangers Beyond Containment," *Commentary* 88:2 (August 1989): 15–22.

Goldbloom, Maurice J. "Foreign Policy," *Commentary* 39:6 (June 1965): 47–55.

Goodman, Paul. "Pornography, Art, and Censorship," *Commentary* 31:3 (March 1961): 203–12.

Goodman, Walter. "The Question of Repression," *Commentary* 50:5 (November 1970): 23–38.

Gourevitch, Philip. "The Crown Heights Riot & Its Aftermath," *Commentary* 95:1 (January 1993): 29–34.

Grenier, Richard. "Bolshevism for the 80's," *Commentary* 73:3 (March 1982): 56–63.

—"The Gandhi Nobody Knows," *Commentary* 75:3 (March 1983): 59–72.

—"The Hard Left and the Soft," *Commentary* 77:1 (January 1984): 56–61.

—"From Eton to Havana," *Commentary* 8:3 (September 1984): 61–4.

—"Clint Eastwood Goes PC," *Commentary* 97:3 (March 1994): 51–3.

Grossman, Anita Susan. "Enemies of Culture," *Commentary* 89:6 (June 1990): 60–2.

Haass, Richard N. "Paying Less Attention to the Middle East," *Commentary* 82:2 (August 1986): 22–6.

Halberstam, David. "Getting the Story Straight in Vietnam," *Commentary* 39:1 (January 1965): 30–4.

Halkin, Hillel. "Israel Against Itself," *Commentary* 98:5 (November 1994): 33–9.

Harries, Owen."The Cold War & the Intellectuals," *Commentary* 92:4 (October 1991): 13-20.

—"The Rise of American Decline," *Commentary* 85:5 (May 1988): 32-6.

Harrington, Michael. "Our Fifty Million Poor," *Commentary* 28:1 (July 1959): 19-27.

—"Slums, Old and New," *Commentary* 30:2 (August 1960): 118-24.

Herrnstein, R. J. "On Challenging an Orthodoxy," *Commentary* 55:4 (April 1973): 52-62.

Hertzberg, Arthur. "Israel and American Jewry," *Commentary* 44:2 (August 1967): 69-73.

Hilberg, Raul. "Nazi Bureaucrats and Jewish Leaders," *Commentary* 33:4 (April 1962): 351-6.

Himmelfarb, Gertrude "From Clapham to Bloomsbury: A Genealogy of Morals," *Commentary* 79:2 (February 1985): 36-43.

Himmelfarb, Milton. "Are Jews Becoming Republican?" *Commentary* 72:2 (August 1981): 27-30.

—"In the Light of Israel's Victory," 44:4 (October 1967): 57.

—"Is American Jewry in Crisis?" *Commentary* 47:3 (March 1969): 33-42.

—"Never Again!" *Commentary* 52:2 (August 1971): 73-6.

—"No Hitler, No Holocaust," *Commentary* 77:3 (March 1984): 37-43.

—"Another Look at the Jewish Vote," *Commentary* 80:6 (December 1985): 39-44.

—"American Jews: Diehard Conservatives," *Commentary* 87:4 (April 1989): 44-9.

Hook, Sidney., Hughes, Stuart, H., Morgenthau, Hans J., and Snow, C. P. "Western Values and Total War: An Exchange," *Commentary* 32:4 (October 1961): 277-97.

Howe, Irving. "Tevye on Broadway," *Commentary* 38:5 (November 1964): 73-5.

—"The New York Intellectuals: A Chronicle and a Critique," *Commentary* 46:4 (October 1968): 29-51.

—"Philip Roth Reconsidered," *Commentary* 54:6 (December 1972): 69-77.

—"America Now: A Failure of Nerve? A Symposium," *Commentary* 60:1 (July 1975): 45-7.

—"Liberalism & the Jews: A Symposium," *Commentary* 69:1 (January 1980): 47-8.

Iannone, Carol. "The Fiction We Deserve," *Commentary* 83:6 (June 1987): 60-2.

—"Feminism vs. Literature," *Commentary* 86:1 (July 1988): 49-53.

"Jewishness & the Younger Intellectuals," *Commentary* 31:4 (April 1961): 305-59.

Johnson, Paul. "Marxism vs. the Jews," *Commentary* 77:4 (April 1984): 28-34.

—"The Race for South Africa," *Commentary* 80:3 (September 1985): 27-32.

—"In Praise of Richard Nixon," *Commentary* 86:4 (October 1988): 50-3.

—"Blessing Capitalism," *Commentary* 95:5 (May 1993): 33-6.

—"Leading Lady," *Commentary* 97:1 (January 1994): 56-8.

—"God and the Americans," *Commentary* 99:1 (January 1995): 25-45.

Kagan, Donald. "World War I, World War II, World War III," *Commentary* 83:3 (March 1987): 21-40.

Kagan, Robert. "Losing in Latin America," *Commentary* 86:5 (November 1988): 45-51.

Kaplan, Fred. "Heller's Last Gag," *Commentary* 79:2 (February 1985): 59-61.

Kass, Leon R. "Death With Dignity and the Sanctity of Life," *Commentary* 89:3 (March 1990): 33-43.

—"Regarding Daughters and Sisters: *The Rape of Dinah*," *Commentary* 93:4 (April 1992): 29–38.

Kedourie, Elie. "Iraq: The Mystery of American Policy," *Commentary* 91:6 (June 1991): 15–19.

Kelman, Steven. "Stalinophilia," *Commentary* 56:1 (July 1974): 67–9.

Kinsley, Michael. "Who Killed Communism?" *The New Republic* (December 4, 1989): 4.

Kirkpatrick, Jeane. "Dictatorships and Double Standards," *Commentary* 68:5 (November 1979): 34–45.

—"U.S. Security & Latin America," *Commentary* 71:1 (January 1981): 29–40.

—"How the PLO Was Legitimized," *Commentary* 88:1 (July 1989): 21–8.

Kramer, Martin. "Islam vs. Democracy," *Commentary* 95:1 (January 1993): 25–42.

—"Islam & the West (including Manhattan)," *Commentary* 96:4 (October 1993): 33–7.

Kramer, Rita. "War Diary," *Commentary* 93:5 (May 1992): 62–4.

Krim, Seymour. "Remembering Harold Rosenberg," *Commentary* 66:5 (November 1978): 65–7.

Kristol, Irving. "The Political Dilemma of American Jews," *Commentary* 78:1 (July 1984): 23–9.

—"Liberalism & American Jews," *Commentary* 86:4 (October 1988): 19–23.

—"The Future of American Jewry," *Commentary* 92:2 (August 1991): 21–6.

—"Why Religion Is Good for the Jews," *Commentary* 98:2 (August 1994): 19–21.

Kristol, William. "A Conservative Looks at Liberalism," *Commentary* 96:3 (September 1993): 33–6.

Laqueur, Walter. "Israel, the Arabs, and World Opinion," *Commentary* 44:2 (August 1967): 49–59.

—"New York and Jerusalem," *Commentary* 51:2 (February 1971): 38–46.

—"Europe: The Specter of Finlandization," *Commentary* 64:6 (December 1977): 37–46.

—"The West in Retreat," *Commentary* 60:2 (August 1975): 44–52.

—"The World and President Carter," *Commentary* 65:2 (February 1978): 56–63.

—"Reagan and the Russians," *Commentary* 73:1 (January 1982): 19–26.

—"Is There Now, or Has There Ever Been Such a Thing as Totalitarianism?" *Commentary* 80:4 (October 1985): 29–35.

—"A Postscript on Finlandization," *Commentary* 95:1 (January 1993): 53.

"Liberal Anti-Communism Revisited: A Symposium," *Commentary* 44:3 (September 1967): 31–79.

Lichter, Linda S. "Home Truths," *Commentary* 97:6 (June 1994): 49–52.

Lichtheim, George. "Vietnam and China," *Commentary* 39:5 (May 1965): 56–9.

Lilla, Elizabeth. "Who's Afraid of Women's Studies?" *Commentary* 81:2 (February 1986): 53–7

Lindberg, Tod. "New York Down, Washington Up," *Commentary* 81:1 (January 1986): 36–42.

Lipset, Seymour Martin and Earl Raab. "The Election & the Evangelicals," *Commentary* 71:3 (March 1981): 25–31.

—"An Appointment with Watergate," *Commentary* 56:3 (September 1973): 35–43.

Lipson, Leon. and Jordan, Nehemiah. "The Cold War," *Commentary* 30:4 (October 1960): 340–4.

Lowenthal, Richard. "Totalitarianism Reconsidered," *Commentary* 29:6 (June 1960): 504–12.

Luttwak, Edward N. "Why Arms Control Failed," *Commentary* 65:1 (January 1978): 19–28.

Lynd, Staughton. "How the Cold War Began," *Commentary* 30:5 (November 1960): 379–89.

Macdonald, Dwight. "Scrambled Eggheads on the Right: Mr. Buckley's New Weekly," *Commentary* 21:4 (April 1956): 367–73.

—"The Candidates and I," *Commentary* 29:4 (April 1960): 287–94.

MacDonald, Heather. "Toward Yugoslavia?" *Commentary* 93:6 (June 1992): 61–3.

Maguire, Timothy. "My Bout with Affirmative Action," *Commentary* 93:4 (April 1992): 50–2.

Mayer, Martin. "Higher Education for All? The Case of Open Admissions," *Commentary* 55:2 (February 1973): 37–47.

Mayfield, Julian. "Challenge to Negro Leadership," *Commentary* 31:4 (April 1961): 297–305.

McCracken, Samuel. "The Drugs of Habit & the Drugs of Belief," *Commentary* 51:6 (June 1971): 43–52.

—"Are Homosexuals Gay?" *Commentary* 67:1 (January 1979): 19–29.

—"'Julia' & Other Fictions by Lillian Hellman," *Commentary* 77:6 (June 1984): 35–43.

Menahem, Milson. "How to Make Pace with the Palestinians," *Commentary* 71:5 (May 1981): 25–35

—"How Not to Occupy the West Bank," *Commentary* 81:4 (April 1986): 15–22.

Meyer, Karl. "Triumph of the Smooth Deal," *Commentary* 26:6 (December 1958): 461–8.

Meyer, Michael A. "Judaism after Auschwitz: The Religious Thought of Emil L. Fackenheim," *Commentary* 53:6 (June 1972): 55–62.

Miller, Stephen. "Totalitarianism, Dead and Alive," *Commentary* 88:2 (August 1989): 28–32.

Morgenthau, Hans. "Asia: The American Algeria," *Commentary* 32:1 (1961): 43–7.

—"Vietnam: Another Korea?" *Commentary* 33:5 (May 1962): 369–74.

Moynihan, Daniel Patrick, "The President and the Negro," *Commentary* 43:2 (February 1967): 31–45.

—"'Joining the Jackals': The U.S. at the UN 1977-1980," *Commentary* 72:2 (February 1981): 23–31.

—"The United States in Opposition," *Commentary* 59:3 (March 1975): 31–44.

—"Was Woodrow Wilson Right? Morality and American Foreign Policy," *Commentary* 57:5 (May 1974): 25–31.

Muravchik, Joshua "Patrick J. Buchanan and the Jews," *Commentary* 91:1 (January 1991): 29–37.

—"Why the Democrats Finally Won," *Commentary* 95:1 (January 1993): 17–22.

—"How the Cold War Really Ended," *Commentary* 98:5 (November 1994): 40–5.

—"Clintonism Abroad," *Commentary* 99:2 (February 1995): 36–40.

—"The Neoconservative Cabal," *Commentary* 116:2 (September 2003): 26–33.

Murray, Charles. "Helping the Poor: A Few Modest Proposals," *Commentary* 79:5 (May 1985): 27-34.

—"The Legacy of the 60's," *Commentary* 94:1 (July 1992): 23-30.

—"What To Do About Welfare," *Commentary* 98:6 (December 1994): 26-34.

Mylroie, Laurie. "How We Helped Saddam Survive," *Commentary* 92:1 (July 1991): 15-19.

Natan Sharansky, "As I see Gorbachev," *Commentary* 85:3 (March 1988): 29-34.

Neuhaus, Richard John. "What the Fundamentalists Want," *Commentary* 79:5 (May 1985): 41-6.

Newman, William. "Time Inc. Offers and Ideology," *Commentary* 28:6 (December 1959): 471-8.

Novak, Michael. "A Radical Feminist," *Commentary* 61:2 (February 1976): 90.

Nuechterlein, James. "Watergate: Toward a Revisionist View," *Commentary* 68:2 (August 1979): 38-45.

—"Neoconservatism & Irving Kristol," *Commentary* 78:2 (August 1984): 43-52.

—"A Farewell to Civil Rights," *Commentary* 84:2 (August 1987): 25-36.

—"The American 80's: Disaster or Triumph?: A Symposium," *Commentary* 90:3 (September 1990): 40-1.

—"The Moynihan Years," *Commentary* 110:3 (October 2000): 29-36.

Patullo, E. L. "Straight Talk About Gays," *Commentary* 94:6 (December 1992): 21-4.

Peretz, Martin. "The American Left and Israel," *Commentary* 44:5 (November 1967): 27-34.

—"Bush, Clinton & the Jews: *A Debate*," *Commentary* 94:4 (October 1992): 15-23.

Perlmutter, Philip. "Balkanizing America," *Commentary* 70:3 (September 1980): 64-6.

Pfaff, William. "The Decline of Liberal Politics," *Commentary* 48:4 (October 1969): 45-51.

Pipes, Daniel. "Arab vs. Arab Over Palestine," *Commentary* 84:1 (July 1987): 17-25.

—"The Ayatollah, the Novelist, and the West," *Commentary* 6:6 (June 1989): 9-17.

Pipes, Daniel and Garfinkle, Adam. "Is Jordan Palestine?" *Commentary* 86:4 (October 1988): 35-42.

Pipes, Richard. "Why the Soviet Union Thinks It Could Fight and Win a Nuclear War," *Commentary* 64: 1 (July 1977): 21-34.

—"Team B: The Reality Behind the Myth," *Commentary* 82:4 (October 1986): 25-40.

—"Gorbachev's Russia: Breakdown or Crackdown?" *Commentary* 89:3 (March 1990): 13-25.

Podhoretz, Norman. "Achilles in Left Field," *Commentary* 15:3 (March 1953): 321-6.

—"Sholom Aleichem: Jewishness is Jews: The Unregenerate Tribe," *Commentary* 16:3 (September 1953): 261-3.

—"The Language of Life," *Commentary* 16:4 (October 1953): 378-82.

—"William Faulkner and the Problem of War," *Commentary* 18:3 (September 1954): 227-32.

—"Jewish Culture and the Intellectuals," *Commentary* 19:5 (May 1955): 451-7.

—"The Issue," *Commentary* 29:2 (February 1960): a, 182-4.

—"The Issue," *Commentary* 29:4 (April 1960): a.

—"The Issue," *Commentary* 29:5 (May 1960): a.

—"The Issue," *Commentary* 30:2 (August 1960): a.
—"Jewishness & the Younger Intellectuals," *Commentary* 31:4 (April 1961): 310.
—"My Negro Problem - and Ours," *Commentary* 35:2 (February 1963): 93–101.
—"Hannah Arendt on Eichmann: A Study in the Perversity of Brilliance," *Commentary* 36:3 (September 1963): 201–8.
—"Speak of the Devil," *Commentary* 51:4 (April 1971): 6–7.
—"Intellectuals at War," *Commentary* 4:4 (October 1972): 6–7.
—"The Intellectuals and the Pursuit of Happiness," *Commentary* 55:2 (February 1973): 7–8.
—"Vietnam and Collective Guilt," *Commentary* 55:3 (March 1973): 4–6.
—"First Things, and Last," *Commentary* 50:1 (July 1970): 27.
—"Laws, Kings, and Cures," *Commentary* 50:4 (October 1970): 30.
—"Like Fathers, Like Sons," *Commentary* 50:2 (August 1970): 21.
—"Laws, Kings, and Cures," *Commentary* 50:4 (October 1970): 30.
—"The New Hypocrisies," *Commentary* 50:6 (December 1970): 5–6.
—"The Tribe of the Wicked Son," *Commentary* 51:2 (February 1971): 6–10.
—"A Note on Vietnamization," *Commentary* 51:5 (May 1971): 6–9.
—"Seducer of the Innocent," *Commentary* 51:6 (June 1971): 4–6.
—"A Certain Anxiety," *Commentary* 52:2 (August 1971): 4–10.
—"'Is It Good for the Jews?,'" *Commentary* 53:2 (February 1972): 7–12.
—"Between Nixon and the New Politics," *Commentary* 54:3 (September 1972): 4–8.
—"McGovern and the Jews: A Debate," *Commentary* 54:3 (September 1972): 43–51.
—"Living with Free Speech," *Commentary* 54:5 (November 1972): 6–8.
—"Laureate of the New Class," *Commentary* 54:6 (December 1972): 4–7.
—"What the Voters Sensed," *Commentary* 55:1 (January 1973): 4–6.
—"Culture and the Present Moment: A Round-Table Discussion," *Commentary* 58:6 (December 1974): 31–50.
—"Making the World Safe for Communism," *Commentary* 61:4 (April 1976): 31–42.
—"The Abandonment of Israel," *Commentary* 62:1 (July 1976): 23–31.
—"The New American Majority," *Commentary* 71:1 (January 1981): 19–28.
—"The Future Danger," *Commentary* 71:4 (April 1981): 29–47.
—"Human Rights and American Foreign Policy: A Symposium," *Commentary* 72:5 (November 1981): 25–63.
—"J'Accuse," *Commentary* 74:3 (September 1982): 21–3.
—"Appeasement By Any Other Name," *Commentary* 76:1 (July 1983): 33–8.
—"The State of the Jews," *Commentary* 76:6 (December 1983): 37–45.
—"The State of World Jewry," *Commentary* 76:6 (December 1983): 37–45.
—"Vietnam: The Revised Standard Version," *Commentary* 77:4 (April 1984): 35–41.
—"Mistaken Identity," *Commentary* 78:1 (July 1984): 56–60.
—"The Hate That Dare Not Speaks its Name," *Commentary* 82:5 (November 1986): 21–32.
—"American Jews and Israel: A Symposium," *Commentary* 85:2 (February 1988): 21–7.
—"Israel: A Lamentation From the Future," *Commentary* 87:3 (March 1989): 15–21.
—"A Statement on the Persian Gulf Crisis," *Commentary* 90:5 (November 1990): 17–20.

—"Enter the Peace Party," *Commentary* 91:1 (January 1991): 17–21.
—"In Israel, With Scuds and Patriots," *Commentary* 91:4 (April 1991): 19–26.
—"After the Cold War," *Commentary* 92:1 (July 1991): 55–6.
—"Rape in Feminist Eyes," *Commentary* 92:4 (October 1991): 29–35.
—"America and Israel: An Ominous Change," *Commentary* 93:1 (January 1992): 21–5.
—"What Is Anti-Semitism? An Open Letter to William F. Buckley, Jr.," *Commentary* 93:2 (February 1992): 15–20.
—"Buchanan and the Conservative Crackup," *Commentary* 93:5 (May 1992): 30–4.
—Editorial Note, *Commentary* 93:6 (June 1992): 21.
—"Why I Thought Perot Would Win," *Commentary* 94:3 (September 1992): 33–6.
—"A Statement on the Peace Process," *Commentary* 95:4 (April 1993): 19–23.
—"Another Statement on the Peace Process," *Commentary* 95:6 (June 1993): 25–30.
—"U.S. Forces on the Golan Heights?: A Special Report," *Commentary* 98:6 (December 1994): 73.
—"The Peace Process So Far," *Commentary* 98:6 (December 1994): 21–5.
—"Comes the Counterrevolution," *Commentary* 99:1 (January 1995): 46–50.
—"Editing *Commentary*: A Valedictory," *Commentary* 99:6 (June 1995): 19–20.
—"In the Matter of Pat Robertson," *Commentary* 100:2 (August 1995): 27–32.
—Contribution to "The National Prospect: A Symposium," *Commentary* 100:5 (November 1995): 23–116.
—"Israel – With Grandchildren," *Commentary* 100:6 (December 1995): 38–47.
—"My war with Allen Ginsberg," *Commentary* 104:2 (August 1997): 27–40.
—"Israel and the United States: A complex history," *Commentary* 105:5 (May 1998): 28–43.
—"The adventures of Philip Roth," *Commentary* 106:4 (October 1998): 25–36.
—"A dissent on Isaiah Berlin," *Commentary* 107:2 (February 1999): 25–37.
—"What Happened to Ralph Ellison," 108:1 (July/August 1999): 46–58.
—"Strange Bedfellows: A Guide to the New Foreign-Policy Debates," *Commentary* 108:5 (December 1999): 19–31.
—"Looking Back at 'Catch-22,'" 109:2 *Commentary* (February 2000): 35–43.
—"Bellow at 85, Roth at 67," *Commentary* 110:1 (July/August 2000): 35–43.
—"Oslo: The Peacemongers Return," *Commentary* 112:3 (October 2001): 21–33.
—"In Praise of the Bush Doctrine," *Commentary* 114:2 (September 2002): 19–28.
—"World War IV: How It Started, What It Means, and Why We Have to Win," *Commentary* 118:2 (September 2004): 17–54.
Puddington, Arch. "The New Soviet Apologists," *Commentary* 76:5 (November 1983): 25–31.
—"The Future of the USSR," *Commentary* 88:3 (September 1989): 60–3.
—"The Anti-Cold War Brigade," *Commentary* 90:2 (August 1990): 30–8.
—"Is White Racism the Problem?" *Commentary* 94:1 (July 1992): 31–6.
Raab, Earl. "Is the Jewish Community Split?" *Commentary* 74:5 (November 1982): 21–5.
Revel, Jean-Francois. "Is Communism Reversible?" *Commentary* 87:1 (January 1989): 17–24.
—"Hastening the Death of Communism," *Commentary* 88:4 (October 1989): 19–23.

Riesman, David and Maccoby, Malcolm. "The American Crisis: Political idealism and the Cold War," *Commentary* 29:6 (June 1960): 461–72.

Roberts, David. Jr., "The ANC in Its Own Words," *Commentary* 86:1 (July 1988): 31–7.

—"Sodomy and the Supreme Court," *Commentary* 82:4 (October 1986): 57–61.

Rose, Louise Blecher. "The Secret Life of Sarah Lawrence," *Commentary* 75:5 (May 1983): 52–6.

Rosenberg, Marjorie. "Inventing the Homosexual," *Commentary* 84:6 (December 1987): 36–40.

Rostow, Eugene V. "The Case Against SALT II," *Commentary* 67:2 (February 1979): 23–32.

—"Why the Soviets Want an Arms-Control Agreement, And Why They Want It Now," *Commentary* 83:2 (February 1987): 19–26.

Roth, Philip. "Writing American Fiction," *Commentary* 31:3 (March 1961): 223–33.

—"Writing about Jews," *Commentary* 36:6 (December 1963): 446–52.

Salmon, Jeffrey. "Greenhouse Anxiety," *Commentary* 96:1 (July 1993): 25–8.

Schumacher, E. F., "A Humanistic Guide to Foreign Aid," *Commentary* 32:5 (November 1961): 414–21.

—"Economism," *Commentary* 36:1 (July 1963): 81–4.

Seabury, Paul. "HEW and the Universities," *Commentary* 53:2 (February 1972): 38–44.

Seltzer, Robert M. "American Jews & Their Judaism," *Commentary* 97:3 (March 1994): 47–50.

Shannon, William V. "Eisenhower as President," *Commentary* 26:6 (December 1958): 462–7.

Shaw, Peter. "Portnoy and His Creator," *Commentary* 47:5 (May 1969): 77–99.

—"The Rise & Fall of Deconstruction," *Commentary* 92:6 (December 1991): 50–3.

Singer, David. "The Record In Latin America," *Commentary* 74:6 (December 1982): 43–9.

Skerry, Peter. "Race Relations at Harvard," *Commentary* 71:1 (January 1981): 62–4.

Sklare, Marshall. "The Greening of Judaism," *Commentary* 58:6 (December 1974): 51–7.

Solotaroff, Theodore. "Harry Golden and the American Audience," *Commentary* 31:1 (January 1961): 1–13.

Spiegel, Steven L. "The Middle East: A Consensus of Error," *Commentary* 73:3 (March 1982): 15–24.

—"Israel as a Strategic Asset," *Commentary* 5:6 (June 1983): 51–5.

"The State of Jewish Belief," *Commentary* 42:2 (August 1966): 71–160.

Stein, Harry. Letter to the Editor, *Bottom Line/Personal* (May 25, 1988) [internet version].

Stelzer, Irwin. "Clintonism Unmasked," *Commentary* 95:5 (May 1993): 21–5.

Sundquist, Eric J. "'Witness' Recalled," *Commentary* 86:6 (December 1988): 57–63.

Tanenhaus, Sam"What the Anti-Communists Knew," *Commentary* 90:1 (July 1990): 32–6.

Tedeschi, Mary. "Infanticide & Its Apologists," *Commentary* 78:5 (November 1984): 31–5.

Tucker, Robert W. "Oil: The Issue of American Intervention," *Commentary* 59:1 (January 1975): 21–31.

Twersky, David. "A New Kind of Democrat?" *Commentary* 95:2 (February 1993): 51–3.

Wattenberg, Ben J. and Scammon, Richard M. "Black Progress and Liberal Rhetoric," *Commentary* 55:4 (April 1973): 35–45.

Weigel, George. "The New Anti-Catholicism," *Commentary* 93:6 (June 1992): 25–31.

—"Their Lustration – And Ours," *Commentary* 94:4 (October 1992): 34–9.

—"Shultz, Reagan, and the Revisionists," *Commentary* 96:2 (August 1993): 50–3.

Wertheimer, Jack. "Family Values & the Jews," *Commentary* 97:1 (January 1994): 30–4.

—"A Jewish Contract With America," *Commentary* 99:5 (May 1995): 31–5.

Williamson Murray, "Munich at Fifty," *Commentary* 86:1 (July 1988): 25–30.

Wilson, James Q. "Against the Legalization of Drugs," *Commentary* 89:2 (February 1990): 21–8.

Wisse, Ruth R. "The Anxious American Jew," *Commentary* 66:3 (September 1978): 47–50.

—"Reading About Jews," *Commentary* 69:3 (March 1980): 41–8.

—"Judaism for the Mass Market," *Commentary* 71:1 (January 1981): 41–5.

—"Philip Roth Then and Now," *Commentary* 72:3 (September 1981): 56–60.

—"Jewish Guilt and Israeli Writers," *Commentary* 87:1 (January 1989): 25–31.

—"A Purim Homily," *Commentary* 93:5 (May 1992): 53.

—"The Might and the Right," *Commentary* 94:3 (September 1992): 48–50.

Wrong, Dennis. 'The Case of the *New York Review*,' *Commentary* 50:5 (November 1970): 49–63.

Zagoria, Donald S. "Communism in Asia," *Commentary* 39:2 (February 1965): 53–8.

—"China's Strategy," *Commentary* 40:5 (November 1965): 61–6.

Letters

Anonymous. Letters, *Commentary* 70:3 (September 1980), 4–12.

—Letters, *Commentary* 76:3 (October 1983), 4–14.

Bar Ilan, David. Letters, *Commentary* 94:3 (September 1992), 2–12.

Bell, Pearl K. Letters, *Commentary* 70:2 (August 1980), 15.

Berman, Paul. Letters, *Commentary* 94:2 (August 1992), 2–21.

Bloom, Jessie S. Letters, *Commentary* 31:6 (June 1961), 528.

—Letters, *Commentary* 32:1 (July 1961), 69–72.

Brantingham, Philip. Letters, *Commentary* 55:4 (April 1973), 32.

Brickner, Rabbi Balfour. Letters, *Commentary* 51:6 (June 1971), 8.

—Letters, *Commentary* 59:3 (March 1975), 18, 20.

Brown, Ronald. Letters, *Commentary* 86:1 (July 1986), 8.

Brownmiller, Philip. Letters, *Commentary* 61:5 (May 1976), 4–12.

Crain, Jane Larkin. Letters, *Commentary* 59:5 (May 1975), 22.

Decter, Midge. Letters, *Commentary* 60:5 (November 1975), 4–15.

—Letters, *Commentary* 76:2 (February 1983), 4–10.

—Letters, *Commentary* 75:4 (April 1983), 12–15.

Denes, Magda. Letters, *Commentary* 62:6 (December 1976), 4–6.

—Letters, *Commentary* 63:1 (January 1977), 18–22.

—Letters, *Commentary* 63:2 (February 1977), 22-5.
Elkoff, Marvin. Letters, *Commentary* 38:2 (August 1964), 8-12.
Elshtain, Jean Bethke. Letters, *Commentary* 99:6 (June 1995), 12-14.
Epstein, Joseph. Letters, *Commentary* 60:5 (November 1975), 4-15.
—Letters, *Commentary* 77:4 (April 1984), 14.
Friedman, Murray. Letters, *Commentary* 69:2 (February 1980), 20.
Glazer, Nathan. Letters, *Commentary* 39:6 (June 1965), 8.
—Letters, *Commentary* 62:3 (September 1976), 4-8.
Gornick, Vivian. Letters, *Commentary* 51:2 (February 1971), 12-36.
Greenberg, Irving. Letters, *Commentary* 59:3 (March 1975), 18.
Irving, Kristol. Letters, *Commentary* 29:4 (April 1960), 345-6.
—Letters, *Commentary* 86:1 (July 1988), 2-10.
—Letters, *Commentary* 87:1 (January 1989), 2-11.
Ivry, Alfred. Letters, *Commentary* 31:5 (May 1961), 443.
Johnson, Paul. Letters, *Commentary* 90:1 (July 1990), 3.
Koenig, Freiderich. Letters, *Commentary* 70:6 (December 1980), 12, 13.
Laqueur, Walter. Letters, *Commentary* 65:5 (May 1978), 6, 8.
Leslie H. Farber, Letters, *Commentary* 39:4 (April 1965), 16-27.
—Letters, *Commentary* 103:3 (March 1997), 3-26.
Levine, Irving. Letters, *Commentary* 54:1 (July 1972), 20-2.
Lind, Michael. Letters, *Commentary* 94:3 (September 1992), 21.
Mayfield, Julian. Letters, *Commentary* 32:1 (July 1961), 72-5.
Patullo, E. L. Letters, *Commentary* 95:3 (March 1993), 2-17.
Pipes, Richard. Letters, *Commentary* 64:2 (August 1977), 4-26.
Podhoretz, Norman. Letters, *Commentary* 30:3 (September 1960), 252.
—Letters, *Commentary* 40:4 (October 1965), 12.
—Letters, *Commentary* 44:6 (December 1967), 6.
—Letters, *Commentary* 51:1 (January 1971), 21-8.
—Letters, *Commentary* 51:6 (June 1971), 8.
—Letters, *Commentary* 60:5 (November 1975), 4-15.
—Letters, *Commentary* 70:3 (September 1980), 4-12.
—Letters, *Commentary* 72:6 (December 1981), 14-23.
—Letters, *Commentary* 74:6 (December 1982), 4-15, 68-80.
—Letters, *Commentary* 96:3 (September 1983), 2-20.
—Letters, *Commentary* 77:3 (March 1984), 2-17.
—Letters, *Commentary* 78:4 (October 1984), 4-17.
—Letters, *Commentary* 88:1 (July 1989), 4-16.
—Letters, *Commentary* 88:3 (September 1989), 8-9.
—Letters, *Commentary* 93:3 (March 1992), 2-8.
—Letters, *Commentary* 93:5 (May 1992), 4-8.
—Letters, *Commentary* 94:3 (September 1992), 2-12.
—Letters, *Commentary* 99:4 (April 1995), 20.
Rose, Louise Blecher. Letters, *Commentary* 76:2 (August 1983), 4-17.
Rosenberg, Marjorie. Letters, *Commentary* 83:2 (February 1987), 2-6.
—Letters, *Commentary* 85:3 (March 1988), 6-12.

Royster, Vermont. Letters, *Commentary* 74:6 (December 1982), 4–15, 68–80.
Rudikoff, Sonya. Letters, *Commentary* 37:4 (April 1964), 6–10.
Samuel, Maurice. Letters, *Commentary* 17:2 (February 1954), 192.
Shaw, Peter. Letters, *Commentary* 48:1 (July 1969), 14.
Silverman, David W. Letters, *Commentary* 40:6 (December 1965), 30.
Steinfels, Peter Letters, *Commentary* 69:6 (June 1980), 6–7.
Syrkin, Marie. Letters, *Commentary* 55:3 (March 1973), 8.
Twersky, David. Letters, *Commentary* 60:4 (October 1975), 7.
—Letters, *Commentary* 63:6 (June 1977), 4–14.
Wasser, Henry. Letters, *Commentary* 18:6 (December 1954), 569–70.
Wertheimer, Jack. Letters, *Commentary* 98:5 (November 1994), 10.
Wrong, Dennis. Letters, *Commentary* 76:2 (February 1983), 4–10.
Yang, Wesley. Letters, *Commentary* 90:6 (December 1990), 8–10.

Index

Abel, Sherry 18, 52
ABM Treaty, The 1
abortion 7, 108, 123, 160, 163 n.50, 168, 169, 188, 214, 243, 260, 262, 263, 269, 290, 312
Abrams, Elliot 1, 98, 114, 122, 166, 167, 168, 171, 173, 190, 193, 200, 220, 221, 236 n.18, 249, 301, 302, 307
Academic Questions 282 n.7
Adelson, Joseph 98, 187, 188
affirmative action 7, 113–16, 121, 123, 168, 169, 190–2, 216, 231, 234 n.6, 257, 261
Afghanistan 150, 166, 175, 228, 250, 304, 307
Africa 150, 200, 205
African National Congress (ANC) 219
Agnew, Spiro 118
Aidid, Mohammed 5
AIDS 205–6, 297
Aiken, Henry 40
Aldridge, John W. 110
Aleichem, Sholom 71
Allen, Richard 170
Allin, Dana H. 250
Alter, Robert 33, 35, 75, 97, 111, 151
Alvarez, Al 268
American Committee for Cultural Freedom 55, 57, 75
American Enterprise Institute 242, 310
American Jewish Committee (AJC), the 3–4, 17, 19, 21, 22, 23, 25, 38, 39, 41–3, 53, 60, 62, 64, 94, 104, 116, 124–6, 138, 155, 178, 188, 191, 207, 216, 235 n.17, 240, 241, 243, 280, 285 n.50, 292, 303–4
American Nazi Party 41
American Spectator, The 166, 236 n.18, 242, 296, 299, 300
Amin, Idi 146
Anderson, Jervis 62, 78
Andropov, Yuri 250
Angola 226, 228
Annan, Noel 294
Another Country 187
anti-Communism 4, 6, 22, 25, 28, 55–8, 60, 68, 75–7, 122, 123, 133–44, 176–7, 194, 218, 289, 296
Anti-Defamation League (ADL) 267
anti-Semitism 36, 64, 73, 74, 75, 77–80, 81, 84, 97, 107, 108, 115, 116, 146, 154, 156, 158, 169, 179, 180, 183, 185, 189, 190, 192, 212–14, 215–16, 217, 220, 230, 235–6 n.17, 253, 265, 266, 267, 272, 295 *see also* anti-Zionism
anti-Stalinism 4, 55, 81, 124
anti-Zionism 79, 108, 146, 151, 180, 185, 265
appeasement 68, 147, 158, 167, 175, 200, 305
Arafat, Yasser 276, 280
Arendt, Hannah 9, 21, 37–9, 41, 127, 294
Argentina 220
Arkansas Project 276

Armey, Dick 290
Atlantic Monthly 25
Atlas, James 296
Auschwitz 64, 73, 185
Australia 173, 235 n.17
Avineri, Shlomo 151
Avishai, Bernard 36

Baker, Gerard 302
Baker, James 272, 274
Balch, Stephen H. 244, 282 n.7
Baldwin, James 50, 62, 65, 66, 78
Banfield, Edward 98
Bar-Ilan, David 208
Barrett, William 57, 97
Bawer, Bruce 295
Bazelon, David 57
Beats, the 54–5, 156
Beattie, Ann 187
Begin, Menachem 154–5, 179, 180, 183, 185, 186, 276
Beichman, Arnold 23, 167, 174
Bell Curve, The 261, 295
Bell, Daniel 21, 23, 39, 40, 41, 57, 76, 81, 85, 86, 98, 118, 124, 127, 144, 233, 289, 295, 322
Bell, Pearl K. 189
Bellow, Adam 296, 313
Bellow, Saul 15–17, 26, 35, 59, 82, 127
Bennett, William J. 127, 192, 301
Berenbaum, Michael 112
Berg, Louis 141
Berger, Peter 295
Berkeley 69, 98
Berkowitz, Peter 312
Berlin, Isaiah 131 n.41
Berman, Paul 253
Berns, Walter 234, 295
Besancon, Alain 223
Bickel, Alexander M. 97, 101
Bin Laden, Osama 309
bioethics 1, 302
Bishop, Joseph W. 98
Bitburg 216, 217

black-Jewish relations 7, 63–6, 77–81, 113–16, 189–90, 192
Black Panthers 77, 94, 96
Black Power 77–8, 79
Blake, Judith 25
Bloom, Alexander 100
Bloom, Harold 106
Bloom, Jessie S. 36
Bloomgarden, Lawrence 25
Blum, Ruthie 193, 208, 209
Blumenthal, Sidney 194, 238 n.50
Bolton, John 312
Boorstin, Daniel 28
Bork, Robert H. 200, 231, 257
Bosnia 297
Bottom Line 206
Bowman, James 318
Brady Education Foundation 241
Brantingham, Philip 115
Breindel, Eric 142, 210, 241
Brezhnev, Leonid 250
Brickner, Balfour 106, 112
Brock, David 166, 207, 224–5, 231, 236 n.18, 286 n.58, 296, 300
Brooklyn 9, 10, 23, 63, 78, 321
Brooks, David 296
Brown, Brenda 97
Brown, H. Rap 75
Brown, Norman O. 28, 40, 41, 53, 86, 99, 110, 156
Brownmiller, Susan 106
Brownsville 9
Brustein, Robert 15
Brzezinski, Zbigniew 154
Buchanan, Pat 213, 244, 271, 286 n.52, 311
Buckley, William F. 124, 137, 267, 290
Bukovsky, Vladimir 272
Bulgaria 228
Burnham, Walter Dean 244
Bush Doctrine, the 1, 303, 305, 312, 313
Bush, George H.W. 148, 215, 231–2, 244, 253, 267, 269, 271, 272, 273–4, 304

Bush, George W. 1, 2, 4, 6, 301–13, 320
Bush, Jeb 301
busing 97, 109, 110, 114, 123, 168

Cambodia 228
Cambridge University 10–12, 27, 41
Camus, Albert 27
Card, Andrew 304
Carl von Clausewitz 273
Carmichael, Stokely 78
Carolina Israelite 35
Carter, Jimmy 122, 146–50, 153–4, 162 n.32, 165–9, 178, 179, 200, 201, 253, 275, 320
Carthage Foundation 241, 282 n.1, 291
Casey, William 172
Castro, Fidel 159
Central Intelligence Agency (CIA) 75–6, 84, 99, 120, 148, 172
Chambers, Whittaker 144
Chase, Richard 52, 55
Chavez, Linda 98
Cheney, Dick 301, 303, 310, 311
Chernenko, Konstantin 250
Chernobyl 227, 247
Chile 150, 220
China 53, 140, 228, 251, 303, 310
Chomsky, Noam 85, 127, 185
Christian Coalition 243, 265, 295
City College of New York 81
civil rights 7, 59, 60–7, 70, 77–81, 113–16, 119, 124, 125, 189–92, 234 n.6, 253, 261–2, 289, 311
Civil Rights Act (1964) 61
Clark, Kenneth 66
Clarke, Jonathan 306, 307
Cleaver, Eldridge 78
Clinton, Bill 6, 274–6, 297, 298, 299, 300, 302, 304, 320
Clinton, Hillary 236 n.18, 276
Coalition for a Democratic Majority (CDM) 121, 146–7

Codevilla, Angelo 225, 273
Cohen, Arthur A. 189
Cohen, Elliot 3, 11, 12, 14, 15, 17–18, 19, 20–1, 23, 24, 25, 28, 29, 30, 32, 33, 34, 35, 36, 39, 40, 41–2, 49–52, 57, 60, 61, 62, 68, 70, 80, 95, 103, 107, 124, 125, 142, 160, 185, 189, 191, 202–3, 292–3, 294, 297, 319, 320–1
Cohen, Eliot A. 301
Cohen, Richard 279
Cold War, the 4, 5, 22, 27, 30–1, 34, 39, 55, 57, 68, 69, 77, 124, 133–44, 145, 149, 172, 186, 200, 224–8, 230, 250, 254–5, 262, 263, 270, 271, 272, 297, 301, 304, 309
   end of 246–9, 254–5, 257–8, 269
Collier, Peter 97, 142, 203
Columbia Review, The 55
Columbia University 10, 11, 12, 40, 41, 55, 77, 84, 305, 320
Commentaire 173
Commentary 2, 3, 4, 6, 11, 12, 14, 15, 16, 17, 19, 21, 30, 31, 49–50, 57, 58
   anti-Communism of 67–9, 76–7, 124, 135–44, 309
   anti-feminism of 104–6, 160, 168, 237 n.36, 257, 260, 293, 305
   circulation figures 43, 99, 233, 281, 291, 300
   early changes under Podhoretz's editorship 23–6
   editorial freedom of 3–4, 7–8 n.5, 22, 95
   fortieth anniversary 202
   high turnover of staff at 90 n.40
   homophobia of 155–9, 160, 205–7, 244, 293, 298
   on Israel 121–2, 151–5, 276–80
   Jewishness of 32–7, 74, 106–9, 126, 155
   Kozodoy becomes editor 291–2, 298–300

Commentary (Cont'd)
  opposition to quotas and affirmative action 113–16, 190–2, 231, 234 n.6, 261
  relationship with the AJC 3, 7–8 n.5, 22, 41–3, 116, 124–6, 178, 207, 240–1, 243, 285 n.50, 292–3
  twenty-fifth anniversary of 94
  under Cohen's editorship 17–18, 20–1, 28, 49–52, 80, 95, 97, 103, 189, 191, 262, 292–3, 294, 296
  as vehicle for neoconservatism 3, 124, 126–7, 133, 248–9
  and Vietnam 31–2, 94, 103, 133–4
Commentary Reader, The 52, 64
Committee for Cultural Freedom (CCF) 75, 193
Committee for the Free World (CFW) 172, 193, 198 n.46, 232, 241, 256, 281
Committee on the Present Danger (CPD) 148–9, 167, 172, 176, 193, 304
Communist Party 241
Congress of Racial Equality (CORE) 115
containment, doctrine of 30–1, 56, 133, 136, 137, 140, 149, 200, 248, 249
Contemporary Jewish Record 34
Contentions 193
Coover, Robert 187
Council of Foreign Relations 32, 136, 193, 267
counterculture, the 6, 55, 69, 84, 87, 93, 96, 97, 103, 110, 117, 123, 127, 133, 156, 158, 204, 275, 278, 305
Crain, Jane Larkin 106
Crittenden, Cathy Danielle 296
Cuba 175, 228
Cuban Missile Crisis 68
Cultural Cold War, the 99, 240
culture wars, the 7, 257–61, 263, 275, 293
Czechoslovakia 153, 228, 246, 251

Dannhauser, Werner J. 70, 71, 84, 118, 169
Davis, Kingsley 25
Dawidowicz, Lucy 63, 143, 180
Decter, Midge 21, 35, 76, 97, 103, 105, 139, 143, 149, 155, 156, 166, 169, 171, 172, 173, 193, 199, 205, 206, 212, 216, 230, 235 n.17, 241, 244, 256, 258, 261, 264, 267, 274, 281, 295, 301, 304
Decter, Moshe 57
Democratic Party, the 116, 117, 121, 122, 131 n.41, 147, 166, 169, 215, 221, 268, 269, 275, 295
Denes, Magda 163 n.50
Dennison, George 78
Dershowitz, Alan 205, 214, 215, 246, 269
détente 122, 123, 137, 201, 225, 250
Dienstfrey, Harris 24, 52, 70, 71
Diggins, John Patrick 147, 248, 249, 309
DiIulio, John 1, 302, 310
Dinkins, David 257
disarmament 31, 57, 224, 226, 228, 231
Dissent 25, 99, 100, 122, 180
Doctorow, E. L. 127, 187
Dorrien, Gary 17, 255, 301
Douglas, Charles 159
Draper, Theodore 57, 98, 123, 159, 173, 218
Dreyfus, Alfred 183
D'Souza, Dinesh 258, 296
Dupee, F. W. 10, 52, 55
Durham, Martin 310

Easterbrook, Gregg 253
Eastwood, Clint 258
Eban, Abba 155
Eberstadt, Nick 222
Edelston, Martin 43
Egypt 122, 153, 272, 277, 306, 310
Ehrman, John 2, 24, 26, 202, 247, 256, 317
Eichmann, Adolph 37, 41, 65

Eisenhower, Dwight D. 26, 27, 28, 35, 119
Ellison, Ralph 81
Elon, Amos 151
Encounter 76, 321
England 12
Epstein, Edward Jay 98
Epstein, Jason 21, 40, 81, 83–4, 85, 93, 98, 99, 101, 294
Epstein, Joseph 110, 111, 156, 157, 171, 187, 189, 206
Equal Opportunities Employment Commission 114
Esquire 41
Ethiopia 228
Ethnics and Public Policy Center, The 170

Fackenheim, Emil 63, 73, 185, 212
Fairlie, Henry 194
Falcoff, Mark 176
Falwell, Jerry 215
Farber, Leslie H. 42, 97, 110
Farfield Foundation, the 76
Farrakhan, Louis 192, 268
Faulkner, William 13, 17, 27
Federal Bureau of Investigation (FBI) 143
Fein, Leonard 179–80
Feith, Douglas J. 1, 302, 312
feminism 7, 104–6, 160, 168, 237 n.36, 257, 260, 293, 305
Feulner, Edwin 199
Fiddler, Stephen 302
Fiedler, Leslie 21, 57
Finlandizaton 147–8, 167, 173, 250
Finn, Chester 98, 171, 234 n.6
First Things 295
Fleming, Thomas 203
Ford, Gerald 145, 148, 198 n.46
Foreign Affairs 136, 137, 149, 177
foreign policy 1, 4, 6, 28, 30–1, 37, 68, 70, 74, 76, 96, 118, 119, 121, 123, 133–40, 147, 173–8, 194, 200–2, 217, 218–28, 256–7, 269–75, 307–8, 310
see also individual countries
Foreign Policy 311
Forster, E. M. 206
France 173, 235 n.17
Frankel, Charles 98
Frankel, Theodore 20
Fraser, Malcom 173
Friedenberg, Edgar 28, 80, 83, 84, 99
Friedman, Milton 245, 296, 302
Friedman, Murray 1, 78, 79, 171, 181, 188, 201
Frum, David 1, 231, 244, 276, 296, 299, 302, 310
Fukuyama, Francis 256, 258, 313
Fumento, Michael A. 205–6

Gaffney, Frank 308
Garment, Leonard 221
Garment, Suzanne 225
Gass, Oscar 59, 68
Gaza 186, 208, 278
Germany 172, 186, 204, 228, 235 n.17, 246, 271, 309
Gershman, Carl 79, 98, 137, 159, 171, 173, 174, 190
Gerson, Mark 40, 57, 58, 59, 103, 290, 298
Gandhi 186
Gandhi 186
Gilder Foundation 241
Gingrich, Newt 245, 281, 290, 296, 298
Ginsberg, Alan 55, 81, 156–8
Ginsberg, H. L. 10
Giuliani, Rudolph 6, 312–13, 320
Glasnost 223, 227
Glazer, Nathan 50, 57, 58, 62, 65–6, 68, 70, 80, 85–6, 97, 103, 114, 116, 117, 118, 124, 141–2, 143, 147, 150, 152, 190, 211, 216, 233, 295, 296
global intifada 4
God That Failed, The 140
Golden, Harry 35, 63

Golden, James 296
Goodman, Paul 28–9, 30, 53, 58, 68, 99, 110, 127, 156, 157, 158
Goodman, Walter 97, 204
Goodwin, Richard 43
Gorbachev, Mikhail 222–3, 225, 226, 227, 231, 247, 248, 249, 250, 251
Gornick, Vivian 105
Gram, Phil 290
Gramsci, Antonio 195
Graubard, Allen 217, 218
Graves, Robert 21
Great Society, the 194, 253
Greece 150
Green, Frances 23, 52
Greenberg, Clement 18–21, 50, 60, 260, 319
Greenberg, Irving 109, 112
Greenberg, Martin 18–21, 52, 60, 319
Greenberg, Moshe 10
Grenada 201, 270, 295
Grenier, Richard 186
Grossman, Edward 97
Gulf, the 1
Gulf War, the 4, 5, 269–74, 297

Hadas, Moses 10
Haft, Harriet 9–10
Halkin, Hillel 151
Halper, Steven 306, 307
Hamas 278
Handlin, Oscar 28
Harper's 82, 319
Harries, Owen 249, 255
Harrington, Michael 28, 39, 50, 85, 87 n.3, 122
Hart, Betsy 296
Harvard 10, 98, 148, 190–1, 244, 260, 290
Haynes, John Earl 98
Heilbroner, Robert 118
Heilbrunn, Jacob 254, 267, 295, 318, 320
Heller, Joseph 120, 187, 189, 294, 318–19

Hellman, Lillian 104, 141–2
Helms, Jesse 213
Herberg, Will 267
Herf, Jacob 295
Heritage Foundation, the 162, 199, 230, 231, 233, 241, 242
Herrnstein, Richard 98, 115, 261–2
Hertzberg, Arthur 155
Herzegovina 297
Heschel, Abraham Joshua 10
Hess, Moses 267
Hickory Foundation 241
Hilberg, Raul 37
Hill, Anita 300
Hill, Herbert 190
Himmelfarb, Gertrude 117, 169, 171, 172, 181, 193, 206, 295
Himmelfarb, Milton 33, 52, 63, 74, 80, 97, 108, 117, 151, 154, 189, 211
Hirst, David 305
Hiss, Alger 144
Hitchens, Christopher 120, 193
Hitler, Adolph 97, 140, 149, 158, 182, 185, 187, 209, 220, 271, 308
Ho Chi Minh 56, 68
Hofstadter Richard 28, 127
Hollywood 186, 242, 260
Holocaust, the 65, 72, 73, 74, 115, 141, 154, 169, 180, 181, 183, 186, 209, 212
homosexuality 7, 55, 155–9, 167, 169, 187, 203, 205–7, 244, 262, 293, 298, 301, 311
Hook, Sidney 23, 39, 40, 57, 62, 66, 76, 117, 126, 141, 158, 167, 174, 203
Hoover Institution 242
Horner, Charles 1, 251, 303
Horowitz, David 1, 97, 142, 203, 302
Horowitz, Irving Louis 193, 232
House UnAmerican Activities Committee (HUAC) 141
Howe, Irving 14, 35, 53, 57, 61, 85, 86, 98, 110–11, 116, 126, 127, 129 n.28, 138, 142–3, 144, 217
A Margin of Hope 143

Hudson Institute 241, 291
Hughes, Stuart H. 28, 57
Hungary 228, 246
Huntington, Samuel 1, 303
Hussein, Saddam 5, 269–71, 272–3, 304, 309
Hyams, Ario S. 214

Iannone, Carol 200, 282 n.7
Independent Women's Forum 304
India 118, 145
Ingraham, Laura 296
Innis, Roy 78
Institute of Peace 303
Intercollegiate Review 229
intermarriage 107–8, 266
Intermediate-Range Nuclear Forces Treaty (INF) 225
International Criminal Court, the 1
Iran 2, 4, 150, 165, 175, 176, 220–1, 228, 306, 310, 312, 313
Iran-*Contra* Affair, the 220–1, 231
Iraq 2, 4, 270–3, 306, 307, 309, 310, 311, 313
Iraq War, the 2, 304, 306, 311
Islam 1, 4, 270, 303, 304, 305, 306, 309
Israel 2, 6, 33, 34, 36, 37, 72–3, 74, 75, 78, 84, 85, 117, 119, 121, 124, 125, 151–5, 165, 169, 173, 178–86, 190, 199, 200–1, 202, 207–10, 211, 213, 216, 230, 235 n.17, 265, 267–8, 270, 271, 272, 274, 276–80, 297, 298, 299, 303, 304, 305, 306, 307, 309–10

J. Howard Pew Freedom Trust 241
Jackson, Henry 121, 122, 176, 213
Jackson, Jesse 78, 190, 215, 265
Jacques, Martin 312
Japan 153, 186, 271
Javits, Marion 43
Jeremiah 305
Jerusalem Post 208
Jewish Almanac, The 189
Jewish Catalog, The 112

John M. Olin Foundation 241, 282 n.1, 291
Johnson, Lyndon B. 43, 59, 67, 84, 119, 124, 194, 289, 290, 302
Johnson, Paul 119, 173, 180, 246, 319
Jones, Le Roi 78
Jordan 208, 277
Jordan, Nehemiah 57
Judaism 6, 10, 15, 21, 35–6, 63, 91 n.45, 106, 108, 109, 111, 126, 189, 212, 213, 216, 217, 246, 262–3, 265–6
Judis, John B. 242
Jumonville, Neil 13, 14, 17, 55, 126

Kadushin, Charles 127
Kagan, Donald 222, 301
Kagan, Robert 1, 303
Kahn, Tom 70
Kaplan, Roger 189
Kass, Leon 1, 262, 302
Kazin, Alfred 17, 21, 52, 57
Kedourie, Elie 273
Kemble, Penn 98, 171, 174
Kempton, Murray 25
Kennan, George 136
Kennedy, Edward 166
Kennedy, John F. 26–7, 32, 42, 43, 59, 87 n.3, 113, 119, 121, 167, 280, 320
Kennedy, Robert F. 43, 84
Kermode, Frank 118
Kerry, John 311
Kerouac, Jack 54, 55, 81
Khrushchev, Nikita 55, 57, 228
Kimball, Roger 296
King, Martin Luther 67, 77, 78, 84, 115, 124, 289
Kinsley, Michael 247
Kirk, Russell 230, 231, 289
Kirkpatrick, Jeane 98, 147, 149, 150–1, 162 n.32, 166, 170–1, 172, 176, 178, 193, 199, 208, 219, 221, 227, 247, 249, 253, 295, 296
Kissinger, Henry 122, 139, 145, 311
Klingenstein, Suzanne 1, 2

Koestler, Arthur 52
Kohl, Helmut 216
Korea 56, 144, 228
Kozodoy, Neal 90 n.40, 97, 101, 169, 291–2, 297, 298–300, 313
Kramer, Hilton 97, 193
Kramer, Leonie 173
Krauthammer, Charles 4
Kristol, Irving 7, 17, 21, 22, 27, 39, 40, 52, 85, 86, 97, 98, 117, 118, 122, 124, 127, 141, 142, 173, 190, 192, 193, 194, 200, 211, 232, 256, 265, 266, 268, 285 n.50, 290, 296, 302, 309, 322
Kristol, Liz 193
Kristol, William 232, 274, 295, 299
Krygier, Richard 173
Kuwait 270, 272, 273
Kyoto Accords, the 1

Laqueur, Walter 98, 109, 147, 151, 152, 159, 173, 200, 222
Lasch, Christopher 139
L.A. Times 215, 235 n.17
Latin America 68, 176–7, 200, 220–1
Leavis, F. R. 10–11, 14, 17, 55
Lebanon 182, 183–5, 186, 200, 201, 306, 310
Ledeen, Michael 1, 220, 303, 308
Lefever, Ernest 162
Lenin, Vladimir 223
Lenkowsky, Leslie 1, 241, 302
Lerner, Michael 216–18, 231, 275
Levin, Michael 282 n.7
Levine, Irving 116
Levine, Philip 25
Lewis, Bernard 1, 303
Lewy, Guenter 195
Libby, I. Lewis 1, 301
Liberator 66, 67
Lichtheim, George 20, 52, 68
Likud 154–5, 186, 193, 274, 276, 279, 309
Lind, Michael 242, 243, 244, 262, 267, 295, 308

Lindberg, Tod 232, 233, 308
Lipman, Samuel 193
Lipset, Seymour Martin 98, 118, 119, 122, 295
Lipson, Leon 57
London Herbert I. 244, 282 n.7
Longstaff, Stephen 241
Loury, Glenn 191, 192, 290, 295
Lowell, Robert 32
Lowenthal, Richard 57
Lucas, Scott 319
Luttwak, Edward 98, 138, 149, 159, 173
Lynd, Staughton 28, 30, 39, 53, 57, 67–8
Lynde and Harry Bradley Foundation 240, 291

Maass, Richard 125
Maccoby, Hyam 265, 295
Maccoby, Michael 31, 39, 57
Macdonald, Dwight 26, 32, 57, 85, 87 n.3, 203, 207
Magid, Marion 60, 70, 90 n.40, 97, 235 n.17
Magnet, Myron 296
Mailer, Norman 14, 25, 28, 41, 53, 54, 80, 84, 85, 86, 99, 109, 127, 156, 158, 294, 305
Malamud, Bernard 12, 13, 26, 35, 50, 111
Mandela, Nelson 219, 253–4
Mann, James 311
March on Washington 67
Marcus, Alfred 112
Marcus, Steven 25, 40, 62
Marcuse, Herbert 28, 53, 86, 99, 127
Master, William 42
Mayer, Martin 29
Maynes, Charles William 177
McCain, John 302, 312, 313, 320
McCarthy, Mary 14, 85, 104, 142
McCarthyism 6, 112, 140–4, 170
McConnell, Scott 98, 241, 278, 311
McCracken, Samuel 97, 104, 142, 157

McGovern, George 116–17, 121, 122, 124, 131 n.41, 147, 148, 165, 186, 258, 275
McLuhan, Marshall 86
Meese, Edwin 220
Meged, Mati 25
Menorah Journal 3
Micklethwait, John 302, 312
Micronesia 147
Middle East, the 1, 2, 5, 68, 73, 122, 137, 151–3, 165, 172, 178–9, 200–2, 207–10, 251, 269–74, 276–80, 303, 305–6, 308, 309–10, 313
Middle East Forum 303
Miller, Arthur 319
Milson, Menachem 182
Milton, Joyce 143
minicons 274, 295
Moment 179–80
Moon, Sun Myung 220
Moral Majority 187, 212–13, 215
Morgan, Hugh 173
Morgenthau, Hans 31–2, 56, 68
Morris, Willie 82
Moynihan, Daniel Patrick, 68, 70, 95, 97, 118, 124, 138, 145–6, 159, 167, 173, 233, 261, 289, 294–5, 322
A Dangerous Place 146
Munson, Naomi 193
Munson, Sam 313
Munson, Steven 193
Muravchik, Joshua 98, 174, 255, 260, 271, 274, 275, 296, 301, 306, 308
Murdoch, Rupert 296, 299
Murray, Charles 245, 261–2
Mylroie, Laurie 272
Myrdal, Gunnar 62, 66

Naim, Moses 311
Nash, George 97, 194, 299
Nation, The 101, 120, 141, 264
Nation of Islam 268
National Association for the Advancement of Colored People (NAACP) 62, 114
National Association of Scholars 282 n.7
National Endowment for the Arts 171
National Endowment for Democracy 171
National Endowment for the Humanities 171
National Interest 242, 255, 256
National Review 102, 124, 137, 146, 203, 207, 230, 232, 267, 299
National Rifle Association (NRA) 243
National Security Council (NSC) 221, 222, 302
Nazism 80, 148, 306
Neoconservatism 1, 23
  and *Commentary* 4, 85
  connections of 193–5
  death of 289–91, 306–8
  definitions of 2, 122–3, 307
  early support for Reagan 166–9
  emergence of 122–4
  foreign policy 1, 2, 123–4, 219, 256–7, 269–75, 307–8, 310
  frozen out by Carter 146–7, 166–7
  and the George W. Bush administration 4, 301–13
  and Old Right/Paleoconservatism 123–4, 168, 228–31, 289–90, 297, 301, 303, 307
  and the Reagan Administration 165, 170–8, 190, 192, 193, 194, 199–202, 222, 250, 252, 257
  younger generation of 295–6
  see also minicons
Netanyahu, Benjamin 208, 280, 301
New Class, the 109–10, 117, 260, 263
New Criterion 193, 242
New Deal 4, 23, 26, 123, 124, 289, 290
New Democrats 274–5
New Frontier 27, 42
New Left, the 28, 30, 53, 56, 57, 68, 69, 70, 71, 75, 77, 78, 80, 81, 83, 84–7, 103, 117, 121, 123, 126, 127, 133, 135, 147, 151, 156, 158, 165, 203, 204, 233, 263, 271, 318
  and Jews 108–13

New Republic, The 100, 138, 166, 205, 247, 264, 306
New Right 232, 245
Newsweek 28, 122, 176, 235 n.17, 253
New York City teachers strike 78–9
New Yorker 37, 62, 65
New York Intellectuals, the 10, 11, 13, 15, 16, 17, 28, 39, 49, 53, 54, 56, 59, 82, 95–6, 99, 124, 154, 195
New York Post 193, 226, 302
New York Review of Books 39, 83, 84, 85, 86, 93, 99–101, 126, 138, 218, 219
  as rival to *Commentary* 99
New York Times 32, 102, 122, 144, 176, 201, 244, 258, 264, 267, 296, 300, 306, 313
Nicaragua 150, 166, 172, 175, 220, 221, 226, 228
Nietzsche, Friedrich 270
Nisbet, Robert 57, 97, 172, 229
Nitze, Paul 149, 172, 250
Nixon, Richard M. 26, 117–20, 121, 122, 131 n.41, 134, 137, 139, 165, 170, 185, 221, 271, 320
Non-Sectarian Committee for Life 163 n.50
non-Zionism 3, 151
North Atlantic Treaty Organization (NATO) 218, 228
North Korea 4
North, Oliver 220, 222
Notley, Paul 157
Not Without Honor 249
Novak, Michael 97, 106, 170, 171, 172, 246
Novak, William 36, 73, 112, 128
Nuechterlein, James 119, 194, 249

Obama, Barack 312
Office of Faith-Based Initiatives 302
Olin Foundation 241
Operation Desert Storm 272–4
Organization of American States 218
Orwell, George 51, 259, 319

Oslo peace agreement 278, 280, 304
Outweek 206
Oz, Amos 151
Ozick, Cynthia 218, 296

Pacino, Al 43
Paleoconservatism/Old Right 6, 123, 168, 228–31, 297, 303, 307
Palestine Liberation Organization (PLO) 169, 184, 190, 208, 233, 255, 277, 278, 306, 310
Panama 270
Paraguay 220
Partisan Review 13, 49, 55, 76, 81, 99, 101, 103, 124
Patullo, E. L. 244
Pawel, Ernst 127
Peace Now 180
Peretz, Martin 75, 274
Perle, Richard 1, 122, 301, 307
Perot, Ross 274
Pew Charitable Trusts 241
Pfaff, William 118
Philanthropic Roundtable 241
Philip Morris Companies 261
Phillips, William 13, 19, 22, 40, 54, 254
Pinochet, Augusto 220
Pipes, Daniel 1, 275, 296, 303, 312
Pipes, Richard 131 n.41, 148, 149, 159, 171, 172, 173, 246, 247, 248, 251
Podhoretz, John 60, 193, 295, 296, 300, 304, 313, 322
Podhoretz, Norman 2, 3, 4, 5, 6, 24
  and the AJC 41–3, 62, 124–6, 178, 188, 235 n.17, 240, 243, 285 n.50
  and Alan Ginsberg 55, 81, 156–7
  and the Beats 54–5, 104, 156, 158
  anti-Communism of 55–8, 69, 93, 101, 102, 133–44, 203, 218
  anti-feminism of 104–6, 160, 168, 237 n.36, 257, 260, 293, 305
  appointment as Editor-in-Chief of *Commentary* 21–2
  awarded Presidential Medal of Freedom 306

Breaking Ranks 59, 167
at Cambridge University 11–12, 27, 104, 320
childhood 9–10, 63, 319, 321
at Columbia University 10, 12, 55, 58, 81, 83, 305, 320
as counterintellectual 27, 69, 101, 145, 194, 279
disappointment with Reagan 199–202, 221, 224–5, 234 n.6, 304
early anti-liberalism of 60–7, 70–81
early changes to *Commentary* 24–6
early reviews 13–17
early years at *Commentary* 12–22
editorial style 24
education 9–12
on Eichmann 37–8
Ex-Friends 199, 294
flirtation with radicalism 25–8, 41, 58–60
and George McGovern 116–17
and Hannah Arendt 37–9, 40, 104
homophobia of 155–9, 205–7, 244, 293
identity crisis 254–6
influence of Elliot Cohen on 51–2
influence of F.R. Leavis on 10–11, 14, 17, 37, 55, 93, 104, 155
influence of Lionel Trilling on 10, 11, 12, 14, 17, 23, 27, 39–41, 55, 56, 95, 196 n.17
Jewishness of 1, 10, 71–2, 106–9
launches attack on New Left 93–102
as literary critic 13–14
Making It 49, 81–4, 99, 101, 144, 167, 318, 319
My Love Affair with America 189
Norman Podhoretz Reader, The 59
opposition to affirmative action and quotas 113–16, 190–2, 211, 231, 234 n.6, 261
parents 9
personality 13, 16–17, 18, 294, 317–22

Present Danger, The 167, 199, 292, 305
The Prophets: Who They Were, What They Are 305
Puritanism of 10, 11, 14, 30, 93, 103–4, 155–6, 160, 187–8, 205
retirement as editor of *Commentary* 7, 291–2, 297
review of *The Adventures of Augie March* 15–17
review of *The Natural* 13
switches vote to the Republicans 117–18
turn against the New Left 71–87
views on Vietnam 31–2, 56, 69, 89–90 n.37, 94, 133–5, 195
Why We Were in Vietnam 195
World War IV: The Long Struggle against Islamofascism 313
Zionism of 71–3, 102, 122, 151–5, 178–86, 207–10
Pointdexter, John 222
Poland 200, 226, 227, 228, 246, 249
Policy Review 241
Political correctness (PC) 204, 243–4, 258, 263–4, 294, 298, 305
Pollard, Jonathan 209–10
Pollock, Jackson 50
Polner, Murray 125, 126
pornography 29–30, 103–4, 109, 110, 123, 165, 170, 187, 188, 203, 214
Portugal 150
Powell, Colin 303
Powell, Jody 235 n.17
Powers, Richard Gid 249, 283 n.20
Present Tense 125–6
Prodemca 171
Project for a New American Century (PNAC) 301, 303, 305
Public Interest, The 118, 124, 193, 242
Public Opinion 193
Puddington, Arch 98, 171, 174, 248, 251, 253

Quayle, Dan 232, 244, 274
quotas 64, 110, 113–14, 115, 117, 123, 168, 169, 191, 211, 216, 234 n.6

Raab, Earl 79, 119
Rabin, Yitzhak 119, 276–9, 280
Rabinowitz, Dorothy 97, 103, 230
race relations 7
Radosh, Ronald 143
Rahv, Philip 14, 40, 104, 319
Ramer, Bruce 304
Ramparts 27, 75
Randolph, A. Philip 67
Ravenal, Earl 138
Ravitch, Diane 97
Ravitch, Norman 265
Reagan, Ronald 6, 120, 124, 162 n. 32, 165, 166–76, 178, 190, 194, 195, 199–202, 203, 210, 211, 216, 217, 219, 220, 221, 222, 224–5, 228, 229, 231, 232, 234 n.6, 238 n.50, 245, 248–53, 271, 274, 294, 295, 300, 301, 304, 305
  Reagan Doctrine, the 171, 221, 249
  Reaganism 6, 201, 213, 253, 260
  Reagan Revolution, the 6, 170, 252
Rekjavik 224
Religious Right 214, 264–8, 290, 295, 307, 310 *see also* Christian Coalition, Jerry Falwell, Moral Majority
Republican Party, the (GOP) 1, 2, 147, 168, 214, 242, 243, 244, 264, 265, 269, 281, 289
Response 36, 112, 127
Revel, Jean-Francois 223, 227, 228
Rice, Condoleezza 303, 304, 310
Richardson, Jack 97
Richardson, Roderic R. 244
Riesman, David 31, 39, 57, 127
Robertson, Pat 244, 265, 267–8, 295
Robinson, David 205
Robinson, Jill 187
Rockwell, George Lincoln 41, 63

Rodman, Peter 1, 301
Roosevelt, Franklin D. 26, 27, 117, 119, 121, 124, 167, 218–19, 289, 299
Roosevelt, Theodore 168
Rosenberg File, The 143
Rosenberg, Harold 38, 57
Rosenberg, Julius and Ethel 143–4, 210
Rosenblatt, Peter 147, 166
Rosenfeld, Isaac 50
Rostow, Eugene 171, 222
Roth, Cecil 20
Roth, Philip 35, 109–11, 119, 129 n.28, 156, 294
  Portnoy's Complaint 109–11
Rove, Karl 302, 303, 311, 312
Rumania 228, 250
Rumsfeld, Donald 198 n.46, 301, 303, 304, 309, 310, 312
Rushdie, Salman 5
Russia 236, 252, 259, 303, 310 *see also* Soviet Union
Rustin, Bayard 67, 70, 78, 81, 97, 115, 159, 172, 173, 174, 177, 207

Sabra and Shatila 183, 185
Sadat, Anwar 122
Said, Edward 208
Saloma, John 242
Samuel, Maurice 189
Sandanistas 220, 221
Sarah Lawrence College 191
Sarah Scaife Foundation 241, 276
Sartre, Jean-Paul 51
Saudi Arabia 201, 270, 272, 274, 303, 306, 310
Scaife, Richard Mellon 276, 282 n.1
Scammon, Richard M. 114
Schickel, Richard 18
Schifter, Richard 245, 274
Schmitt, Gary 303
Scholem, Gershom 108
Schrag, Peter 170
Schumacher, E. F. 58

Schwartz, Stephen 1, 303
Scowcroft, Brent 303
Scrutiny 11
Seabury, Paul 98, 114
Second World War, the 7, 38, 79, 122, 149, 184, 203, 217, 218, 228
separation of church and state 1, 266, 285 n.50, 290
September 11, 2001 1, 302, 303, 304, 306, 307, 308, 320
Serbia 297
Shamir, Yitzhak 186, 208
Sharansky, Natan 222
Sharon, Ariel 182, 309–10
Shaw, George Bernard 294
Shaw, Peter 282 n.7
Shechner, Mark 202
Sherry, Michael 149
Short, Thomas 191
Shub, Anatole 50, 52
Shulevitz, Judith 305
Shultz, George 172, 201, 225
Silvers, Robert 83, 127
Singer, Isaac Bashevis 52
Singer, Max 200
Six Day War, the 71–5, 78, 84, 85, 122, 280
Sklare, Marshall 112
Slawson, John 125
Smith-Richardson Foundation 241, 244
Snow, C. P. 21
Sobran, Joseph 230
Solotaroff, Ted (Theodore) 24, 27, 28, 30, 35, 43, 52, 63, 68, 70, 80, 84
Solzhenitsyn, Alexander 251
Somalia 5
Sontag, Susan 21, 80, 127
South Africa 172, 178, 219, 253–4
Soviet Union 25, 30, 53, 55–6, 57, 108, 122, 123, 135, 137, 138, 140, 145, 147, 148–9, 150, 156, 172, 174–5, 201–2, 203, 210, 219, 222–8, 231, 233, 246–51, 256, 257, 269, 270, 277, 309

Sowell, Thomas 191, 261, 275
Spain 150
Spectator, The 321
Spiegel, Steven L. 201
Stalin, Joseph 55, 57, 140, 142, 218
Starr, Roger 98
Star Wars 175, 226, 238 n.50, 255 *see also* SDI
Staub, Michael 63, 108
Steel, Ronald 139
Steele, Shelby 191
Steinfels, Peter 101, 127, 159, 194
Stelzer, Irwin 275, 307
stem cell research 1
Stern, Sol 27, 112
Stern, William 250
Stone, Robert 187
Stonewall 155
Strategic Arms Limitations Talks 123,148–9
Strategic Defense Initiative (SDI) 225–6, 238 n.50, 244, 249, 250, 255, 270 *see also* Star Wars
Strauss, Leo 70
Stroessner, Alfredo 220
Stroock, Alan 41
Students for a Democratic Society 54, 98
Student Nonviolent Coordinating Committee (SNCC) 75, 78
Sullivan, Andrew 264
Sultan of Brunei 220
supply-side economics 1, 244, 289, 307
Supreme Court, the 119, 188, 200, 206, 257, 311
Syria 2, 4, 264, 278, 306, 310
Syrkin, Marie 110, 189

Tacitus 321
Tanenhaus, Sam 248, 254
Taylor, General Maxwell 56
tax cuts 1, 194, 245, 252, 289
Team B 148, 172, 250
Tedeschi, Mary 188

Teres, Harvey 61
Thatcher, Margaret 249, 252, 265, 274
theoconservatives 295
Thompson, John 62
This World 193
Tibet 228
Tikkun 217, 237 n.36, 275–6
Time 122, 176
Times Literary Supplement 24–5, 83
Tomes, Frederick 133
Tonsor, Stephen J. 229
Trilling, Diana 22, 39–41, 55, 76, 77, 104, 141, 294
Trilling, Lionel 10, 11, 12, 14, 15, 17, 23, 27, 28, 30, 39–41, 52, 55, 56, 72, 76, 77, 81, 127, 196 n.17, 203, 294
Trotsky, Leon 229
Truman Doctrine, the 135, 137
Truman, Harry S. 26, 119, 121, 124, 289, 290
Tucker, Robert W. 98, 137, 138, 159, 173, 295
Twersky, David 154, 275, 281

Uganda 146
Uhler, Walter C. 251
United Federation of Teachers 79
United Nations, the (UN) 145–6, 151, 170, 171, 193, 199, 218, 295, 310, 312
University of Chicago 24
Updike, John 156, 187
Uris, Leon 35
US Information Agency (USIA) 172, 193, 199
Ussery, Wilfred 78

Van Doren, Mark 10
Vidal, Gore 156, 158, 206, 235 n.17
Vietnam 31–2, 68, 71, 76, 82, 84, 86, 103, 109, 117, 119, 123, 133–5, 138, 139, 140, 145, 151, 153, 166, 180, 187, 195, 228, 270, 271, 305

see also Commentary and Podhoretz, Norman
Vietnamization 134
Vietnam syndrome, the 123, 138, 139, 158
Village Voice, The 105

Wallace, Henry 81, 117
Wall Street Journal 102, 183, 193, 242, 296, 297
Walsh, Lawrence 222
Warburg, Paul 267
War on Poverty 50, 87 n.3
Warshow, Robert 11–12, 50
Washington Post 32, 149, 203, 235 n.17, 279
Washington Times 193
Waskow, Arthur 111
Watergate 119–20, 125, 165, 170, 185, 220, 221
Wattenberg, Ben 114, 167, 171, 193
Wattenberg, Danny 193
Weather Underground 94
Weaver, Paul 98
Weaver, Suzanne 98
Weekly Standard 233, 236 n.18, 299, 300
Weinberger, Caspar 201
Weiss-Rosmarin, Trude 112, 128
West Bank 179, 182, 183, 186, 208, 273, 274, 278
Whitewater scandal 300
Wick, Charles Z. 199
Wiegel, George 301
Wilford, Hugh 76
Williams, William Appleman 68
Wills, Gary 162
Wilson, Clyde 229
Wilson, Edmund 94
Wilson, James Q. 1, 98, 302
Wilson, Woodrow 124
Wilsonianism 1, 2, 5, 30, 124, 219, 307
Winik, Jay 249

Wisse, Ruth 34, 100, 110, 111, 160, 189, 217, 296
Wolfe, Bertram 61
Wolfe, Tom 99, 103
Wolfowitz, Paul 1, 301, 302, 312
Women's Liberation 96, 106, 123
Woolridge, Adrian 302, 312
World Bank 312
Worsthorne, Peregrine 321
Wrong, Dennis 97, 99–100, 126
Wyschogrod, Michael 20, 319

Xiaoping, Den 255

Yale University 3, 101
Yalta 218–19
Yemen 228
Yoder, Edwin M. 235 n.17
Yom Kippur War, the 122
Young, Andrew 78, 147, 169
Young People's Socialist League 98
Yugoslavia 257, 264

Zionism 75, 122, 124, 151–5, 265, 267–8
Zola, Emile 183